Arguments in Syntax and Semantics

Argument structure – the pattern of underlying relations between a predicate and its dependents – is at the base of syntactic theory, and the theory of the interface with semantics.

This comprehensive guide explores the motives for thematic and event-structural decomposition, and its relation to structure in syntax. It also discusses broad patterns in the linking of syntactic to semantic relations, and includes insightful case studies on passive and resultative constructions. Semantically explicit and syntactically impartial, with a careful, interrogative approach, Williams clarifies notions of *argument* within both lexicalist and nonlexicalist approaches.

Ideal for students and researchers in syntactic and semantic theory, this introduction includes:

– A comprehensive overview of arguments in syntax and semantics
– Discussion points and suggestions for further reading in each chapter
– A glossary with helpful definitions of key terms.

Alexander Williams is Assistant Professor in the Departments of Linguistics and Philosophy at the University of Maryland, College Park, where he teaches semantics, syntax and philosophy of language.

KEY TOPICS IN SYNTAX

"Key Topics in Syntax" focusses on the main topics of study in syntax today. It consists of accessible yet challenging accounts of the most important issues, concepts and phenomena to consider when examining the syntactic structure of language. Some topics have been the subject of syntactic study for many years, and are re-examined in this series in light of new developments in the field; others are issues of growing importance that have not so far been given a sustained treatment. Written by leading experts and designed to bridge the gap between textbooks and primary literature, the books in this series can either be used on courses and seminars, or as one-stop, succinct guides to a particular topic for individual students and researchers. Each book includes useful suggestions for further reading, discussion questions and a helpful glossary.

Already published in the series:

Syntactic Islands by Cedric Boeckx

Clause Structure by Elly van Gelderen

Arguments in Syntax and Semantics by Alexander Williams

Forthcoming titles:

The Clitic by Francisco Ordóñez

Ellipsis by Kyle Johnson

Syntactic Agreement by Roberta D'Allesandro

The Evolution of Syntax by Brady Clark

Studying Syntactic Change by Thomas McFadden

The Syntax–Semantics Interface by Terje Lohndal

Variation in Syntax by Joanna Nykiel

Arguments in Syntax and Semantics

ALEXANDER WILLIAMS

CAMBRIDGE
UNIVERSITY PRESS

CAMBRIDGE
UNIVERSITY PRESS

University Printing House, Cambridge CB2 8BS, United Kingdom

Cambridge University Press is part of the University of Cambridge.

It furthers the University's mission by disseminating knowledge in the pursuit of education, learning and research at the highest international levels of excellence.

www.cambridge.org
Information on this title: www.cambridge.org/9780521151726

First published 2015

A catalog record for this publication is available from the British Library

Library of Congress Cataloging in Publication data
Williams, Alexander (Linguist)
Arguments in syntax and semantics / Alexander Williams.
        pages   cm.
Includes bibliographical references.
ISBN 978-0-521-19096-1 (Hardback) – ISBN 978-0-521-15172-6 (Paperback)
1. English language–Syntax.   2. English language–Semantics.   3. Persuasion (Rhetoric)
I. Title.
PE1369.W53 2015
425–dc23   2014021009

ISBN 978-0-521-19096-1 Hardback
ISBN 978-0-521-15172-6 Paperback

For Marcel and Melissa

Contents

Acknowledgments

I wrote this book. But that is true only because verb meanings don't traffic in relations as boring as causation. I was just the writer. Many others caused my book to come about, and quite directly so. Chief among these are Norbert Hornstein, Paul Pietroski, Jeff Lidz, Valentine Hacquard, Tonia Bleam and Dave Embick. These friends have taught me a lot, and done me many favors. But the greater gift has been their faith in me, which, like every great gift, is completely inexplicable. Thank you.

I have had many wonderful colleagues at the University of Maryland. From the faculty this includes Amy Weinberg, Bill Idsardi, Chris Morris, Colin Phillips, David Poeppel, Ellen Lau, Erin Eaker, Georges Rey, Juan Uriagereka, Naomi Feldman, Peter Carruthers, Rachel Singpurwalla and Sue Dwyer. From the students it includes Alex Drummond, Alexis Wellwood, Angela He, Annie Gagliardi, Brad Larson, Brendan Ritchie, Brock Rough, Chris Vogel, Dave Kush, Ewan Dunbar, Johannes Jurka, Matt Wagers, Michaël Gagnon, Mike McCourt, Quinn Harr, Rachel Dudley, Scott Fults, Shannon Barrios, Shevaun Lewis, Stacey Trock, Tim Hunter and Yu Izumi. All of you have made work both interesting and fun, thereby contradicting what I had previously taken to be an analytic truth.

I would also like to thank Lu Nelson, Bas van Fraassen, Gil Harman and John Burgess for starting me in this direction; Rajesh Bhatt, Robin Clark, Jim Huang, Ed Keenan, Angelika Kratzer, Richard Larson and Roger Schwarzschild for their encouragement; and Marcus Kracht for his support of this book.

I am grateful to the Department of Linguistics at the University of British Columbia, especially Henry Davis and Lisa Matthewson, for granting me a summer office. Thanks also go to Muffy Siegel, Ted Fernald and Jared Klein for their support at Temple University, Swarthmore College and the University of Georgia, respectively.

Independently of their help with this book, Jeff, Tonia and Valentine are dear friends. Through laughter and understanding, they have allowed me to be a person, even myself, when I least expected to be. Then when I was all-too-human, Valentine managed to restore my balance. Here I feel not only gratitude but joy.

At the core is my family, Melissa and Marcel Ho. Melissa has supported me with hard work and boundless patience. Marcel has inspired me with sweetness and wit. There is no better pair of people, and I work to be worthy of you both.

Abbreviations

1s	first person singular
2s	second person singular
3s	third person singular
3sS	third person singular subject
3sn	third person singular neuter
ANP	Arguments Name Participants
ART	article
BAT	Base Argument Theory of passives
BVC	Bound Verb Complement; the BVC is a nominalization of the verb group in Igbo, sometimes serving only to satisfy the requirement that a verb group in the factative not be clause-final
CLS	classifer
COP	copular verb
DAT	dative
DET	determiner
DOR	Direct Object Restriction
ERG	Ergative
EXIST	existential; roughly, this marks a noun phrase in St'át'imcets as indefinite.
EXPL	Expletive
FACT	factative; roughly, an Igbo predicate in the factative has past time reference when eventive, and nonpast time reference when stative.
FUT	future
NEG	negation
NMOD	adnominal modifier
NOM	nominative
NOMZ	nominalizer
OBL	Oblique object
PAM	Participant-to-Argument Matching
PASS	passive

PFV	perfective
PPL	past participle
PRES	present tense
REFLEX	reflexive
RIG	Role Iteration Generalization
S	subject
TAM	Tense Aspect Mood affix
TRANS	transitive

Term in bold face have an entry in the Glossary.

Introduction

1.1 ARGUMENT STRUCTURE

Verbs have meanings, and occur in meaningful contexts. What is the relation between the verb and the contexts it privileges, seen from the viewpoint of meaning? Theories of argument structure contribute to an answer, focussing on satellites of the verb that bind participant roles it implies. Constellations of the verb and such satellites are argument structures, our topic in this book.

Any clause centered on carry, for example, concerns an event of carrying – this much is a consequence of what the verb means. Any carrying involves both a carrier and what is carried, two participant roles – this much follows from what a carrying is like, no matter what we say about the verb. And now in (1), carry inhabits a transitive clause, with a subject and an object. True uses of the sentence require that, in the carrying it reports, Navin is the carrier and the chair is what he carried.

(1)   Navin carried the chair.

These last facts – that carry can occur in a transitive clause, and that the clause has just this interpretation – are consequences of the grammar, nothing else. And it is facts like this that we aim to describe theoretically, in terms that allow for fertile generalizations. What exactly are the relations that the satellites bind in the meaning of the clause? What exactly are the relations that mediate this in syntax? And what exactly are the properties of the verb such that it can enter these dependencies?

A theory of argument structure answers these questions for each context a verb may occur in. In carry's case, this includes sentences like (1), and also those of the sort listed in (2).

(2)   a Navin carried the chair down Beverly Drive.
      b His knapsack carried a thermos.
      c Those chairs don't carry so easily.
      d The chair was carried by Navin.
      e Constantly carrying the chair will wear Navin down.

1

The theory should also account for those contexts that do not allow the verb. Carry is excluded from the contexts in (3), for example.

(3) a * Navin carried.[1]
         'Navin carried something.'
     b * The chair carried.
         'Something carried the chair.'
     c * Navin carried the chair his thermos.
         'Navin carried the chair and his thermos.'
     d * Navin carried his elbow sore.
         'Navin made his elbow sore by carrying something.'

This all paves the way for questions of greater generality. Surely the facts about carry are instances of broader patterns, both within English and cross-linguistically. Our analysis should be in a vocabulary that allows us to state these. The goal, as always, is to put the analysis in terms that help us to understand the human capacity for language, and the way we acquire a language in childhood (Chomsky 1965).

In studying argument structure, therefore, we study the relation between predicates and their arguments, generally abstracting both from details of morphology, and from non-local syntactic dependencies, areas covered by other books in the Key Topics series.

1.2 OUR APPROACH

This book is not a treatise on one theory of argument structure, or an impartial review of several. It is an analysis of the elements for any such theory, both syntactic and semantic. Textbooks on syntax or semantics can only skim our topic quickly. Monographs may drop us into the middle of a debate among specialists. There is a need, I think, for something in between, a book that engages the specialist's issues by concentrating on fundamentals, building from the ground up. This approach has two different purposes. One is to provide a foundation on which

---

[1] Judgments of acceptability are always relative to a given interpretation. The asterisk in (3a) indicates that Navin carried cannot be used in exactly the same way as Navin carried something. There are other interpretations, however, relative to which Navin carried is an acceptable sentence. Relative to a game of basketball it can mean that Navin dribbled the ball after allowing it to come to rest in his hands. In the argot of American gun law, it can mean that Navin carried a gun. And sometimes it can be used anaphorically, exploiting a contextually given restriction on what is carried; for example, when discussing a task known to involve two components, carrying boxes and loading boxes, one can use Navin carried to mean that Navin carried boxes. Yet none of these possibilities changes what is reported in (3a).

diverse hypotheses about argument structure can be understood and evaluated, neutralizing parochial differences. The other is to stimulate new thoughts on what the right theory might look like. Sometimes the biggest ideas come from scrutinizing what seems elementary.

In particular I will focus more than usual on the argument relation itself, taking my inspiration mainly from Dowty (1989), Parsons (1990), Schein (1993, 2002, 2012), Kratzer (1996, 2000, 2002, 2003, 2005) and Pietroski (2005a). What sorts of relations, syntactic and semantic, go under the heading of *argument*? What sorts of semantic interpretations are associated with arguments? And how do these match up with the syntax? These are my main interests, and I think they deserve a sustained but introductory treatment in contemporary terms. They also provide a basis for further issues. What semantic classes of verbs occur in which argument structures? What is the right analysis for a particular argument structure, such as unaccusative, passive, middle or resultative? And are some argument structures derived syntactically from others? I will address some aspects of these questions in later chapters. But they are already a central focus of many excellent books, including Jackendoff (1990), Goldberg (1995 and 2006), Levin and Rappaport Hovav (1995 and 2005), Hale and Keyser (2002), Borer (2005) and Ramchand (2008). Again, I would like to add something that I think is missing: a guide to the elements of argument structure.

Two aspects of my perspective are best flagged at the outset, to prevent disorientation: it is both less lexical and more semantic than one might expect, given the topic. Argument structure is sometimes presented in isolation from phrasal syntax and semantics, as a part of the theory of the lexical items. But this can be misleading. What the theory aims to describe are relations between verbs (or other predicates) and satellites elsewhere in the clause. These are phrasal, clause-level dependencies. To describe such dependencies, we must of course fix the properties of the words they involve. But this is an intrinsic part of phrasal grammar, and not something separate. It goes hand in hand with designing the rules of syntactic and semantic composition: the two tasks are complementary. Certainly it may turn out in the end that the properties we assign to the words are complex and demand further analysis, lest generalizations be missed; and this will indeed put us in the province of Lexicon, a level of analysis whose domain is the primitives of Syntax. But this is just one possible outcome of the theory of argument structure, and not a necessity. It should not be mistaken for a definition of the topic. The topic is relations within phrases between predicates and semantically related satellites.

This attitude will express itself in many ways, and I will note two here. First, I deal openly and regularly with the compositional semantics. Without this, it is simply not possible to understand what an argument structure is, or might be. As my medium, I use the predicate calculus, supplemented with lambda abstraction (as in Dowty 1979) and Davidsonian event variables (as in Parsons 1990). This notation is familiar, highly expressive and also perfectly clear, with a settled, textbook interpretation. This enforces an important standard of explicitness, not shared by all notations, but essential for stating and evaluating hypotheses. I present a brief primer in chapter 2; richer background can be found in Chierchia and McConnell-Ginet (1990), Gamut (1991) or Heim and Kratzer (1998).

Second, I do not simply presuppose that argument structures 'project' from the verb, rather than from other items in whose company the verb occurs. Instead I take this to be one of our major questions: is a given argument relation 'introduced' by the verb, or by a structure that the verb occupies? The first approach is expressed in many landmark works since the mid 1970s, including Dowty (1979), Chomsky (1981), Stowell (1981), Jackendoff (1990b), Grimshaw (1990), Hale and Keyser (1993) and Levin and Rappaport Hovav (1995). But the second is brought to the fore in Carlson (1984), Dowty (1989), Schein (1993), Borer (1994 and 2003), Goldberg (1995), Kratzer (1996), Marantz (1997) and Pylkkänen (2002), often echoing the earlier perspectives of Lakoff (1965, 1971) and McCawley (1971), which went briefly into abeyance after Dowty 1979 and Chomsky 1981. I feel the issue is not as well understood as it might be, and discuss it periodically throughout the book. It is the exclusive topic of Chapter 9.

1.3 CHAPTER SYNOPSIS

This book has four parts. Chapters 1–2 provide a background in syntax and semantics. Chapters 3–5 characterize the notion of argumenthood. Chapters 6–11 concern the semantic and syntactic analysis of argument relations. The book finishes with two case studies in Chapters 12 and 13. Let me now describe this in more detail.

I begin in Chapter 1 with the very general perspective I take in talking about syntax. I view grammar as the derivation of a 'big' expression from 'smaller' ones. Besides any features that serve to restrict the phonetic or semantic values of its tokens, any expression has a syntactic category, comprising features to which the rules of syntax may refer, generally having to do with distribution. I observe that theories of syntax most often share two properties that shape the theory of argument structure: they presume that the rules of syntax do not refer to very specific categories, such as 'transitive verb,' and that every primitive of syntax is phonetically interpreted, if only as silence. But neither property is necessary, and their absence characterizes what are sometimes called construction-based theories.

Chapter 2 is a primer on relevant aspects of semantics. Getting clear here is essential. We talk about 'meaning' in many different ways, and the differences often matter to theories of argument structure in particular – far more than to theories of movement, for example. I distinguish between objectivist and mentalist theories; between meaning, value and semantic representation; between derived and underived structure; between semantic consequence and analyticity; and between various forms of indeterminacy, such as ambiguity and polysemy. At the end of the chapter, I establish my notation, namely the predicate calculus with lambdas and event variables, and review common rules of semantic composition.

With this background in place, the next three chapters explore three uses of the term *argument*: syntactic arguments, semantic arguments and implicit arguments. First up in Chapter 3 is syntax. Here arguments are dependents in a phrase that are 'selected' in relation to its head, as distinct from adjuncts. The most common implementation of this idea treats the 'selection' relation as projecting from the head, giving a lexicalist encoding of the argument relation. But nonlexicalist encodings are also possible, and I will review this alternative. Then I quickly discuss optionality and the internal–external distinction, as well as "Θ-roles," which are syntactic indices of semantic argumenthood. I finish with a review of how the argument–adjunct distinction might (and might not) be expressed observationally.

Chapter 4 concerns argumenthood in the domain of semantics. Here usage is detrimentally diverse, and distinctions need to be made. A dependent is a **functional argument** of a predicate when the predicate expresses a function that has the meaning of the dependent as an argument. A **content argument** of a predicate instantiates a relation that the predicate introduces into the derivation. A **participant argument** merely names a participant in the event that the predicate denotes.

Then in Chapter 5 we come to understand some of what goes under the heading of **implicit arguments**. Any clause entails many relations that correspond to no obvious part of its syntax. This alone warrants no grammatical recognition. So when is an entailed relation furthermore an implicit argument? This is a rich question that is often passed over, especially in introductory literature. In addressing it, I explore the important distinction between *existential* and *definite* implicit arguments, assembling and developing insights from Fillmore (1986), Partee (1989) and Condoravdi and Gawron (1996), among others. I then discuss the two major diagnostics of bona fide implicit argumenthood. First, the availability of covarying readings in the scope of a quantifier, as in (4). Much of the data here is not widely known.

(4) a Nobody who put chips on a prime number won.
        'No person$_k$ who put chips on a prime number won the bet he$_k$ placed in doing so.'
     b * No ship purchased by a gangster was sunk less than three days later.
        'No ship purchased by a gangster$_k$ was sunk by him$_k$ less than three days later.'

Second, the possibility of controlling infinitival adjuncts, as in (5). I foreshadow the claim I develop in Chapter 12 that the well-known argument on this basis is unsound: sentences like (5) do not necessitate a syntactic or semantic argument for the demoted subject of the passive.

(5) The ship was sunk to collect the insurance. (Roeper 1987)
     'The ship was sunk so that its sinker might collect the insurance.'

Chapters 6–11 concern semantic analysis and how it matches up with syntax. The most common type of analysis is in terms of **thematic relations**. In Chapter 6 I say what these are, and why one might or might not want to use them. The chapter ends with a quick review of some popular inventories of relations. Chapter 7 follows on with a longer discussion of the most popular relations, Agent and Patient, the former as seen through the lens of instrumental subjects, as in This knife sliced the salami.

Chapters 8 and 9 consider how thematic relations align with the syntax. In Chapter 8, I ask why **role iteration**, as in (6), is impossible. Except perhaps in some special cases, the same semantic relation is never associated with two distinct dependents.

(6) * Nik smacked the table the chair.
       'Nik smacked the table and the chair.'

Standard accounts follow Fillmore 1968 and Chomsky 1981 in excluding this via a grammatical constraint against assigning the same relation twice, such as Chomsky's "Theta Criterion." I argue against this, and instead defend the (partly) semantic account from Carlson (1984), Dowty (1989) and Schein (1993), according to which each dependent is interpreted as *exhausting* its semantic role, naming all of its satisfiers. On this view, (6) is unacceptable for the same reason that (7a) does not entail (7b).

(7) a Tony and Geezer lifted the amp and the piano.
     b Tony lifted the amp.

In Chapter 9 I consider the choice between **projection** and **separation** of thematic relations: are they are introduced by the verb, or separately, by other items in whose context the verb occurs? I take the position of a partisan, and review several arguments in favor of separation (Carlson 1984, Schein 1993, Goldberg 1995, Kratzer 1996, Borer 2003). But I do this critically, as in my view the most familiar arguments for separation are often among the weakest, while the strongest are the least-known. I try to give separation a fair hearing by criticizing the weak arguments and clarifying the strong.

In Chapter 10, I return to semantic analysis, with a discussion of **event structures**. An event structure is a decomposition of a predicate meaning into a relation between several distinct events. I review general arguments for and against such structure in the semantics, as well as the question of whether it is derived in syntax, reprising the issue of projection versus separation. Throughout, I focus on transitive clauses expressing changes, such as Floyd melted the glass. These are very often analyzed as meaning that one event caused another. But I give reasons to reject this analysis, following Pietroski 2005a.

Chapter 11 covers two topics. First, how do semantic relations instantiated by a dependent, such as Agent or Patient, align with grammatical relations, such as Subject or Object? This is the issue of **linking** or *alignment*. I review the common theories of linking, which agree in relating an ordering of semantic relations to an ordering of grammatical relations. They disagree in whether the semantic ordering is over traditional thematic relations (Gruber 1965, Fillmore 1968, Jackendoff 1972, Baker 1997), "aspectual" relations (Tenny 1987, Grimshaw 1990, Ramchand 1998, Borer 2005) or causal and mereological relations between events (Van Valin and LaPolla 1997, Rappaport Hovav and Levin 1998, Croft 2012). They also disagree in whether the mapping between orderings is "relative" or "absolute" (Baker 1997). A relative mapping relates a *set* of thematic relations to a pairing of these with grammatical relations, while an absolute mapping, as proposed in Baker's (1988) "Uniformity of Theta Assignment Hypothesis," relates each thematic relation to a single grammatical relation.

The second topic of Chapter 11 is **framing**. What are the argument structures in which a particular verb can occur, and how does this relate to its meaning? For instance, as Fillmore (1970) asked, why is hit acceptable in both (8) and (9), but not break?

(8) a John hit the fence with a stick.
    b John broke the fence with a stick.

(9) a John hit a stick against the fence.
    b * John broke a stick against the fence.
       'John broke the fence with a stick.'

Here there are important cross-linguistic patterns. For example, we do not find a verb like the hypothetical scarry in (10), that means 'carry' but occurs in these sorts of contexts.

(10)   a * The chair scarried Navin (down Beverly Drive).
            'Navin carried the chair (down Beverly Drive).'
       b * Navin scarried (down Beverly Drive).
            'Navin carried something (down Beverly Drive).'
       c * There scarried (down Beverly Drive).
            'People carried things (down Beverly Drive).'

These generalizations in turn suggest hypotheses about language acquisition. Might the cross-linguistic patterns reflect learning biases in young children?

Chapters 12 and 13 conclude the book with case studies on passives and resultatives, giving us a chance to exercise what we have learned. In the chapter on passives, Chapter 12, my focus is on the status of the 'demoted subject,' the implied role corresponding to the subject of the active. Commonly, sentences such as (5) are taken to show that this role has (in some way) the status of ordinary argument, just one that is not realized with the form it has in actives. I develop a case against this conclusion, generally in agreement with Landau (2000). It leaves many facts unexplained, such as the implicit control of the infinitival clause in (11), and what does explain those facts also explains those which initially motivate the implicit argument theory.

(11) The ship was sunk. People were horrified. The only goal was to collect the insurance.

The chapter on resultatives, Chapter 13, focusses on their event structure, and the relation between arguments of the main verb and arguments of the complex predicate it inhabits. Resultatives like (12) suggest that there is a distinction, since the direct object of the clause is not an argument of sing, the main verb.

(12) Ozzy sang his throat hoarse.

Given this, we must say what an 'argument of the complex predicate' is, and how it relates to the main verb in cases like (13), where the cutlet seems also to be an argument vis-à-vis pound.

(13) Al pounded the cutlet flat.

As we will see, this modest question bears directly and consequentially on many issues discussed in earlier chapters: the syntactic distinction between lexical and structural arguments (Chapter 3); the semantic distinction between between participant arguments and content arguments (Chapter 4); the utility of highly general thematic predicates (Chapters 6 and 7); projection versus separation of thematic relations (Chapter 9); the event structure of change (Chapter 10); and the realization of thematic relations in syntax (Chapter 11).

Part I
Background

1 Syntax

1.1 INTRODUCTION

A theory of argument structure tells us how arguments relate syntactically to predicates. In this chapter I introduce a few aspects of syntax that matter to this. My intention is to provide not a theory of syntax, but a general framework within which different views can be discussed, neutralizing somewhat the diversity of perspectives in this area. I start with a view of grammar as derivation (Section 1.2) before distinguishing Syntax from Lexicon (Section 1.3). I then briefly discuss syntactic category (Section 1.4) and displacement (Section 1.5). Section 1.6 concludes with a delicate but consequential distinction between lexicalized and nonlexicalized syntax. Further relevant issues, such as case and grammatical relations, are discussed by other authors in the Key Topics series.

1.2 GRAMMAR AS DERIVATION

A grammar analyzes big items into smaller ones. The analysis is done at different levels, with the unanalyzed primitives of one level perhaps undergoing analysis at another. In this book I choose to talk about analysis in terms of *building* structure, assembling bigger expressions out of smaller ones. For each level, we specify its primitives and its rules of combination. Accordingly I choose to talk in *derivational* terms, rather than in terms of constraints on structures. That means I will speak of a rule of combination taking one or more expressions as inputs and yielding a new expression as an output.

For example, take (1) and (2) to be two expressions, carry and the chair, respectively. Each expression pairs a phonological feature structure, /keɹi/ or /ðə.tʃeɹ/, with a syntactic feature structure, V[N] or N. For now I ignore meaning.

(1) ⟨/keɹi/, V[N]⟩

(2) ⟨/ðə.tʃeɹ/, N⟩

(3) informally defines a rule of combination, Check. The rule takes two expressions as inputs and yields a third as its output. The phonological features of the output concatenate those of the inputs. The syntactic category of the output is X, if those of the inputs are X[Y] and Y.

(3) Check[⟨/α/, X[Y]⟩ , ⟨/β/, Y⟩] $=_{\text{def}}$ ⟨/αβ/, X⟩

In (4) we feed this rule the inputs (1) and (2), carry and the chair. The output is the bigger expression in (5), carry the chair. Thus the analysis of this bigger expression consists in (4), its derivation from (1) and (2) under application of Check.

(4) Check[(1), (2)] = (5)

(5) ⟨/keɹi.ðə.tʃeɹ/, V⟩

This derivation of carry the chair can be depicted graphically in various ways. One is given in (6), where lines connect the inputs to the output of Check. That is, the daughter nodes are inputs to Check and the mother node is the output. Another common notation would label the top node just with its syntactic category label, as in (7).

(6)   ⟨/keɹi.ðə.tʃeɹ/, V⟩

        ⟨/keɹi/, V[N]⟩   ⟨/ðə.tʃeɹ/, N⟩

(7)   V

        ⟨/keɹi/, V[N]⟩   ⟨/ðə.tʃeɹ/, N⟩

I will say that the parts of a derivation, or the **derivational parts**, are the token primitives it uses, as well as each application of a derivational rule. In derivation trees like those above, the parts are therefore all the terminal nodes, plus each step that connects a node to its daughters. Suppose that carry the chair is derived by combining the with chair under Check, and then combining the result with carry as in (4). This derivation would have five parts: tokens of carry, the, and chair, plus two applications of Check.

1.3 SYNTAX AND LEXICON

Linguistic expressions have phonological and semantic properties, in virtue of which they constrain the form and meaning of their uses.

Some expressions can be used as sentences, to do things like make assertions, give orders or ask questions. Syntax is the level of analysis with these expressions in its purview, perhaps among others. Thus Syntax derives at least sentential expressions from smaller ones, assigning them the properties that its rules of combination may refer to, such as NOUN, VERB, PLURAL or TRANSITIVE.

The primitives of Syntax are the **lexical items**. I will not use the term to mean anything more than that: lexical items are items that can bottom out a derivation in Syntax. In particular, I will not limit the term to any traditional notion of *word*. What the lexical items are is wholly a result of the syntactic theory; for us in this book, this is by definition. The set of lexical items is *the lexicon*.

In many grammatical theories, but not all (Sproat 1985, Halle and Marantz 1993, Marantz 1997, Fodor and Lepore 1998, Embick and Noyer 2007), lexical items may in turn be analyzed at another level, which I will call **Lexicon**, opposing this to Syntax. Modifying a term from McCawley 1971, I will talk about Lexicon as the **prelexical syntax**, a derivational level which builds lexical items (its outputs) out of **prelexical items** (its primitives). This perspective allows me to generalize smoothly over both **lexicalist** and **nonlexicalist** models of argument dependencies, which we will discuss below. Roughly, what the lexicalist does in Lexicon the nonlexicalist does in Syntax. It is therefore easier to recognize formal equivalences between these approaches if the two levels of analysis are both described in terms of constructive derivations. For my purposes in this book, this advantage trumps the well-known stigma of a Lexicon described derivationally: overgeneration. To recover just the small set of actual lexical items, the derivational perspective requires that the much larger set of derivable lexical items be extravagantly filtered. For this reason many linguists who use a Lexicon prefer to describe it as a network of relations, "lexical redundancy rules" (Chomsky 1970), over the set of lexical items. However, such rules tend to darken analogies that I would like the opportunity to highlight.

1.4 SYNTACTIC CATEGORY

An expression has features to which the rules of syntax may refer. Call these features collectively the **syntactic category** of the expression. Linguists often divide syntactic category broadly into two parts, major versus minor. In general I will write the category of an expression as "C[S]" where C is the value of the major category feature and S represents some (sequence of) minor category feature(s). To indicate that expression E has category C[S] I will sometimes write "E:C[S]."

Major category features encode a pattern of great generality, typically in where the expression can occur as an argument. An example is the major category of VERB in English. Roughly, expressions of this category are those that can be an argument in an expression headed by an auxiliary like will or might. I will explain what it means to **head** an expression, and what it means to be a **syntactic argument**, in Chapter 3.

Minor category features encode more specific distinctions. Among the verbs, there is the minor category of transitives. Only these verbs can be the sole verb in a transitive clause, with a subject and object. Among the clauses, there is the minor category of interrogatives. Only these clauses can be the object of the verb wonder, for example. Among the nouns, there is the minor category of plural. Many sorts of nouns combine with a determiner, but only plurals combine with the plural determiner these.

Contextual features (Chomsky 1965) are one kind of minor category feature. Relative to the rules of the syntax, the contextual features of a lexical item B encode what sorts of expressions occur as dependents in an expression that B heads. That is, they encode its argument structure. There are different senses in which contextual features 'encode' an argument structure, leading to different sorts of theories. These are the topic of Chapter 3. Traditional phrase structure grammars use contextual features such as "TRANSITIVE" (Chomsky 1957, 1965). Also familiar are the "subcategorization frame" feature of Government and Binding Theory (GB) or the analogous "SUBCAT" (or also "VALENCE") feature in Head-driver Phrase Structure Grammar (HPSG) (Manning and Sag 1998, Sag and Wasow 1999).

By distinguishing major from minor category, we allow for generalizations that simplify the grammar (Chomsky 1965). The grammar is simplified, for example, if it can refer to all *verbs* at once, with a single symbol, rather than needing to refer individually to the transitive-verbs and the nontransitive-verbs, treating these as formally unrelated categories.

1.5 DISPLACEMENT IN SYNTAX

Theories of argument structure focus on local relations between heads and dependents, such as the relation between carry and Navin or the chair in (8). Local relations are always within a single clause, and sometimes within the phrase of a single predicate. In Chapter 3 we will discuss the basic local relations of head, argument and adjunct.

(8) Navin carried the chair.

Theories of argument structure therefore ignore long-distance **displacements**, such as those in (9) – where what and the chair are syntactically and semantically related to carry, but displaced from it by intervening predicates.

(9) a What did Marie hear that the dog saw Navin carrying?
    b The chair tends to seem to be easy to carry.

But displacement is not always long-distance: some theories employ local displacement, within the domain of a single predicate, or a single clause. And in at least two cases, this relates importantly to the theory of argument structure: argument structure alternations and the interpretation of quantifiers. For this reason let me be explicit about my assumptions.

1.5.1 Alternations and movement

Local displacement may be invoked in the account of *argument structure alternations*. In an alternation, the 'same' predicate occurs in two apparently distinct arrays of arguments. The pair in (10), from Fodor (1970), illustrates the so-called 'causative alternation.'

(10) a Floyd melted the glass.
     b The glass melted.

Here a verb pronounced "melt" occurs in two different contexts, contributing a shared nugget of meaning to both. In (10a) the thing melted is named by the direct object of a transitive clause, while in (10b) it is named by the subject of an intransitive clause.

In cases like (10) it is plausible to assimilate the two alternates at an unpronounced level of 'underlying syntax.' At this level the glass has the exact same grammatical relations to melt in both (10a) and (10b): in both it is the 'underlying object.' This analysis implies that, for the latter sentence, the underlying syntax is then related to the surface (pronounced) syntax via local displacement of the glass, which is the subject of the clause at the surface.

This is still a very general idea. There are various ways it can be executed, depending on what content is given to the notions of 'underlying syntax' and, correspondingly, of 'displacement.' I will generally assume a transformational implementation, under which the pronounced syntax is derived from the underlying syntax by movement. Let me say what this means.

A syntactic operation on an expression is **transformational** when it refers to the syntactic parts of that expression – either a part of its derived form or a part of its derivation. For example, the expression melted the glass has the glass as a syntactic part, in one or the other sense of the term. So any operation on melted the glass that refers to the glass is transformational. **Movement** operations are transformational operations which take a syntactic part A of an expression E and attach it elsewhere.[1] I will maintain the most common assumption, that A attaches to E itself, i.e., at its root.[2] For simplicity I will assume that, when movement targets A, it replaces A with a *trace*, written as *t*. A trace of movement is interpreted phonetically as silence (at least usually) and semantically as a variable bound by the moved expression.

Example (11) shows a simplified scheme for applying movement to melted the glass. Here bracketing indicates the syntactic parts of an expression. A movement operation called Move targets the glass, a syntactic part of melted the glass. It replaces the glass with a bound trace *t*, and attaches it back to the verb phrase. The trace being interpreted as a bound variable, the result means 'the glass *x* is such that *x* melted,' which boils down to 'the glass melted.'

(11)   Move⟨ [melted [the glass]] ⟩ = [[the glass]$_k$ [melted t_k]]

Under this analysis, the syntactic analysis of both (10a) and (10b) includes a verb phrase with the glass as its object. What is common across both alternates is therefore represented in the syntactic derivation.

1.5.2 Quantifiers and movement

The second reason we must attend to displacement is the semantics of quantifiers. Any semantic theory must account for the interpretation of dependents both when they are pronouns, like she and her in (12), and when they are quantifiers, like every ewe and at least one vixen in (13).

---

[1] There are many ways of formulating movement, sometimes with important differences. Here I am abstracting to what I think is the most general case.

[2] Under this assumption, movement produces (by convention) a derived tree in which the moved expression A c-commands its original position in E. In such cases we say that movement is 'upwards.' The operation of "Sidewards Movement" (Nunes 2001, Hornstein *et al.* 2005) may produce derived trees in which movement is not upwards, but "sideways." It takes a part A of expression E and attaches it to D, an expression which may not overlap with E. Occasionally it will matter that I ignore Sidewards Movement, and I will indicate this in footnotes.

(12)   She kicked her.

(13)   Every ewe kicked at least one vixen.

Some theories deploy different rules of semantic composition for the two cases. Others assimilate one of the two cases to the other. I will assume an account of the latter kind, assimilating the two cases through *quantifier raising* or *QR* (Lakoff 1970, Lewis 1970, McCawley 1972, Montague 1973, May 1977, Heim and Kratzer 1998).

Given QR, sentences with quantifiers are not interpreted semantically with the quantifiers in the positions where they are pronounced. Instead they are interpreted with the quantifiers at the edge of their clause, and a trace in their surface position. Example (13) is given a syntax something like (14), where coindexation indicates movement. The trace is interpreted as a variable over the domain of the quantifier, and raising is interpreted as binding of that variable. Thus (14) means (15).

(14)   [[Every ewe]$_k$ [[at least one vixen]$_j$ [t_k kicked t_j]]]

(15)   'For every ewe x, there is at least one vixen y, such that x kicked y.'

Pronouns too are interpreted as variables, so that (12), she kicked her, means 'x kicked y.' Consequently the two immediate dependents of the verb in (14), subject and object, are now semantically equivalent to those in (12): they are all interpreted as variables over individuals. The only difference is in binding. In the interpretation of (12) the variables are free, while they are bound by the quantifiers in the interpretation of (14). Free variables are assigned a value 'by context.'

Given this assimilation, we can usually (though not always) ignore quantifiers in the theory of argument structure, and pretend that all nominal dependents are pronouns – or rather, we can assume that all nominal dependents are interpreted, like pronouns, as individuals in the domain of discourse. Accordingly, in my example data, nominal dependents will usually be pronouns, proper names and definite descriptions, all of which I will assume are not quantifiers, and are interpreted as individuals. This is not to say that quantifiers are theoretically unimportant; they are extraordinarily important. It is only to say that we can bracket this while attending to other matters.

1.6   LEXICALIZED AND NONLEXICALIZED SYNTAX

The common theories of argument structure are deeply connected to the standard styles of syntax. The connection is deepest in two basic assumptions made by most theories of syntax since the 1970s: first, the rules of combination are general, and second, the primitives are **lexicalized**. Understanding these assumptions helps us to understand the common theories of argument structure, and also to see what sorts of alternatives there might be.

1.6.1 General and specific rules

Rules of combination are **general** when they do not refer to specific syntactic categories, like 'transitive verb'. Thus the rule expressed by "•" in (16) is general, here taking X and Y to be variables that range over values of syntactic category features. This rule isolates the purely syntactic (non-phonological) component of Check in (4).

(16) $X[Y] \bullet Y[] = X[]$

Rule (16) allows two expressions of any major categories X and Y to make a larger expression of major category X, as long as the minor category feature of the first matches the category feature of the second in value.

The rule expressed by "⊛" in (17), on the other hand, says something much narrower: expressions specifically of categories V[t] and N can combine to make a larger expression of category V. Rule (17) is therefore not general, but **specific**.

(17) $V[t] \circledast N[] = V[]$

By definition, a rule that is general cannot encode dependencies among categories that are specific. So if all the rules of the syntax are general, we cannot state any such specific dependencies in the rules of combination. Rather they will have to be encoded in structured features of the primitives, the lexical items (Bar-Hillel 1953, Lyons 1966, Chomsky 1970, 1981, 1995, Jackendoff 1977, Bresnan 1980, Stowell 1981, Keenan and Stabler 2003, Joshi 2004). Thus instead of having a rule that says "combine a transitive verb with a noun phrase," for example, we will associate each transitive verb with features that, in the context of the grammar, mean 'combine me with a noun phrase.' In such a system, grammatical dependencies therefore **project** from lexical items, since the rules of combination merely express phrase structure patterns that are explicitly encoded in the lexical features of a single lexical item. So a syntax with only general rules will project syntactic patterns entirely from lexical items.

The assumption that rules are general defines the basic character of GB, Minimalism, HPSG, Lexical Functional Grammar (LFG), Construction Grammar and all varieties of Categorial Grammar, which is arguably the historical source (Ajdukiewicz 1935, Bar-Hillel 1953).

In these frameworks, phrase structure patterns project from lexical items. In contrast, the grammars in Chomsky 1957 and 1965 make use of specific rules. For instance, to analyze or build a transitive verb phrase, Chomsky (1957:26) has (18), which refers to specific categories such as "Verb" and "NP."

(18) "VP → Verb + NP"

1.6.2 Lexicalized and nonlexicalized grammars

Let us call the primitives of syntax lexicalized when they are candidates for phonological expression (Joshi and Schabes 1997). More precisely, lexicalized primitives are interpreted by the phonology, if only as the empty string. A primitive of syntax that is lexicalized is therefore in one very traditional sense a *word*, a basic unit of the syntax that can be pronounced and have a meaning. Consider (19) for example.

(19) a ⟨ /keɹi/, V[N] ⟩
      b ⟨ /ɛ/, V[V] ⟩

Assume that these are two lexical items, each of which pairs phonological with syntactic features. The phonological features are interpreted phonologically, specifically as [kʰeɹi] and silence, respectively. Thus both lexical items are lexicalized.

A syntax is lexicalized when all its lexical items are lexicalized. Every primitive of a **lexicalized syntax** has a pronunciation, if only as silence. Today, most of the common frameworks for syntax are lexicalized: GB and Minimalism, HPSG, LFG and all varieties of Categorial Grammar. Lexicalization is also entailed by the traditional structuralist idea of syntax, under which it consists in the distributional categorization of sound-strings, possibly including the empty string. If everything with a syntactic category is also a sound-string, then the syntax is therefore lexicalized.

But a lexicalized syntax is not the only possibility. In a **nonlexicalized syntax** the set of primitives includes some items that have a syntactic category, and also a semantic interpretation, but contribute nothing to be read by the phonology. In effect, such items are phrase structure rules rendered as lexical items, the primitives of syntactic composition. One variety of nonlexicalized syntax is offered in the "Construction Grammars" of Kay, Fillmore, Goldberg, Croft and Sag (see Boas and Sag 2012). Since much work on argument structure is done under this rubric, it is worth having some grasp of the idea, so let us walk through an example.

To make a nonlexicalized syntax vivid, it helps to think of Syntax as building, not categorized sound strings, but categorized trees (Joshi 1987). Suppose that the four trees in (20–23), the first of depth-two and the others of depth-zero, are the primitives of our syntax. Thus (20) is *not* a graphic representation of a derivational history, but rather a structured lexical item, the 'transitive construction.'

(20)

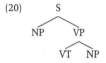

(21)   VT, /keɹid/
(22)   NP, /ɪt/
(23)   NP, /nevɪn/

Here nodes are decorated with category labels. The depth-zero trees in (21–23) have, in addition, phonological features, listed after the comma. These are the words carried, it, and Navin. The depth-two tree in (20), however, contributes nothing to phonology; it is 'purely structural,' and because of this our syntax is nonlexicalized.

This tree in (20) illustrates how in a nonlexicalized syntax one can state category-specific grammatical patterns separately from any particular 'word.' Here the fact that VTs combine with two NPs to form an S is encoded in (20), separate from anything pronounced "carried." Furthermore, since this specific information is encoded in the primitives, and not the rules of combination, those rules can be kept highly general. The basic rule is just substitution of a tree whose root is labeled X for a node labeled X in a second tree. Thus we can assemble our four primitive trees to make one pronounced "Navin carried it." We substitute tokens of (21), (22) and (23) into matching nodes of the structural tree in (20). This yields (24), a sentential expression. Remember, this is not a graph of the derivation, but the derived expression itself.[3]

(24)

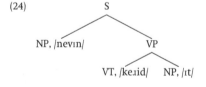

---

[3] Here the structure of the derivation differs from that of the tree derived, regardless of how it is graphed. The derivation involves three instances of tree substitution. The derived structure has only two sisterhood relations.

Now let us translate the grammar of (20–23) into a broadly similar grammar that is fully lexicalized. The only difference is that the S tree, (20), and the VT tree, (21), are conflated into one, (25).

(25)

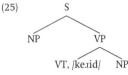

(26) NP, /nevɪn/

(27) NP, /ɪt/

Now each primitive of the grammar is a traditional word, pairing phonological features with a syntactic category, here represented by its tree. So the word that will be pronounced "carried," (25), has the syntactic category of a sentence with its subject and object missing. To build the final sentential tree in (24), we substitute tokens of (27) and (26) for the relevant nodes in tree (25). This yields the exact same output as does the derivation under the first grammar. But it involves one step less, since the combination of "carry" and its category is, so to speak, precompiled in Lexicon.

In Chapter 3, I will compare lexicalized to nonlexicalized treatments of argument structure, and briefly discuss the reasons why lexicalized grammars are presently dominant.

DISCUSSION POINTS

1 In (2), [the chair] is treated as a single object. What might the categories of the and chair be, such that they combine via Check to yield (2)?

2 Suppose that the derivation of Mo might cook has three primitive parts (lexical items), namely Mo, might and cook. Does its derivation also have just three parts, as "derivational part" is defined in this chapter? What is the smallest number of derivational parts it might have? Is there a largest number of derivational parts it might have?

3 Provide both a lexicalized and nonlexicalized analysis of (1) below.

(1) Tony gave the guitar to Geezer.

4 Follow the logic in §1.5 to argue that it would be reasonable to regard (2a) and (2b) as being related by transformations. Then give a mini-grammar that will derive these two sentences under a

transformational perspective. How would you derive the two sentences without transformations?

(2) a Tony gave the guitar to Geezer.
     b Tony gave Geezer the guitar.

5 How can you tell whether the structure of an expression is built in Syntax or in Lexicon? Why is it common to assume that there is Lexicon, distinct from Syntax? That is, that phonological words with internal structure are built at a different level of analysis than sentences are?

6 Can you think of transformational operations that are not movements?

7 As observed in the text, "by distinguishing major from minor category we allow for generalizations that simplify the grammar." Make sure you understand why. Now ask, should we have minor category features that are shared across different major categories? For instance, are there transitive nouns, in addition to transitive verbs? Can you think of any other possible cases?

8 Is it attractive to assume that derivational rules of Syntax are general? Why?

SUGGESTIONS FOR FURTHER READING

Koopman, Sportiche and Stabler 2013 and Culicover 2009 are superb general introductions to syntactic analysis. On syntax in the context of the Minimalism Program, see Hornstein, Nunes and Grohmann 2005 and Stabler 2010. For a view of syntax from a high level of abstraction, see Keenan and Stabler 2003.

2 Semantics

2.1 INTRODUCTION

A theory of argument structure tells us, among other things, how dependents relate to a predicate semantically. So our goal in this chapter is a preliminary understanding of semantics, in those aspects which matter to our topic. I first discuss various notions of meaning (Sections 2.2 and 2.3), structure (Section 2.4), entailment (Section 2.5) and indeterminacy (Section 2.6). I then introduce specifics: the notation I use for stating meanings (Section 2.7), the common rules of semantic combination (Section 2.8), and the basics of event semantics (Section 2.9).

2.2 VALUES

The meaning of an expression token, under one use of the term, is something outside of language to which the expression is related. Call a meaning of this sort a **semantic value**, or just a value. Two broad views of semantic values are most familiar in linguistics, each in important variants.

On the first view, semantic values are in general outside the mind. They include things such as Barack Obama, the event of his election, the property of having won, the actual world and possible alternatives, the truth values True and False, or various sets and pairings of these things. For example, we might say that the value of Obama is Obama; the value of won is a set of ordered pairs that pair a person with a truth value; and the value of Obama won is a truth value. Thus for some expressions, such as Obama, the semantic value may be (or include) the very thing we use the expression to talk about. Call this view **objectivist**.

The other view is **mentalist**. It sees all values as concepts or thoughts in the mind, such as the mental concept of being Obama, the mental concept of having won, the mental concept of being actual or possible, or the thought that Obama won the election. On this view, whereby the semantic value of Obama is not Obama, the values of expressions are not (in general) the things we use the expressions to talk about. Consequently semantics alone, regarded as just the theory that associates expressions with values, does not explain how we convey information about Obama by using the word Obama. To explain that, we will need supplementary theories, to do with the function and content of mental states and also acts of language use.

I would like to keep both views, objectivist and mentalist, within the scope of our discussion. Accordingly I will try to generalize over both, most often without comment. But the distinction sometimes makes a difference that I will pause to point out.[1]

2.3 MEANINGS

As linguists we are often more interested in expressions themselves than in their uses. Therefore in general we do not consider semantic values directly. Instead we consider just the invariant contribution an expression makes to restricting or determining the values of its token uses. This contribution is also often called the **meaning** of an expression – and this is the usage I will follow in this book, thereby reserving the simplest term for the main object of interest.[2] When I talk about the *meaning* of an expression, I am not talking directly about the value of any of its uses, but rather about the contribution the expression makes to restricting those values. Deviations from this usage will happen, I hope, only where it will cause no confusion.

The meaning abstracts from any contributions to the value made at the tokening or use. These contributions will include at least the

[1] One important view of semantics denies that all expressions *stand for* something, whether mental concepts or things in the world. Rather, sentences are true (or satisfied) under certain conditions, and semantics takes the form of a truth theory that recursively specifies truth (or satisfaction) conditions in terms of the syntactic derivation. This gives us no reason to suppose that a predicate, such as won, stands for anything; it just contributes to the satisfaction conditions of its sentence. This view has a classic source in Davidson 1967c, which builds on Tarski 1944 and Quine 1953. Larson and Segal 1995 develop a contemporary version, adapted into a broadly Chomskyan and mentalist perspective. I will not address this third view directly here, however. Most of what I say, though not all, will apply straightforwardly to a transformation of the Davidsonian view that reifies the lexical axioms of its truth theory as meaning specifications. The transformation is far from theoretically innocent. But it does not much distort what I would like to say here in this book.

[2] The same terminological choices are made in Neale 1990.

resolution of indexicals, such as me and now. In some semantic theories they will also include "pragmatic enrichments" not formally indexed in the expression itself (Perry 1986, Sperber and Wilson 1986, Bach 1994, Carston 2002, Recanati 2004), or even some contribution of background assumptions and cultural practices (Searle 1978, 1980).

Given this definition of the term, an expression cannot fail to have a meaning, so long as some of its uses have a semantic value, and the expression is a factor in determining those values. For example, if every communicative use of the simple symbol "⋆" has Obama as its value, then "⋆" has a meaning, consisting in the very fact that its uses all evaluate to Obama.

Meanings are therefore not "semantic representations." On careful uses of the term (Dowty 1979), a **semantic representation** is a symbolic representation *of* the meaning or the value, distinct from the meaning itself, used to state some grammatical generalization. The representation is taken to be either an additional part of the expression itself, or instead just part of the language in which the relevant grammatical generalization is stated. In our example there is no semantic representation associated with "⋆," no part of "⋆" or further symbol to which it is related, which represents the fact that it stands for Obama, or represents Obama himself.

If semantic representations are not meanings, what use are they to linguists? Here is a quick but representative example. The distribution of verbs is somehow related to what sort of event satisfies them. For example, kill and sing occur in different sorts of clause in part because killings are relevantly different from singings. To state generalizations about this, we will need to describe the satisfiers of verbs in a certain general format. For example, we might say that a verb will occur exclusively in transitive clauses if it describes events where "someone CAUSES something to CHANGE," using CAUSE and CHANGE as primitives of our format. But now, importantly, this description need not itself be the meaning of any verb. We can still say, if we like, that the meaning of kill consists just in the fact that its value is always the set of killings. So our generalization does not require that the meaning of kill have CAUSE and CHANGE as parts. It requires only that killings themselves can be described in these terms. And this description, inasmuch as it is not the meaning itself, but is used in stating a grammatical generalization, can be called a semantic representation.[3]

---

[3] Here is another example of how linguists use semantic representations, as distinct from meanings. Suppose we were to make two initial assumptions. First, every use of the word ewe has as its value the set of ewes (an objectivist assumption).

2.4 DERIVATION, STRUCTURE AND DECOMPOSITION

When an expression has meaningful parts in Syntax or in Lexicon, its meaning is therefore **derived**. The meaning of carry the chair is derived, because it is due to carry, the and chair, plus their syntactic arrangement. Similarly if harden has hard and -en as prelexical parts, then these and their arrangement give it its meaning; its meaning too is derived. The theory of derived meanings is **compositional semantics**.

Having a derived meaning does not imply having a **structured semantic value**. The meaning of carry the chair is derived. But its value may not have structure to match the derivation. For example, in the most common style of objectivist semantics, tokens of carry the chair will have as their value a function. A function, on one common definition, is a set of ordered pairs. The pairs in the carry-the-chair function associate those who carry the chair with True and everyone else with False. This set has no structure to match that of carry the chair. So to say that an expression has a structured semantic value is to say more than just that its meaning is derived.

Among linguists of an objectivist stripe, structured semantic values are these days uncommon. Such linguists rely mainly on sets of ordered pairs – pairs of individuals and truth values, pairs of possible worlds and truth values, and so forth – and these sets have no structure to match that of the expression. But objectivism is not tied conceptually to structureless values. An objectivist can say, with no appeal to psychology, that the value of Obama won is a structure, comprising Obama and the property of victory, that matches the subject–predicate form of the clause (Russell 1903, Soames 1987, King 1995, 1996).

Among mentalists, structured semantic values are the norm. It is standard for a mentalist to assume that the value of a complex expression is a concept or thought with much the same structure. The value of Obama won, for example, might be a sentence-like mental structure, perhaps in a "language of thought" (Fodor 1975), comprising (mental symbols for) the concept of Obama and the concept of victory (Sperber and Wilson 1986, Jackendoff 1990b, Carston 2002, Pietroski 2010, 2011).

Therefore its meaning consists in the restriction of every value to that set. And yet, second, every use of ewe entails tokening the concepts FEMALE and SHEEP in the mind. The first assumption cannot explain the second, so, if we did want to explain the second assumption, we would have to say more. One thing we might say is that ewe, besides standing for the ewes, also has a semantic representation which includes symbols that stand for the mental concepts FEMALE and SHEEP. In this way, the semantic representation might be used to encode the cognitive significance of the expression, in theories where the value and meaning alone do not.

These distinctions matter in discussions of **semantic decomposition**. We speak of semantic decomposition when a meaning is described using more predicates than there are audible words in the expression. Parsons (1990:139), for example, says that (1a) means (1b). And while (1a) has only one predicate audibly, break, (1b) involves many more: Agent, Theme, Culminates, Cause and Breaking. (We will learn how to read such formulas in Section 2.7.)

(1) a Mary broke the window.
  b $\exists e[$ Agent$(e,$ Mary$)$ & Culminates(e) & $\exists e'[$ Breaking(e')
      & Culminates(e') & Theme$(e',$ the window$)$ & Cause(e, e') $]]$

Dowty (1979) describes the semantic value of transitive harden with the formula in (2). The verb is syntactically simple, but Dowty's description of its value is complex, with the several predicates Cause, Do and Become, in addition to Hard.

(2) $\lambda y \lambda x[$ $\exists P[$ Cause$(Do[x, P(x)],$ Become$[Hard(y)])$ $]]$

Parsons and Dowty are themselves very clear about what they mean the 'additional' structure in these formulas to indicate. But in principle it might be meant in any of three ways, importantly different: semantic decomposition may be **strict**, **representational** or **metasemantic**.

Semantic decomposition is **strict** when it ascribes structure to the meaning of the expression itself. This structure may in turn be resolved in any of the ways discussed just above. It may be derived, either in Syntax or Lexicon; all but one of the predicates in (1b) would then come from inaudible parts of the syntactic derivation, or from prelexical parts of the verb break. This is how Parsons means (1). Alternatively, the meaning of the expression may be structured but not derived. Some primitive must then have a structured semantic value: perhaps the verb break has no prelexical parts, but nonetheless stands for a complex mental concept, for example. The decomposition is then both strict and underived.

Semantic decomposition is **representational** when the structured formula is meant as a name, not for the meaning itself, but for a semantic representation. Supposing that there are such things, a semantic representation is a particular symbolic representation *of* the meaning or value of an expression, somehow active in the grammar (Section 2.3). Importantly, however, where a semantic representation cannot be active is in the compositional semantics, which by definition operates on meanings (or indeed values) and not on representations of them.

The third view is that of Dowty (1979). Dowty sees little use for semantic representations. And in proposing (2), he says neither that the value of harden has any interesting structure, nor that harden has prelexical parts to which the parts of (2) devolve. Instead, he intends his complex "translations" of lexical items as part of a theory *about* the semantics – about the language – and not a part of the semantics or language itself. The decomposition is entirely **metasemantic**. Its purpose is only to claim that the semantic value of the lexical item, itself just an unstructured set of ordered pairs, *can* be described in *at least* this way. This alone is interesting, argues Dowty, because if very general predicates such as Cause and Become can be used to specify the values of many different verbs, it constitutes a substantive generalization about the attested meanings for verbs in the language. But, to repeat, this is not a claim of structure in either the derivation or the value of the verb.

2.5 ENTAILMENT AND ANALYTICITY

I can use (3) to claim that Cy struck out Ty in a certain round of baseball, at some time and place. If Cy did indeed strike out Ty in the relevant circumstances, then the claim I make is a true one.

(3) Cy struck out Ty.

It is also convenient to say that the sentence, (3) itself, is then true as well. I don't know if it's also right to say that, but it is at least a usefully brief way of saying that the claim made in using the sentence is true. Let us leave aside the question of what, relative to a context, properly bears truth: sentence types, sentence tokens, sentence uses, speech acts or their content.[4]

In any circumstance where one sentence is true, many others will be true as well. For example, whenever (3) is true, so are (4) and (5); or at any rate let us presume that this is so, fixing our understanding of strike out in the context of baseball.

(4) Cy threw a ball.

(5) Ty held a bat.

In such cases, where Y is true whenever X is, we can say that X **entails** Y. So (3) entails (4) and (5). They are therefore among its

---

[4] On that matter it is helpful to consult, among others, Austin 1950, 1961, Searle 1980, Perry 1986, Bach 1994, Travis 1996, Stanley 2000, Borg 2004, Recanati 2004, Cappelen and Lepore 2005a, b, Burgess and Burgess 2011, and Pietroski, to appear a.

entailments. Another term I will use with the same definition is **semantic consequence**. To indicate the relation of entailment or semantic consequence, I will use "⊨," as in (6).

(6)   Cy struck out Ty ⊨ Cy threw a ball

Many entailments will not arouse much interest in the linguist. Take (7) and (8), for example. These are among the entailments of (3), since they cannot be false while (3) is true. Indeed they cannot be false in general.

(7)   Anything with color is extended in space.

(8)   The circumference of a circle is proportional to its diameter.

But some entailments feel special, in seeming to reflect a relation of meaning. Cy struck out Ty entails (7) and (8) only because the latter are true in nearly all imaginable circumstances. But why does it entail Cy threw a ball? Seemingly because their meanings are importantly related, though their forms are quite different. Specifically, Cy struck out Ty seems to somehow include the meaning of Cy threw a ball, though without containing throw or ball. We may have similar thoughts about (9). It is tempting to say that the entailment holds because ewe has 'sheep' as a part of its meaning, even though it does not have sheep as a part of its derivation.

(9)   Eunice is a ewe ⊨ Eunice is a sheep

In the jargon, such entailments are the ones that appear to be **analytic**. Analytic entailments are those underwritten by meaning inclusion, in some sense that a theory of analyticity needs to develop.

We can distinguish between **covert** analyticities and **overt** analyticities. An analytic entailment is **covert** when the allegedly included meaning is not part of an audibly included subexpression. Our first two examples, (6) and (9), are both covert: throw is not an audible part of strike out, nor sheep of ewe. An analyticity is **overt** where there is a relevant overlap in form. Thus the entailment in (10) is potentially an overt analyticity.

(10)   Eunice is a female sheep ⊨ Eunice is a sheep

When a putative analyticity is overt, the semantics should ideally state the meanings so that the entailment comes out as formally valid. In the best case an overt analyticity should be not merely an entailment but also a **syntactic consequence**, one that can be proven just in terms of logical structure, with no reference to nonlogical content. I will use "⊢" for the relation of syntactic consequence. Thus, suppose that Eunice is a female sheep and Eunice is a sheep are analyzed as having the meanings in (11a) and (11b).

(11)   a   Female(Eunice) & Sheep(Eunice)
       b   ⊢ Sheep(Eunice)

Then we render (10) as not only a semantic but also a syntactic consequence. Example (11b) can be proven from (11a) using just the rule of Conjunction Elimination, a standard rule of logical inference. In such cases I will say that the entailment is represented as **strictly** analytic, or as a **strict analyticity**. So $X \vDash Y$ is strictly analytic just in case $X \vdash Y$.[5]

Overt analyticities don't arouse much controversy. But a claim of covert analyticity is always hard to justify. All ewes are sheep, but how does one show that the word ewe has sheephood in its meaning? Ewes would be sheep regardless of what we say about ewe, except that it stands for ewes. Maybe everything we call water contains H_2O, maybe everything we call singing involves patterned vibrations in a fluid, and maybe every chair contains protons. But it is not obvious that these facts belong to the meanings of water, singing or chair – if only because people who know nothing of chemistry and physics can use these words to talk about water, singing and chairs. Putting it generally, it is not obvious how to distinguish matters of meaning from matters of non-linguistic fact, theory or social convention.[6]

To claim that a covert analyticity is strict requires a further sort of daring. When ewe does not include sheep as part of its form, how could Eunice is a ewe have Eunice is a sheep as a provable consequence? If the meanings are as in (12), it can't. No general rule of inference will prove

---

[5] Within formal semantics there is a history of identifying analyticity with necessary truth, reductionistically. Following Carnap (1956:9), David Lewis (1970:34) writes: "a sentence meaning is *analytic* ... iff it is true at every index," where an "index" is a circumstance relative to which the sentence is interpreted. Relatedly, many linguistic semanticists characterize the meaning of a sentence solely in terms of its entailments, those things which are true whenever the sentence is true. On this view, an "analytic" consequence could only be an entailment. But then any sentence would have every necessary truth as an "analytic" consequence; for instance, Cy struck out Ty would have as an "analytic" consequence the proposition that the circumference of a circle is proportional to its diameter. This is odd, since the sentence has nothing to do with circles (Foster 1976). One way to preserve some of the term's original sense, ultimately following Frege 1884, is to limit the use of "analytic" to those entailments that are provable syntactic consequences, those I call the *strict* analyticities. This is what I do here.

[6] The issue has engaged many thinkers since Locke, Hume and Kant, importantly including Frege, Carnap and Quine. For relevant contemporary discussion, see Fodor and Lepore 1998, 2006, Harman 1999b, Pietroski 2003, Juhl and Loomis 2010, and Rey 2013.

$Q(a)$ from $P(a)$. So, as stated in (12b), Sheep(Eunice) is not a syntactic consequence of Ewe(Eunice).

(12) a Ewe(Eunice) ⊨ Sheep(Eunice)
     b Ewe(Eunice) ⊭ Sheep(Eunice)

One has to say that the sentence in the premise has more structure in its meaning than is manifest on the surface in its form. Only then can its meaning formally include that of the conclusion. So, for example, if we say *Eunice is a ewe* has the meaning in (13a), (13b) will follow as a syntactic consequence, and (9) will be a strict analyticity.

(13) a   Sheep(Eunice) & Female(Eunice)
     b ⊢ Sheep(Eunice)

So a covert analyticity, to be strict, requires some nonapparent level of structure, where the sentences have more parts than they seem to on the surface: semantic decomposition. If the added structure is in the syntax, the decomposition is syntactically derived. Otherwise we have lexical decomposition, and thereby commit either to a derivational Lexicon or to lexical items whose values have underived structure.

These distinctions are subtle, but also quite important. In theories of argument structure, claims of covert but strict analyticity, and therefore of syntactic or semantic decomposition, are very common. Many linguists would assign (14) a meaning like (15); and this is to say that (14) has "Navin is an Agent in some event" as a covert but strict analytic entailment. There is no audible part of (14) whose meaning is Agent, and yet this predicate is a separate conjunct in (15), licensing (16) as a syntactic consequence.

(14)   Navin carried the chair.

(15) $\exists e[$ Agent(e, Navin) & Carrying(e) & Patient(e, the chair) $]$

(16) $\exists e[$ Agent(e, Navin) $]$

2.6 INDETERMINACY

As I use the term "meaning," the meaning of an expression is part of its identity. So a single expression always has a single meaning and not more. But this is not how we speak informally. We do sometimes say that one "word" may have several "meanings." This informal talk covers several different phenomena, all under the broad heading of semantic **indeterminacy**. It will be useful to quickly distinguish four, since all of these come up regularly in discussions of argument structure: ambiguity, generality, vagueness, and polysemy.

I use **ambiguity** only to describe the homophony of two distinct expressions, like the franks with mustard and the Franks with mustaches. Homophones are two expressions that have the same pronunciation but differ in their meaning (each makes a different contribution to the semantic values of its tokens). The other terms (generality, vagueness and polysemy) all apply to a single expression.

A predicate is **general** in relation to some others just when its meaning subsumes those of the others. For example, the predicate teacher is general in relation to the predicates math teacher and history teacher. Anything that satisfies the latter two predicates satisfies teacher as well. And if the values of these predicates are sets of individuals, the value of teacher has these sets as subsets.

A predicate is **vague** when the boundaries of its application are indeterminate. A woman is considered *tall* in today's America if she is 5 foot 8, but not if she is 5 foot 4. The boundary between tall and not tall is blurry, however. Surely we would say that a woman is tall if she is 5 foot 7.9 and also if she is 5 foot 7.8. Eventually these marginal subtractions will yield a woman who is not tall. But the question of exactly *when* has no nonstipulative answer. And for this reason tall is vague. It is best to use the term "vague" with just this meaning, rather than as a hypernym for several sorts of indeterminacy.

Sometimes we talk as if a single expression always has only a single semantic value, the same at each use. But this is a simplification. Different uses of the same expression may have different values. This is obvious with demonstrative or indexical expressions, like she, this or me: one use of she may have Mo as its value, while another has Lee.

There are different and more subtle cases, however, some of which may fairly be put under the rubric of **polysemy**. Consider the word France (Austin 1962). It can be used to talk about either a political or a territorial body, as in (17).

(17)   France is a republic and France is hexagonal.

Yet this is not homophony; there is just one word pronounced "France", not two.[7] Still it is not plain that we should recognize a single semantic

---

[7] Here is one reason to believe that France is unambiguous. When a sound X is ambiguous, anaphors dependent on the word pronounced X do not preserve the ambiguity independently. One cannot say Jean loves to eat franks because they were his ancestors, meaning to explain Jean's affection for hot dogs in terms of his European heritage. The interpretation of they follows that of its antecedent. Yet it

value for every token of the word, a value which is both a political and a territorial body. For if we do, the relative oddity of (18) is left unexplained (Pietroski 2005b). Example (18) differs from (17) in having only a single use of France, and consequently in requiring that the semantic value of this one France is both a hexagon and a republic. Its oddity suggests that there is no single value of France which has both properties.

(18) ? France is a hexagonal republic.

Perhaps we should say, therefore, that some tokens of France have the (concept of the) republic as their value and others have (the concept of) the territory, these being two among the possible values that tokens of France may have (Searle 1978, Carston 2004, Pietroski 2005b, Wilson and Carston 2007, Recanati 2010). On this view, then, different uses of a single expression can have different values, even if the values for pronouns and indexicals are fixed. Accordingly, an expression has a single value only relative to a resolution of polysemy. This is controversial (Kracht 2011:7). On the orthodox view it is ruled out as a matter of principle. See Recanati (2012) for an overview of the dispute.

While the distinctions between ambiguity, generality, vagueness and polysemy are more or less clear in principle, it is often unclear, for a given case of semantic indeterminacy, which of these four bins it should be put in. This is often important in disputes over argument structure. For example, suppose we want to say that the subject relation in (19) is interpreted by the Agent relation in the semantics. Then what should we say about (20), when opening the door involves the locksmith and the blue key in very different ways?

(19) The locksmith opened the back door.
(20) The blue key opened the back door.

Is the subject relation ambiguous, sometimes meaning Agent and sometimes meaning Instrument? Or is it polysemous, with a single structure taking different but related values on different occasions? Is the Agent relation simply general as to the involvement of the locksmith and the key? Or is the Agent relation vague, with (20) being just a borderline case of agency? None of this is at all clear at the outset (see Chapter 7).

---

is fine to say: France is a republic and it is hexagonal, talking thereby first about a government and then about a landmass.

2.7 NOTATION

2.7.1 Values and meanings

Double brackets, $[\![\cdot]\!]$, yield the semantic value of the expression they enclose. The circumstance c relative to which the expression is evaluated may be given as a superscript. Thus (21) says that, relative to circumstance c, carry the chair has a certain set as its value. The members of the set are ordered pairs of a person and a truth value.

(21) $[\![\text{carry the chair}]\!]^c = \{\langle \text{Marie}, \text{False}\rangle, \langle \text{Navin}, \text{True}\rangle, \langle \text{Patty}, \text{False}\rangle, \ldots\}$

We might also describe the value of carry the chair in other ways, such as (22). This second way of presenting the value is no different from (21), if indeed Navin carried the chair, but Marie and Patty did not, and so forth.

(22) $[\![\text{carried the chair}]\!]^c$ = the function that pairs those who carried the chair in c with True and everything else with False

In stating hypotheses about meanings it is often convenient to use a formula F with at least as much structure as the expression E has in Syntax or Lexicon. This will help us to state and to develop hypotheses about how its meaning is derived, by assuming that each part of E contributes at least one part of F. Structure in F may also serve to represent underived structure in the semantic value, if there is any.

To that end let me introduce some very loose but occasionally useful notation. I will say that E and F are *semantically congruent*, written E $\cong$ F, when E and F have not only the same semantic value relative to any circumstance, but also 'congruent logical forms.' The idea is, all structure in formula F indicates semantic structure in E, either in its derivation or in its value. I won't be too precise about this. But, roughly, if E and F have congruent logical forms, three conditions must hold. First, each minimal part of E's derivation corresponds to at least one minimal part of F's form (modulo notational simplification). Second, no minimal part of F's form corresponds to more than one minimal part of E's derivation. Third, if some minimal part, A, of E's derivation contributes more than one minimal part of formula F, then these several parts of F represent either underived structure in the semantic value of A, or possibly, when A is a lexical item, in its lexical derivation. These conditions set semantic congruence apart from the "translation" relation in Montague Grammar (Dowty *et al.* 1981), though very often the latter is used for similar expository purposes.[8]

When E and F are semantically congruent, they have the same semantic value in every circumstance, up to polysemy. So (23) will entail (24). The interpretation of logical formulas like these will be reviewed just below, in Section 2.7.2.

(23)   carry the chair $\cong \lambda x \exists e [$ Agent(e, x) & Carrying(e) & Patient$(e,$ the chair$)$]

(24) $[\![$ carry the chair $]\!]^c = \lambda x \exists e [$ Agent(e, x) & Carrying(e) & Patient$(e,$ the chair$)$]

But the reverse is not true: sharing a semantic value does not entail semantic congruence. Strictly speaking, (24) says nothing at all about semantic structure in carry the chair; it just says that carry the chair stands for whatever the following formula stands for. So (23) and (24) make importantly different claims. And very often in discussions of argument structure, it is the kind of claim made by (23), a claim of semantic congruence, that matters more.

2.7.2 The predicate calculus with lambdas

The formulas I will use to represent meanings and to refer to semantic values are formulas of the predicate calculus supplemented with lambda abstraction, such as the formula in (25), carried over from (23) and (24) above.

(25) $\lambda x \exists e [$ Agent(e, x) & Carrying(e) & Patient$(e,$ the chair$)$]

Such formulas have a standard interpretation, given at length in textbooks.[9] I will review this interpretation by going step-by-step through the formula in (25). Then, in Section 2.7.3, I will outline some unorthodox ways of reading these formulas, with which we can accommodate alternative semantic assumptions.

Any formula $\ulcorner \lambda x[\phi] \urcorner$ names a function. A function, under one standard definition, is a set of ordered pairs. So $\ulcorner \lambda x[\phi] \urcorner$ names a set of ordered pairs. The set named by $\ulcorner \lambda x[\phi] \urcorner$ consists of exactly one pair

---

[8] In Montague Grammar there would be no theoretical significance whatsoever to translating a lexical item with a complex formula. But if a lexical item is semantically congruent to a complex formula, this indicates semantic structure in the lexical item, either in its lexical derivation or in its semantic value. Thus, in order to generalize over all sorts of semantically relevant structure, whether syntactic or lexical, in the derivation or in the value, it is useful to have the broader notion of congruence.

[9] See, for example, Chierchia and McConnell-Ginet 1990, Partee *et al.* 1990, Gamut 1991 or Heim and Kratzer 1998.

for each element d in what is called the *domain* of the function. Each of these pairs is of the form $\ulcorner \langle d, [\![\phi]\!]^{[x/d]} \rangle \urcorner$. $[\![\phi]\!]^{[x/d]}$ is the value of the formula ϕ when each free occurrence of x in ϕ is given the value d.

Formula (25) has the shape of $\ulcorner \lambda x[\phi] \urcorner$ with ϕ as in (26).

(26) $\exists e[\text{Agent}(e, x) \ \& \ \text{Carrying}(e) \ \& \ \text{Patient}(e, \text{the chair})]$

Thus (25) is a name for a set of ordered pairs, each pair matching some object d with (27), which is the value that (26) takes when d serves as the value for the variable x.

(27) $[\![\ \exists e[\text{Agent}(e, x) \ \& \ \text{Carrying}(e) \ \& \ \text{Patient}(e, \text{the chair})] \ ]\!]^{[x/d]}$

This is in turn a truth value. It is the truth value True just in case there is at least one value for the variable e that makes (28) yield the value True, again with x standing for the chosen object d. Otherwise it is False. This is a consequence of the definition of "$\exists$," the existential quantifier.

(28) $[\![\text{Agent}(e, x) \ \& \ \text{Carrying}(e) \ \& \ \text{Patient}(e, \text{the chair})]\!]^{[x/d]}$

In turn, due to the definition of "$\&$," (28) yields True just in case all three items in (29) do. Otherwise it yields False.

(29) a $[\![\text{Agent}(e, x)]\!]^{[x/d]}$
      b $[\![\text{Carrying}(e)]\!]^{[x/d]}$
      c $[\![\text{Patient}(e, \text{the chair})]\!]^{[x/d]}$

So, in sum, (25) names a set of pairs of objects and truth values. Each pair matches object d in the domain with True just in case there is some e such that, with d as the value for x, it is true that Agent(e, x), Carrying(e), and Patient(e, x). Otherwise the pair matches d with False. More prosaically, (25) names a function that maps to True anything that is the agent of a carrying with the chair as its patient.

Suppose then that this function maps only Navin to True, not Marie, Patty or anybody else. Then (25) is a name for the same set that is sketched in (30). And in that case (24) and (21), repeated here, make exactly the same claim.

(30) $\{\langle \text{Marie, False} \rangle, \langle \text{Navin, True} \rangle, \langle \text{Patty, False} \rangle, \ldots\}$

(24) $[\![\text{carry the chair}]\!]^c = \lambda x \exists e[\ \text{Agent}(e, x) \ \& \ \text{Carrying}(e) \ \& \ \text{Patient}(e, \text{the chair}) \ ]$

(21) $[\![\text{carry the chair}]\!]^c = \{\langle \text{Marie, False} \rangle, \langle \text{Navin, True} \rangle, \langle \text{Patty, False} \rangle, \ldots\}$

This helps make clear why (24), given the standard interpretation of lambda terms, says nothing about the semantic structure of carry the chair – why it does not say that some part of carry the chair has the relation Agent as its value, for example. The lambda term in (24) is just one way of naming the same set that is named by (30), and that set does not have the Agent relation as a part.

2.7.3 Heterodox interpretations

The example above shows that, when we use a formula like (25) to name a semantic value, the standard interpretation has two implications. First, it implies an objectivist view, since a set of pairs of objects and truth values is not something internal to the mind (even if some of the objects in the set are mental). Second, it implies that semantic values typically lack the structure of the expression: a set of pairs does not have the structure of carry the chair.

These implications may be welcome, or even correct. But I would not like my notation, chosen mainly to be familiar and clear, to decide anything in advance. So while I will use the idiom of the standard interpretation, I would also like to permit unorthodox ways of reading the formulas, when appropriate. Here I will outline three possible dimensions of heterodoxy.

First, one might read the formulas as describing a semantic value with structure that matches the structure of the formula. For example, one might take (25) to name a 'conjunctive' constellation of three objective properties, or of three mental concepts: Agent, Carrying and Patient.

Second, one might read the formulas as indicating concepts or thoughts in the mind, rather than as mind-external objects. So instead of taking (25) to stand for a set of objects and truth values, one can take it to stand for a mental concept, and instead of taking (26) to stand for a truth value, one can take it to stand for a thought.

Third, one might read the predicates in our formulas not as standing for a single value, but as a pointer to a family of related values, from which one must be chosen in interpreting tokens of the expression. That is, one might assume that different tokenings of a single predicate in the meaning may take different values, even if they contain no demonstratives or indexicals. This freedom may be useful in the representation of polysemy (Chomsky 2000a, Wilson and Carston 2007, Pietroski, to appear a, and compare Kracht 2011 for concerns), as discussed in Section 2.6.

These unorthodox readings betoken importantly different perspectives, each of which demands careful development and justification. But this book is not the place for that, and my notation does not mark a preemptive decision. For thorough pursuit of related issues, see Pietroski (to appear a).

Finally, it is worth repeating the cautions in Dowty (1979). The formulas we use to state hypotheses about meaning do not necessarily have any further theoretical status. They need not themselves be objects at a distinct level of representation. To describe a meaning is not to claim further that one's description is a distinct property of the expression, a semantic representation, over which certain linguistic principles are defined. Perhaps there is a theoretically significant level of semantic representations, populated by structured symbols that represent the meaning or value of the expression. But this is not implied just by the use of structured formulas to describe meanings.

2.8 SEMANTIC COMBINATION

In Syntax, an operation is *transformational* just in case it refers to the internal structure or derivational history of its operand (Chapter 1). In (31) the operation Move maps one tree onto another; and it is transformational because it manipulates a subpart of the input tree, the embedded quantifier everyone.

(31)   Move([Al [loves [everyone]]]) = [everyone$_k$ [Al [loves t_k]]]

Let us say exactly the same about semantic operations. Were a semantic operation to refer to the structure or derivational history of an operand, it would be transformational. This is a new but useful extension of the jargon. The hypothetical semantic operation Smove in (32) is transformational. Its operands are two meanings (or values, rather) f and $[g, y]$, where the latter is a structure with parts g and y. Its output is the structure $[[f, y], g]$, with the parts $[f, y]$ and g. Thus the output of Smove depends on the internal structure of the second operand.

(32)   Smove($f, [g, y]$) = [$[f, y], g$]

Such an operation would be handy for derivation (33), if we wanted to associate pound semantically with cutlets (Chapter 13), even though no step in the derivation combines them.

(33)   pound cutlets flat

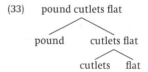

Suppose Smove has access to the derivation of cutlets flat, or that the value of cutlets flat has the structure [[[cutlets]], [[flat]]]. Then, as shown in (34), Smove can associate pound with cutlets to the exclusion of flat, as desired. Consequently the meaning of pound cutlets flat, (34), will not preserve the structure of its derivation, (33).

(34)   Smove⟨ [[pound]], [[[cutlets]], [[flat]]] ⟩ = [[[[pound]], [[cutlets]]], [[flat]]]

I will take for granted that no semantic operation is transformational. All are blind to structure in their operands or in their derivation. This is a widely shared assumption, standard across frameworks, and therefore enormously important. The syntax may or may not be transformational, but the semantics is always **nontransformational**. This rules out anything like Smove, and implies that meanings will preserve the structure of the derivation. Usually this is viewed as *compositionality*, the premise that the meaning of a whole is a function of its parts and their mode of combination. But it is more specific than that, since a derivation can be compositional and yet semantically transformational, if its semantic operations can refer to the structure or history of their inputs.[10]

With this foundation in place, let us review some common rules of compositional semantics. As we have seen, it is common to talk about semantic values of predicates as functions, following Frege and Montague. Functions are sets of pairs. The first member of each pair is drawn from the **domain** of the function, and the second is drawn from its **range**. If f is a function, and a is in the domain of f, there is exactly one x in the range such that the pair $\langle a, x \rangle$ is a member of the set f. Within this view rules of semantic combination are generally operations on functions. The two most common are **Application** and **Conjunction**. The latter is called "Predicate Modification" in Heim and Kratzer (1998).

Application is defined in (35). Conventionally Application$[f, a]$ is written as $f(a)$, and the second operand, a, is called the *argument*.

(35)   a Application$[f, a]$ is defined if and only if there is exactly one x such that
           $\langle a, x \rangle \in f$
        b Application$[f, a] = b$ if and only if: $\langle a, b \rangle \in f$

The first clause of (35) says that $f(a)$ is defined just in case f is a function with a in its domain. The second clause says that $f(a) = b$ just in case the pair $\langle a, b \rangle$ is a member of f. Items (36) and (37) give two examples. The lambda expression in (36a) names a function that pairs any number

---

[10] See Kracht 2011 for discussion of many related issues.

n with n^2. This is the set adumbrated in (36b). Since $\langle 3, 9 \rangle$ is in that set, Application of the function to 3 yields 9, as in (36c).

(36) a $\lambda n[\, n^2 \,]$
      b $\{\langle 1,1 \rangle, \langle 2,4 \rangle, \langle 3,9 \rangle, \ldots\}$
      c Application$[\; [\![\lambda n[n^2]]\!], [\![3]\!] \;] = 9$

Next, suppose that the semantic value of won is the function named by the lambda expression in (37a). This pairs those who won with True and everything else with False. Suppose that this function is the set of pairs hinted at in (37b). Since $\langle \text{Obama}, \text{True} \rangle$ is in this set, Application of the won function to $[\![\text{Obama}]\!]$ (namely, Obama) yields True in (37c).

(37) a $\lambda x\,[$ True if and only if x won, and otherwise False $]$
      b $\{\langle \text{Obama}, \text{True} \rangle, \langle \text{Romney}, \text{False} \rangle, \langle \text{Biden}, \text{True} \rangle, \langle \text{Ryan}, \text{False} \rangle, \ldots\}$
      c Application$[\; [\![\text{won}]\!], [\![\text{Obama}]\!] \;]$ = True

Conjunction$[f, g]$ is an operation over two functions f and g. The operation yields a new function, h, equivalent to $\lambda x[fx \,\&\, gx]$. For example, if the values of won and cried are functions that yield True just for those who won and those who cried, respectively, then the Conjunction of those two values is a new function that yields True just for those who both won and cried. The operation is defined in (38).

(38) a Conjunction$[f, g]$ is defined if and only if f and g share the same domain, and both have as their range the truth values True and False
      b Conjunction$[f, g]$ = the function h such that, for any x in the shared domain of f and g:

      i $\langle x, \text{True} \rangle \in h \leftrightarrow [\langle x, \text{True} \rangle \in f]$ and $[\langle x, \text{True} \rangle \in g]$, and
      ii $\langle x, \text{False} \rangle \in h \leftrightarrow [\langle x, \text{False} \rangle \in f]$ or $[\langle x, \text{False} \rangle \in g]$, and
      iii nothing else is in h.

The first clause requires that the two operands of Conjunction be functions of the same sort. They must share the same domain, and have as their range the truth values. Conjunction of f and g then yields a new function h. For any member x of the shared domain, h includes $\langle x, \text{True} \rangle$ just in case both f and g do as well. On the other hand h includes $\langle x, \text{False} \rangle$ just in case either f or g does.

A few times in this book, I will also refer to the operation of FunctionComposition, or just **Composition**. By definition, Composition$[f, g]$ is equivalent to $\lambda x[f(g(x))]$. For example, Composition$[\lambda y[3y], \lambda x[x^2]]$ is equivalent to $\lambda x[3(x^2)]$, the function which triples the square of any input number.

As defined, these operations presuppose an objectivist semantics. Sets of pairs are objects outside the mind. But both operations have mentalist analogues. The objectivist's function corresponds to the mentalist's one-place mental concept, with the function mapping to true those things that fall under the mental concept. Conjunction of two functions corresponds to formation of a complex 'conjunctive' concept, under which a thing falls just when it falls under both its constituent concepts. Thus while I will generally write in the objectivist idiom, I will presume that the reader can provide mentalist translations.

2.9 EVENT SEMANTICS

In this book I usually take sentence meanings to be descriptions of events, following Davidson (1967b). Specifically, I take the meaning of any sentence to be specified by a formula with the outlines of (39), where "ϕ" is some string of event predicates; this is the defining assumption of an **event semantics**. The initial ellipsis ("…") may include a sequence of quantifiers or propositional operators. For simplicity, I freely translate proposals from the literature into these terms, hopefully without important distortion.

(39) $\ldots \exists e [\, \phi(e) \,]$

The main motive for this choice is practical. Event-based representations are both expressive and easy to understand. Most helpfully, they provide an intuitive and first-order way of analyzing the meaning of a sentence into parts. Namely, the parts can be rendered as conjoined predicates of the same event variable. For example, suppose we want to say that the meaning of (40a) involves the thematic relations Agent and Patient for its subject and object. Then we can use (40b) to do so.

(40) a Navin carried the chair.
      b $\exists e [\, \text{Agent}(e, \text{Navin}) \,\&\, \text{Carrying}(e) \,\&\, \text{Patient}(e, \text{the chair}) \,]$

This is a first-order formula, each of whose conjuncts is easily understood. A formula like "Agent(Navin, [Patient(the chair, Carrying)])" would be opaque in comparison, if at all sensible.

Of course, an event semantics also has more substantive motives. Lucid presentation of these can be found in Parsons (1990), Larson and Segal (1995) and Landman (2000). Davidson's own motive was to provide a satisfactory and non-intensional semantics for adverbial adjuncts.

If sentences have a logical form like (39), we can treat adverbs as predicates of the quantified event, like quietly in (41).

(41)   a Navin quietly carried the chair.
       b $\exists e$[Agent(e, Navin) & Carrying(e) & Patient(e, the chair) & Quiet(e)]

This will explain why dropping or permutation of certain adverbs preserves truth. Sentence (40a) preserves the truth of (41a); and if we interpret these two sentences as (40b) and (41b), the inference is just a case of Conjunction Elimination within the scope of an existential quantifier, validated by logical syntax alone. It is attractive to treat the inference in this way, as a syntactic consequence, since the inference does not seem to depend on the particular meaning of the adverb. It seems rather to be an instance of a more general pattern.

Now, both the practical and logical motives for Davidsonian meanings have to do with the utility of treating the verb and its dependents as separate predicates of the same variable. But this says nothing about what values such variables take. Conventionally we say that the values of the e's in Davidsonian formulas are *events*. But it might be better to coin a new term. Maybe we should just call them E's or Eventh's. The reason is, none of the arguments for Davidsonian meanings require that these variables range over a particular ontological category that we would pretheoretically call *the events*. Rather, the domain for our e variables must be whatever will support the predicates we apply to them. And we cannot be sure that what we would otherwise call *events* will serve well in this role.

An example will help to motivate this caution. Suppose we say that (42a) and (43a) have interpretations specified by (42b) and (43b). Then the values of our e's must be items to which one can have an Agent relation.

(42)   a Lee bought the book.
       b $\exists e$[Agent(e, Lee) & BuyingOf(e, the book)]
(43)   a Mo sold the book.
       b $\exists e$[Agent(e, Mo) & SellingOf(e, the book)]

This already excludes one very simple notion of events as regions of spacetime (Quine 1985). If Lee bought the book from Mo, the buying and selling would seem to occupy the same chunk of the world. So if our e's were merely regions of spacetime, Lee and Mo would both be agents of the same thing (Parsons 1990, Landman 2000). To avoid this, our e's must instead range over objects individuated by finer criteria, at least fine enough to distinguish buyings from their correlated sellings. The buying that verifies (42a) cannot be the same 'e' as the selling that verifies (43a). Therefore if we call our *e*'s events, there will be some conflict with ordinary diction, since it is natural to say that (42a) and (43a) are just two ways of talking about the very same event. As we will see in Chapter 6, this is one reason why some linguists reject the use of general thematic relations such as Agent.

For further thoughts on what the Davidsonian *e*'s really are, see, for example, Lombard (1986), Bennett (1988), Parsons (1990), Landman (2000), Schein (2002) and Pietroski (to appear b).

DISCUSSION POINTS

1 Explain why "a set of pairs of objects and truth values is not something internal to the mind."

2 What does it mean to say that the semantic value of an expression E lacks the structure of E?

3 The predicate illegitimate applies to children whose parents were unmarried at their birth. Does it follow that the meaning of illegitimate has the same structure as its definition, with parts for 'parent of *x*,' 'at birth of *x*' and 'unmarried'? If not, is there then some reason that illegitimate should have, in addition to its meaning, a semantic representation with such structure?

4 No common semantic theory is transformational. Why?

5 There are words that don't seem to stand for anything in the world, such as or, not, Pegasus, the largest prime number and the average American. What can we say about their meanings from an objectivist perspective? What can we say from a mentalist perspective? Are the examples I chose importantly different from one another?

6 What would a mentalist interpretation of Application and Conjunction look like? How would this interpretation differ from an objectivist interpretation? How would the two interpretations be alike?

7 Does (1a) below entail (1b)? Do they have the same meaning? Why or why not? What about (2)?

(1) a Montana borders Alberta.
    b Alberta borders Montana.

(2) a The circumference of a circle is proportional to its diameter.
    b The area of a square is a function of the length of its sides.

8 Hal has walked uphill, and therefore Hal has walked. In walking uphill, Hal sent a signal to Sal. But Hal did not signal Sal *uphill*

(Taylor 1985). That is, the signalling was not uphill. What (if anything) does this show about the notion of 'event' that is relevant to our representation of adverbial modifiers?

9 Is it possible to treat both quickly and nearly in (3) as event modifiers, predicates made true by events? Why or why not?

    (3)   a John quickly closed the door.
          b John nearly closed the door.

10 Consider a yellow-fleshed watermelon covered in mud. With different purposes in mind, one could either affirm or deny that it is yellow, that it is green, or that it is dun. How should we think of this indeterminacy? Are there several homophonous words "green?" Or just one that is general? Is it vague? Is it polysemous? Does green have a meaning 'green like so,' where 'so' indicates some topical standard of color? Or is the indeterminacy not a semantic matter at all? (See, e.g., Kennedy and McNally 2010, Clapp 2012 and extensive references there.)

SUGGESTIONS FOR FURTHER READING

Elbourne 2011 is a beautiful introduction to thinking about meaning. On truth and meaning, read Burgess and Burgess 2011, and, on analyticity, see Rey 2013. Excellent textbooks for compositional semantics include Chierchia and McConnell-Ginet 1990, Gamut 1991, Larson and Segal 1995, and Heim and Kratzer 1998. Parsons 1990 is an invaluable guide to event semantics. For a mentalist and eventish semantics in a Chomskyan framework, see Pietroski (to appear a,b). Dowty 1979 and Fodor and Lepore 1998 provide a clear view on semantic decomposition and its commitments. Gillon 2004 has a careful discussion of semantic indeterminacy.

Part II
Kinds of arguments

3 Arguments in Syntax

3.1 INTRODUCTION

In this chapter I discuss the notion of *argument* as it is used in syntactic theory. I begin with the observation that expressions have a head and perhaps some dependents (Section 3.2). Among the dependents only some are 'specified' or 'licensed' by some derivational part of the expression, in relation to features of the head. These are the syntactic arguments, and the others are the syntactic adjuncts (Section 3.3). I then discuss two different theoretical implementations of argumenthood, lexicalist and nonlexicalist, in two more technical sections (Sections 3.4–3.5). Next I discuss optionality (Section 3.6), the syntactic notion of a Θ-role (Section 3.7), and the dichotomy between external and internal arguments (Section 3.8). Finally, I come to the possible 'observational' consequences of syntactic argumenthood, the 'surface data' that might be used to recognize this syntactic status (Section 3.9).

3.2 HEAD AND DEPENDENTS

An expression may inherit its category from one of its parts. Consider cook sausage tonight in (1). It belongs to the category of expressions, *verb*, that go together with auxiliaries such as might or will. And it has this property specifically because of cook, a verb. The words sausage and tonight have nothing to do with it. For this reason cook is the *head* of the larger expression.

(1) Mo might cook sausage tonight.

Suppose that expression B is an immediate part of expression C. I will say that B **heads** C when C inherits its major category from it. An expression C **inherits** its category from B when the rule of derivation that yields C sets the category of C to that of B. The inverse of inheritance is *transmission*.

47

(2) Head
Expression B *heads* C, when B is an immediate part of C from which C inherits its major category.

Heading will be transitive: if B heads C, and C immediately heads D, then B heads D as well. So cook heads cook sausage tonight in (1). If B heads C, and B is a lexical item, then B is also *the head* of whatever it heads. Thus cook, a lexical item, both heads and is the head of cook sausage tonight.

(3) The head
B is the head of C if and only if B heads C and B is a lexical item.

An immediate part of C that does not head C is a **dependent** in C.

(4) Dependent
An immediate part of C that does not head C is a dependent in C.

So sausage and tonight are each dependents in their parts of cook sausage tonight. Both are also dependents in the whole expression, given something like transitivity. If A is a dependent in C, and C immediately heads D, then A is a dependent in D.

Recall, these terms name relations in a syntactic analysis; they are not observational **argument diagnostics.** We come to their application in Section 3.9.

Expressions seem never to have more than one head. For example, cook sausage tonight does not inherit the category of both cook and sausage. Because of cook it can combine with might in (1). But its inclusion of sausage, an expression of category *noun*, does not make the phrase partly nominal. It does not, for instance, let the phrase combine with a determiner, as in (5a), as sausage itself can in (5b).

(5) a * [the [cook sausage]]
     b   [the [sausage]]

This generalization – call it **Single Headedness** – (6), is among the most important in linguistic theory (Pinker 1994). Human languages would be very different than they are, if expressions instead blended the categories of their parts, inheriting (for example) the union of the categories of their constituents.

(6) Single Headedness
Expressions do not have more than one head.

Endocentricity is a further hypothesis, (7). It says that every expression with syntactic parts has a head.

(7) Endocentricity
     Every expression with syntactic parts has a head.

This seems in general to be correct, despite some challenges.[1] But even if Endocentricity is correct, it is not always clear which part of an expression is its head, an issue that arises often in the study of argument structure. Typical problems can be illustrated using the example of *clauses*.

At first blush it is not clear that clauses, such as (1) above, even have a head. But closer study shows that certain parts of a clause do decide which sorts of syntactic contexts it occurs in. A clause with the auxiliary *will* can be independent (8a), but cannot be a complement to the verb *force* (9a). Yet the opposite is true of a clause with infinitival *to* in the place of *will*, as shown in (8b,9b).

(8) a   Mo will cook sausage.
     b * Mo to cook sausage.
(9) a * Lee forced Mo will cook sausage.
     b   Lee forced Mo to cook sausage.

It is a good hypothesis, therefore, that *will* and *to* are the heads of their clauses here, deciding whether the clause has the minor category of *finite* or *infinitival*. Similarly (10) and (11) suggest that the complementizers (*why, whether* and *that*) head the bracketed expressions in these sentences, deciding whether the expression has the minor category of *interrogative* or *declarative*.[2]

(10) a   Lee wonders [why Mo might cook sausage]
      b   Lee wonders [whether Mo might cook sausage]
      c * Lee wonders [that Mo might cook sausage]

(11) a * Lee thinks [why Mo might cook sausage]
      b * Lee thinks [whether Mo might cook sausage]
      c   Lee thinks [that Mo might cook sausage]

But with (12) a source of uncertainty arises.

(12) a   Lee thinks [that Mo might cook sausage]

---

[1] For example, the conjunction of two expressions headed by a verb also has the category *verb*, (1). But then which verb is its head? Insofar as the answer is unclear, something special needs to be said about conjunction – for instance, that conjunctions inherit the categories of their arguments.

   (1) Mo will cook sausage and mix drinks.

[2] The judgments describe my own English. Other people's judgments may differ.

    b * Lee thinks [that Mo to cook sausage]
    c   Lee thinks [Mo might cook sausage]

The complementizer that goes with finite clauses (12a) but not with infinitival clauses (12b), and a clause with might is finite. As a result, the presence of both might and that indexes finiteness redundantly. This makes it unclear, at least initially, which of the two to choose as the head of the bracketed expression in (12a). In the end the best answer is that the complementizer is the head; in turn, expressions headed by that must have a finite clause as a dependent, leading to the redundancy. But now what about (12c), where no complementizer is audible? Is might now the head of the bracketed expression? Or is there instead a complementizer of the same minor category as that, but silent? Both options are plausible, and the choice will have to be made by empirical argument.

    With this lesson in mind let us revisit cook sausage tonight. The best initial hypothesis is that this is headed by cook. But this might be wrong. It might be that cook is like might in (12c), a required verbal dependent in an expression with a silent head, as in (13) for example. Here a silent expression ("ϵ") of category v heads a phrase with two dependents, cook and sausage. Similarly it might make sense to say that sausage pronounces a complex expression with a silent determiner as its head (14). We will consider such hypotheses periodically throughout this book.

(13)   [$_v$ [$_v$ [$_v$ ϵ] [$_V$ cook]] [$_N$ sausage]]
(14)   [$_D$ [$_D$ ϵ] [$_N$ sausage]]

    Finally, it is important to say why heading requires only transmission of major category. The expression cook sausage tonight has the same major category as cook, if cook is its head. If the categories of the two expressions were wholly identical, both major and minor, the syntax could not distinguish them. Syntactically, cook would be everywhere replaceable by cook sausage tonight, leading to such strings as (15).

(15) * Mo might cook sausage tonight sausage tonight sausage tonight.

To prevent this, we can say that cook has the contextual feature of TRANSITIVE, but cook sausage does not. And because of this distinction, the syntax will be able to treat the two expressions differently and (15) will not be generable. Heading should therefore require only that the major category of an expression be inherited from its head, in ways to be discussed below. The minor category may or may not be transmitted. And, as we will now see, this modification of minor category, between an expression and its head, is the basis for the syntactic notion of argument.

3.3 ARGUMENT AND ADJUNCT

Dependents are nonheads. The verb phrase in (1), repeated as (16), gets its category neither from sausage nor from tonight. Thus neither is the head of cook sausage tonight, and both are dependents.

(16) Mo might cook sausage tonight.

We now make a further syntactic distinction between two kinds of dependents, **syntactic arguments** and **syntactic adjuncts**. There is a common and rough idea of the difference. The presence of a syntactic argument is somehow specified, explicitly permitted, by some derivational part of the expression in which it is a dependent. The presence of a syntactic adjunct is not. So one might talk about syntactic arguments and syntactic adjuncts as specified and unspecified dependents, respectively. In the rest of this chapter, I will use the terms "argument" and "adjunct" with "syntactic" understood.

More technically, where arguments differ from adjuncts is in their effects on the transmission of minor category from the head to the phrase, specifically in the transmission of contextual features. As a matter of definition, an argument affects the contextual features of its phrase, while an adjunct does not. What effect it has is some function of the categories of the head and the argument.

(17) Syntactic Argument
      When A and B are immediate parts of C, and B heads C, A is a syntactic argument in C if and only if C differs from B in some contextual feature.

(18) Syntactic Adjunct
      When A and B are immediate parts of C, and B heads C, A is a syntactic adjunct in C if and only if it is not a syntactic argument in C.

For example, suppose that cook has the contextual feature TRANSITIVE, while cook sausage does not. Then this makes sausage a syntactic argument in the latter expression. Suppose further that both cook sausage and cook sausage tonight have exactly the same syntactic category. Then tonight is an adjunct in the latter expression. Here too let us assume a kind of transitivity. If A is an argument in C, and C heads D, then A is an argument in D. Likewise for adjuncts.

It may help to repeat this in the abstract. Suppose that two expressions, A and B, combine to make C. Suppose also that B heads C and has category X[Y]. If A is an adjunct, then C will share both the major and the minor category of B, as in (19), creating a purely recursive structure.

(19) Adding an adjunct
      B:X[Y] + A:W[ ] = C:X[Y]

But if A is an argument, then C will share only the major category of B, as in (20). Its minor category will be different, some Z not equal to Y, determined by the syntax as a function of the categories of A and B.

(20) Adding an argument
      B:X[Y] + A:W[ ] = C:X[Z]

An argument thus makes for a structure that is recursive only in part, with inheritance of some minor category blocked.

Now I would like to walk through two illustrations of this distinction, with a minimal difference that I will discuss directly in Sections 3.4 and 3.5. The first derives our example, cook sausage tonight, using the grammar made of (21) and (22). Here "⊛" is our rule of syntactic combination, partially defined by (21).

(21) a V[t] ⊛ N[X] = V[ ]
      b V[ ] ⊛ N[Y] = V[ ]
(22) a cook:V[t]
      b sausage:N[ ]
      c tonight:N[ ]

I specify a single contextual feature by listing its value inside square brackets. One such value is t (meant to evoke *transitive*, but only initially and vaguely). X and Y range over all possible values. Empty brackets signify the absence of this feature, or a distinguished 'null' value for it.

This grammar yields the derivation in (23) for cook sausage tonight. Joining sausage to cook with rule (21a) yields an expression which lacks the minor category, t, of its head. But rule (21b) has no such effect in joining tonight with cook sausage. Thus sausage is an argument in this expression, but tonight is an adjunct.

(23)   V[ ]

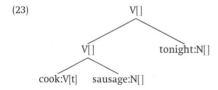

Our second illustration uses the grammar made of (24) and (25) instead. This approximates the rule schemata of a generic Minimalist

Grammar, or any other grammar driven by checking of lexical features, such as a Categorial Grammar or HPSG.

(24)   a $X[\langle Y, \ell \rangle] \bullet Y[\wp] = X[\langle \ell \rangle]$
       b $X[\langle \ell \rangle] \bullet Y[\wp] = X[\langle \ell \rangle]$

(25)   a cook:$V[\langle N, N \rangle]$
       b sausage:$N[\langle \rangle]$
       c tonight:$N[\langle \rangle]$

Here X and Y are variables over category labels, among which are V and N. Cursive ℓ and $\wp$ range over lists of category labels, possibly null. Crucially, and different from (21), the relevant minor category feature within the square brackets is now an ordered list of category labels. Call this an **a-list**, mnemonic for *argument-list*. I describe this bit of jargon more explicitly below (Section 3.4).

This second grammar yields the derivation in (26) below. Joining sausage to cook with rule (24a) yields a phrase that lacks the minor category of its V head. It inherits only the noninitial portion of its a-list. But rule (21b) has no such effect in joining tonight with cook sausage, which inherits all the properties of cook sausage alone. So again sausage is an argument and tonight is an adjunct.

(26)

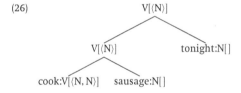

Thus, under either of these two grammars, the derivation of cook sausage includes a part that permits an N dependent in relation to some feature of its head, cook, yielding a larger expression that lacks the same feature. This is why both make sausage an argument. Where the grammars differ is in which part of the derivation does this. Under the first, (21), it is a phrase structure rule, while under the second, (24), it is cook itself. I will discuss this further in the next two, more technical sections.

3.4   LEXICALIST ENCODINGS

For cook sausage in (16) we have decided that sausage is an argument. So far this means only that sausage is a syntactic part of an expression headed by cook, and that cook sausage does not have the minor category of cook itself. We are committed, that is, only to a derivation of (27) that is something like (28), with X and Z distinct.

(27)   cook sausage

(28)   V[Z]

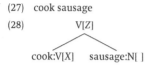

cook:V[X]   sausage:N[ ]

Two things are yet to be decided. What are X and Z, and what rule of syntax effects the change from one to the other? *Lexicalist* and *nonlexicalist* encodings are defined by their different answers. The difference is already illustrated in the examples I gave above: grammar (21) is nonlexicalist and grammar (24) is lexicalist. But now I discuss the difference directly. Roughly, it is in whether the argument is mentioned directly in the contextual features of the head, or instead only in the rules of Syntax. I describe lexicalism here and nonlexicalism in the next section.

A lexicalist encoding of arguments does two things. First, it endows the head of an expression with a structured group of contextual features whose values are category labels.[3] Item (29) endows cook with a list of such features, expressed by listing the values of the features within angle brackets. It begins with a feature valued N, and continues with some list ℓ, possibly null.

(29)   cook:V[$\langle$N, $\ell\rangle$]

Second, a lexicalist encoding uses a certain kind of highly general rule for syntactic combination, that I will call an **a-checking rule**, mnemonic for "argument checking." Such a rule eliminates (blocks inheritance of) a contextual feature on the head when its value matches the category of the dependent.

(30)   A-checking Rule
       A rule of syntactic combination is an a-checking rule if and only if its output lacks a minor category feature of the head just when the value of that feature matches the category of the dependent.

The rule named Check in (31) is an example. This has the same effect that "•" has in (24a) above. Here I ignore the phonological or semantic effects of Check, and consider only its effects on syntactic category.

(31)   Check($X[\langle Y, \ell\rangle]$, $Y[\ldots]$) = $X[\langle\ell\rangle]$

---

[3] One might also allow for a disjunction of category labels, underspecifying the category of the argument. This choice matters to some things I say, but not much.

Check combines two expressions. One has category X and a list of minor features $\langle Y, \ell \rangle$, while the other has category Y, matching the value of the first feature in the list. The result of their combination inherits category X, but only the noninitial portion of the list. Inheritance of the initial portion is blocked. Using Check to combine the cook of (29) with sausage gives us the derivation in (32), an exemplary lexicalist instance of the argument schema in (28).

(32)   cook sausage:V[$\langle \ell \rangle$]

cook:V[$\langle N, \ell \rangle$]   sausage:N[ ]

In the context of an a-checking rule, I will refer to those features of the head that are targeted by the rule as **a-features**, short for "argument features." A list of a-features will be an **a-list**.

(33) A-features
      Features of a head that can be targeted by an a-checking rule.

And when we talk about an expression "having an argument" in the syntax, this is what we should have in mind. An expression **has a syntactic argument** when and only when it has an a-feature. So according to (29), cook has a syntactic argument.

(34) Having a syntactic argument
      An expression has a syntactic argument if and only if it has an a-feature.

In addition an expression **is a syntactic argument of** another when and only when the first eliminates an a-feature of the second under application of an a-checking rule.

(35) Being a syntactic argument of something
      In the derivation of C from immediate parts A and B, A is a syntactic argument of B if and only if it eliminates an a-feature of B.

Sausage is therefore a syntactic argument of cook in (32), since in this derivation it eliminates the a-feature of cook under application of Check. When A is a syntactic argument of B, I will say that A *satisfies*, or also *realizes* an argument of B. Our transitivity assumptions apply in the usual way.

Importantly, having a syntactic argument is not yet having a distributional requirement. Even in a syntax with Check as its only rule, a word with an a-feature valued X is not yet required to occur in the company of an X. To see this, notice that Check allows the derivation in (36). Here the cook of (29) is an argument of a (silent) morpheme of category K and a-list $\langle V \rangle$. The result has no inclination to combine with N.

(36)   cook:K[⟨⟩]

ε:K[⟨V⟩]   cook:V[⟨N, ℓ⟩]

It takes further work to turn an argument into a distributional requirement. We have to ensure that no derivation yields a licit expression
unless every a-feature is eliminated in an application of Check. This can
be achieved in various ways. In theories within the Minimalist Program
(Chomsky 1995, 2000b), for example, it is done by assuming that only
a derivation which eliminates all a-features yields an expression that
can be pronounced. But there are other possibilities. Notably, no such
further step is taken in standard Categorial Grammars (Dowty 1988,
Jacobson 1990, Steedman 2000, Moortgat 2012), which allow derivations like (36).

The lexicalist approach to arguments is favored in the common
syntactic frameworks of today, including Minimalism, HPSG, LFG and
various Categorial Grammars. Landmarks in its explicit definition
are Ajdukiewicz (1935) and Bar-Hillel (1953), among the founding
works of Categorial Grammar. Work in the GB framework uses two
connected a-lists: the "subcategorization frame," which annotates an
a-list with syntactic restrictions, and the "Θ-grid" (Stowell 1981:34),
which indexes the elements of an a-list to their semantic interpretation;
see Section 3.7. HPSG likewise has analogous "SUBCAT" or "VALENCE"
lists (Manning and Sag 1999). Categorial Grammars build an a-list
into a structured category label, such as (S\N)/N (Bar-Hillel 1953,
Steedman 2000). Meanwhile our a-checking rule Check is a version of
what is sometimes called Functional Application in Categorial
Grammars, a rule type Bar-Hillel (1953) compared to multiplication
of fractions. Very similar is the basic rule of syntax in Minimalist
grammars, namely Merge (Chomsky 1995, Stabler 1997, 2010).

The main formal attraction of lexicalism is its clear expression of
headedness (Lyons 1966:226–7, Jackendoff 1977). As discussed above,
expressions in general (or always) have a head. Headedness is expressed
directly by a general rule of derivation that projects the major category
from one of its inputs to its output, no matter what that category is.
Thus a rule of derivation that would express headedness directly must
be neutral as to major category. In any lexicalist syntax the basic rule
of derivation is an a-checking rule like our Check; and such rules are
easily rendered as category-neutral. The reason is, a-features are themselves very specific. With their values drawn from the set of category
labels, they explicitly restrict or determine the category of the argument. This degree of specificity in the minor category features leaves

the major category of the head with no further work to do in encoding the particular dependency between head and argument. For instance, to say that cook can occur with an argument of category N, we need not say both that cook has some contextual feature X and that it is a verb. It is enough to specify its contextual feature, namely the a-list $\langle N, \ldots \rangle$. Thus an a-checking rule is easily stated as category-neutral, and such a rule – to repeat – permits a direct expression of headedness in a rule of syntactic derivation. Since headedness is among the most important facts about the syntax of human languages, this is attractive.

3.5 NONLEXICALIST ENCODINGS

A nonlexicalist encoding of arguments lacks the defining properties of the lexicalist alternative. A head is not endowed with a-features that have category labels as their values, to be matched with the category of a dependent. For example, a nonlexicalist grammar might endow cook with value V for its major category and t for a minor, contextual feature, as in (37), where t is not the label of any major category.

(37)   cook:V[t]

Correspondingly there is no general rule, like Check, that matches the category label of an argument with the value of a contextual feature on the head. Instead a nonlexicalist grammar states dependencies between specific pairs of features – say, t and N, or t and P. The contextual features of a lexical item are consequently less informative: they do not 'on their own' imply what context the item will occur in.[4]

These specific dependencies between contextual features and category features may be stated in either of two different ways: in a rule of Syntax, or in a nonlexical primitive, a term I will shortly explain. This difference gives us two different kinds of nonlexicalism, which I call rule-based and constructional, respectively.

3.5.1 Rule-based nonlexicalism

Rule-based nonlexicalism is familiar from traditional phrase structure rules, such as those in Chomsky 1957. It encodes argument dependencies in specific rules of syntactic combination. Item (38) provides an

---

[4] Strictly speaking, no feature on its own implies anything. The informational content of a feature is always decided by the rules of the grammar. But when the rules are maximally general, they make no great contribution.

example, with a rule I call the t/N-Rule. This generalizes the effects of "⊛" in rule (21a) above.

(38)   t/N-Rule[X[t], N[...]] = X[i]

This rule refers specifically to the contextual features t and i – meant to evoke *transitive* and *intransitive*, but, again, only vaguely and initially – and the category feature N. Here X is a variable over category labels. Thus (38) allows any X expression with minor category t to combine with an N to make a bigger X with minor category i. Using this to combine the cook of (37) with sausage yields the derivation in (39).

(39)   cook sausage:V[i]

            cook:V[t]   sausage:N[ ]

Derivation (39) entails that sausage is a syntactic argument in cook sausage, according to the usage set out in Section 3.3, for cook sausage does not share the minor category of cook, making (39) an instance of the schema in (28).

Yet we should not say in this case that cook itself "has a syntactic argument," or that sausage "is a syntactic argument of" cook, or that it "realizes" one. These terms I reserve for heads with a-features and the dependents that check them. A word with the feature t does not carry explicit information about what arguments it may be paired with. This comes from elsewhere, here the rule in (38). Adding still further rules, like (40) and (41), will emphasize this moral.

(40)   t/P-Rule[X[t], P[...]] = X[i]

(41)   t/∅-Rule[X[t]] = X[i]

The t/P-Rule in (40) allows an $X[t]$ and a P to make an $X[i]$. The t/∅-Rule in (41) allows an $X[t]$ to make an $X[i]$ all on its own. Plainly, in a syntax with all three of these rules, endowing cook with t does not mean just that it licenses an N argument. A word with t does not carry information about what arguments it may be paired with. Its collocation with an N or P dependent is instead licensed by the rules of the syntax, t/N or t/P.

3.5.2 Constructional nonlexicalism

Constructional nonlexicalism differs less drastically from lexicalism. Like lexicalism, and unlike rule-based nonlexicalism, it keeps the rules of Syntax general, and instead does its work in the primitives. The difference is, here the primitives may be nonlexicalized (Chapter 1). Recall that these are primitives of Syntax that are not phonologically interpreted, not even as silence. Thus, in effect, they are category-specific rules of Syntax, such as the t/N or t/P rules from above, rendered as primitives – that is, as lexical items. Sometimes nonlexical primitives are called *constructions* (Goldberg 1995, Kay 2002, Sag 2012, Michaelis 2013).

One way to represent a nonlexical primitive is as a tree, all of whose leaves are category labels, as in (42), a constructional version of the t/N-Rule in (38). The tree has no phonological features and will have no phonological value, audible or silent.

(42)   X[i]
         ╱‾‾╲
       X[t]   N

We then take the syntax to be a routine for building big trees out of smaller ones (Joshi 1987). For example, tree (42) can be combined with the trees for sausage and cook, which I will take to be the one-node trees in (43) and (44), as before.

(43)   sausage:N

(44)   cook:V[t]

Now suppose the combination is done by a highly general rule that substitutes one tree for some leaf in another, provided that the leaf matches in some feature with the label on the root of the substituted tree. We then substitute (43) and (44) for the leaves of (42), deriving the output tree in (45). (Keep in mind, this is not a graph of the derivation, but rather the derived expression cook sausage. In this syntax, a derived expression has the morphology of a tree and not a string.)

(45)   V[i]
            ╱‾‾‾‾‾╲
      cook:V[t]   sausage:N

Item (45) is an expression with category V[i]. Thus it shares its major but not its minor category with cook, a V[t]. The shift in minor category coincides with the presence of the category-N dependent, sausage. Consequently, the derivation of the expression in (45) is another instance of the argument schema in (28); for simplicity I will not go through the details. But again we should be careful about our terminology. Sausage is an argument *in* cook sausage, and an argument *in relation to* cook, because cook is why cook sausage has category V. Yet under our nonlexicalist encoding of these argument relations, sausage is not an argument *of* cook, which itself has no arguments.

One primitive of this syntax does have arguments in precisely the lexicalist sense, however, and that is the nonlexical primitive in (42), call it the t/N construction. Our general rule of tree substitution is rather like the lexicalist's rule Check. It will combine (42) with any expression whose category matches the label of a leaf node, eliminating that leaf in the process. Each leaf is therefore an a-feature and the label is its value. Structure (42) has two categorized leaves, thus two a-features, and thus two arguments: an X[t] and an N. Correspondingly, both cook and sausage are syntactic arguments *of* structure (42) in the derivation of (45). And yet, to repeat, we are nevertheless equipped to say that sausage is an argument in relation to cook, in accord with (28). This sort of example justifies the generality of the argument definition in Section 3.3. Without it, one would have to say that nonlexicalists forfeit the distinction between a head and an argument in a phrase, quite unnecesarily.

3.5.3 The history of nonlexicalism

Rule-based nonlexicalism was presumed in earlier Transformational Grammar (Chomsky 1957). It is also permitted in the work of Montague (1974), though exploited only in some cases. Latter-day versions of constructional nonlexicalism are advocated in, for example, Goldberg (1995) and Kay (2002). And recently, several works, including Goldberg (2006) and Sag (2012), have promoted a kind of *hybrid constructional nonlexicalism*. Such grammars include nonlexical primitives, analogous to our tree in (42), and for this reason they are nonlexicalist. But they also specify a list of possible arguments on the lexical primitives of the grammar, such as the verb cook. The lexical primitives are then permitted to occur in nonlexical constructions, so long as their argument lists are compatible; the two argument lists are, so to speak, superimposed. See the papers in Boas and Sag (2012).

But pure lexicalism has been dominant since the 1970s, if with increasingly liberal use of silent lexical items. The best reason for this is headedness. As discussed above, lexicalist grammars express headedness in a single rule of syntactic derivation, a rule like our Check. In a genuinely nonlexicalist grammar, this is not possible. Here headedness could only be expressed in a principle (a meta-rule) over the set of syntactic rules (on a rule-based approach) or over the set of nonlexical primitives (on a constructional approach). One must say that any rule of syntax, or any nonlexical primitive, yields an expression that inherits the category of just one input to the rule, or of just one argument of the construction, respectively. So *if* the best way to understand headedness is as a property of syntactic derivation, rather than as a property of its primitives, this is unattractive. In my opinion it is not plain that this concern is fatal, however – though this opinion is certainly in need of defense.

3.6 OPTIONAL ARGUMENTS

It is sometimes assumed, as a matter of theory, that arguments of a head are obligatorily realized. That is, if a head has an argument, its phrase must include a dependent to satisfy it. Let me apply this assumption to examples (46) and (47).

(46) Lee robbed Mo of a necklace.

(47) Lee robbed Mo.

For illustration, suppose that *of a necklace* in (46) satisfies an argument of *rob* here. Then if arguments are obligatorily realized, the *rob* of (47) cannot be the *rob* of (46). The verbs are homophonous and both concern robbings, but the first must have an argument that the second does not. The two verbs must differ in their a-lists.

Obligatory realization does not follow from our basic understanding of arguments, however. There is nothing incoherent in saying that a head has a syntactic argument that is not satisfied by any dependent in the course of the derivation. The rules of syntax can be arranged to allow for nonrealization, without this changing our basic understanding of argumenthood. In lexicalist terms, one can allow members of an a-list to be marked as optional, with a diacritic that allows the a-checking rule to pass them over. And if this path is chosen, one can say that both (46) and (47) do contain exactly the same verb, with the same list of arguments. In (46) the argument of *rob* that tells you what the thief stole, the 'Loot argument,' is satisfied by a dependent phrase, but in (47) it is *unsatisfied*.

The choice between these two views is subtle. But there is one kind of evidence that would favor the second. Suppose we find a phrase that patterns syntactically as if it contained an argument dependent, when in fact there is no such dependent present. For example, suppose that (47) were to pattern as if it has a syntactic argument in the role of Loot, despite the evident absence of a dependent linked to that role. We can then say that the head of the phrase has an unsatisfied argument. This will explain the facts if the relevant grammatical pattern is stated not in terms of dependents, but rather in terms of the head's lexical arguments.

As we will see in Chapters 5 and 12, this sort of reasoning has been used in the case of short passives, such as (48). It is suggested

(Williams 1985, Grimshaw 1990, Jackendoff 1990b, among others) that
the verb phrase has an unsatisfied argument corresponding to the overt
by-phrase in a long passive, such as (49).

(48) The ewe was killed.
(49) The ewe was killed by a wolf.

The suggestion rests in part on the observation that the short passive
patterns just like the long passive with respect to control of infinitival
"rationale clauses" (Faraci 1974, Jones 1985, Roeper 1987), as in (50).
Here the understood survivor of the winter can be the killer of the ewe.

(50) The ewe was killed (by a wolf) to survive the winter.
      'The ewe was killed (by a wolf) so that the killer might survive the winter.'

Sometimes it is supposed that control of rationale clauses is determined
with reference to syntactic argumenthood. From this it follows that
the unrealized role of killer in (48) must correspond to a syntactic
argument. A short passive has no obvious dependent in that role.
And therefore a short passive must contain either a non-obvious
dependent, or instead just a predicate with an unsatisfied argument.
If for some reason the first option is ruled out, one has to conclude
that the syntactic arguments of a predicate are not always satisfied. See
Chapter 12.

3.7 Θ-GRIDS

Work in the tradition of GB (Chomsky 1981) describes the a-list of a
predicate in terms of two connected lists: a *subcategorization frame* and a
Θ-*grid* (Stowell 1981:34). Sometimes the Θ-grid is called the "argument
structure" (Williams 1985, Grimshaw 1990). The members of a Θ-grid
are called **Θ-roles**.

(51) carry: V [SubcategorizationFrame : ⟨N, N⟩, ThetaGrid : ⟨θ, θ⟩]

The two lists differ in the properties that they entail for their satisfiers. The subcategorization frame restricts the form or syntactic category of the dependent that satisfies the argument. For example, it
may require that the satisfier of the argument be a noun phrase, or
a prepositional phrase. The subcategorization frame in (51), ⟨N, N⟩, lists
two arguments, both required to have category N.

Membership in the Θ-grid, on the other hand, marks a syntactic argument as being a semantic argument as well – an argument on which
the predicate imposes a semantic relation (see Chapter 4). On a few

accounts, members of the Θ-grid also bear a label indicating what sort of semantic relation interprets the argument, for example the labels AGT or PAT to mark an Agent or Patient interpretation syntactically.

When an expression with Θ-roles heads a phrase, its Θ-roles are paired off with the dependents, according to their order in the Θ-grid. A dependent that satisfies a Θ-role in the derivation of a phrase is said to be *assigned* that Θ-role. Typically this is represented by eliminating the Θ-role from the features that the head transmits to the phrase that it heads.

In the normal case, the two lists coincide: a dependent that satisfies the first item on the Subcategorization Frame satisfies the first item in Θ-grid, and so forth (Chomsky 1981:35-6). We might make this explicit by coindexation, as in (52).

(52)   carry: V [SubcategorizationFrame : $\langle N_1, N_2 \rangle$, ThetaGrid : $\langle \theta_1, \theta_2 \rangle$]

But in principle there may be atypical cases. A head may restrict the syntactic category of an argument without taking it as a semantic argument. For example, the head may require that its argument be expletive *there*. But then an expletive is not in the relevant sense a semantic argument, and therefore the subcategorization frame will have a member that does not correspond to a Θ-role. Conversely, if the head imposes no specific restriction on the syntactic category of a syntactic argument, allowing any category at all, one might choose to remove the argument from the subcategorization frame, leaving it only in the Θ-grid.[5] The division of the a-list into these two components therefore permits some theoretical freedom.

The Θ-grid is a syntactic object, but it serves to indicate whether a syntactic argument is also a semantic argument. Use of the Θ-grid, and its members the Θ-roles, is therefore motivated only if semantic argumenthood matters to some pattern in Syntax. Are there such patterns? Facts such as (53) have been taken to show that there are: the direct object of a verb cannot move into the position of its subject.

(53)   * Lee$_k$ criticized t_k.
         'Lee criticized herself.'

In the dominant tradition, this fact is taken to show that a movement dependency cannot span two positions that both instantiate a semantic argument. In turn this idea is written into the syntax by means of

---

[5] The alternative is to have members of the Subcategorization Frame that do not restrict the category of their satisfiers.

Θ-roles. A dependent that instantiates a semantic argument of a lexical predicate is also assigned a Θ-role. To rule out (53), one can then stipulate (principles which imply) that a single expression cannot satisfy more than one Θ-role, as stated in (54) from Chomsky (1981:36). This is one half of the "Theta Criterion." Example (53) will then be syntactically underivable, since a single expression cannot move between two positions that are both assigned Θ-roles.

(54)   Theta Criterion (part 1)
       "Each argument bears one and only one Θ-role[.]"

Alternatively one can deny (54), allow movement to span two positions with Θ-roles, but then say that in such cases the lower Θ position, the launching site of movement, when it is also assigned Case, is pronounced as a reflexive pronoun, as in (55), and not as silence, as in (53). This idea is developed in Lidz and Idsardi (1998) and Hornstein (1999), who treat the relation between Lee and herself in (55) as one of movement.

(55)   Lee$_k$ criticized herself$_k$.

But either way, the account of (53)'s unacceptability appeals to Θ-roles, and these are regarded as syntactic indices of semantic argumenthood.

    Lastly, a note on optionality. Chomsky (1981) proposes that Θ-roles are obligatorily satisfied, via the restriction in (56), the second half of the "Theta Criterion."

(56)   Theta Criterion (part 2)
       "Each Θ-role is assigned to one and only one argument."

In Chapter 8, I discuss the relevance of saying that each Θ-role is assigned to *only* one argument. This is thought to help explain why a sentence like (57) is impossible, with the given type of interpretation.

(57)   * Mo might cook sausages bacon.
       'Mo might cook sausages and bacon.'

Here I want only to note the requirement that each Θ-role be assigned to an argument, at least one. Other theorists have rejected this and allowed for unsatisfied Θ-roles (Williams 1985, Roeper 1987, Manning and Sag 1998). The empirical motive for this is as stated in the previous section. It allows an account of cases where a phrase behaves syntactically as if it included an argument, and yet no argument is manifest. Again, a classic case is the short passive, where we might say that the unrealized 'deep subject role' corresponds to an unsatisfied Θ-role of the verb. See Chapters 5 and 12 for more discussion.

3.8 EXTERNAL AND INTERNAL ARGUMENTS

Some theories divide the syntactic arguments of a head into two classes, *external* and *internal*. There is at most one external argument, and all nonexternal arguments are internal. When a head has both, the dependent that realizes the external argument is structurally more remote from the head than any other argument; or at least this is so in those cases that the theory treats as basic, such as simple active clauses. I will represent the distinction by having the first member of the a-list be the list of internal arguments, as in (58).

(58) ⟨⟨Internal Arguments⟩, External Argument⟩

Suppose for the moment that in (59) and (60) both the subject and object realize syntactic arguments of the verb.

(59) Ozzy sang *Paranoid*.
(60) Ozzy shattered the goblet.

Given the internal/external distinction, one would then say that the subject realizes the external argument, while the object realizes an internal argument, giving the verbs the a-lists in (61) and (62).

(61) sing:[⟨⟨N⟩, N⟩]
(62) shatter:[⟨⟨N⟩, N⟩]

What is the use of this distinction, over and above the ordering of arguments? Importantly, it allows for a dichotomy among heads with only a single argument: in some the single argument is external while in others it is internal. This split has several theoretical uses, but one is most common. It is used to encode, in the lexical properties of the verb, a distinction between unergative and unaccusative clauses: we can say that the subject realizes an external argument of the verb in the former but an internal argument in the latter.

An *unergative clause* is an intransitive whose subject patterns in some relevant respect like the subject in a transitive clause with a verb of action. Example (63) is a candidate for unergativity, since its subject is interpreted like the subject of transitive (59), as naming the singer.

(63) Ozzy sang.

An **unaccusative clause** is an intransitive whose subject patterns in some relevant respect like the object in a transitive clause. Item (64) is a candidate for unaccusativity since its subject is interpreted like the object of (60), as naming what is shattered.

(64)   The goblet shattered.

Thus to encode the semantic equivalence between the subjects of (59), Ozzy sang Paranoid, and (63), Ozzy sang, we can say that both realize the external argument of sing, and link this argument to the role of Singer in the semantics. Likewise, to encode the equivalence between the object of (60), Ozzy shattered the goblet, and the subject of (64), The goblet shattered, we can say that both realize an internal argument of shatter, and link this argument to the role of Shattered. This may require two verbs "shatter" and two verbs "sing," but even then the relations between them would be captured in their argument lists.

Attractively, this affords a fixed alignment of semantic with syntactic relations (Hall 1965, Perlmutter 1978). The role of Singer links unconditionally to the external argument relation, and the role of Shattered links unconditionally to the internal argument relation. This would not be possible without something like the external versus internal division, since the semantic relations do not align uniquely with the surface relations of subject and object: the role of Shattered goes with surface object in (60) but the surface subject in (64). The same point applies to any other, nonsemantic aspects of the distinction between unergative and unaccusative clauses, such as differences in case marking or in what transformations may apply to each class. We will discuss such contrasts more in Chapter 11. See also Levin and Rappaport Hovav (1995), and the overview in Alexiadou *et al.* 2004.

We should observe, however, that the utility of the division is lessened if we drop the assumption that all the relevant arguments project from the very same head, the verb. For if, instead, they are arguments in relation to different heads, this alone will be sufficient to make the desired distinctions and generalizations.

For example, on one popular theory, to be reviewed at length in Chapter 9, the subject of a clause with a verb of action, transitive or unergative, is not a syntactic argument in relation to the verb (Schein 1993, Borer 1994, Kratzer 1996, Marantz 1997). It is an argument in relation to another head, often called "AG" and put in category v. The arguments of AG do not include either the object in a transitive clause or the subject in an unaccusative clause. Thus sentence (59) has a derivation like (65), and that of (63) would be the same minus Paranoid.

(65)

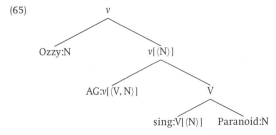

What was formerly an external argument of the verb is now distinguished as the argument of AG. As a result, no two-way division *among* the arguments of the verb is necessary. It is therefore unclear whether such a division is ever required. It may be enough that the arguments are ordered, something that is more widely presumed and does not imply the internal/external distinction.

A note of caution about jargon. Sometimes the term "external argument of the verb" is still used for a subject phrase that is not even a syntactic argument of the verb, as in (65). Under this usage the term does not mark an independent theoretical distinction. It is informal shorthand for the conjunction of two properties: the subject is generated outside of the verb phrase, and yet semantically it is related in some way to the event of the verb; see Chapter 4.[6]

3.9 CONSEQUENCES AND CORRELATES OF ARGUMENTHOOD

What are the 'surface' consequences of the syntactic distinction between arguments and adjuncts? There can be no full answer without a complete grammatical theory and a complete grammar of the language in question, including its semantics and pragmatics. But partial answers are possible if we provisionally grant certain premises, if only for the sake of argument.

Sections 3.9.1–3.9.3 will trace a few such partial answers. Given certain premises, we expect arguments to contrast with adjuncts in the possibility of omission, iteration and susceptibility to 'stranding' under transformational operations. The remaining sections, 3.9.4–3.9.5, will

---

[6] When the distinction between internal and external arguments was first introduced, it was assumed that external arguments were generated *externally* to the phrase headed by the predicate. This was later rejected, in favor of the assumption that an argument is always within the phrase headed by its predicate. On our understanding of arguments, this follows from the basic premise that an expression inherits only the category features of its head.

then indicate some patterns that correlate with the argument/adjunct distinction, if for indirect reasons.

First let me single out two ideas that will serve as potential premises in our reasoning, even if we think they are wrong. The first is Argument Necessity: syntactic arguments of a head are obligatorily satisfied. So suppose the sound "cook" in (66a) pronounces a verb with two syntactic arguments, here satisfied by Mo and sausage. Argument Necessity then requires, in (66b), either that "cook" pronounces a different verb, or that the clause has a silent direct object to satisfy cook's first argument.

(66)   a Mo might cook sausage.
      b Mo might cook.

Second, Lexical Uniqueness: a single pairing of sound and 'basic meaning,' within a single major syntactic category, corresponds to a single lexical item. In both (66a) and (66b) "cook" pronounces a verb that basically means 'to prepare food.' Lexical Uniqueness therefore requires that it pronounces exactly the same lexical item in both cases. The same lexical item has the same syntactic arguments. So if sausage satisfies an argument of cook in (66a), Argument Necessity and Lexical Uniqueness jointly imply that (66b) too includes a direct object, though here it is evidently silent.

3.9.1 Omissibility

By definition, adjuncts have no effect on category. Removing an adjunct therefore cannot affect whether or not an expression is syntactically licit in a certain context. If C comprises head B and adjunct A, and the syntax permits C in context K, then it must also permit B in context K. Contrapositively, if the syntax forbids omission of a particular dependent, then that dependent must not be an adjunct.

So if removing a dependent results in *unacceptability*, this is good initial evidence that the omitted dependent is an argument. Item (67b) is good initial evidence that the chair in (67a) is an argument. It is a separate question whether the chair is an argument *of* the verb carry, or rather of some other, silent part of carry the chair's derivation.

(67)   a Navin carried the chair.
      b *Navin carried.

The converse is not on equal footing, however. If a dependent can acceptably be omitted, it need not be an adjunct, since nothing in the minimal idea of a syntactic argument requires that arguments be realized. But this changes if we stipulate Argument Necessity. Then modulo Lexical Uniqueness, a genuinely omissible dependent would have to be an adjunct. Data like (68) would be good evidence that tonight is an adjunct in cook sausage tonight.

(68)   a Mo might cook sausage tonight.
       b Mo might cook sausage.

Even then the initial evidence would not be decisive if the relevant dependent could be present, but silent. Logically, it is possible to say that cook has a temporal argument in both (68a) and (68b), for example, but that in (68b) it is silent. Here this seems the less plausible option, but see Creary *et al.* (1989).

3.9.2 Iterability

Again, adjuncts don't alter category. So if the syntax permits B in context K, and we *add* an adjunct A to B to make C, then the syntax must also permit C in K. Adjuncts can be iterated freely without any effect on syntactic well-formedness. But acceptability is more than that: it also expresses phonological, semantic and pragmatic factors. Often it's hard to decide whether a string is bad because of its syntax, rather than something else.

This caution is not idle. Adding an adjunct, while it will never have a syntactic effect, will often have an effect on the distribution of a phrase among the acceptable strings of the language – one effect in particular. Doubling up on any semantic relation is generally forbidden, whether the relation is associated with an argument or an adjunct (Chapter 8). Consider (69). Presumably tomorrow is an adjunct in (69a). But its presence keeps the verb phrase from collocating acceptably with tonight in (69b), as it otherwise could. This is comparable to (70), a pattern one might take to show that sausage is an argument in (70a).

(69)   a Mo might cook sausage tomorrow.
       b # Mo might cook sausage tomorrow tonight.[7]
(70)   a Mo might cook sausage.
       b * Mo might cook sausage bacon.

We will return to this pattern at length in Chapter 8. Here I note only that (69) and (70) leave us with a choice. Either tomorrow is an argument in (69a), so that adding tomorrow changes minor category; or there is no change, and tomorrow is indeed an adjunct, but (69b) is unacceptable for reasons that are not strictly syntactic. If the latter option is correct, as I think it is (Chapter 8), this will not void the theoretical

---

[7] A prefixed hash-mark (#) indicates that the following string, if it is a syntactically derivable expression, has a meaning that is in some way odd.

distinction between 'selected' and 'unselected' dependents, arguments and adjuncts. But it will efface what would otherwise be a widespread reflection of the distinction in surface distributions. Adding an adjunct won't always create an expression with the same surface distribution as its host.

We can only expect iteration to be a diagnostic over a very narrow domain. Suppose that C has a dependent A in semantic role R; then if adding a dependent D to C with the same role is acceptable, D is presumably an adjunct. It is hard to say what "the same role" means here. But maybe calmly and quietly bear the same role to cook sausage in (71). If that's right, then we have good evidence that at least one of the two is an adjunct here.

(71)   Mo might calmly cook sausage quietly.

3.9.3 Strandability

Rules of Syntax are defined over syntactic categories. So if a rule, Rule, applies acceptably to expression B, it will also do so to [B A] when A is an adjunct, as stated in (72a). The same is not true for arguments, since adding an argument A to B results in an expression of different minor category. As stated in (72b), a rule that applies to B may not apply to [B A], or conversely.

(72)   a If Rule(B) is syntactically licit and A is an adjunct, then Rule([B A]) is syntactically licit.

       b If Rule(B) but not Rule([B A]) is syntactically licit, or vice versa, then A is an argument.

This is the basis for some common diagnostics. We start with a C for which Rule(C) is acceptable – this might be an ellipsis rule that silences C, for instance. Now suppose C has two immediate parts, A and B, with B the head. We then attempt Rule(B), silencing B but not A, for example. If this works, it suggests that B shares its category with C, and therefore that A is an adjunct. On the other hand, if Rule(B) is unacceptable, and there is no obvious nonsyntactic account of why, it suggests that the categories of B and C differ, and so that A is an argument.

The ellipsis test illustrated in (73) and (74) can serve as an example, given the judgment in (74c). First we need a few premises. Assume that sausage and tonight in (73a) are both dependents in a phrase headed by cook, and that neither can move out of that phrase. Do the same for sausage in (74a). Next assume that all the other sentences are derived from (73a) and (74a) by a rule, call it Ellipsis, that silences a certain kind of constituent.

(73) a Mo might cook sausage tonight.
     b Mo might.
       'Mo might cook sausage tonight.'
     c Mo might tonight.
       'Mo might cook sausage tonight.'
(74) a Mo might cook sausage.
     b Mo might.
       'Mo might cook sausage.'
     c * Mo might sausage.
       'Mo might cook sausage.'

Now we can make some inferences. In (73), `Ellipsis` applies equally to cook sausage and cook sausage tonight. So tonight in (73a) is probably an adjunct. But `Ellipsis` distinguishes cook from cook sausage, in the contrast between (74b) and (74c). So sausage in (74a) is probably an argument. These inferences will not be sound, however, absent any of our premises. For instance, they will not hold if tonight can extrapose rightward, outside of the phrase headed by cook. In that case our conclusion will be sound only relative to the assumption that adjuncts but not arguments can undergo this kind of extraposition.

3.9.4 Substitution by pro-forms

Subsitution by a pro-form is often used diagnostically. The contrast between (75b) and (76b), for example, might be taken to show that tonight is an adjunct and sausage is an argument. Here the pro-form is do so, or perhaps just so.

(75) a Mo might cook sausage tonight ...
     b ...and Lee might do so tomorrow.
(76) a Mo might cook sausage ...
     b * ...and Lee might do so bacon.

This would be a consequence of the basic argument/adjunct distinction, were substitution by pro-forms to be a syntactic operation, a rule that changes the phonological features of an already assembled expression. In that case it would be just like `Ellipsis`, except that it substitutes a pro-form and not silence.

But nowadays this is not the standard account of pro-forms. They are treated as lexical items in the syntactic derivation. Thus our logic does not apply, and the contrast in stranding is not a consequence of the fundamental distinction between arguments and adjuncts. Explaining (75b) and (76b) will require a different rationale.

Here is one reasonable option: postulate that a pro-form never has syntactic arguments (Panagiotidis 2003). Any dependent in a phrase headed by a pro-form must then be an adjunct. So bacon would have to be an adjunct in (76b). Since (76b) is ungrammatical, it follows that no phrase in the predicate of this sentence – that is, no phrase in the maximal expression pronounced do so – can host bacon as an adjunct. Analogy then implies that no phrase in the predicate of (76a) could host sausage as an adjunct either. Consequently sausage must be a syntactic argument in cook sausage – and the substitution diagnostic is serviceable, given our initial postulate. Whether sausage is an argument in a phrase headed by cook, and if so whether it is furthermore an argument of cook, are as usual additional questions.

3.9.5 Extraction

Displacement, or extraction, is sometimes worse out of an adjunct than out of an argument. Most notably, it is often forbidden out of adjunct clauses but permitted out of clauses in object position (Cattell 1976, Huang 1982). For example, after Lee insulted Mo is presumably an adjunct in (77), and (78) shows that wh-movement and relativization out of this clause are unacceptable.

(77)   She noticed it after Lee insulted Mo.

(78)   a * Who did she notice it after Lee insulted?
       b * That's the guy who she noticed it after Lee insulted.

Meanwhile in (79) the clause is the direct object, and now in (80) the analogous extraction is fine.

(79)   She noticed that Lee insulted Mo.

(80)   a Who did she notice that Lee insulted?
       b That's the guy who she noticed that Lee insulted.

Thus extraction can sometimes be used to distinguish adjunct clauses from direct object clauses. It will not distinguish adjunct clauses from subject clauses, however, where extraction is generally horrible, as shown in (82).[8]

---

[8] Sometimes extraction seems to distinguish argument from adjunct PPs within an indefinite noun phrase. Certainly (1) is better than (2).

(1)   What shop did you burn a photograph of?

(2)   ?*What shop did you burn a photograph from?

But this is not perfectly reliable, since extraction is often bad even out of putative argument PPs. To me the two strings in (3) are equal in (un)acceptability, even though of what would be regarded as an argument and from where, as an adjunct.

(3)   a ? What did you kiss a teacher of?
      b ? Where did you kiss a teacher from?

(81) That Lee insulted Mo came as no surprise.

(82) a * Who did that Lee insulted come as no surprise.
      b * That's the guy who that Lee insulted came as no surprise.

Relatedly, a long-distance dependency to an argument is sometimes better than the same kind of dependency to an adjunct. Huang (1982) observes contrasts such as (83) in Mandarin Chinese. This string can mean (83a) but not (83b).

(83) Ni   xiang zhidao shei zenme xiuhao nei bu   che?
      you want   know   who   how   fix   that CLS car
      a 'About whom do you wonder how he fixed the car?'
      b * 'What is the method about which you wonder who fixed the car that way?'

Meaning (83a) makes the whole sentence a question about the fixer of the car, a role associated with the subject of the lower clause. Thus a dependency between the whole sentence and an argument in the lower clause is licit. On the other hand, the meaning in (83b) requires the same kind of dependency to an adjunct in the lower clause, zenme 'how.' And this is ungrammatical.

Contrasts such as these have been encoded in various ways.[9] But as yet there is no fully satisfactory explanation for them. We don't know *why* adjuncts should sometimes obstruct long-distance dependencies.

In any case, whatever relation there might in fact be between extraction and argumenthood, it probably should not be written too deeply

---

[9] Chomsky 1986 simply stipulates that an expression blocks extraction if it is not "L-marked," and that only syntactic arguments are L-marked.

Hunter 2011, and (following Kroch 1987) Frank 2002, among others, have tried to provide a more explanatory account. Hunter stipulates a condition on "Spellout," his name for phonological and semantic interpretation. The condition entails that an expression with an adjunct cannot be Spelled Out if the adjunct has a *wh*-phrase within it whose features require it to move. Attractively, the same condition entails a prohibition on extracting out of a moved constituent, deriving the "Freezing Effect" of Wexler and Culicover 1981, and thereby giving the account some explanatory power.

Frank works in the framework of Tree Adjoining Grammar. Here the contrast in extraction is not derived from a constraint, but is rather a formal consequence of how long-distance displacement is represented. Suppose X is moved out of phrase XY, and over expression B, to yield XBY. In Tree Adjoining Grammar this is analyzed as B taking XY as a syntactic argument, with the morphological effect of infixing B into its argument. Thus movement *ipso facto* happens only out of arguments; movement out of an adjunct is an incoherent notion. This is a very strong explanation – but perhaps too strong, since movement out of non-clausal adjuncts is typically possible.

into the syntax. Extraction out of non-clausal adjuncts is often acceptable. In particular, when a PP is an adjunct to VP, extraction of its object is generally acceptable, as in (84).

(84) a What did you open this with?
      b Who did you sing that song with?
      c What day do you leave on?
      d Which tree is he sitting behind?
      e What is he standing next to?

The minimal contrast in (85) is striking.

(85) a Which song did you leave after?
      b * Which song did you leave after started?
      c ?? Which song did you leave after the conductor announced?

So we cannot expect contrasts in extraction, except when the dependent is a clause. For this reason it is not plain that any restriction on extraction should be a direct consequence of the basic distinction between arguments and adjuncts. Some room needs to be left for the possibilities in (84). Unfortunately, it is far from clear how this should be done. The contrast in (85) has no settled account.

Thus, while the apparent sensitivity of long-distance dependencies to the distinction between syntactic arguments and syntactic adjuncts is surely among the most interesting observations in linguistics, and also among the best reasons for believing that the distinction is important, it is neither well understood nor very sturdy as a diagnostic.

DISCUSSION POINTS

1 Provide evidence that cook is the head of cook sausage tonight in Mo might cook sausage tonight.

2 Example (1) below is ungrammatical. Does the grammar comprising (21) and (22) above account for this? Does the grammar in (24) and (25)? If either of them fails, how would you amend them?

(1) * Mo might cook tonight sausage.

3 Many syntactic theories presume that an adjunct cannot combine with an expression that has unsatisfied syntactic arguments. Thus a head with arguments must take them all, before its phrase can host an adjunct. Is there some good reason to presume this? What further diagnostics of the argument/adjunct distinction does this presumption allow? In considering these questions, keep in

mind the existence of displacement phenomena (represented by movement).

4 For each example below, decide whether the italicized phrase is an argument or an adjunct. Provide evidence for your conclusion using tests from the chapter. Are the test results all consistent?

(2) a Al cooked a fish *in the backyard*.
  b Al put the fish *on the grill*.
  c The garden swarmed *with bees*.
  d Bees swarmed *in the garden*.
  e Al elbowed *his way* into the room.

5 Every event of cooking happens at a time and place. Write a syntax that treats in the backyard and at 5 p.m. in (3) as arguments in the cook phrase (ignoring tense on cook). Does treating these as arguments cause any problems?

(3) Al cooked a fish in the backyard at 5 p.m.

6 Example (4) has a subject (Matt) and three different kinds of objects: two noun phrases (me, $5) plus a finite declarative clause (that ewes suck fenceposts for fun). All the other dependents are prepositional phrases.

(4) In the lunchroom, before every meeting, just for Al's amusement, Matt wagers me $5 that ewes suck fenceposts for fun.

This illustrates a broad generalization about human languages. Clauses tend to have no more than four dependents, call them *core dependents*, that don't require something like a preposition to support them. Does this show us anything about the argument/adjunct distinction? Does it by itself imply that the non-core dependents are adjuncts in their phrases? Why or why not? What do you think explains this generalization?

7 Many of our argument/adjunct diagnostics rely on what I called "Lexical Uniqueness," the assumption that a single pairing of sound and 'basic meaning,' within a single major syntactic category, should correspond to a single lexical item. How compelling is this assumption? When should we adhere to it, and why?

8 Can you think of any syntactic pattern in a language you study that requires reference to the distinction between arguments and adjuncts? Can you think of any syntactic patterns that are sensitive to whether or not an expression is meaningful (as opposed to expletive or idiomatic)?

9 Can a nonlexicalist encoding of argument relations do justice to headedness?

SUGGESTIONS FOR FURTHER READING

Lexicalized syntax based on argument-taking has important antecedents in both logic and structuralist linguistics, among them Ajdukiewicz 1935 and Tesnière 1959, respectively. The two strands merge in Bar-Hillel 1953. Dowty 2003 is an excellent discussion of both the standard view and its challenges; see also Bierwisch 2003 in the same volume. For a recent textbook treatment, with exercises, see Koopman *et al.* 2014. Hornstein and Nunes 2008 reflect provocatively on our poor understanding of the argument/adjunct distinction. Bresnan 1980 and Stowell 1981 were important moves towards explicit lexicalization in mainstream syntax. On the practical virtues of lexicalized syntax, read Joshi 2004. See Boas and Sag 2012 for recent exploration of nonlexicalized syntax.

4 Arguments in Semantics

4.1 INTRODUCTION

There is a general notion of *semantic argument*. It says that A is a semantic argument of B when it instantiates a term (fills a slot) in a relation expressed by B. But under this rubric fall several more specific ideas, all commonly evoked, that need to be distinguished. In this chapter I will discuss four, which I call functional arguments (Section 4.2), content arguments (Section 4.3), entailed role arguments (Section 4.4) and participant arguments (Section 4.5). In Section 4.6, I will review common ideas on the correspondence of semantic and syntactic arguments.

The need for distinction reflects actual diversity in usage. The term "argument" is used with more variety in semantics than it is in syntax, and for a reason. In syntax it is clear what sort of fact the distinction between arguments and adjuncts is meant to account for: namely, different effects on distributional category. The string carry the chair slowly has nearly the same distribution as carry the chair, but these two strings both differ substantially in distribution from carry on its own. The claim that the chair but not slowly is an argument is meant to encode this. In semantics, however, the distinction between arguments and non-arguments finds no single agreed explanandum that is equally clear. Consider (1).

(1) Mo might cook sausage in the kitchen with our blowtorch.

Its meaning relates Mo, sausage, the kitchen and our blowtorch all to an event of cooking. If any single aspect of this fact demands a purely semantic distinction between arguments and adjuncts, it is not clear at first blush. Any distinction we might care to make will therefore be based on observations that are subtle or even tendentious – nothing so plain as a difference in string distributions.[1] And with no single kind of fact to be accountable to, usage of "semantic argument" is correspondingly diverse. Linguists feel free to use it in any of several different ways. In the interests of clarifying conversation, I will now put labels to a few of these uses.

4.2 FUNCTIONAL ARGUMENTS

Linguistic semantics inherits its notion of argument from mathematics, where an argument is an 'input' to a function. The direct analogue of this in semantics is what I call a **functional argument**. In deriving an expression C with immediate parts A and B, A is a functional argument of B just in case the semantic values of the two combine by Application (or any similar rule) with A as the argument, as stated in (2). So if the phrase kiss Mo has its value derived as in (3), Mo is a functional argument of kiss.

(2) Functional Argument
    In an expression C with immediate parts A and B, A is a functional argument of B if and only if $[\![\,[\,B\,A\,]\,]\!] = \text{Application}([\![B]\!],[\![A]\!])$

(3) $[\![\,[\,\text{kiss Mo}\,]\,]\!] = \text{Application}([\![\text{kiss}]\!],[\![\text{Mo}]\!])$

We can think of Application in terms of variable substitution. By substituting certain variables in a name for f with a name for a, we produce a formula that names the result of applying of f to a. Many semantic frameworks deploy some such substitution operation, providing a value to some open slot in a meaning. Inasmuch as these can all be construed as 'versions' of Application, (2) has wide coverage.

---

[1] There is a popular idea that certain dependents, the semantic arguments, are required to express a 'complete thought' while others are not. Presumably the idea is not just that omitting these yields a nonsentential string of words, or one that (the grammar being what it is) is not of a truth-evaluable semantic type. Rather, it must be that no grammar could produce a truth-evaluable sentence with words that evoked the same concepts, since these concepts jointly fail to make a 'complete thought.' But surely this is nonsense. That there was an event of cooking is itself a complete thought, just like the thought that Mo was a teacher. There is no conceptual reason that Cooked is not a sentence on par with Mo was a teacher, expressing the complete thought that there was a cooking. To say that as a matter of fact it does not express a complete thought, but only (say) a relation, just begs the question. And though we might express more specific thoughts by adding that the cooking was by Mo, and that Mo was a teacher of math, such additions need not be treated as completions. So, in general, dependents cannot ultimately be motivated by the need to complete a thought. See Kracht 2011:116ff. for discussion.

The inverse of being a functional argument is **taking a functional argument**. B **takes** A as a functional argument exactly when A is a functional argument of B. So if Mo is a functional argument of kiss in kiss Mo, then kiss correspondingly takes Mo as a functional argument. In these terms we can also say what it means for a single expression to itself *have* a functional argument. Expression B **has a functional argument** just in case there is a licit derivation in which it takes a functional argument, as stated in (4).

(4) Having a functional argument
Expression B has a functional argument if and only if the grammar permits a derivation that yields an expression [B A], order irrelevant, and the semantic value of this expression is Application($[\![B]\!]$,$[\![A]\!]$)

The extension to multiple arguments is straightforward. Suppose that B has a functional argument. Suppose further that when B takes any A as an argument, the resulting expression [B A] itself has a functional argument. In that case we say that B has *two* functional arguments. The second is just the argument of those functions that are in the range of B – that is, those functions expressed by [B X] for any argument X. Likewise for further arguments: the third, fourth and so on. Each dependent B takes as an argument is itself an argument of B.

As an example, let kiss have the semantic value in (5). Then, if (6) is syntactically derivable, it also has the licit semantic derivation in (7). Therefore we can say that the kiss of (5) has at least two arguments, corresponding to the kisser and the kissed.

(5) $[\![$ kiss $]\!] = \lambda y \lambda x \lambda e[$ KissingByOf$(x,y)(e)$ $]$

(6) [Lee [kiss Mo]]

(7) a $[\![$ [Lee [kiss [Mo]]] $]\!]$
  b$=$ Application($[\![$kiss Mo$]\!]$, $[\![$Lee$]\!]$)
  c$=$ Application(Application($[\![$kiss$]\!]$, $[\![$Mo$]\!]$), $[\![$Lee$]\!]$)
  d$=$ Application(Application($\lambda y \lambda x \lambda e[$ KissingByOf$(x,y)(e)$ $]$, Mo), Lee)
  e$=$ $\lambda e[$ KissingByOf(Lee, Mo)(e) $]$

The result in (7e) is itself a function: it pairs any event *e* with True if *e* is a kissing by Lee of Mo. Does this mean that the kiss of (5) has a third argument, corresponding to the event of kissing? According to our definition, that depends on the grammar. Does the grammar permit a derivation in which some expression, naming an event, is a functional semantic argument of expression (6), interpreted as (7e)? If it does, then expression (6) has a functional argument, and the kiss of (5) correspondingly has three. But otherwise the sentence does not have an argument and kiss has only two.

This highlights the fact that the definition in (4) is not purely semantic. It does not say just that B has a functional argument if its value is a function. It also requires that there be a licit derivation in which B takes a functional argument. In this light consider English nouns. Plausibly, the semantic value of ewe is a function that yields true when applied to a ewe, (8).

(8) $[\![\text{ewe}]\!] = \lambda x[\text{Ewe}(x)]$

And yet it isn't clear that ewe can ever take an argument, since (9) is ungrammatical. If this is the right conclusion, then, according to (4), we cannot say that ewe has a functional argument. We can only say that its value is a function.

(9)   *She ewe.

To me it seems more natural to say that ewe stands for a function but has no arguments, than to say instead that it does have an argument, but can never take one. Still, many other authors do use the term differently, and say that an expression has a semantic argument so long as its value is a function.

Historically, linguistic semantics inherits the analysis of expression meanings into functions and arguments from Frege (1891, 1892), whose idea that predicates were 'incomplete' or 'unsaturated' was developed in new directions by Russell (1905, 1911, 1918), Ajdukiewicz (1935) and many relevant others. See Ramsey (1925) for a sharp early critique. The Fregean approach to semantics was widely popularized following the work of Montague (1974), influentially including Lewis (1970). For opposition to this current, see Davidson (1967c).

4.3 CONTENT ARGUMENTS

The notion of a functional argument is tied to one particular step in a semantic derivation: a function applies to an argument. What I will call a **content argument** has only to do with the 'source' of the role bound by that argument, in the derivation.

I will characterize this loosely, and by walking through an example. Let expression B have a value like (10), with a functional argument in term x of relation R.

(10) $[\![\text{B}]\!] = \ldots \lambda x[\ldots R(\ldots x \ldots)]$

In the simplest case, B might be a one-place predicate like ewe in (11). Or it might be carry in (12), for example, with functional arguments in the roles of carrier and carried.

(11) $[\![\,ewe\,]\!] = \lambda x[\ Ewe(x)\ ]$

(12) $[\![\,carry\,]\!] = \lambda y \lambda x \lambda e[\ CarryingByOf(e, x, y)\ ]$

Now, B may occur in derivations which 'transmit' the relevant functional argument to a containing expression D, so that D itself has a value like (13), with a functional argument binding the same term in R.

(13) $[\![\,[_D\ldots B\ldots]\,]\!] = \lambda x[\ \ldots [R(\ldots x \ldots)]\ ]$

Technically, this can happen in various ways. Here is one example: our D is black ewe, derived as in (15) from (11) and (14) under Conjunction.

(14) $[\![\,black\,]\!] = \lambda x[\ Black(x)\ ]$

(15) Conjunction$(\![\,black\,]\!], [\![\,ewe\,]\!]) = \lambda x[\ Black(x)\ \&\ Ewe(x)\ ]$

Conjunction here **transmits the argument** of ewe to black ewe. Intending to make the same point, let us also say that in this derivation, the argument of black ewe is *inherited* from ewe, and that ewe *contributes* an argument to black ewe. If we want to say that the adjective black has an argument, we can also say that it contributes this argument to black ewe as well: an expression can inherit from any of its parts. These notions, inheriting and contributing, are not easy to define for the general case. But for our purposes, I think the example alone will do.

Next, suppose that D takes some A as a functional argument, combining under Application to yield C, as in (16).

(16) $[\![\,[_C\ A\ [_D\ldots B\ldots]]\,]\!] = $ Application$([\![D]\!], [\![A]\!])$

For instance, let A be Eunice (17), and disregard is a as morphological noise. Then our D, black ewe, can take our A, Eunice, as a functional argument, as in (18). The whole sentence, (17), is our final expression C.

(17) Eunice is a black ewe.

(18) $[\![(17)]\!] = $ Application$((15), Eunice) = Black(Eunice)\ \&\ Ewe(Eunice)$

Due to this derivation, the value of our A (Eunice) is said to satisfy the value of our D (black ewe). Thus Eunice is said to be a black ewe. Satisfaction of black ewe relates to ewehood because of how it was derived from ewe; our D expresses the relation it does because of its derivation from B. We therefore said that black ewe 'inherited' an argument from ewe – or also one from black. For the same reason, let

us now also say that, in deriving (17), Eunice is a *content argument* of
ewe, or also of black. The limiting case of a content argument, where
D = B, is a functional argument; so Eunice is also a content argument
of black ewe.

In brief, A is a content argument of B just when B has a functional
argument it contributes to D, and D takes A as a functional argument.

(19) Content argument
      When C has immediate parts A and D, A is a content argument of B just in case
      A is a functional argument of D, and the argument it satisfies is *inherited* from
      B, perhaps among other parts of D.

Eunice is a content argument of ewe, or also of black. But, of course,
syntactically, black and ewe are not on a par, since ewe is the head of
its phrase and black is a dependent. Maybe there is also a correlated
conceptual difference between their values, Black and Ewe, since the
first expresses a quality and the second a sortal. But neither difference
is reflected in (18). In the semantic derivation, Eunice has the same relation to both: it is a content argument. Notably, it is a functional argument of neither – exhibiting the descriptive utility of our new rubric.

The main use of the rubric, however, is in being able to articulate the
strong claim that some A is *not* a content argument of some B. Importantly, A is not a content argument of B just because the sentence they
inhabit entails some relation between whatever they describe. Example
(20) entails that Navin is in some relation to a carrying.

(20) Navin carried the chair.

Surely it is Navin that names Navin, and carry that tells us that the event
of the clause was a carrying. But from this it does not follow that Navin
is a content argument of carry. Why? Because in (20)'s derivation, the
relation bound by Navin may not be contributed by the verb. To see
this, just suppose that carry the chair has the value in (21), namely the
relation between a carrying and what is carried in it.

(21) $\llbracket$ [carry the chair] $\rrbracket$ = $\lambda y \lambda e$[CarryingOf(e, the chair)]

Next imagine that the subject–predicate relation means 'agent of,' with
a semantic rule like (22).[2] Combining Navin and carried the chair under
(22) yields (23).

(22) $\llbracket$ [$_S$ NP VP] $\rrbracket$ = $\exists e$[Agent(e, $\llbracket$NP$\rrbracket$) & $\llbracket$VP$\rrbracket$(e)]

(23) Navin carried the chair $\cong$ $\exists e$[Agent(e, Navin) & CarryingOf(e, the chair)]

---

[2] Rule (22) might be reinterpreted as a nonlexical primitive; see Chapters 1 and 3.

So Navin was the agent of a chair-carrying. But the relation Navin bound came from rule (22), not carry the chair or carry. To describe this, we can say that Navin is not a content argument of the carry phrase, or its head. The same point can be made with the syntax in (24), which includes a silent lexical item of category v.

(24) [Navin [[$_v$ ϵ] [carry the chair]]]

Following Kratzer (1996), let this v have the value in (25), the Agent relation.

(25) $[\![$ [$_v$ ϵ] $]\!] = \lambda z \lambda e[$ Agent(e, z)]

Simple rules of composition will then again yield (23), and, as before, Navin fails to be a content argument of carry. The two expressions are semantically related in several looser senses. The sentence entails a relation between the referent of Navin and an event that satisfies carried the chair. Navin even binds a relation to that event. But that relation is not introduced by the verb.

4.4 ENTAILED ROLE ARGUMENTS

Any sentence S carried O entails that there was an event of carrying. And like events in general (Strawson 1959, Kim 1976), any event of carrying necessarily enters certain relations to other individuals. For instance, any carrying is related to a carrier and a thing carried. Such relations are **entailed roles** of carry, as defined in (26).

(26) Entailed role
Relation R is an entailed role of expression B if and only if, necessarily, for any B'ing (alternatively, any B), there is an x that has relation R to that B'ing (or to that B).

The parenthesized alternatives here allow us to talk also about the entailed roles of predicates that express properties of ordinary objects, rather than events, such as sausage or pet dog. The relation of Keeper is an entailed role of pet dog, inasmuch as every pet dog has someone who is its keeper.

Many relations one can have to a carrying or a pet dog are not entailed roles of carry or pet dog. As Navin carries the chair, his dog follows him. But not every carrying has an accompanying animal, and not every pet dog accompanies someone carrying something. So these relations are not entailed roles of carry or pet dog.

Sometimes linguists use the term "semantic argument" to talk about dependents that instantiate entailed roles, in a very broad use of the term. To be clear we can call these the **entailed role arguments**, defined in (27).[3]

(27) Entailed role argument
>   When C has immediate parts A and B, A is an entailed role argument relative to B if and only if, in the semantic derivation of C, A instantiates a relation that is an entailed role of B.

It will be useful to generalize to the parts of B, when B is complex, as carried the chair is. Let me again do this loosely. If A instantiates an entailed relation for B, and B entails this relation 'because' one of its parts does, then A is also an entailed role argument for that part. Then we can say that Navin is an entailed role argument both for carry the chair, and for carry – and that is so on almost any analysis of the sentence, since Navin surely binds a role that is entailed by carry.

4.5 PARTICIPANT ARGUMENTS

Linguists are rarely concerned with all of a predicate's entailed roles. More often what we have in mind is a small subset that are of special grammatical or psychological importance: what I will call the **participant roles**. A dependent that instantiates a participant role is a **participant argument**.

(28) Participant argument
>   In an expression C with parts A and B, A is a participant argument relative to

---

[3] Here is a possible recent example of this usage. John Beavers (2010:823, fn.1) writes: "I consider an argument to be any participant necessarily entailed to be part of the event by the predicate." In the context, Beavers seems to mean that an "argument" is any individual in a relation of a type that the event must enter, if it satisfies the predicate. There may be more to it, however, depending on what it means to be "part of the event."

The terminological association between "semantic arguments" and "entailments" has been encouraged by Dowty's 1989 influential definition of "thematic roles" as "a cluster of entailments," via the assumption that "thematic roles" interpret semantic arguments. This is unfortunate, however, since for Dowty himself it is not true that any individual in an entailed relation occupies a "thematic role." The reason is, for Dowty a "thematic role" is not just a cluster of entailments, but a cluster of entailments "shared by certain arguments of certain verbs ... that plays a special role in linguistic theory" (1989:76–7). And this restriction to "arguments," basically subjects and objects, as well as relations with a "special role in linguistic theory," narrows things down enormously.

B, if and only if, in the semantic derivation of C, A instantiates a relation that is a participant role for B.

Individuals in participant roles for B are **participants** in the event, viewed as a B.

Casual usage of the term "participant" in linguistics is varied. Often it is used just to mean 'thing in a somehow relevant relation to an event.' On that use, even the dog that accompanies Navin might be called a participant in Navin's carrying of the chair. But the term does have a stricter and theoretically significant use, guided by a common idea. The idea is, predicates in natural languages do not just have satisfaction conditions or entailments. Each is also associated – in some as yet unsettled way – with a particular representation of the things that satisfy it. Call this representation a **sketch**. The sketch provides a psychological perspective on things that satisfy the predicate, perhaps engaged by default when one thinks of a thing *as* a satisfier of the predicate. The few entailed properties that are represented explicitly in the sketch – that is, those which correspond to distinct constituents of the representation, like the eyes and mouth in "☺" as a representation of my face – are ipso facto foregrounded in this perspective. Others are not. My face has a nose, even if I didn't draw it. And now the claim is, the explicit constituents of the sketch include only some of the entailed roles, and these are the ones we call *participant roles*. The other entailed roles, while entailed, do not correspond to distinct constituents of the sketch, and so are not in the foreground of the associated perspective.

(29) Participant role
    R is a participant role of a predicate B just in case it is an entailed role of B, and it is furthermore an explicit constituent of the *sketch* associated with B, a privileged representation of those things that satisfy B.

So the participant roles of a predicate are exactly the formal constituents of its associated sketch. Should we dare to say that the sketch is in some relevant sense an aspect of meaning (or perhaps even is its meaning), the participant roles would therefore be those that a predicate entails *analytically* in virtue of its sketch.

Participanthood as understood here is not a category of discourse pragmatics. It is independent of distinctions between topic and comment, focus and background, given and new, or anything similar. Participant arguments and non-participant adjuncts can equally play any of these roles in discourse. Suppose that Carrier and Carried are the only participant roles for carry. The sentence in (31) can nevertheless serve as the answer to either question in (30). It can be used in a conversation about Navin and the chair, or in a conversation about 1979 and North Beverly Drive.

(30)   a What can you tell me about Navin carrying the chair?
       b Did anything interesting ever happen here on Beverly in 1979?

(31)   Navin carried the chair on North Beverly Drive in June of 1979.

So participant roles are not what one *talks about* in using the predicate. They are the constituents of a representation that is somehow associated with the predicate, and is therefore constant across all of its tokens. The contexts a predicate occurs in may differ significantly from one another in their effects on discourse, making some roles salient and not others. The various sentences in (32) will differ in the attention they direct to the participants in a stealing. Still, to view an event as a stealing is to view it as featuring Thief, Loot and Victim, no matter what sentence we use to discuss it.[4]

(32)   a Lee stole a necklace.
       b A necklace has been stolen.
       c This necklace is stolen.
       d The constant stealing bothers me.

Not every linguist embraces the psychological commitments of this category, the participant roles. But for those who do, intuitive judgments about which entailed roles pick out participants are stable in most cases. In the remainder of this section, I will discuss which entailed roles are commonly counted as singling out participants.

The participant roles for carry would surely include those of Carrier and Carried; so the sketch associated with carry would have the Carrier and Carried as constituents, as they are in (33). Indeed it would generally be assumed that the participant roles always include those associated with core dependents in the clause: subject, object, and in some cases an indirect object.

(33)   Sketch for carry: | Carrying | Carrier || Carried |

Just as surely, the participant roles for carry would not include Time or Place. These roles are entailed, since any carrying happens at a time and place. But they would not typically be regarded as participants

---

[4] For this reason, the category of *participant role* does not align with the notion of a "profiled" role developed in Langacker 1984 and deployed in Goldberg 1995, among other places. This latter notion seems to include the pragmatic effects of overt mention, in addition to the categorization of entailed relata that is provided by the sketch associated with a predicate.

relative to the verb carry. Thus, in (31), the participant arguments would include Navin and the chair, but not North Beverly Drive or June of 1979.[5] In using sentence (31) the speaker would draw attention to the roles of Time and Place, perhaps even mean to discuss them. The claim here is only that these roles are not explicit in the representation of carryings provided solely by the verb carry on its own, in its sketch.

Not every role linked to an adjunct picks out a nonparticipant, like Time or Place. Some do seem prominent in the event concept provided by the verb. In (34), from Mo is syntactically an adjunct. Semantically, it expresses an entailed role of steal, since every stealing has a victim from whom some loot is taken. But beyond this, it also seems natural to say that the victim is prominent in our psychological representation of stealings, alongside the thief and the loot. For me it is harder to think of a stealing without thinking of its victim than it is to do so without thinking of its time or place.

(34)   Lee stole a book from Mo.

There are similar intuitions about (35) and (36). To jimmy a window is to open it with with a short lever, and to bean someone is to throw a projectile that hits him or her on the head. So the lever and projectile are entailed roles of these verbs. But beyond this, it is hard – so certain intuitions might tell us – to think about a jimmying as a jimmying, or about a beaning as a beaning, without thinking of these roles. They seem to be psychologically prominent, on par with the jimmier and the jimmied, or the beaner and the beaned, and not with the time or place.

(35)   Al jimmied the window with a screwdriver.

(36)   Mo beaned Lee with a pebble.

Adjuncts are optional, so we can use steal or jimmy without introducing the victim or lever as topics of conversation. Likewise for the time and place. But again, participanthood is not about conversational dynamics.

The question now arises, whether the participant roles of a predicate can be predicted from its satisfaction conditions, its truth-conditional content. Initially, it may seem that they can be. The participant roles for steal include Thief, Loot and Victim, but not Time or Place. This contrast

---

[5] The time and place of an event are often taken to be among the *identity conditions* of an event, which imply whether or not two descriptions can apply to the same event (Kim 1976, Taylor 1985). But there is no reason to assume that criteria for identity should be of any psychological or grammatical significance, and therefore no reason that Time or Place should be participant roles. Similar comments would apply to any suggestion that participant roles are those that are metaphysically 'essential' to the event.

hints that the participant roles are those that are specific or idiosyncratic to the predicate. The victim is involved in a stealing in a way
that is relatively specific to stealings, and very differently from how the
projectile is involved in a beaning, for example. But Time and Place are
involved quite similarly across many different types of events, stealings
or beanings, carryings or swimmings.[6] So perhaps the participant roles
include only those entailed roles that are in this sense idiosyncratic.
Koenig *et al.* (2002) and Conklin *et al.* (2004) make a similar claim for a
subset of the participant roles that they call "lexically encoded," which
they "define ... as information that is highly activated upon recognition of the verb" (Conklin *et al.* 2004:222), and measure behaviorally
with reading-time responses.[7]

But this does not seem sufficient. Not every role that is entailed and
idiosyncratic seems intuitively to be a participant role, or to be "highly
activated." Every strike-out involves a ball and a bat and at least three
pitches. Every singing takes place in a fluid medium. These are idiosyncratic facts about strike-outs and singings. They isolate entailed roles
that are at least as specific to their event-type as the role of a lever in a
jimmying or a projectile in a beaning. We can talk about these roles as
in (37) and (38), where they may even be central to the conversation.

(37)   Cy struck out Ty on a fastball and two sliders.

(38)   Ozzy sang *Paranoid* into liquid cocaine.

But few linguists would treat all of these relations as participant roles,
or expect that they are all "highly activated" in the sense of Conklin
et al. (2004). If this is right, it implies that an entailed role is not a
participant role, or "highly activated," solely because it is specific to
the event type. There must be more to it.

What more there is will surely admit of further generalizations, all
of them worth working to discover. Nevertheless, it is odd to expect at
the outset that the participant roles of a predicate should be uniquely

---

[6] This is not to say that it is always easy to say what the time or place of an
event is. See Dretske 1967, Thomson 1971b and Hacker 1982, among others, for
complications.

[7] If what Conklin *et al.* 2004 call the "lexically encoded" or "highly activated" roles
are a subset of the participant roles, the subset is by definition proper. Typical
usage of "participant" implies that a verb implies the same number of participants,
no matter what grammatical context it occupies. But the "highly activated" roles
are not constant across contexts. For example, Mauner and Koenig 2000 argue that
the agent role of a verb may be "highly activated," and hence "lexically encoded,"
when a verb occurs in a passive (this chair was carried) but not when it occurs in
a middle (this chair carries easily). In this way the "lexically encoded" roles may be
more similar to what Goldberg 1995 calls the "profiled" roles, following Langacker
1984.

determined by its satisfaction conditions alone.[8] The participant roles reflect a certain psychological perspective, one informed by perceptual biases and human interests. It would be surprising if our minds and our interests allowed only a single perspective on a certain class of things, and still more surprising if this were to follow from some feature of language itself.

Why not have a verb, schtrike out, with exactly the satisfaction conditions of strike out but where the pitches are participants, or perhaps just the last pitch? The schtrike-outs are all and only the strike-outs, but with schtrike out the attention to pitches conveyed by the full sentence in (37) is expressed already in the sketch associated lexically with the verb. It also seems easy to imagine verbs that are truth-conditionally equivalent to our current verbs but have Time or Place as participant roles. I presume that the actual verb sleep in English does not have Time and Place as participant roles. But it is easy to imagine a verb, call it schleep, that applies exactly and only to the events of sleeping, but foregrounds both the sleeper and the time of rest: think of your night as a sleeping, and you see only yourself, eyes closed, but think of it as a schleeping, and you also see six dark hours. Of course, what is easy to imagine may not be true. But at the outset I see no good reason to presume that there are necessary and sufficient conditions which select the participants from among the entailed roles.

4.6 CORRESPONDENCE OF SYNTAX AND SEMANTICS

To conclude this chapter, let us briefly consider the possible correspondences between syntactic arguments and functional arguments.[9] Under what is perhaps the most common view, call it the **canonical correspondence**, every syntactic argument of an expression is a functional semantic argument, and vice versa. So if carry has a syntactic category like (39a) it will have a semantic value like (39b), and conversely. The syntactic arguments in the a-list of carry correspond to functional semantic arguments in its meaning.

(39) a carry:V$[\langle N, N \rangle]$
      b $[\![$ carry $]\!] = \lambda y \lambda x \lambda e [$ CarryingByOf$(x, y)(e)]$

Likewise, if carry were granted no syntactic arguments, one would expect that it has no functional semantic arguments either, as in (40).

---

(40) a carry:V[t]
      b ⟦ carry ⟧ = λe[Carrying(e)]

From this perspective, having a syntactic argument goes hand in hand with having a functional semantic argument. This symmetry is attractive – for reasons that will become clear in comparing the alternatives – and most often it is taken for granted.

Mixed views are logically possible, however, and also attested. The first possible mixture is a nonlexicalist syntax with a lexicalist semantics, as in (41).

(41) a carry:V[t]
      b ⟦ carry ⟧ = $\lambda y \lambda x \lambda e$[CarryingByOf($x, y$)($e$)]

According to (41a), carry has no syntactic arguments; it is just a verb of subcategory t. Its combination with the chair will be licensed by a phrase structure rule, or a nonlexical primitive. Still the semantics of carry in (41b) is relational. The verb has the carrier and carried as functional arguments. Thus in carry the chair the relation imposed on the chair projects from the verb.

Something like this, I believe, is implicit in much work within Transformational Grammar before the mid 1970s. It combines a phrase-structural syntax with the idea that verbs express relations, whose terms are instantiated by the subject and object. This mixture is no longer common, however, in part for this reason: the syntactic category of the verb allows it to occur in contexts that will not provide appropriate arguments for its meaning. For example, a grammar that includes (41) might also include the rule in (42), allowing any verb to co-occur with a PP. This would allow us to derive the string in (43) without any further adjustments to the syntax.

(42) VP → V PP

(43) carry across Beverly Drive

But in such a case the semantics would require ad hoc complications. We would want (43) to mean not that 'across Beverly Drive' is what got carried, but that the carrying was across Beverly Drive. Given the semantics for carry in (41b), this would require a semantics for (42) that is specific to transitive verbs and in no way motivated by the syntax of the construction.[10] This mismatch between simplicity in the syntax

---

[10] For example, we could say that a VP constructed under rule (42) can mean (1), with abstraction over the two lexical arguments of the verb. Yet this abstraction –

and complication in the semantics is unattractive. And, for this reason among others, mixtures like (41) are presently unpopular.

The second possible mixture is represented by (44). Here the syntax is lexicalist and carry projects syntactic arguments. But semantically the verb is just a predicate of events and has no functional arguments.

(44) a carry:V[⟨N, N⟩]
      b 〚 carry 〛 = λe[Carrying(e)]

This view has some adherents, particularly within the Minimalist Program. It is explicit in Hunter (2011), for example, who follows suggestions in Pietroski (2005a). Hunter projects syntactic arguments from an a-list associated with the head. But the head does not contribute the semantic relations imposed on its dependents. These come from rules of semantics, which interpret the entire phrase as such, assigning "Internal" and "External" roles to its inner and outer arguments, respectively. The semantics here is motivated by arguments for 'Separation' of thematic relations from the verb (Chapter 9). The syntax is consistent with the lexicalized framework of work in the Minimalist Program, which countenances neither nonlexical primitives nor rules of composition that are category-specific. The result is a nontraditional, mixed view in which syntactic and semantic arguments do not go hand in hand. But this second kind of mixture lacks the immediate problems of the first. The carry of (44a) is required to occur in the syntactic context of two N arguments, and the semantic rules can be specified to interpret these appropriately, for example as Agent and Patient in relation to the event of the head. So this lexical item, (44a), cannot occur in a context that would necessitate semantic complications. The semantics involves a rule of interpretation that is more particular than Application; but this need not be seen as a theoretical blemish.

DISCUSSION POINTS

1 Sentence (1) below entails that Ozzy was naked while singing *Paranoid*. Given this, how would you describe the relation between Ozzy and naked, in the terms of this chapter? Is Ozzy a functional argument of naked? A content argument? An entailed role argument? A participant argument? If your answer is "No" for any

which would be appropriate for transitive carry but not for intransitive walk – bears no conceptual relation to the fact that the construction adds a PP.

(1)   λyλxλe[〚V〛(y)(x)(e) & 〚PP〛(e)]

of these questions, what would it take, grammatically, for the answer to become "Yes?"

(1)   Ozzy sang *Paranoid* naked.

2 Suppose we find a language, Emblish, with a verb, prive, which occurs only in intransitive clauses like (2), with the English translation as given in the gloss. How many 'semantic arguments' does prive take? Discuss this in the terms of this chapter. How is prive like or unlike the English verb dribble, as this verb is used in the context of basketball?

(2)   Sam prived.
      'Sam drove a car.'

3 What are the entailed role arguments in the sentences of (3)?

(3)   a April broke the airplane.
      b Betty buttered the bread.
      c Sal spread the jam.
      d Sal spread the jam on the toast.
      e Sal spread the jam on the toast with a knife.

4 One cannot head a soccer ball except with one's head. Therefore both Mo and her head are in an entailed relation to the event of (4).

(4)   Mo headed the soccer ball.

Moreover, reflecting on headings as such, I find the head of the header to be foregrounded in my mind's eye. Should we therefore say that the verb head has three participant roles, including the player's head plus the player and the ball? If "Yes," how might you try to support this hypothesis? If "No," why not? Is there a general principle behind your answer, to do with the relation between the two roles, Player and Head? (See Koenig *et al.* 2008 for relevant discussion.)

5 Using the different semantic notions of argument presented in the chapter, how would you clarify a claim that adverbs like quickly do (or do not) take semantic arguments? Once you have formed some clear questions out of this vague beginning, try to answer some of them. Is there some kind of evidence you would need to answer these questions?

6 Do any of the semantic notions of argument explain any grammatical phenomena that you know of? Do any of these line up perfectly with notions of syntactic argument? Can you predict on the basis of semantics whether a given role will be syntactically expressed?

SUGGESTIONS FOR FURTHER READING

For fluency in the mechanics of functional arguments, study Heim and Kratzer 1998. Klein and Sag 1985 is perhaps the modern apogee of the Fregean ideal. Dowty 1989 clarifies many things, including the difference between functional arguments and content arguments. Kracht (2011: ch. 4.1) is germane to several of the distinctions in this chapter. Many uses of "argument" in the sense of participant argument find inspiration in Jackendoff's (1983, 1987, 1990b) mentalist semantics, where values are highly structured mental concepts. Related ideas have been explored in an experimental setting by Koenig and collaborators; see Koenig *et al.* 2008 and references there.

5   Implicit arguments

5.1   INTRODUCTION

One use of "argument" is particularly subtle, and that is in the context of "implicit argument." In this chapter we will try to understand some of what falls under this heading. I begin (Section 5.2) with the rough idea: an implicit argument is an entailed but *unrealized* role that is in some way like an overt argument. Then (Section 5.3) I will justify and explicate a division of unrealized roles, URs, into two types, existential and definite. Next I observe (Section 5.4) that the availability and interpretation of a UR cannot be predicted just on the basis of a predicate's satisfaction conditions. The upshot of these two sections (5.3–5.4) is the conclusion that all definite URs, at least, must be regarded as implicit arguments in some broad sense. The next two sections, 5.5 and 5.6, concern arguments for treating certain URs as implicit arguments in a narrower sense as well. Section 5.5 shows that definite, but not existential, URs are prone to covarying readings in the scope of a quantifier, a semantic dependency otherwise limited to overt dependents. Section 5.6 foreshadows a case study on the unrealized deep subject role of a short passive, to be developed at length in Chapter 12.

Before setting out, let me quickly warn that I will not be discussing the central cases of *pro*, like Mandarin (1); or of PRO, like (2,3); or of what are called "middles" in traditional grammar (Kemmer 1993), like (4,5).

(1)   [*pro*]   qu   -le   Beijing.
      x   go   -PFV   Beijing
      'I/you/he/she/it/they went to Beijing.'

(2)   Mo$_k$ promised Lee [PRO$_k$] to cook sausage.

(3)   [PRO] to cook sausage would be a good idea.

(4)   Lee and Mo met [= each other] for lunch.

(5)   Lee shaved [= herself].

I do allow, however, that some of the implicit arguments I will discuss might involve non-central instances of these categories. For

94

example, it may be that (6) and (7) have some sort of PRO or *pro* instantiating the roles of 'stealer' and 'location of arrival,' respectively (Baker *et al.* 1989, Stanley 2000).

(6)   The necklace was stolen from Lee.

(7)   Val arrived.

5.2   IMPLICIT ARGUMENTS

Let us start with a very broad category: an **unrealized role**, or UR, is an entailed relation which is bound by no obvious derivational part of the clause. A derivational part is obvious when it is either pronounced or manifestly present on syntactic grounds. Sentence (8) describes a theft. Every theft has some loot, something that was taken from the victim. Yet the Loot relation is bound by no audible part of (8), in contrast to (9). Nor does the syntax of (8) suggest that it is bound by an inaudible part either, not at first blush. So the role of Loot is here **unrealized**, while in (9) it is realized.

(8)   Mo robbed Lee.

(9)   Mo robbed Lee of a necklace.

Unrealized roles are common. A predicate may entail all sorts of relations and in general these are unrealized. Every swimming has a velocity and a fluid medium, in addition to a time, a place and a swimmer, among many other things. But sentences with swim in general leave all but the role of Swimmer unrealized. All money is related to some guarantor of its value, but noun phrases with money do not in general realize the Guarantor. It would be outlandish to suggest that every single entailed relation receives some specific representation in the grammar. And so in general there is no need for the grammarian to say anything about a UR.

But sometimes the facts do suggest that a certain UR is explicitly specified in the grammar. Some phenomenon – syntactic, semantic, pragmatic or psychological – distinguishes it from a mere entailment. For any such case let us say that the UR then counts as an **implicit argument in the broad sense**.

By this lax standard, any UR that counts as a participant role, for example, is an implicit argument, since not every entailed role is a participant role (see Chapter 4). Thus, if Loot is a participant role for rob it might be called an implicit argument in (8) just on these grounds alone. Or take the example of (10), from Perry (1986).

(10)   It is raining.

I don't know whether Place ought to be a participant role for rain. But, according to Crimmins and Perry (1989:699), "[i]f I say [(10)] you understand me as claiming that it rains at that time at some place the context supplies." The place, they propose, is a "constituent" of the proposition one asserts in using (10), just one that is "unarticulated" in not being contributed by any derivational part of the sentence (Recanati 2002, Neale 2007). If this is right, then (10) has Place as an implicit argument, in this first and very broad sense, since there surely cannot be a propositional constituent for absolutely every relation entailed by the verb (Cappelen and Lepore 2007).

Often "implicit argument" is used more strictly, however, just for cases where the UR participates in some grammatical dependency, semantic or syntactic, that otherwise only an overt dependent can enter (Bhatt and Pancheva 2006). In these cases, let's say that the UR counts as an **implicit argument in the narrow sense**.

Which dependencies matter is a topic of dispute. But two that have been much discussed are covariation with a quantifier (Partee 1989), as in (11), and control of a nonfinite predicate (Zubizaretta 1982, Keyser and Roeper 1984, Williams 1985, Roeper 1987), as in (12). In (11a) the contest entailed by win is understood to covary with the men placing bets. In contrast, the loot entailed by rob in (11b) cannot be understood exclusively as covarying with the kids waxing cars.

(11) a   No man who placed a bet on me won.
          'No man who placed a bet on me won the bet he placed.'
      b * No kid who waxed a car robbed its owner.
          'No kid who waxed a car robbed its owner of the car he waxed.'

Owing to this contrast one might say that the Contest role for win in (11a) is in the narrow sense an implicit argument, while the Loot role for rob in (11b) is not (Dowty 1981, Partee 1989, Stanley 2000). We will discuss this further in Section 5.5. The pair in (12) illustrates a contrast in 'control' of a nonfinite clause. We can use (12a), from Roeper (1987), to say that the intended collector of insurance was the entailed sinker of the ship. But we cannot use (12b) to say that the intended collector was the entailed victim of the theft, even if that victim hired the crook for this purpose.

(12) a   The ship was sunk to collect the insurance.
          'The ship was sunk so that that the sinker might collect the insurance.'
      b * A hired crook stole the ship to collect the insurance.
          'A hired crook stole the ship so that *the victim of the theft* might collect the
          insurance.'

Again, for this reason one might say that the Sinker role in (12a) is in the narrow sense an implicit argument (Keyser and Roeper 1984), but the Victim role in (12b) is not. This will be the topic of an extended study in Chapter 12.

In either the broad or the narrow sense, then, an implicit argument is, to repeat, more than just an entailment. The theorist who says that an unrealized role R is an implicit argument in expression E must therefore accord it some further status. The role, or its entailed satisfier, must correspond to a distinct constituent at some level of theoretical description, whether syntactic, semantic, psychological or pragmatic.

There are many ways this might be done. Eight are listed and labeled below. Each is attested in the literature, if sometimes only implicitly. Only a few of these options are mutually exclusive; several are jointly consistent. For simplicity I illustrate each using the same example expression, the intransitive clause Ron won, focussing on the unrealized role of Contest: if Ron won, then he won some contest. I will occasionally refer to this list throughout the present chapter.

1 Silent syntactic part
  The expression E with unrealized role R includes a *silent syntactic part* whose semantic value either is or instantiates R (Baker *et al.* 1989, Stanley 2000). For example, the sentence Ron won may include a silent predicate that stands for the Contest relation, or a silent noun phrase that binds this relation.

2 Unsatisfied argument
  R is the interpretation of an **unsatisfied argument** of E. An unsatisfied argument is an argument not satisfied by any dependent (Chapter 3). Thus for Ron won we might claim that the verb win has an unsatisfied item in its 'thematic grid' or 'argument structure,' linked to the role of Contest. This approach was influentially enunciated by Edwin Williams (1985:314): "Implicit arguments are not the mysterious shadowy presences they are sometimes made out to be. They are really nothing more ... than unlinked argument roles."

3 Lexically removed argument
  R has no special status in either the syntactic category or the meaning of E on its own. But E is derived from a homophonous predicate E* in Lexicon, and this E* does have a syntactic argument linked to role R. For example we might say that there are two verbs pronounced "win," one transitive and the other intransitive, the latter derived from the former in Lexicon. Transitive win$_1$ has as its semantic value a relation between

Winners and Contests, while the value of derived intransitive win_2 is a one-place predicate of Winners (Bresnan 1978, Dowty 1981; compare Gillon 2012).

4 Silent prelexical part

The lexical item E that entails R has structure in Lexicon, and its lexical derivation has a part whose semantic value is R. Thus the UR is contributed by a *silent prelexical part*. For example, perhaps the verb won is the output of a prelexical derivation that combines three prelexical items: a predicate true of winnings, a predicate true of winners, and a predicate true of a contest won.

5 Semantic constituent

The semantic value of E has structure, and R is a distinct constituent of that structure (Jackendoff 1990b), hence a *semantic constituent*. For example, it might be that the value of Ron won has a structure roughly like that of the formula in (13) (with or without the quantifier in curly brackets) where the role of Contest is a part.

(13) $\exists e[\text{Winner}(e, \text{Ron}) \ \& \ \text{Winning}(e) \ \& \ \{\exists x\}\text{Contest}(e, x)]$

6 Semantic variable

E has in its meaning a free *semantic variable* in role R (Partee 1989, Condoravdi and Gawron 1996, Stanley 2000). On this view Ron won, rather like Ron won it, means 'Ron won x,' where x is a free variable whose value is given 'by context' (or, in formal terms, by the assignment of values to variables).

7 Participant role

E is associated with a psychological representation of things that satisfy E, and R is a constituent of that representation. R is therefore a *participant role* for E, as this was defined in the previous chapter. For example, perhaps win is associated with a psychological representation of winnings in which the role of Contest is a distinct constituent.

8 Unarticulated constituent

Direct speech acts performed in using E have R, or its satisfier, as a constituent of their content, and yet no part of E has this constituent as its value. Instead it is contributed by general pragmatic processes. In that case R, or its satisfier, is called an "**unarticulated constituent**" (Perry 1986) of the speech act content. For example we might say that, while no part of Ron won has the relevant contest as its semantic value, the contest is nonetheless a constituent of what one asserts in using the sentence (Sperber and Wilson 1986, Carston 1988, Bach 1994, Recanati 2002, Neale 2004), perhaps because talk of winning invites interest in what was won (Cappelen and Lepore 2007).

5.3 EXISTENTIAL AND DEFINITE UNREALIZED ROLES

5.3.1 Initial contrasts

Unrealized roles can be divided into at least two classes. Some are **existential** while others are **definite** (Fillmore 1971b, 1986, Shopen 1972, Gillon 2006, and many others). The difference lies fundamentally in their relation to the context of use.

The existential understanding is initially approximated by adding a phrase with indefinite reference such as stuff or something or somebody, as (14b) adds stuff to (14a) in the role of Loot, or (15b) adds somebody to (15a) in the role of Victim.

(14) a Mo robbed Lee.
      b Mo robbed Lee of stuff.
(15) a Mo stole a bag of money.
      b Mo stole a bag of money from somebody.

A sentence with an existential UR may be felicitous – successfully used to make a direct speech act whose comprehension puts no unusual inferential demands on the hearer – even in a discourse that implies no relevant filler for its role. Sentence (16b) is felicitous after (16a) even without any hint of who Mo has stolen the money from.

(16) a Check it out, Mo has a new car!
      b She stole a bag of money.

In this way (15a), like the paraphrase in (15b), does not have the same conditions on its use as does (15c), below, where the role of Victim is filled with a pronoun, demonstrative or definite description.

(15) c Mo stole a bag of money from {them / there / the people / the place}.

Use of (15c) is felicitous only if the discourse model, in concert with common knowledge and the environment of use, supplies or implies a relevant victim.

Things go exactly the other way on the definite understanding of a UR. This understanding *can* be approximated by adding a phrase with definite reference, such as a definite description (the thing), pronoun (it), demonstrative (that) or indexical (here). For example, (17a) has a fair first paraphrase in (17b), thus differing quite strongly from (17c) (Fodor and Fodor 1980, Dowty 1981, Fillmore 1986).

(17) a Mo noticed.
      b Mo noticed that.
      c Mo noticed something.

Sentence (17a), like (17b) and unlike (17c), is felicitous only when the discourse model, in concert with common knowledge and the environment of use, supplies or implies something relevant that Mo might have noticed. To the extent that it doesn't, one fails to make a clear assertion in using the sentence (Gillon 2006). Sentence (18) provides another example, concerning the role of Contest that is implied by win. Sentence (18a) is like (18b), and not like (18c).

(18) a Ron won.
      b Ron won the contest.
      c Ron won a contest.

The difference comes out in (19). After (19a) we can felicitously use (19b), intending to explain how Ron might have acquired his new car. But we cannot use (19c) to convey the same thing. Indeed, like (18b) and unlike (19b), use of (19c) isn't felicitous unless the context provides some relevant contest that Ron might have won.

(19) a   Check it out, Ron has a new car!
      b   He won a contest.
      c # He won.

The contrast between (19c) and (16b), in relation to the lead-ins of (19a) and (16a) respectively, shows the sharp pragmatic difference between existential and definite URs. Sentences with definite URs share a basic characteristic of sentences which overtly include a definite description, demonstrative, unbound pronoun or indexical. In some sense, delicate but significant, we cannot know what claim they are being used to make without some knowledge of the context.[1]

This pragmatic contrast between existential and definite URs provides a basis for a useful diagnostic (Sgall et al. 1986, Recanati 2010). If an unrealized role R is understood existentially, it is usually fine to say that no one knows who or what instantiates R, as in (20a); an interrogative follow-up, as in (20b), is analogous.

---

[1] For simplicity, this statement presumes, with Frege 1892 and Strawson 1950, that definite descriptions are expressions whose uses stand for an individual.

(20) a Mo robbed Lee, but no one has a clue what she took.
  b Mo robbed Lee, but does any of us have a clue what she took?

This is usually unacceptable, however, if the UR is definite, as in (21a) or (21b). Such URs require a discourse model or environment of use that supplies or implies a filler for their role. Since the interlocutors are expected to be aware of the model and the environment, the result is generally infelicitous.

(21) a # Mo noticed, but no one has a clue what she noticed.
  b # Mo noticed, but does any of us have a clue what she noticed?

A more semantic expression of the contrast emerges in negative contexts (Hankamer and Sag 1976, Gillon 2006). Negation of an existential results in a very strong statement, while the negation of a statement about a particular individual does not. In (22a) what is baked is understood existentially; the sentence is nearly synonymous with (22b) (Fillmore 1986).

(22) a Lee baked this morning.
  b Lee baked stuff this morning.

And now consider (23b) as a follow-up to (23a). It implies that Lee baked nothing at all. This is much stronger than what is implied by any of the options in (23c). With these we can say only that Lee did not bake the beautiful cupcake.

(23) a On the coffee table I saw the most beautiful cupcake!
  b Lee didn't bake this morning.
  c Lee didn't bake {it / that / the thing} this morning.

Similarly in the wake of (24a), use of (24b) implies that Mo didn't rob Lee of anything, at least not while they were on the subway. This is in contrast to (24c), with which one can only say that Mo didn't rob Lee of some particular topical thing.

(24) a Mo was on the subway with Lee.
  b Mo didn't rob her.
  c Mo didn't rob her of {that / the thing}.

The same goes for the unrealized 'agent' role in a negated short passive. In the context of (25a), use of (25b) implies that the necklace was not stolen from Lee by anybody, at least not during the subway ride. The same implication does not attend use of (25c) – unless we take them to stand for everyone on the subway.

(25)   a Lee was on the subway.
        b The necklace was not stolen from her.
        c The necklace was not stolen from her by {him / them}.

And now compare a definite UR, as with intransitive notice. (26b) can be used to say that Mo failed to notice that Ron was on the subway. But it cannot readily be used to say that Mo noticed *nothing at all*. In this way it is like (26c).

(26)   a Ron was on the subway with Mo.
        b Mo didn't notice.
        c Mo didn't notice that.

Sentence (27b) has intransitive win, where the entailed role of Contest is unrealized. Following (27a), this can be used to say that Ron didn't win his bet on number 17, as can (27c).

(27)   a Ron placed a bet on number 17.
        b He didn't win.
        c He didn't win it.

But (27b) is not readily used to say that Ron won nothing at all, as it would be if the role of Contest were understood existentially.[2] So the UR is definite.

This book focuses on verbs. But existential and definite URs are found in all categories. Any man who satisfies the noun father is related to a child, and any event that satisfies robbery is related to a thief, a victim and some loot. In (28) and (29) these various roles are unrealized and interpreted existentially: felicitous use of (28) does not require that any children be relevant, and neither does (29) require relevant fillers for the roles of Thief, Victim or Loot.

(28)   Mo prefers not to rob fathers.

(29)   Lee witnessed a robbery.

Examples (30) and (31), both adapted from Partee (1989), have an adjective and then an adverb with definite URs. These are felicitous only in contexts that imply a relevant alternative strategy and a relevant reference time, respectively.

(30)   The general tried the opposite strategy.

---

[2] There are indeed circumstances in which one can use Ron didn't win to convey that Ron won no relevant contest at all. These are circustances in a which a particular set of contests is sufficiently topical that one could refer to them demonstratively, perhaps with those contests. But this just illustrates the point: Ron didn't win contrasts in this way with Ron didn't win anything, for which one doesn't need this background.

(31) The thief abandoned the car afterwards.

Finally, (32) has an indexical UR, as ago always means 'before the time of speech.'

(32) Ron argued with his wife two hours ago.

There is a great deal more to be said, about both semantics and syntax. The unrealized roles of nouns have been particularly important in the development of Binding Theory, for example (Williams 1985, 1987, Rizzi 1986a, Safir 1987, Clark 1990, among many others). But I cannot discuss all the pertinent issues here.

5.3.2 Contrasts with initial paraphrases

As we have just seen, expressions with existential URs have an initial paraphrase with a simple indefinite, while those with definite URs have an initial paraphrase with a pronoun or demonstrative. But in both cases the paraphrases are inaccurate. Existential URs differ from overt indefinites in at least three ways: they cannot antecede a pronoun, they do not imply a new discourse referent, and the entailed existential quantifier always has narrowest scope. Definite URs, meanwhile, differ from pronouns and demonstratives in one main way. They do not require a referent that is evoked by an overt antecedent, or is salient in the setting of the conversation, but only one that is "inferable" (Prince 1981), or can be "accommodated" (Condoravdi and Gawron 1996), given the discourse model. We will now discuss these differences in turn.

5.3.2.1 Contrasts with indefinites

An overt indefinite can by itself antecede a subsequent pronoun (Karttunen 1976, Kamp 1981, Prince 1981, Heim 1982, Groenendijk and Stokhof 1991). In (33a) the indefinite stuff introduces a new item into the discourse model, the stuff Lee baked, and this stuff can be the referent for it in (33b).

(33) a Lee baked stuff.
      b Sev ate it.

The same is not true for existential URs. They cannot by themselves provide a referent for a subsequent pronoun (Koenig and Mauner 2000). Removing stuff from (33a) makes the pronoun in (33b) less felicitous: we are at first puzzled about what its referent might be. The same point is made by the contrasts below.

(34) a Al cooked stuff before it had thawed.
      b # Al cooked before it had thawed.

(35) a   Mo robbed Lee of something, and it was very expensive.
      b   # Mo robbed Lee, and it was very expensive.
(36) a   Al jimmied the window with something, and its tip snapped off.
      b   # Al jimmied the window, and its tip snapped off.
(37) a   The ewe was killed by something, but evidently it didn't eat her.
      b   # The ewe was killed, but evidently it didn't eat her.

In the (a) examples, we can use a pronoun to refer to the entailed food, loot, lever and killer respectively, without putting any special inferential demands on the hearer. Not so in the (b) examples. The pronoun in the second clause is not readily taken to refer to this unrealized participant from the first. This is the first of our contrasts.

Second, overt indefinites not only can introduce a new item into the discourse model, they also usually do (or, at least, the item-under-a-guise is new). Usually, that is, we understand the domain for an indefinite to exclude all individuals already in the discourse model (Strawson 1950, Karttunen 1976, Prince 1981, Heim 1982). To see this, consider (38).

(38) Mo saw Lee on the subway and stole a necklace from somebody.

Use of (38) would defeasibly imply that Mo did not steal a necklace from Lee; the presumed domain for somebody would exclude Lee, since she is already in the model.

But existential URs are different. In (39) the unrealized role of Victim is understood existentially: the sentence implies that Mo didn't steal a necklace from anybody.

(39) Today Mo didn't steal a necklace.

And yet use of (40) does not exclude Lee from the likely victims of the theft. Indeed, it is compatible with wanting to suggest that Mo did steal the necklace from Lee.

(40) Mo saw Lee on the subway and stole a necklace.

In this way (40) contrasts with (38). Use of a sentence with an existential UR does not imply that the de facto filler of the UR is new to the discourse. The following examples support the same point, as the reader can work out.

(41) a   Mo was on the subway when Lee's necklace was stolen by somebody.
      b   Mo was on the subway when Lee's necklace was stolen.
(42) a   Al saw a screwdriver on the counter and jimmied the window with something.
      b   Al saw the screwdriver on the counter and jimmied the window.

These observations raise a question about our semantic assumptions. If a UR is understood existentially, how can it be used to talk about a familiar discourse referent? Should we perhaps revise our account, and say that in cases like (40) the unrealized role may be understood definitely, like the pronoun or description in (43)?

(43)   Mo saw Lee on the subway and stole a necklace from {her / the girl}.

I don't think so. As emphasized by Grice (1969), Kripke (1977) and Neale (1990) in defense of Russell's (1905) account of descriptions, an existential statement can be made with the intent of conveying a claim about a specific individual who verifies that statement. So an anaphoric semantics for Mo stole a necklace in (40) is unnecessary, given a general understanding of communicative intentions. Nor is an anaphoric semantics desirable, since it would require an implausible ambiguity, given that (40) seems clearly to have one 'reading' that is not anaphoric.

Therefore what we should conclude from the contrast between (40) and (38) is no more than this: overt indefinite noun phrases are associated with the function of introducing new discourse referents, but existential URs are not.

The third contrast has to do with scope. An overt indefinite can sometimes take scope over structurally higher quantifiers. In (44), for example, the scope of the indefinite exactly three girls can include the interpretation of every boy, to say that there are exactly three girls from whom every boy stole a book. Similarly (45) can be used, it appears, to say that there are exactly three girls from whom Mo didn't steal a book, with the quantifier scoping over negation.

(44)   Every boy stole a book from exactly three girls.

(45)   Mo didn't steal a book from exactly three girls.

A UR understood existentially, on the other hand, always has narrowest scope (Bresnan 1978, Fodor and Fodor 1980, Dowty 1981).

(46)   Every man stole exactly three books.
        'Each man stole exactly three books total, no matter from whom.'

(47)   Exactly three students baked this morning.
        'For exactly three students, there was stuff that they baked this morning.'

(48)   Mo didn't steal any books.
        'Mo did not steal books from anybody at all.'

These sentences have only the meanings in the given glosses. They do not allow the meanings that would be possible if an existential quantifier binding the UR were to take wide scope. Sentence (46) cannot mean that, for each man, there is at least one person from whom he stole exactly three books. Sentence (47) cannot mean that there was some particular baked good that exactly three students baked this morning. And (48) cannot mean just that there is at least one person from whom Mo didn't steal any books.

Perhaps related to this contrast is another one in effects on aspectual type (Mittwoch 1982). Example (49) is an *activity* sentence (Vendler 1957, Dowty 1979): the event description it provides applies equally to any temporal subpart of its event. Correspondingly it accepts a temporal for-PP as in (50), and validates the inference in (51).

(49) Sev ate.

(50) Sev ate for five minutes.

(51) Sev was eating, therefore Sev ate.

But for (52), where we have added the explicit singular indefinite, another interpretation is available. This can be understood as an *accomplishment* sentence (Vendler 1957, Dowty 1979), meaning that Sev ate all of some particular thing. Sentence (53) then has the odd implication that Sev ate the entirety of one thing repeatedly for five minutes (Mittwoch 1982:115). Also, it is then possible to judge (54) false, since Sev may have been eating something and yet not finished it.

(52) Sev ate a thing.

(53) ?? Sev ate a thing for five minutes.

(54) # Sev was eating a thing, therefore Sev ate a thing.

These contrasts are explained directly if an existential UR is simply an entailment of the verb. They are not explained directly if an existential UR corresponds to a silent quantifier in the syntax. We would then need to say why the interpretive effects of the silent and overt quantifiers differ.

5.3.2.2 Contrasts with pronouns

A definite UR gets its value, in some important sense, from the discourse model or environment of use. For this reason paraphrases with pronouns or demonstratives, as in (55), are initially fair.

(55) Ron won.
      'Ron won {it / that}.'

Nonetheless they are flawed. In some settings an expression with a definite UR cannot be replaced by its pronominal or demonstrative paraphrase without semantic effect. As observed by Condoravdi and Gawron (1996), following Partee (1989), the better paraphrase is generally with a definite description. The paraphrase is better in (56) than in (55).

(56)   Ron won.
       'Ron won the contest.'

Example (57) shows why. Sentence (57a) can mean that Lee won the contest in which she put chips on 17. So can (57b), where the role of contest is instantiated by a definite description. But (57c) cannot.

(57)   a   Lee put chips on 17 and won.
       b   Lee put chips on 17 and won the bet.
       c   # Lee put chips on 17 and won {it / that}.

With the pronoun in (57c), the contest must be 'salient.' Typically, salience requires explicit prior reference (Heim 1982, Elbourne 2005). But this is not necessary with a definite UR (Partee 1989). It is enough if the discourse model, given world knowledge, permits the uncontroversial inference that there was a contest. The contest needs only to be "inferable" (Prince 1981) or easily "accommodated" into the domain of discourse (Condoravdi and Gawron 1996).

Sentences (58–60) give three more examples. Omitting *for it* from (58), we can use the sentence to mean 'applied for the job.' What is applied for is not the ad but the advertised job, not referred to explicitly, but implied in relation to the ad. This reading is difficult with the addition of *for it*, however. The sentence then seems to say that people applied for an ad, and not for a job.

(58)   Mo saw an ad for dish washers and applied (?#for it).

Likewise it is only without the pronoun that we can easily use (59) to mean that the implied presentations were started early.

(59)   Lee was on the schedule of presenters, and she started (#it) early.

And while (60a) can be used to mean that Ozzy was not ready for his performance, it seems that (60b) can only be used to say that Ozzy was not ready for the festival.

(60)   a   Ozzy was up last in the festival, but he still wasn't ready.
       b   Ozzy was up last in the festival, but he still wasn't ready for it.

For more contrasts and further discussion, see Williams (2012), which collects observations from Condoravdi and Gawron (1996), ter Meulen (2004), Francez (2010) and Gauker (2012). These works make it clear that the correct semantics for a definite UR cannot assimilate them to pronouns or demonstratives.

5.3.3 Encoding the contrast

In principle, an existential UR may be no more than an entailment of the predicate. And an entailment per se needs no explicit representation in the grammar. Nothing in the grammar needs to tell us that events of stealing have victims.

However, it does not follow from the general sense of a predicate, nor from when the predicate is likely to be used, that it has a definite UR. Is there a reason why the unrealized Contest role for *win*, in particular, should be definite rather than existential? Or why the unrealized Victim role for *steal* should be existential rather than definite? There have been no satisfactory answers to such questions (Bach 1994; cf. Cappelen and Lepore 2007), and it seems to me that there is no choice but to stipulate definite interpretations explicitly in the grammar.

For example, we cannot just say that Ron won has the semantic value in (61), and postulate that an event satisfying WinningBy(Ron) is related to some contest. This would give us only an existential interpretation.

(61)   ⟦ Ron won ⟧ = ∃e[WinningBy(Ron)(e)]

Rather, Ron won must be assigned a meaning and usage conditions that make it roughly equivalent to Ron won the thing. There are many ways to do this. One is developed by Condoravdi and Gawron (1996). They treat a definite UR as a free variable in the meaning of the host expression, as in (62).[3] Then crucially they assume that the domain of values for this variable is broader than it would be for a pronoun or demonstrative. It includes not only the individuals that are salient, but all those in the discourse model, plus those that are "inferable" given common knowledge.

(62)   ⟦ Ron won ⟧ = ∃e[WinningByOf(Ron, y)(e)]

In turn, the postulated free variable might have either of two sources. It might come from the lexical meaning of the verb itself (Partee 1989), as in (63). The definite UR is then no more than a *semantic variable* (see Section 5.2).

(63)   ⟦ win ⟧ = λxλe[WinningByOf(x, y)(e)]

Second, the free variable might be provided by some silent part of the syntax (Stanley 2000). For example Ron won might have the syntax in

---

[3] Compare the treatment of definite descriptions in Heim 1982.

(64), where pro_d is a silent noun phrase that introduces the required sort of variable.

(64)   [Ron [won pro_d]]

In (64) the silent syntax is just a lexical item. This is consistent with the observation that an implicit argument never behaves syntactically like a verb phrase or clause (Hankamer and Sag 1976, Grimshaw 1979, Depiante 2000), even with verbs such as find out or notice, where the implicit satisfier of the UR is a sentence-meaning. The evidence includes data like (65) versus (66). Sentence (65b) shows that there can be no extraction 'out of' a definite UR, so to speak. Sentence (66b) shows in contrast that there can be extraction of a clause within a VP that has undergone ellipsis. Thus while targets of ellipsis behave syntactically like complex phrases, definite URs do not.

(65)   a Who$_k$ have the investigators found out [t_k] was lying?
     b It's much more important who$_k$ you have found out *([t_k] was lying).

(66)   a Who$_k$ have the investigators found out [t_k] was lying?
     b It's much more important who$_k$ you have (found out [t_k] was lying).

Some writers have denied both of these options and made a very different suggestion (Perry 1986, Sperber and Wilson 1986, Recanati 2002, Carston 2004, Neale 2004). They suggest that definite URs are "unarticulated constituents," parts of the content of the speech act that are contributed not by the meaning of the expression used in that act, but rather by general pragmatic processes. Yet this seems to imply that definite interpretations for URs are generally available, to any predicate, modulo what is pragmatically sensible. And if it is not clear already that this is incorrect, I believe it will become so after Section 5.5.

Thus definite URs are implicit arguments in at least the broad sense, since they must be distinguished from mere entailments. In the narrow sense, however, a role is an implicit argument only if it participates in some grammatical dependency otherwise limited to overt dependents. And so far in this chapter we have not yet seen that. In Section 5.5, however, we will see some potential evidence that points in this direction, from the interpretation of definite URs in the scope of a quantifier. Then in Section 5.6 we will see evidence for one particular sort of existential UR being an implicit argument in the narrow sense, namely the unrealized deep subject role in a short passive. Before then, I would like to note two ways in which unrealized roles are lexically idiosyncratic.

5.4 *LEXICAL IDIOSYNCRASY*

5.4.1 Restricted roles

For both existential and definite URs, the role may be more restricted when unrealized than when realized (Fillmore 1986). For example, (67a) means that what Lee baked were baked goods, such as breads or cakes, but (67b) does not.

(67) a Lee baked this morning.
      b Lee baked an apple and a chicken this morning.

Similarly, while one can win either a contest or a prize, (68c) is understood like (68b) and not like (68a). The definite UR ranges over contests and not prizes.

(68) a Ron won a prize.
      b Ron won the contest.
      c Ron won.

And while one can notice an object or notice a fact, the UR in (69c) can be used to mean (69b) but not (69a). That is why (70b) is odd as a follow-up to (70a). It would not be odd if (70b) could mean 'I noticed Jo's nose,' as (70c) can.

(69) a   Mo noticed Jo's nose.
      b   Mo noticed that Jo's nose was broken.
      c   Mo noticed.
(70) a   Is something wrong with Jo's nose?
      b   # I noticed, but didn't see anything unusual.
      c   I noticed it, but didn't see anything unusual.

In all such cases, let us say that the UR is **restricted**. If we have the same lexical item with or without the UR, a restricted UR is an implicit argument in at least the broad sense, since we need to stipulate its restriction.

5.4.2 Unrealized role or not

Most events of finding something out are also discoveries. But find out lets what is found out go unrealized, while discover does not (Fillmore 1986), as shown in (71).

(71)   Mo stole a necklace, but no one found out / *discovered.

Three more such examples are shown in (72–74), from Bach (1994). When one reaches a place, one arrives there, but in (72b) we can only use arrive, not reach, to mean that the king showed up at the castle. Similar comments apply to (73) and (74).

(72) a I just phoned the castle.
      b The king has arrived / *reached.
(73) a I talked to Navin about who wrote the letter.
      b He confessed / *admitted.
(74) a There is no more need to worry about Hal's book.
      b He has finished / *completed.

With existential URs we have similar contrasts. The victim must be realized with rob but not steal, and the eaten must be realized with devour but not with eat.

(75) a * Mo robbed (of many things).
      b   Mo stole many things.
(76) a * Al devoured.
      b   Al ate.

So the satisfaction conditions of a verb do not on their own decide whether a certain role may go unrealized (Fillmore 1971b, Shopen 1973, Hankamer and Sag 1976, Dowty 1981). This depends in part on some further property of the verb. Minimally, the semantically similar verbs must differ in syntactic category.

Plausibly, the two similar verbs have exactly the same participant roles: both find out and notice have the Observer and the Observed as participant roles; both rob and steal have the Thief, Victim and Loot; both arrive and reach have the Destination; and so on. If that is correct, then the relevant UR for notice, rob, steal or arrive counts as an implicit argument in at least the very broadest sense.

At the same time, some writers feel that such syntactic contrasts between semantically similar verbs reflect a perspectival difference in how they represent their events psychologically. For example Goldberg (1995), following Langacker (1984), says that rob represents thefts differently from steal. Both represent thefts as involving three participants, but rob "profiles" the victim and not the loot, while steal "profiles" the loot and not the victim; for related thoughts, see Fillmore (1982).

This is plausible, but perhaps unnecessary. The apparent differences may be just the pragmatic effects of an arbitrary difference in syntax. Since rob but not steal requires the company of a dependent naming the victim, only the latter can be used (as a verb) without mentioning the victim explicitly. Since the UR for arrive is furthermore definite, arrive but not reach is limited to contexts where a destination is topical. Pragmatic contrasts such as these would obtain even without any additional difference in psychological representation. So before positing that difference, we might ask for more evidence.

5.5 IN THE SCOPE OF QUANTIFIERS

5.5.1 Definite unrealized roles

When a definite UR occurs in the scope of a quantifier, it may be understood as dependent on that quantifier. We will discuss three kinds of examples. In the first two, the values of the UR covary with the members of the quantifier's domain. In the third kind – not available to every predicate with a definite UR – the UR is itself bound by the quantifier, finding its values within its domain.

Partee (1989) gives us example (77a), to which we can add (77b).

(77) a Every man who shaves off his beard expects his wife to notice.
      b Every man who shaves off his beard expects his wife to forget.

Here the quantifier's domain is men who shave off their beards. The verb notice occurs within its scope. What is noticed or forgotten is a certain fact, not a shaved man. Yet the noticed or forgotten fact *varies* with the choice of man. For every man *x* who shaves his beard, what *x* expects *x*'s wife to notice or forget is the fact that *x* shaved off *x*'s beard. In a case like this let us say that the UR *covaries with the quantifier* and has a **covarying reading**.

In this first example the UR is similar to a donkey pronoun, like it in (78). A *donkey pronoun* is a pronoun that occurs in the scope of a quantifier (or similar operator) and finds its antecedent within that quantifier's restriction. In (78), the scope of the quantifier is grooms it regularly and the restriction is man with a beard.

(78) Every man with a beard grooms it regularly.

Dowty (1981:90) discusses a similar but distinct type of example, (79).

(79) Every secretary made a mistake in his final draft. The good secretary corrected his mistake. Every other secretary didn't even notice.

Here again what is noticed covaries with a quantifier; the noticed fact is the fact that the relevant secretary had made a mistake in the final draft. But now the antecedent is not within the restriction of the governing quantifier. It is outside, in a previous clause. This is definitive of a *paycheck pronoun*, such as the it in (80).

(80) The wise woman gave her paycheck to her husband. Every other woman gave it to her lover. (Dowty 1981:88)

A paycheck pronoun covaries with a superordinate quantifier, but gets its descriptive content from outside the restriction (or scope) of that quantifier (Karttunen 1969).

So definite URs can function like both donkey and paycheck pronouns. In addition, some predicates with a definite UR allow the role to be directly bound by a quantifier. More precisely, some URs allow interpretations which *can* be represented by means of a quantifier binding the role. For example, (81a) and (82a) are easy to hear as synonyms of (81b) and (82b), respectively, where the pronoun it is bound by every contest or no task.

(81)   a   Every contest turned out to have been rigged by the person who won.
      b   Every contest turned out to have been rigged by the person who won it.

(82)   a   No task is impossible for a person who is ready.
      b   No task is impossible for a person who is ready for it.

Let's say that these are **bound readings** of the UR. Bound readings are not available to every predicate with a definite UR. As observed in Williams (2012), they are not available to notice or forget, for example. Sentence (83) cannot mean what (84) does, reading it as bound by nothing.

(83)   # Nothing was forgotten by the person who had first noticed.

(84)   Nothing was forgotten by the person who had first noticed it.

The problem for bound readings with notice is not a general ban on binding a variable that is entailed to stand for a proposition. In (85) and (86) the quantifiers bind the object of find out, and any sentence X finds out Y entails that Y names a proposition. One can find out that a restaurant is good, but one cannot find out a restaurant.

(85)   Nothing I found out seemed interesting to others who had already noticed #(it).

(86)   I wish that nothing would ever be found out by the enemies of those who first notice #(it).

I am not aware of any explanation for this contrast between notice and win (though see Williams 2012 for discussion). That the contrast exists does make the new suggestion, however, that definite URs do not have a uniform analysis. There must be some difference between win and notice that explains the difference in binding.

5.5.2 Existential unrealized roles

Unlike definite URs, existential URs resist both covarying and bound readings in the scope of a quantifier. In (87–90), each of the (a) sentences allows for donkey anaphora; the pronoun covaries with the quantifier and finds an antecedent in its restriction. Yet the same interpretations seem not to remain in the (b) sentences. In my judgment these make a

stronger claim than do the sentences in (a), a judgment sharpened by
the use of a negative quantifier.

(87) a No kid who waxes a car robs its owner of it.
      b No kid who waxes a car robs its owner.
(88) a No kid who hates his neighbor steals a car from him.
      b No kid who hates his neighbor steals a car.
(89) a No rooster eaten by a vixen is killed by her more than two days before.
      b No rooster eaten by a vixen is killed more than two days before.
(90) a No baker who had a cupcake for lunch baked it this morning.
      b No baker who had a cupcake for lunch baked this morning.

For example, (87b) is false if some kid who waxed a car robs its owner
of his gold watch. But this would have no effect on the truth of (87a).
Likewise (89b) is false if one rooster eaten by a vixen is killed one week
earlier *by a wolf.* But this alone would not falsify (89a). The contrast is
particularly clear in (90).

Existential URs also resist bound readings. In my judgment (91b)
makes a stronger claim than (91a): (91b) but not (91a) is made false by
a father who criticizes a child who steals liquor *from his uncle.* Similarly
(92b) lacks the bound reading available to (92a), and therefore only the
first presupposes that a single student baked anything (see Martí 2006
contra Recanati 2002).

(91) a No father criticizes a child who steals liquor from him.
      b No father criticizes a child who steals liquor.
(92) a No cake was praised by the student who baked it.
      b No cake was praised by the student who baked.

There may appear to be counterexamples, sentences in which a UR
seems to be intended as a bound variable. Certainly one can use (93) to
talk about a world in which every kid who waxes a car robs its owner *of
that car.*

(93) Every kid who waxes a car robs its owner.

But in light of the various contrasts observed above, the best response
is to treat these as cases of the hearer inferring more than the speaker
says. The literal meaning of (93) is just that every kid who waxes a car
robs its owner. This entails that the kid robs its owner of something.
From that we might infer that what he robs the owner of is in particular
his car, and this might even be what the speaker intended. But that
additional inference makes no difference to the semantics (Grice 1969,
Kripke 1977, Neale 1990, Bach 2000).

5.5.3 Encoding the contrast

Quantified contexts illuminate a surprising contrast: definite URs have bound or covarying readings, but existential URs do not. In this way definite URs enter semantic dependencies that are otherwise available only to overt dependents, and not to just any entailed role. So they are implicit arguments in the narrow sense.

It is not plausible that the availability of bound or covarying readings should derive in every single case from pragmatic reasoning (though see Carston 2004, Neale 2007 and Elbourne 2008 for relevant discussion). Therefore it is correspondingly implausible that both types of UR should have the very same treatment in the semantics (as suggested in Cappelen and Lepore 2005a, for example). Rather, a semantic distinction appears to be necessary. As already concluded in Section 5.3.3, a definite interpretation must be explicitly specified in the grammar.

The new contribution of the data from quantified contexts is that the representation of definite URs must be such as to permit covarying and (when appropriate) bound readings. The suggestion (Partee 1989, Condoravdi and Gawron 1996, Stanley 2000) that definite URs correspond to a bindable variable in (at least) the meaning of their host, as in (62), repeated in (94), is among those that are sufficient to this task.

(94) $[\![\text{Ron won}]\!] = \exists e [\text{WinningByOf}(\text{Ron}, y)(e)]$

5.6 SHORT PASSIVES

A short passive, such as (95), does not realize its **deep-Subject role**, the role associated with the subject in the active. This UR is understood existentially, so that the initial paraphrase of (95) is 'The ewe was killed by something.'

(95) The ewe was killed.

It is reasonable to say that when we use a passive, we do not only describe an event that has a participant in the deep-Subject role: we also describe that event *as* having that participant. Sentence (95), for example, is about a killing, and every killing involves a killer. But in using (95) do we not also represent this killing *as* involving a killer? I feel less inclined to say the same about (96).

(96) There was a killing.

Dixon (1988) describes a contrast in Fijian between short passives, such as (97), and intransitives where the same verb occurs in its root form, such as (98).

(97) sa   motu'i   a   pua'a.
      TAM   club.PASS   ART   pig
      'The pig is being clubbed.' [Dixon's translation]

(98) sa   motu   a   pua'a.
      TAM   club   ART   pig.
      'The pig is being clubbed.' [Dixon's translation]
      Perhaps better: 'The pig is undergoing clubbing.'

In both (97) and (98), the clubbed beast is named by the surface subject. Both sentences also entail that there was a clubber, since this is
common to all clubbings. So how do they differ in use? Dixon reports
the intuitions of a native speaker: "He said that if you saw someone hit
a pig, then it would be felicitous to use the passive: [(97)]. But if you
could only tell the animal was being killed through hearing its cry,
some way off, then the intransitive verb would be employed, [(98)]."
Thus the passive seems to draw attention to the agent in a way that
the simple intransitive does not. One uses the passive to talk about the
event *as* one that has an agent.

If any such observations are correct, they distinguish the unrealized
deep-Subject role in a short passive from a mere entailment in *some*
way, at least pragmatically or psychologically. The role would therefore
be an implicit argument in at least the broad sense of the term.

But for English this UR is also regarded as a parade case of an implicit
argument in the narrow sense, one that needs to be treated like an
ordinary argument. The motive for this conclusion does not come from
quantifiers, where the UR of a passive does permit covarying readings,
as we have seen (despite Bruening 2012). Rather, it comes from the
construction exemplified in (99) (Roeper 1987).

(99) The ship was sunk to collect the insurance.
      'The ship was sunk so that the sinker might collect the insurance.'

In (99) the implied sinker of the ship can be the intended collector of the
insurance. On these grounds Williams (1985), Roeper (1987) and others
have argued that the deep-Subject role has a grammatical status that is
normally accorded to manifest arguments. I will review this conclusion
at length in Chapter 12 on passives, where we will see good reasons to
doubt it.

DISCUSSION POINTS

1 We use (1) below to say that Mo's height does not reach a certain
  standard, and (2) to say that certain rules forbid the fork from
  being on the right. Does this show that tall enough and cannot

have implicit arguments for standards or rules? Why or why not? Can you construct tests to support your position?

(1) Mo is not tall enough.

(2) The fork cannot be on the right.

2 Francez (2010) observes that (3a) but not (3b) can be used to say (3c), even without any further context. What does this show about the role of Location, associated with there was a famine, that is bound by the demonstrative there in (3b) but unrealized in (3a)? Can you construct examples where the Location role has a covarying reading in the scope of a quantifier?

(3) a Jacob fled to Egypt because there was a famine.
   b Jacob fled to Egypt because there was a famine there.
   c Jacob fled to Egypt because there was a famine where he fled from.

3 Williams (1985) and Safir (1987) discuss (4). Here stoned can describe the discussants only when of the issue is present. Does this show that discussion of the issue, but not discussion, has an implicit argument for the discussants? Why or why not?

(4) Yesterday's discussion *(of the issue) stoned didn't clarify matters.
   'Yesterday's discussion (of the issue) by stoned discussants didn't clarify matters.'

4 Hankamer and Sag (1976) and Grimshaw (1979) discuss patterns like (5). The direct object of care can be an interrogative clause, (5a), but not a DP, (5b). In (5c), however, the guy's name in the first clause lets us understand the second clause as (5a). Does this show us anything about the unrealized role for care in (5c), the role that gives the content of caring?

(5) a Syl doesn't care what the guy's name is.
   b * Syl doesn't care the guy's name.
   c Ro wants to know the guy's name, but Syl doesn't care.

5 Recall the contrast between arrive and reach in (6a). Can this be explained by the subsequent data? If so, how? Do your thoughts about (6) extend to finish versus complete, find out versus discover, or confess versus admit?

(6) a The king has { arrived / *reached }.
   b The king { arrived / *reached } at the castle.
   c The king { reached / *arrived } it / the castle.
   d The king { arrived / *reached } there.

6 Lidz (2001) observes a pattern in Kannada (Dravidian). The verb much 'close' can occur either with or without the so-called

'reflexive morpheme' koND, (7). Either way the sentence just means 'the door closed.' With koND the sentence does not mean 'the door made itself close.' But only with koND can a dative adjunct, here gaaLige 'wind.DAT,' name a cause of the door closing, (8). Does this mean that koND introduces an implicit argument in the role of Cause? Why or why not? What else would you like to know to answer this question? In thinking of this, keep in mind English (9).

(7) baagilu   much   (-i-koND)   -itu.
     door.NOM   close   -PPL-REFLEX   -PAST.3sn
     'The door closed.'

(8) gaaLige   baagilu   much   *(-i-koND)   -itu.
     wind.DAT   door.NOM   close   *(-PPL-REFLEX)   -PAST.3sn
     'Because of the wind, the door closed.'

(9) The pot is oily (from the soup).

7 When notice has an overt direct object, it can refer either to an object, or to a fact. But when it does not, what is noticed must be a fact (Section 5.4.1). Must we therefore say that there are at least two distinct lexical items, both pronounced "notice?" Why or why not? Does your answer imply anything about the representation of the unrealized role for the (surface-)intransitive notice?

SUGGESTIONS FOR FURTHER READING

Bhatt and Pancheva 2006 is a marvelous overview of the linguistic literature on implicit arguments. Gillon 2006 is also excellent. Williams 1985, Fillmore 1986 and Partee 1989 are classics. Recanati 2012 is a clear review of pertinent discussion in philosophy of language, concerning the line between semantics and pragmatics, and staking a middle ground between Stanley 2000 and Cappelen and Lepore 2007.

Part III
Analysis of argument relations

6   Thematic relations

6.1   INTRODUCTION

Sometimes a dependent is claimed to instantiate a *thematic relation*.[1]
Familiar labels for very general thematic relations include Agent,
Patient, Experiencer, Instrument, Source, Location and Goal. Besides
these there are specific thematic relations such as 'thing carried in
a carrying.' For the linguist who uses thematic relations, there are
two big questions. What is the justification for using any thematic
relation? And if there is a thematic relation in the meaning of an
expression, exactly which relation is it? I discuss the first question in
Sections 6.3 and 6.4, and the second briefly in Section 6.5. The next
chapter (Chapter 7) then concentrates specially on Agent and Patient.
Before all this (Section 6.2), I clarify what we are talking about.

6.2   WHAT ARE THEMATIC RELATIONS?

What is it that makes a relation thematic? On classic uses of the term,
it is something grammatical: thematic relations are predicated of just
one dependent and not more. They do not relate the meanings of two
dependent expressions, both the subject and the object for example,
but rather interpret just a single dependent in relation to the head.
When a dependency is interpreted by a thematic relation, its interpretation is *separate* from that of any other (Schein 1993).

To see the point, compare (1) and (2) below. These are two distinct
hypotheses about the meaning of the same sentence. In (1), a single

---

[1] The term is credited by Jackendoff (1972:29) to Richard Stanley. It derives from
Gruber's use of "Theme" to describe the relation borne by a participant whose
location or movement are described by the verb. Nominally, therefore, thematic
relations are relations that are like *Theme*. Connotations of the normal word
thematic do not apply.

relation, called CarryingByOf, is predicated both of the subject and of the object. Because this relation is predicated of both dependents, it is not a thematic relation, not in the classic sense to which I will adhere.

(1) a Navin carried the chair.
     b $\cong \exists e[$ CarryingByOf(e, Navin, the chair)]

Now contrast (2). Here the subject and the object provide terms in two separate relations: Navin names a term in the CarryingBy relation, but the chair does not, while the chair names a term in the CarryingOf relation, and Navin does not.

(2) a Navin carried the chair.
     b $\cong \exists e[$ CarryingBy(e, Navin) & CarryingOf(e, the chair)]

Because each relation in (2) is predicated of just a single dependent, both may be classed as thematic.[2]

Under this rubric we can fit more specific proposals about the semantic type and content of thematic relations. What sorts of relations serve as thematic relations? Today the most common answer treats them as two-place relations between an event and an individual (Castañeda 1967, Carlson 1984, Dowty 1989, Parsons 1990, Landman 2000), like the CarryingBy relation in (2), or the Agent and Patient relations in (3), a third possible hypothesis about our example.[3]

(3) a Navin carried the chair.
     b $\cong \exists e[$ Agent(e, Navin) & Carrying(e) & Patient(e, the chair)]

Furthermore, the term is generally applied only to those relations that are entailed relations for the relevant verb. A dog who watches Navin carry the chair has some relation to the carrying, as does a woman who laments it. But it is not entailed by the truth of Navin carried the chair that the carrying has a watcher or lamenter. For this reason one would not usually say that Watcher or Lamenter are thematic relative to carry. In fact, common usage is often still stricter, with only some of the entailed relations being called thematic. For example, Dowty (1989) definitionally restricts the term only to relations associated with arguments, such as the subject or the object.

---

[2] A non-thematic relation might entail a thematic relation. CarryingByOf(a, b)(e) might entail Agent(e, a), for example. But that doesn't make CarryingByOf itself a thematic relation. A relation need not have the properties of everything it entails.

[3] It is not necessary that thematic relations be relations between individuals and events. Dowty 1979 treats some as relations between individuals and propositions. Schein 2002 treats them as relations between individuals, an event and a "scene," for reasons discussed in Section 6.4.

When we say that thematic relations involve individuals and events, this reflects an objectivist semantics. If the Agent relation involves Navin and a carrying, it involves two things that are not inside anybody's head. But our labels can be transposed into a mentalist perspective; the mentalist can use the term "thematic relations" for a class of mental concepts that represent relations in the world. To say that Navin is interpreted by the Agent relation in Navin carried the chair is then to say – this is one version of the mentalist perspective – that the semantic value of the sentence is a complex thought, one of whose constituents is the thought that Navin was an agent in some event, as that event is viewed under the concept named by the verb. The connection that these thoughts and concepts have to the nonmental world is, on the mentalist view, outside the domain of linguistic semantics. As we will see in Section 6.4, many take this to be the only feasible view of thematic relations. The reason is, these relations resist definition in objectivist terms, and seem to depend essentially on the psychological perspective expressed by the verb (Huddleston 1970, Jackendoff 1976, 1987, Delancey 1991).

Either way, the use of a thematic relation is often a claim of semantic decomposition, and thus covert analyticity, since this part of the meaning is not pronounced by a separate part of the audible form (see Chapter 2). In (3), for example, there is no audible word whose meaning is Agent, nor one whose meaning is Patient. It is therefore important to remind ourselves of the distinction between strict versus representational or merely metasemantic decomposition. These ascribe structure to three different sorts of things. For strict decomposition, it is the actual meaning of the expression. For representational decomposition, it is some grammatically active representation of its meaning, and not the meaning itself. And for metasemantic decomposition, it is just a description of the expression in the language of the theorist, not anything in the object language. This matters because many popular arguments for thematic relations warrant no more than a claim of metasemantic or representational decomposition. It takes more to conclude that the decomposition is in the meaning of the expression itself. And yet, when a linguist uses thematic relations, it is most often, I believe, the stronger hypothesis of strict decomposition that is intended.

Finally, and for similar reasons, let me emphasize an important (though vague) division between *specific* and *general* thematic relations. Specific relations can hold of very few sorts of events. Very few sorts of events, perhaps only carryings, involve carriers. So Carrier, rendered as CarryingBy in (2), is near the limit of specificity. In contrast, relations like Agent and Patient are highly general. Many sorts of events involve an agent or a patient, if any do at all: not only carryings, but also smackings, dancings and so on. Near the limit of generality is the relation of Participant, which relates any sort of event at all to its participants.

Usually, general thematic relations are seen as abstracting out common aspects of certain verb-specific thematic relations. For example, the Agent relation abstracts out what is common to Carriers, Cookers, Kickers, Stealers and so forth. Dowty gives one influential articulation of this view. He says that any thematic relation is "a cluster of entailments and presuppositions shared by certain arguments of certain verbs" (Dowty 1989:76); or again, a thematic role is "a set of entailments of a group of predicates with respect to one of the arguments of each" (Dowty 1991:552). Any verb will underwrite a number of entailments about the values of its dependents. For example, because of the verb carry, Navin carried the chair entails that Navin supported the weight of the chair. Some of these entailments will be of notable generality, and shared across a large number of verbs. The shared entailments that prove useful in stating some grammatical regularity, says Dowty, are the thematic relations of linguistic theory, what he calls the "L-Thematic Role Types." Again, this is just to say that general thematic relations collect common aspects of certain verb-specific thematic relations, especially those that are useful in capturing linguistic generalizations. Dowty's particular contribution is to state this formally within a firmly objectivist semantics, with no psychological commitments.[4]

Methodologically speaking, the distinction between general and specific relations matters for one big reason: several common arguments both for and against the use of thematic relations in semantics apply only to highly general relations, and leave specific relations untouched, as we will now see in Sections 6.3 and 6.4.

6.3 MOTIVATION FOR THEMATIC RELATIONS

6.3.1 Grammatical patterns

The most popular motivation for thematic relations is grammatical. Certain thematic relations allow us to state grammatical generalizations that govern broad semantic categories, generalizing over clauses

---

[4] Of course it is a further question whether Dowty's objectivist project of defining the desired relations in terms of entailments does or even could succeed. See Delancey 1991 and Wechsler 1995, among many others, for doubts.

with many different verbs. Many of these are "linking" generalizations (Carter 1976), which link grammatical with thematic relations, in partial independence of the verb (Chapter 11). There is a generalization that transitive clauses with verbs of action have subjects that name the action's *agent*, for instance, and stating this will require the predicate Agent, at some level of linguistic description. Important arguments of this kind were made by Gruber (1965), Fillmore (1968), Jackendoff (1972), Carter (1976), Perlmutter (1978) and many others after them.

This kind of argument is often compelling, but also limited in scope. First, it can only motivate highly general relations, such as Agent or Theme, since it is exactly their generality that makes the generalization possible. Second, such arguments leave open 'where' in the theory the thematic relations are supposed to be active. There are three options, importantly different, according to whether the implied decomposition is metasemantic, representational or strict.

The metasemantic approach commits to almost nothing. It requires only that we linguists have the term "agent" available in the theoretical jargon we use to talk about entailments (Dowty 1979). Our linking principle is only that, in general, transitive clauses entail that there was an event with a participant which we can describe in our jargon as its agent, and the subject names that agent. This does not require that 'agent' be in any sense a part of the language itself.

The representational approach says a bit more. The linking generalization, and consequently 'agent' as well, is in some way a rule in the language itself. It deploys a certain representation of the events denoted by the verbs in its domain: verbs denoting *events with agents* have a certain distribution. But notice, this does not require that any verb has Agent as a constituent of its meaning. Consider an analogy. Only nouns that name things with hair will sound natural with blond, for obvious reasons. This correctly distinguishes the nouns child and diameter, since children but not diameters have hair. But from this we needn't conclude that child has 'with hair' as a constituent of its meaning, in any sense. Granting this, one might nevertheless insist that the further commitment – that Agent be part of the verb's meaning – is required for the linking rule to be useful psychologically, for example to the child acquiring language. But is that so? The rule will be useful so long as the child can recognize that a certain verb denotes events with agents, i.e., that it entails an agent. Recognizing an entailment does not, indeed *cannot*, require treating it as a strict analyticity.

Only the third approach commits to strict semantic decomposition. Here the linking generalization says that a typical transitive clause has the Agent relation as a separate constituent of its meaning, and that in deriving this meaning, Agent is always instantiated by the subject. The thematic relation of Agent is then as much a part of the expression itself as is the subject relation. This is the strongest possible hypothesis. But, by the same token, it is not supported by the mere existence of the linking generalization, for which representational decomposition would be sufficient.

6.3.2 Inferential patterns

A second motive for thematic relations is logical. In the wake of Davidson (1967b), it was observed by Castañeda (1967), Carlson (1984), Parsons (1990) and others that thematic relations permit a nice account of inferences like those in (4–6).

(4)   a   The mule kicked Otis.
      b   ⊨ The mule kicked.
(5)   a   Brutus stabbed Caesar.
      b   ⊨ There was a stabbing.
(6)   a   Lee stole the necklace from Mo.
      b   ⊨ Lee stole the necklace.

With thematic relations, we can render (4–6) as (7–9), respectively. Dropping a dependent in the syntax is thereby treated as dropping a conjunct in the semantics.

(7)   a   ∃e[Agent(e, the mule) & Kicking(e) & Patient(e, Otis)]
      b   ⊢ ∃e[Agent(e, the mule) & Kicking(e)]
(8)   a   ∃e[Agent(e, Brutus) & Stabbing(e) & Patient(e, Caesar)]
      b   ⊢ ∃e[Stabbing(e)]
(9)   a   ∃e[Agent(e, Lee) & Stealing(e) & Patient(e, the necklace) & From(e, Mo)]
      b   ⊢ ∃e[Agent(e, Lee) & Stealing(e) & Patient(e, the necklace)]

The inferences hereby come out as formal validities, syntactic consequences that require no reference to the identity of the predicates. This is attractive, insofar as the inferences do not seem to depend on the meanings of the particular words in the sentence. There is an additional attraction to treating them, in particular, as cases of Conjunction Elimination. This affords a nice match between syntactic and semantic complexity (Carlson 1984). The absence of a subject, object or oblique corresponds to the absence of a conjunct in the meaning.

Without thematic relations, we can still treat the inferences as valid, by representing them as in (10–12). The difference is, we cannot treat them as cases of Conjunction Elimination. Instead, we have to treat them as cases of Existential Generalization. Rather than dropping a conjunct, we introduce a quantifier (Dowty 1981).

(10) a   ∃e[KickingByOf(e, the mule, Otis)]

  b ⊢ ∃y∃e[KickingByOf(e, the mule, y)]

(11) a   ∃e[StabbingByOf(e, Brutus, Caesar)]

  b ⊢ ∃y∃x∃e[StabbingByOf(e, x, y)]

(12) a   ∃e[StealingByOfFrom(e, Lee, the necklace, Mo)]

  b ⊢ ∃y∃e[StealingByOfFrom(e, Lee, the necklace, y)]

But there are two objections to this. First, the removal of something from the syntax corresponds to the addition of something in the semantics (Carlson 1984), raising questions about how this is to be implemented; on this issue see Gillon (2012).

Parsons (1990:97) has a tougher objection, our second. He observes that the existential quantifier does not always give us the right truth conditions. Formula (10b) is supposed to translate (4b), The mule kicked, but (10b) entails that the mule kicked something, while (4b) does not. A mule can kick without kicking anything. Sometimes, therefore, inferences involving the removal of a dependent cannot be modeled by Existential Generalization. And this now forces a compromise that Parsons finds unattractive: without thematic relations, Existential Generalization is the only way that such inferences can be represented as formally valid, and therefore, without thematic relations, some such inferences cannot be represented as formally valid.

Let me repeat this objection, a bit more slowly. We need to avoid a logical implication from The mule kicked to The mule kicked something. To do this, we must represent The mule kicked as in (13), with a relation that has no slot for a thing kicked. It is not a syntactic consequence of this formula that the mule kicked anything.

(13) ∃e[KickingBy(e, the mule)]

Now turn to the transitive clause, The mule kicked Otis. If we had a thematic relation available for Otis, perhaps Patient, we could translate this sentence as in (14), using the same two-place predicate, KickingBy, that now occurs in (13).

(14) ∃e[KickingBy(e, the mule) & Patient(e, Otis)]

But a thematic relation for Otis is not on the menu. So the transitive must be represented, as before, with (15); without thematic relations, we need to use a single relation, here KickingByOf, that has slots for both the kicker and the kicked.

(15) ∃e[KickingByOf(e, the mule, Otis)]

Now compare the conclusion to its premise, rendered as (13) and (15) respectively. They contain two different predicates, KickingBy versus

KickingByOf. So the inference is not underwritten by logical syntax. We can stipulate that it is nonetheless a semantic consequence, by saying that, as it happens, whenever $\langle e, x, y \rangle$ satisfies KickingByOf, $\langle e, x \rangle$ satisfies KickingBy; and we can repeat this for every other verb that behaves just like kick. But without thematic relations, we lose the opportunity to treat the inference as formally provable, and to regard its validity as reflecting a general fact about the interpretation of dependents. Some proponents of thematic relations, including Parsons (1990) and Schein (2002), find this unattractive, extending Davidson's attitude about adverbs. But compare Dowty (1989) or Kracht (2011).

As usual, what one makes of these arguments depends on whether or not one regards the proposed decomposition as strict. For Dowty (1979), as for Davidson (1967b), it is not strict. It is instead a way of 'formalizing' the observed inferences. Other analysts take the decomposition to be strict. In that case the argument from inference patterns requires that these inferences are valid relative to a 'natural logic' that is internal to the language, in a sense that deserves clarification (Lakoff 1972).

6.3.3 Syntactic separation

If two dependents instantiate thematic relations, then by definition they instantiate two separate relations: each instantiates a term in its relation but not in the other. For example, if the subject and object both instantiate thematic relations in Navin carried the chair, then its meaning, in our strictest sense, has the structure of (16).

(16)   Navin carried the chair $\cong \exists e[\ P(e, \text{Navin}) \ \& \ \dots \ \& \ Q(e, \text{the chair})]$

Since the two relations are separate, it is possible that they are introduced by separate parts of the derivation, whether lexical items or rules. The decomposition is then syntactically derived (Chapter 2). Call this **(syntactic) separation** of the relations, adapting a term from Schein (1993). Without thematic relations, syntactic separation is ipso facto impossible; two dependents related to the same predicate will then instantiate terms in one and the same relation, not two that are separable. Evidence for syntactic separation is therefore the best evidence for thematic relations.

There are several arguments for separation, including those in Carlson (1984), Parsons (1990), Schein (1993), (1997), (2012), Borer (1994), (2003), Kratzer (1996), Marantz (1997), Pietroski (2005a) and Williams (2008a). These are the topic of Chapter 9. Here I will just emphasize two tactical advantages of such arguments, in comparison to those from grammatical or inferential patterns. First, they don't depend on the content of the thematic relation, nor on whether it is general or specific. Thus they are largely unaffected by objections to very general thematic relations, to be described in Section 6.4. Second, they are, by definition, arguments specifically for strict decomposition, syntactically derived; and strict decomposition is always an empirically stronger hypothesis than representational or metasemantic decomposition.

6.3.4 , Psychological primitives

Finally, one might be attracted to thematic relations for their possible role in non-linguistic cognition. Plausibly, some highly general participant relations have a privileged cognitive role. It may be that we naturally perceive or understand events in terms of agents, for example (Leslie 1994, Gao and Scholl 2011).

These privileged categories will be reflected, to some degree, in what sorts of words we have. Surely it is neither an accident nor a quirk of grammar that we have a verb, hug, meaning 'x wraps his arms around y,' but no verb schug meaning 'z is with a person who wraps his arms around y.' Rather, this presumably reflects the fact that agency draws our attention more than accompaniment. Viewing a scene in which x hugs y while with z, we are likely to exclude z, the mere companion of the agent x, from our gloss on what happened: Gordon (2003) has shown this even in 10-month-old infants. Correspondingly, it is more likely that a verb's satisfaction conditions can be described in terms of agency than in terms of accompaniment. In turn, this provides at least a good initial motive to use the Agent relation as a constituent of sentence meanings, now using 'meaning' in its narrow sense.

But this initial motive is nowhere near decisive. That the satisfaction conditions of a sentence can be described using a predicate R does not mean that R is, in the narrow sense, a separate constituent of its meaning. What makes (17) true?[5]

(17)   Cashew apples are fruits and pumpkins are vegetables.

In answering this, I will mention many properties that typically belong to fruits or vegetables. Some will reflect perceptual categories and practical interests that are important in human life, such as sweetness and cooking. But it doesn't follow that each property I mention corresponds to a separate constituent in the meaning of (17). So, again,

---

[5] Sentence (17) is indeed true under common usage of fruit and vegetable. But it is false under the definitions used by botanists, according to which pumpkins are 'fruits' but cashew apples are not.

while the cognitive centrality of certain thematic relations may explain why these can often be used in explicating the content of a verb, this alone does not entail these relations are separate constituents of its meaning (Dowty 1979, 1989, 1991). This claim would have to be otherwise justified.

Maybe one day the methods of psycholinguistics will provide clear evidence for or against certain thematic analyses, and show, for example, whether or not tokening Navin carried the chair *consists* partly in tokening the Agent concept. But our present methods are nowhere close to distinguishing between semantic constituency and even incidental association. It might be that whenever I token football player I also token the concept 'strong,' but this does not itself put 'strong' in the meaning of the expression. It is therefore hard to make stick any psychological argument for thematic relations.

6.4 OBJECTIONS TO GENERAL THEMATIC RELATIONS

6.4.1 Obscurity

There are problems with the use of general thematic relations. The first, reviewed most influentially in Dowty (1991), is obscurity.

What are the general thematic relations? There is no agreed list, and criteria for inclusion are unclear. It is furthermore difficult to say when we have one relation or two, since even the commonly used relations, such as Agent or Theme, lack agreed definitions. This is not for want of trying. The terms, whatever their intuitive resonance, simply resist substantive definition.

The obscurity does not end with a compromise on a rough-and-ready list. We still have to say which dependents bear which thematic relations. Here again there is much disagreement, but no clear standards for resolution. For example, do (18a) and (18b) impose different thematic relations on Hal? What about a and b in (19), or in (20)?

(18) a Hal received a package.
      b Al sent Hal a package.
(19) a Hal resembles Al.
      b Al resembles Hal.
(20) a Hal is opposite Al.
      b Al is opposite Hal.

We may want to say that they do, since our linking generalizations generally presume that the subject and object instantiate distinct semantic relations. But if these relations are supposed to be general, it is difficult to distinguish the two relations by their truth conditions (Huddleston 1970), without begging important questions. So if relations are differentiated only by their truth-conditions, the two cannot be the same. Thus a commitment to truth-conditional semantics is pitted against an interest in rich grammatical generalizations – for many linguists an uneasy conflict.

Dowty (1991) therefore proposes to do away with thematic relations, at least the very general ones. His rejection has two aspects. First, general thematic relations play no role in meanings, in our technical sense of the term. The meaning of *Navin carried the chair*, for example, either involves no thematic relations at all, as in (21); or, if it does, the relations are highly specific, as in (22). Thus no sentence entails analytically that its subject-referent satisfies Agent, or its object-referent, Patient.

(21) $\exists e[$ CarryingByOf(e, Navin, the chair)]

(22) $\exists e[$ CarryingBy(e, Navin) & CarryingOf(e, the chair)]

Second, general thematic relations play no role even in the theoretical metalanguage that linguists use to describe truth-conditions and entailments. Thus for Dowty there simply are no general relations answering to Agent or Patient, none that can be suitably defined. Rather, there is rough, pairwise classification of specific relations as being (in my words) more agent-like or more patient-like. The properties in (23) make a relation more agent-like, while those in (24) make one more patient-like (Dowty 1991:572). These he calls "Proto-Agent properties" and "Proto-Patient properties," respectively (Dowty 1991:576).[6]

(23) Proto-Agent properties

    a volitional involvement in the event or state

    b sentience (and/or perception)

    c causing an event or change of state in another participant

    d movement (relative to the position of another participant)

    e (exists independently of the event named by the verb)

(24) Proto-Patient properties

    a undergoes change of state

    b incremental theme[7]

---

[6] See the earlier Foley and Van Valin 1984 for thoughts in a similar spirit.

[7] Dowty characterizes an **incremental theme** as a thematic relation that maps each part of individual *x* to a temporal part of the event *e*. Lawn-mowing has an incremental theme, since for each bit of the lawn that gets mowed, there is a part of the mowing. The idea is, each increment of change in the theme corresponds to temporal progress in the event.

c causally affected by another participant

d stationary relative to movement of another participant

e (does not exist independently of the event, or not at all)

This has come to be called the "Proto-Role" theory, but the name can be misleading. Dowty's classification is not a definition of two hyper-general relations, Proto-Agent and Proto-Patient. It contributes nothing to the stock of semantic primitives. It just provides a scheme for comparing two very specific relations with reference to some opposition. For Dowty a relation that has more properties from (23) than from (24) is more typically like one we would informally classify as an Agent relation, while one with more from (24) than from (23) is more typically like one we would informally classify as a Patient relation. And to say that is not to define two new very general thematic relations.

With general thematic relations gone, the problems that attend their use of course do not arise. But this leaves the challenge of accounting for the observations that motivated them in the first place. Dowty focusses on linking generalizations, what he calls principles of "argument selection." Foremost among these is the generalization that, in transitive clauses that describe actions, subjects name agents and objects name patients. According to Dowty, this generalization does not show that the meanings of transitive clauses typically include Agent and Patient, or anything of equal generality. Instead it shows a typical difference between the *specific* semantic relations associated with subjects and objects in a transitive clause. Of these two specific relations, the subject relation tends to be more agent-like than the object relation, and the object relation tends to be more patient-like than the subject relation. Thus Dowty gives the "Argument Selection Principle" in (25).

(25) In predicates with grammatical subject and object, the argument for which the predicate entails the greatest number of Proto-Agent properties will be lexicalized as the subject of the predicate; the argument having the greatest number of Proto-Patient entailments will be lexicalized as the direct object. (Dowty 1991:576)

Here there is no reference at all to thematic relations, either at the level of meaning or in the description of truth-conditions. There is only the rough pairwise classification of entailments provided by the scheme of Proto-Agent and Proto-Patient properties.

This theory secures some wiggle room that Dowty considers important. If two thematic relations have the same number of Proto-Agent or Proto-Patient properties, their association with grammatical relations is undetermined. So for such predicates we expect some variation in the realization of their arguments. In this way Dowty proposes to handle some cases that otherwise seem anomalous, such as (26).

(26) a Arguments please Al.
    b Al likes arguments.

What pleases Al has more or less the same properties as what Al likes (though see Wechsler 1995 and Pesetsky 1995). So why are pleasers subjects when the liked are objects? For Dowty, it is because the pleasers and the pleased, as well as likers and the liked, do not differ much in how agent-like or patient-like they are. The Argument Selection Principle is therefore indifferent as to their linking.

6.4.2 Logical problems

Obscurity alone may leave you unmoved. There are few definitions of any interesting concepts, and few agreed taxonomies of any basic linguistic relations. If we haven't yet found satisfactory answers, this needn't be taken as evidence that we have the wrong agenda. On the contrary, it might just show that the demand for truth-conditional explication is pointless. Thematic relations reflect flexible categories of human psychology, perceptual, conceptual and practical, and why expect that such categories can be explicated wholly in terms of mind-external satisfaction conditions? Their resistance to such characterization gives us no reason not to use them in linguistic theory. Or so it is fair to argue, especially within a mentalist semantics.

Yet there is a second challenge that demands a more engaged response. General thematic relations engender logical flaws that cannot be ignored as problems of detail or resolution. The clearest come from predicates that are (nearly) inverses of each other, such as buy and sell, or also symmetrical predicates, such as resemble or be opposite to (Huddleston 1970). Consider (27a) and (28a). The linguist who uses general thematic relations is likely to assign the same general relation to the subject of both sentences: each will name the agent of some event, as in (27b) and (28b).

(27) a Mo bought Fido from Lee.
    b $\exists e[$ Agent(e, Mo) & Buying$(\ldots)(e)\ldots]$
(28) a Lee sold Fido to Mo.
    b $\exists e[$ Agent(e, Lee) & Selling$(\ldots)(e)\ldots]$

And now suppose we use both sentences to talk about the same transaction. It is then reasonable to say that both sentences must be verified by the same event, that the buying and the selling are the very same thing. But if thematic relations are relations directly to events, this will have an incorrect consequence. With the predicates in both (27a) and (28a) true of one and the same event, this event will have both Lee and Mo as agents, and will be both a buying and a selling. So (27a) and (28a) should together imply (29) and (30), contrary to fact.

(29)   Lee (and Mo) bought Fido.

(30)   Mo (and Lee) sold Fido.

This does not immediately falsify the premise that in both (27a) and (28a) the subject names an agent. For the other premises of the argument are open to doubt. I will distinguish two broad lines of response; there are several others.

First, one can deny that a buying is identical to the corresponding selling (Parsons 1990, Landman 2000). They are intimately related, but not the same. Then the agent of a buying is not immediately the agent of a selling. The upshot is a very fine-grained ontology for the so-called 'events' that are in the domain of thematic relations. A great many events that are 'intimately related' will occupy the same stretch of time and space. Such multiplication of events may offend common sense, which perhaps counsels that the buying and selling are not two events, but just one event described by two different verbs. On this point my own intuitions are haphazard. But the retort from common sense is hard to resist with predicates that provide their own inverse: the symmetrical predicates. Example (31) is from Huddleston (1970).

(31)   a   The post office is opposite the bank.
         b   The bank is opposite the post office.
         c   # The post office is opposite the post office.

Certainly (31a) and (31b) do seem to describe the very same state. If that is correct, and the subject in these sentences is assigned a thematic relation, then (31a) and (31b) should jointly entail (31c) as a matter of logic. But they don't. Our first line of defense for general thematic relations thus counsels something that does indeed offend common sense. It counsels that we deny the problematic identity, and say that (31a) and (31b) describe two different events.

The second response is to assume that thematic predicates hold only relative to a *perspective* on an event, given (either sometimes or always) at least in part by the verb (Huddleston 1970, Jackendoff 1976, Fillmore 1978, Delancey 1991, Schein 2002). This is done most simply by giving thematic relations an additional term, so that they relate an individual x to both an event e and a perspective π.[8] What satisfies $\lambda x[\text{Agent}(e, \pi_1, x)]$ need not satisfy $\lambda x[\text{Agent}(e, \pi_2, x)]$, when $\pi_1 \neq \pi_2$. Therefore the agent of e relative to the buy perspective need not be the agent of e relative to the sell perspective, even if the buying and the selling are one and the same event. Thus what we are talking about or mentally representing – namely the events – remains simple, and only the way we talk about them becomes more complex. Locating the complexity in the representation in turn raises questions for the compositional semantics. Thematic relations have an additional term. Do some predicates in the clause modify the perspective and others the event? Can different thematic relations in the same clause share an event but not a perspective? For reflection on these issues see Schein (2002) and (2012); for a deeper critique, see Pietroski (to appear b).

6.5 KINDS OF THEMATIC RELATIONS

There cannot fail to be specific thematic relations. But if there are also general ones, we need to ask which ones there are. The general relations most commonly invoked are Agent, Experiencer, Instrument, Location, Goal, Source, and Patient or Theme. In (33–39) I give a rough sketch of how linguists use these terms. The names are themselves a good indication of the intended content, with the exception of "Theme." See Andrews (1985) and Jackendoff (1987) for fuller details.

(32) An **Agent** is a thing viewed as bringing about the event. Traditionally this included only volitional actors (Gruber 1965, Jackendoff 1972), but now this condition is often dropped (Baker 1997; cf. Van Valin and Wilkins 1996).

(33) An **Experiencer** is the sentient locus of a mental event.

(34) An **Instrument** is a thing viewed as assisting the agent in bringing about the event (Nilsen 1973, Koenig *et al.* 2008).

(35) A **Location** is the location of an event.

(36) A **Goal** is a thing or place towards which a certain participant in the event moves.

(37) A **Source** is a thing or place from which a certain participant in the event moves.

(38) A **Patient** is a thing viewed as undergoing an event passively.

(39) The term **Theme** was introduced in Gruber (1965) for a participant whose location or movement (whether in a physical or an abstract space) is described

---

[8] Absent this third term, we would have to give our meaning-formulas a noncompositional or 'context-sensitive' interpretation, and say that Agent(e, x) can be evaluated only with consideration of other 'nearby' subformulas involving e or x.

by the verb. These days it is often used with much broader meaning, often interchangeably with Patient. Commonly, any subject or object that does not name Agent or Experiencer is said to name a Theme.

Sentence (40) gives us an opportunity to practice the argot, under the supposition that each of its noun phrases instantiates a thematic relation from our list. The list in (41) gives one possible labeling of the thematic relations assigned to the noun phrases here.

(40) Lee thinks that Al pushed the puck from the door to the closet with a broom in the foyer.

(41)   a Lee: Experiencer relative to think
       b Al: Agent relative to push
       c the puck: Patient or Theme relative to push
       d the door: Source relative to push
       e the closet: Goal relative to push
       f a broom: Instrument relative to push
       g the foyer: Location relative to push

This is more or less the standard inventory of thematic relations, historically and still today. But it is just one. Many others have been proposed, varying in heterodoxy. Here I will mention two interesting alternatives, from Wechsler (1995) and Jackendoff (1987). Others will come up incidentally in later chapters (Grimshaw 1990, Tenny 1994, Van Valin and LaPolla 1997, Borer 2005).

Wechsler classifies argument relations in terms of three semantic classes, named Notion, Nuclear and Part. In (43–45) I paraphrase the condition for being in each of these three classes. These are stated relative to the assumption that we have a transitive clause with the meaning in (42), where P and Q are thematic relations, possibly specific to the verb.

(42) $\exists e[\ P(e, x)\ \&\ \text{Verbing}(e)\ \&\ Q(e, y)\ ]$

(43) $P \in$ Notion iff (42) entails that x has an idea about y
     $Q \in$ Notion iff (42) entails that y has an idea about x

(44) $P \in$ Nuclear iff (42) entails that e ends with a particular change in x
     $Q \in$ Nuclear iff (42) entails that e ends with a particular change in y

(45) $P \in$ Part iff (42) entails that x is a proper part of y
     $Q \in$ Part iff (42) entails that y is a proper part of x

The sentences in (46) give examples. Sentence (46a) entails that John has an idea about Mary, but not that Mary has an idea about John. Sentence (46b) entails that the event ends with a change in the metal, not necessarily the acid. And (46c) entails that the sugar is a proper part of the toothpaste, not vice versa.

(46)   a John fears Mary.
    b The acid dissolved the metal.
    c The toothpaste contains sugar.

Wechsler argues that this taxonomy is in two ways better than the standard. First, its primitives are less obscure: it is relatively clear what it is to have an idea, to undergo a change or to be part of something – clearer than what it is to be an Agent, for example. Second, it affords a linking theory that is no less satisfactory, roughly as in (47). See Wechsler (1995) for the full story, and discussion of challenges.

(47)   a A +Notion relation must link to the subject
    b A pair of +Nuclear and −Nuclear relations must link to the object and subject, respectively.
    c A pair of +Part and −Part relations must link to the object and subject, respectively.

Jackendoff (1987) objects that the traditional inventory of thematic relations is insufficiently expressive. It both fails to describe the interpretation of every dependent for every verb, and misses generalizations that cross-classify its various roles. In response he proposes more decomposition: the relation a dependent instantiates may comprise the conjunction of several different predicates, and these may relate to several different events. This conjunctive structure is taken to be underived, and present only in the semantic value of the verb, which for Jackendoff is a complex mental concept. Formula (49) is a Jackendovian meaning for (48) (Jackendoff 1990b:59), here translated into event-theoretic terms.

(48)   Lee sold Fido to Mo for $100.
(49)   a $\exists e_1 \exists e_2[$ InExchangeFor(e_2, e_1) & Going(e_1) & Going(e_2)
    b & $[\lambda x[\text{Goer}(e_1, x)]]$(Fido)
    c & $[\lambda x[\text{From}(e_1, x)$ & To$(e_2, x)]]$(Lee)
    d & $[\lambda x[\text{Goer}(e_2, x)]]$($100)
    e & $[\lambda x[\text{To}(e_1, x)$ & From$(e_2, x)]]$(Mo)]

The sentence describes two events, one in exchange for the other. The first, e_1, is an event of Fido going from Lee to Mo, and the second, e_2, of $100 going from Mo to Lee. In (49c), Lee instantiates a relation that is analyzed as a conjunction of two predicates: a From relation to e_1, and a To relation to e_2. Likewise, in (49e), Mo instantiates the conjunction of the inverse relations.

This decomposition serves both of Jackendoff's aims. First, it recognizes commonalities across semantic relations that the traditional inventory treats as unrelated. For example, with the traditional palette we might say that, in (48), Lee names the Agent of selling and Mo names its Goal, these being two unrelated primitives of the semantics. But (49) isolates a commonality: both name terms in From and To relations (that is, the two are both Sources and Goals), just relative to two different events. Second, by allowing for conjunction of the primitive predicates, and also for multiple related events, the decomposition promises a larger number of possible relations that might be assigned to a dependent.[9]

In Chapters 10 and 11, I will touch on a third alternative to the traditional thematic analysis, related to Jackendoff's, which relies explicitly on "event structure" (Dowty 1979, Foley and Van Valin 1984, Van Valin and LaPolla 1997, Croft 1998, Rappaport Hovav and Levin 1998). In short, where the traditional analysis has (50a), this event-structural alternative has (50b).

(50)   a $\lambda x \lambda e_1 [\ \Theta(e_1, x)\ ]$
        b $\lambda x \lambda e_1 [\ \exists e_2 [\ \Theta^*(e_1, x)\ \&\ R(e_1, e_2)\ ]]$

DISCUSSION POINTS

1 Using the list of roles in (33–39), say what roles are assigned to each NP in (1).

(1)   a Arnold visited Willis.
       b Fletch chased Stanwyk from LA to Provo.
       c The spill deleted the files from my harddrive.
       d Jo dislikes Blair.
       e Tootie bothers Rudi.

2 How do Al likes arguments and Arguments please Al differ in meaning? How do the differences affect the plausibility of saying that Al binds different thematic relations in the two sentences?

3 How would you describe (2a) and (2b) in terms of thematic relations? Which noun phrases name agents? In answering, consider (3a) and (3b).

(2)   a   I fled the guard dogs.
       b   The guard dogs chased me.
(3)   a   I fled the scene of the crime.
       b # The scene of the crime chased me.

[9] With n primitive predicates, there are 2^n possible conjunctions of them (excluding negations). The number of relations grows even larger when, as in (49c), these predicates may express relations to different events; see Chapter 10.

4 If Mo bought Fido from Lee quietly with a credit card, it does not follow that Lee sold Fido to Mo quietly with a credit card (Landman 2000). Does this affect the argument against thematic relations given in Section 6.4.2? Why or why not?

5 Searle (1978:211ff.) observes that, in unusual circumstances, we might find it hard to judge whether it is true or false that *the cat is on the mat*. For example, is the cat on the mat if "each, cat and mat, [is] suspended on an intricate series of invisible wires so that the cat, though slightly in contact with the mat, exerts no pressure on it?" Likewise it may not be clear that Mo has obeyed Lee's order to cut the birthday cake if she runs over it with a lawnmower (Searle 1980). Do these observations affect the objection from Section 6.4.1 that general thematic relations, such as Agent, are illegitimate, because obscure? Why or why not?

6 Verb-specific thematic relations, such as Carrier and Carried, are in no way obscure. So are there any reasons *not* to use them, say in describing the meaning Navin carried the chair? To answer this, suppose first that we use them to describe the semantic value of carry, as in (4). What claims might we be making with this semantic decomposition of a lexical item? What does it mean to write "Carrier" and "Carried" separately here, in describing the semantic value of carry?

(4) $[\![\text{carry}]\!] = \lambda y \lambda x \lambda e [\text{ Carrier}(e, x) \ \& \ \text{Carried}(e, y)]$

Next suppose that we use them to describe the values of the subject and object relations, respectively, roughly as in (5). What will then happen when the verb is not carry, but cook? Is this a problem? Why or why not?

(5) a $[\![\ [_S \ \text{NP VP} \ ] \ ]\!] = \lambda e [\text{Carrier}(e, [\![\text{NP}]\!]) \ \& \ [\![\text{VP}]\!](e)]$
     b $[\![\ [_{VP} \ \text{V NP} \ ] \ ]\!] = \lambda e [\text{Carried}(e, [\![\text{NP}]\!]) \ \& \ [\![\text{V}]\!](e)]$

7 Compare the traditional thematic role labels to the system given by Wechsler, described in the text. Consider the examples in (46). Describe these first in the traditional terms, and then in Wechsler's. Explain how Wechsler's linking rules would apply here. Now consider (6) and (7).

(6) a Al poured salt into the soup.
     b Al filled the soup with salt.

(7) a Al gave the house a new coat of paint.
     b The house has a new coat of paint.

Say how Wechsler's linking theory would account for the relative positions of the arguments in (6). Does the theory need modification to explain the alternation? If so, provide it.

Turning to (7), do the house and a new coat of paint stand in the same relation to each other in (a–b)? Are these the ±Part relations described by Wechsler? If so, how might we generalize Wechsler's linking theory to account for the parallel pattern in (7)?

Suppose that in (7a) there is a secondary predicate with a subject and object that expresses the possession relation stated explicitly in (7b). This is one way to maintain Wechsler's rule (47c). What difficulties might adopting such an abstract theory of the grammatical relations pose for children acquiring their first language, who use syntactic position as a cue for thematic relations (Chapter 11)?

SUGGESTIONS FOR FURTHER READING

Davis 2011 is a brilliant synopsis of the vast literature on thematic relations. Besides this, one should read Fillmore 1968, Jackendoff 1987, Dowty 1989 and 1991, Parsons 1990 and Baker 1997 at least every other year. Delancey 1991 is a poignant retort to Dowty 1991. On the importance of thematic relations in the semantic analysis of plurality, read Schein 1993, 2002, Lasersohn 1995 and Landman 2000.

7 Agent and Patient

7.1 INTRODUCTION

This chapter concerns Agent and Patient (or Theme), the most popular thematic relations. Many linguists have not yielded to Dowty's (1991) polemic against highly general thematic relations. Some have instead been moved to conclude that, lest important generalizations be missed (Chapter 6), there must be at least two core relations – call them Agent and Patient – that are extraordinarily general (Van Valin and Wilkins 1996, Baker 1997). This dialectic leaves us with many questions. Here I review just a few in some detail. Section 7.2 investigates the putative generality of Agent with a study of instrumental subjects; this includes some discussion of relations between agency and causation. Section 7.3 discusses problems with Patient in the context of changes and non-changes, and finishes with a note on telicity.

7.2 AGENTS

7.2.1 Agents and actors

Typically in sentences that describe nonstative events, the subject names a participant that is conceived, relative to the description of the event provided by the verb, as directly involved in bringing it about. Sentences (1–5) provide examples.

(1) Floyd described the glass.
(2) Floyd collected the glass.
(3) Floyd melted the glass.
(4) The heat melted the glass.
(5) The oxyacetylene torch melted the glass.

Despite disagreements in jargon, the term "agent" is an appropriate rubric for such relations, since in ordinary usage it has very broad application. We speak of antimicrobial agents, thickening agents, FBI agents, agents of change, agents of disease, and agents of the Czar, in addition to moral agents, intentional agents, and agents of collecting, melting or carrying. Many linguists prefer less mundane names for the broad category comprising (most or all of) these roles, such as "Effector" (Van Valin and Wilkins 1996), "Originator" (Borer 2005) or "Initiator" (Ramchand 2008).

Under this heading there is an assortment of cases. In (1–3) the subject names an individual capable of action: Floyd, the hero of Fodor (1970). In addition, these sentences can be used to say that Floyd performed an *act*, an event that stems from the will or is "intentional under some description" (Davidson 1971). Often the term "agent" is reserved exclusively for cases like these. I find it more clear to say that the agent here is furthermore an **actor**, employing a term whose usage is less diffuse. An actor is the performer of an act, and acts, whatever they are, cannot be performed by things like heat or wind, stones or torches. The categories of Actor and Act have a deep role in our thinking. Philosophers are accordingly interested in when something counts as an actor (Anscombe 1957, Davidson 1971, Thalberg 1972, Thomson 1977, Ginet 1990), and psychologists in when we perceive something as an actor (Leslie 1994, Gergely *et al.* 1995, Gao and Scholl 2011, Beier and Spelke 2012).

This does not settle the semantics, however. Floyd is capable of acts but the heat is not: it does not follow that Floyd and the heat instantiate different semantic relations in the meanings of (3) and (4). Even when (3) is used to talk about a melting that Floyd instigates deliberately, its subject may still be interpreted by exactly the same relation as that of (4), as claimed in (6).

(6) a Floyd melted the glass ≅ ∃e[. . . Θ(. . .)(Floyd)(e)]
     b The heat melted the glass ≅ ∃e[. . . Θ(. . .)(the heat)(e)]

I will assume without argument that (6) is correct. As for Θ, this might be as specific as Melter, or as general as Agent. I will suppose the latter for concreteness.

What I do want to discuss are sentences like (5): The oxyacetylene torch melted the glass. To me this seems the more difficult case, and what we learn from it can be applied to simpler cases such as (4). In using (5) we are most likely talking about an event in which the torch is wielded as an instrument, with no hint that the torch is by itself responsible for melting the glass. And now our question is more interesting. When this is what the speaker means, does the oxyacetylene torch nevertheless instantiate the same thematic relation in the meaning of (5) as Floyd does in (3), as claimed in (7)?

(7) a Floyd melted the glass $\cong \exists e[\ldots \Theta(\ldots)(Floyd)(e)]$
   b The oxyacetylene torch melted the glass $\cong \exists e[\ldots \Theta(\ldots)(the torch)(e)]$

We will explore both possible answers in Sections 7.2.3–7.2.5. Before that it will help to comment on the relation between agents and causation.

7.2.2 Agents and direct causation

When do we count an object *x* as satisfying Agent in relation to an event *e* described by verb V? This question is particularly difficult if Agent is not defined in terms of acts and intentions.

One partial answer is that Agent(e, x) holds only if *x* participates in some other event e^* that *causes* the event *e* of the verb (Davidson 1967a, Thomson 1977, Dowty 1979, Pietroski 2000, Wolff 2003, among countless others). This is reasonable, since (8a) entails (8b).

(8) a   Floyd melted the glass.
   b ⊨ Events involving Floyd caused the glass to melt.

But it is also insufficient, since the converse inference, (9), is invalid (Hall 1965, Fodor 1970, Jackendoff 1972, Morreall 1976, Shibatani 1976, McCawley 1978).

(9) a   Events involving Floyd caused the glass to melt.
   b ⊭ Floyd melted the glass.

There are many things Floyd can do that cause the glass to melt, but far fewer that permit us to say that he melted the glass. Nor does it help much to restrict the events involving Floyd to those in which he is an actor. If Floyd's enthusiastic frying of bacon causes a fire that melts the glass in his neighbor's apartment, one still cannot truly assert (9b) (Hart and Honoré 1959, Fodor 1970, Thomson 1977).

So what further factors do permit this? What lets us say that Floyd is a participant in that melting, and even its Agent? It is common to answer that the causal relation between the cause and effect must be somehow "**direct**" (Fodor 1970, Shibatani 1976, McCawley 1978, Delancey 1984, Bittner 1999, Wolff 2003), and this resonates with certain intuitions. But the notion of "directness," I think it is fair to say, has never been defined to anyone's satisfaction (Fodor and Lepore 1998, Pietroski 2005a:185ff.). Were the matter settled, we would spend much less time arguing about whether a corporation that has caused many deaths has furthermore killed many people.

We can point to some things that do interrupt directness. Here is an example adapted from Thomson (1977). Floyd hits a button that spreads a reactive cleansing powder all over his kitchen floor: this may be enough to say truly that Floyd cleaned the floor. We can say also say this if he spreads a mass of small insects that eat kitchen filth and are then swept away – though here it also becomes possible to object that the bugs cleaned the floor, not Floyd. But if Floyd does no more than order his friend Kermit to spread the powder, or the bugs, we would not agree that Floyd has cleaned the floor – unless Kermit is in some way his proxy, perhaps an employee. The difference seems to be in the intervention of a potentially intentional actor. Kermit is a possible actor, the soap is not, and the bugs are somewhere in between. Evidently this matters a great deal to the use of verbs describing causal processes (Thomson 1977, Ginet 1990, Wolff 2003). But this insight does not amount to a definition of causal directness. There is much more work to be done, since some wildly indirect relations between Floyd's acts and the clean floor will let us say that Floyd cleaned the floor, and some perfectly direct relations will not.[1] As Pietroski (2005a:184) writes, in asking what the "right way" might be for one event to cause another, so as to allow for description using a transitive 'causal' verb: "What counts as a right way is presumably a vague, context-sensitive, and verb-sensitive matter [even if it] is entrenched in both common sense and common law." Without any explication of directness, entailments like (8) do little to inform our explication of the Agent relation. Should this cause despair? In the spirit of Waismann (1945), Searle (1978:211) observes that we find it hard to say exactly when we would judge it true that a cat is *on* a mat. Why expect more from Agent than from on?

In any case, as we will see in Chapter 10, there are good reasons to think that the meaning (in the narrow sense) of sentences with so-called 'causal verbs' does not involve a relation of causation.

7.2.3 Instrumental subjects

Sometimes the subject of a clause refers to the de facto instrument of its event. The sentences in (10) can be used to talk about exactly the same situations as those in (11), or also (12), and these are all situations in which the key or the knife were wielded. They need not be used to say that the key or the knife, fantastically, acted alone.

---

[1] We can say that Nora melted the candy by flicking a switch on an elaborate contraption that harnesses the power of sunlight and rivers, depends on the barking of nearby dogs to function, and takes days to do its job. Meanwhile, we would not say that the sunlight melted the candy if it started a brush fire near a cooler that contained it.

(10) a The blue key opened the back door.
     b The porcelain knife sliced the salami.
(11) a Bo used the blue key to open the back door.
     b Al used the porcelain knife to slice the salami.
(12) a Bo opened the back door with the blue key.
     b Al sliced the salami with the porcelain knife.

Let us therefore say that sentences like (10), when used to talk about the wielded instrument of an action, have **instrumental subjects**, not committing thereby to any claim about their meaning. Sentences with the same verbs are otherwise understood to have *noninstrumental subjects*, as in (11) or (12).

Instrumental subjects are not always acceptable, as we will see below. Their acceptability also varies by language; many languages are not as permissive as English, for example. To get a sense for when they are acceptable in English, it helps to see that they have at least two common uses, which I call **success** uses and **result** uses. Take (10b). On the success use of this sentence, the speaker means to convey that the porcelain knife contributed importantly to success in slicing the salami, which might not have been easy to slice with some other relevant knives. In contrast on the result use of (10b), the speaker means to convey that the slicing had a noteworthy result on the knife. This is what would be intended in (13), for instance.

(13) The porcelain knife sliced the salami. So don't use it to cut the peaches.

Presumably the two uses do not constitute an ambiguity. They just reflect two probable reasons one might have for using a sentence with an instrumental subject. Other possible reasons might be implied by the surrounding context, as in (14). Here the point seems to be neither success nor result, but rather that the porcelain knife in particular made the process or result of slicing the salami more pleasing.

(14) I really liked how the porcelain knife sliced the salami.

That there are instrumental subjects in this sense is just an observation of fact. It leaves open more specific questions about meaning. In the meanings of the sentences in (10), do the subjects instantiate exactly the same relations as do their counterparts in (11) or in (12)?

Any answer must take account of four further facts. First, clauses with instrumental subjects are often somewhat awkward with instrumental PPs, as in (15).

(15) a ? The blue key opened the back door with a magnet in its shaft.
     b ? The porcelain knife sliced the salami only with the heel of its blade.

Second, like all active clauses, they reject agentive by phrases, as in (16).

(16)   a   * The blue key opened the back door by Bo.
       b   * The porcelain knife sliced the salami by Al.

Third, conjunct subjects are not easily interpreted as combining an instrument with an agent, as in (17). Notice that (17) is odd even if one intends it to be about two distinct events of cutting.

(17)   # Al and the porcelain knife cut the bread and the salami, respectively.

Fourth, what is acceptable as an instrumental with-PP may not be acceptable as an instrumental subject (Delancey 1984, Schlesinger 1989). Indeed, most likely it will not be. For example, the truth of the sentences in (18) does not itself make the sentences in (19) acceptable, reading the latter as having instrumental subjects. The sentences are acceptable only under a fantastical reading not at all suggested by (18).

(18)   a   Jo figured out the square root of 1369 with a slide rule. (Adapted from Schlesinger 1989:197)
       b   I changed the lightbulb with the ladder. (Schlesinger 1995:92)
       c   Mo played the banjo with his metal pick.
(19)   a   # Jo's slide rule figured out the square root of 1369.
       b   # The ladder changed the lightbulb.
       c   # Mo's metal pick played the banjo.

Semantic theories of instrumental subjects can be divided into two groups, **ambiguity theories** and **nonambiguity theories**. In ambiguity theories, the semantics assigns different relations to instrumental and noninstrumental subjects for the same verb. Thus the two ways of understanding a subject, as instrumental or as noninstrumental, correspond to two different derivations, differing in what relation the subject binds. The nonambiguity theories deny this: instrumental and noninstrumental subjects do not correspond to different derivations. Thus at the level of meaning (in the strict sense) there is no difference. The difference is outside the grammar, in the thoughts the sentences are used to communicate. I will discuss a classic version of the ambiguity theory, from Fillmore (1968), in Section 7.2.4, and then develop a nonambiguity theory in Section 7.2.5.

7.2.4 Ambiguity theories

According to Fillmore (1968), instrumental subjects instantiate the thematic relation of Instrument, the same relation expressed by instrumental with-PPs, while noninstrumental subjects instantiate Agent.

(20) a Al sliced the salami with the porcelain knife.

  b $\exists e[$ Agent(e, Al) & Slicing(e) & Patient$(e,$ the salami$)$
     & Instrument$(e,$ the knife$)$]

(21) a The porcelain knife sliced the salami.

  b $\exists e[$ Instrument$(e,$ the knife$)$ & Slicing(e) & Patient$(e,$ the salami$)$]

This proposal offers a satisfactory explanation for three of our four facts. The first fact was illustrated by (15), which showed that instrumental subjects may exclude certain instrumental with-PPs. For Fillmore this is explained by assuming that the same relation is never assigned to two distinct dependents; see Chapter 8. Second, (16) showed that instrumental subjects cannot co-occur with agentive by phrases. This is explained by assuming that by phrases express the Agent relation, and by stipulating that, in an active clause, any dependent so interpreted must surface as the subject. Third, (17) showed that a conjunct subject cannot mix an instrument with an agent. Suppose that the Instrument relation is in general not true of an action's agent, while the Agent relation is in general not true of an action's instrument. Then a mixed conjunction will always lead to falsity, and perhaps for some reason this is infelicitous.

The fourth fact is a clear problem, however: why are the sentences in (19) unacceptable, when those in (18) are fine? I repeat one pair of these examples here.

(18) a Jo figured out the square root of 1369 with a slide rule.

(19) a # Jo's slide rule figured out the square root of 1369.

In Fillmore's view, (18) shows that the slide rule, ladder and pick satisfy Instrument in relation to the events figuring out, changing and playing. He also assumes that this same relation can interpret the (surface) subject of a clause. But then, since the sentences in (19) are bad, there must be an additional condition, besides satisfaction of the Instrument relation, on when an Instrument can surface in the subject. If this condition were to follow from entirely general properties of subjecthood – for instance, a tendency to refer to the discourse topic – we could still say that Fillmore's position is fully explanatory.[2] But to me it does not seem that it does.

---

[2] By way of contrast, the pragmatics of subjecthood might somehow explain why (1a) below is strange when (1b) is not.

(1) a # Chairman Mao looks like my husband.

  b My husband looks like Chairman Mao.

7.2.5 Nonambiguity theories

A nonambiguity theory denies that, in deriving the meaning of the clause, instrumental and noninstrumental subjects bind different relations. For concreteness let us say that they both bind the general relation of Agent, as in (22) and (23).

(22)   a   Al sliced the salami with the porcelain knife.
       b $\cong$ $\exists e$[Agent(e, Al) & Slicing(e) & Patient(e, the salami)
             & Instrument(e, the knife)]

(23)   a   The porcelain knife sliced the salami.
       b $\cong$ $\exists e$[Agent(e, the knife) & Slicing(e) & Patient(e, the salami)]

The contrast between (18) and (19) – for instance, the contrast between changing a lightbulb with a ladder and a ladder changing a lightbulb – now comes as no surprise. We have no reason to expect that an instrumental with-PP will make for an acceptable instrumental subject, since the two dependents are interpreted by distinct relations. Instead we expect only that an instrumental subject will be acceptable when we can use Agent to talk about its referent. More precisely, an instrumental subject S will be acceptable with verb V just when the referent of S, besides being the instrument in some event e_1 of V'ing, can *also* be regarded as satisfying Agent in relation to an event e_2 of V'ing. The two events of V'ing, e_1 and e_2, may not be identical, but they must both be closely related, at least overlapping in space and time.

From this perspective, the acceptability conditions of instrumental subjects are a subcase of the more general issue discussed above in Section 7.2.2: when can we use Agent to talk about x in relation to an event e described by verb V? Here we just add the wrinkle that – as a matter of fact but not meaning – x also satisfies Instrument in relation to a related V'ing. If Al sliced the salami with the porcelain knife, what further factors let us talk about this same chunk of history using a sentence which says that the knife was an agent? Here we might have intuitions about causal relevance: somehow the knife seems causally more relevant to the cutting than does the slide rule to the calculation. But we can't have much confidence that 'relevance' will receive a satisfactory explication, any more than 'directness.'

We can say truly that the farmer plowed the field, even when he did it by driving his mules, (24a). But then it also seems true that the mules plowed the field, (24b). And to me it seems wrong to insist that this sentence, (24b), used to describe the very same chunk of history, has an instrumental subject.

(24) a The farmer plowed the field by driving his mules.
      b The mules plowed the field.

The mules need not be seen merely as instruments, even if they were under the farmer's very firm control; consult Thomson (1977). Both they and the farmer were involved directly and importantly enough in what happened for them to count as plowers in what went on. This may compel us to say that there were two distinct 'events,' both called plowings, one by the farmer and one by his mules. But so be it.

Now return to Al and his porcelain knife. How different is this from the farmer and his mules? The knife is not a possible actor, but then a farmer may handle his mules with as much control as a child does a knife. So does the mere capacity to perform acts require a difference in semantics? For the nonambiguity theorist the answer must be No – and this is at least plausible, since the empirical motives for requiring a capacity for acts are in any case unclear: witness (25).

(25) a Al dulled his knife cutting the bone.
      b The bone dulled Al's knife.

The same history may verify both sentences, and yet there is no question at all of calling the bone an instrument. But neither is the bone an actor, or a natural force envisioned as one, like the erosive flow of a river. The bone simply resists the action of the chef who cuts it. Being the agent of a change does not even require being an agent in the event that brings it about. And, given this, it is hard to deny on conceptual grounds alone that Al's knife might satisfy Agent in our examples.

So let us grant that there is a case to be made for the main claim of the nonambiguity theorist: instrumental and noninstrumental subjects of the same verb instantiate the same semantic relation. Still, even then, this theorist cannot stop after saying that Agent is a very *general* predicate, expressing a single concept that may be satisfied either by instruments or by actors. This would leave no answer for the challenge of conjunct arguments in (17), repeated here.

(17) # Al and the porcelain knife cut the bread and the salami, respectively.

General predicates do not cause this sort of oddity. There is nothing odd about (26), for example. There are many different ways of being a teacher, but they all fall under the single general concept of 'being a teacher.'

(26) Mo and Al are both teachers. Mo teaches pottery to senior citizens every third Saturday of the month, and Al teaches Uyghur to spies.

Ambiguity, in contrast, is always resolved uniformly over conjuncts (Zwicky and Sadock 1975, Gillon 2004). Thus the ambiguous pens must be interpreted the same way with respect to both conjuncts in the subject of (27).

(27) # What I have in my hand and what I have in my yard are both pens.

The ambiguity theorist has a ready explanation for (17): it is just like (27), since the subject relation is ambiguous. But the nonambiguity theorist has a problem here.

In response he must insist that the oddity of 'mixing senses' is not always and only a sign of ambiguity. This is not crazy; there is also pressure to resolve polysemy uniformly. A common example of polysemy, as distinct from ambiguity, comes from names for political bodies. They can be used to talk either about the political body as such, (28a), or about its territory, (28b). Presumably there is just one word Kansas, since one can also say (28c), and anaphora does not preserve ambiguity. Yet (28d) is odder than any of (a–c). It is odd to use a single token of the word with the intent of conveying both its senses at once. Sentence (29) makes the analogous point with predicative uses of France. I don't know whether (29d) is true, but it doesn't strike me as odd in the way that (29c) does (Pietroski 2005b).

(28) a   Kansas is a democracy.
      b   Kansas is a rectangle.
      c   Kansas is a democracy, and it is a rectangle.
      d   ? Kansas is both a democracy and a rectangle.

(29) a   This hexagonal landmass is France.
      b   The republic once led by de Gaulle is France.
      c   ? This hexagonal landmass and the republic once led by de Gaulle are both France.
      d   Both the republic led by de Gaulle and the kingdom ruled by Louis XIV are France.

Lyons (1977:407) raises a similar issue with (30). The sentence suggests that John likes brunettes and marshmallows in the same way. This is not odd if we can think of one very general way of liking both, say for their color. But one tends to think of distinct and more specific modes of liking for each, namely sexual and gustatory. To that extent the sentence sounds odd.[3] But we should hesitate to say that "like" is therefore ambiguous, pronouncing two different words.

(30)   ? John likes brunettes and marshmallows.

So the nonambiguity theorist has some account of (17): perhaps (25) has a derivational part whose meaning we initially gloss as 'Agent', but which we can use to evoke distinct, though related, concepts, just as we do with Kansas or like. A sentence whose meaning we describe as 'Agent(e, x) & Slicing(e),' for example, can be used to express a wielded knife, or about the knife wielder. But this is not a sign of ambiguity. It shows only that the subject relation is in this sense polysemous; it is unambiguous and not general, yet can be used to express quite distinct concepts. This conception of polysemy demands clarification. But it has its proponents (including Searle 1980, Sperber and Wilson 1986, Bach 1994, Carston 2004, Cappelen and Lepore 2005a,b, and Pietroski, to appear b) who have developed it in a number of different ways, all of them reasonable.[4]

What remains are the challenges of (15) and (16), partly repeated here.

(15)   b   ? The porcelain knife sliced the salami only with the heel of its blade.
(16)   b   * The porcelain knife sliced the salami by Al.

Recall, Fillmore takes (15) to show that instrumental subjects have the same thematic relation as an instrumental with-PP. But it seems equally plausible that such sentences, in those cases where they are odd, are odd only to the degree that one uses them to say what obviously

---

[3] Cruse 1995 (who swaps brunettes for blondes) observes that (1) below lacks the oddity of (30). This indicates that likes in (1) is understood as 'likes in some way or other.' Each of the two adverbial adjuncts then specifies the mode of liking further. Such adjuncts are less easily added when the conjunct direct object, blondes and marshmallows, is clefted as in (2). The addition in (2b) changes the presupposition, besides being awkward. Sentence (2c) is of course ungrammatical. For this reason a cleft like (2a) is a more effective vehicle for the point Lyons makes.

(1)   John likes marshmallows for their taste and blondes for their beauty.
(2)   a   It is marshmallows and blondes that John particularly likes.
      b   It is marshmallows and blondes that John particularly likes (?for their taste and their beauty, respectively).
      c   It is marshmallows (*for their taste) and blondes (*for their beauty) that John particularly likes.

[4] On this view, when we hear The knife sliced the salami as magically personifying the knife, this is just another thought we can use the very same sentence to express.

cannot be true. If a certain with-phrase can be construed only as naming
a wielded instrument, it will to that extent be unacceptable with an
instrumental subject that is inanimate, since an inanimate object
cannot wield an instrument. But otherwise the sentence might be
used to say something sensible – for example, that a certain part of
the subject's referent, identified in the with-PP, was instrumentally
important to the achievement of the event. The examples in (15) are in
this latter category. They are only moderately unacceptable, and this
seems to be because the with-PPs here identify an 'instrument' that is
not wielded.[5]

As for (16), this is as straightforward as (15) is for Fillmore. If the subject is assigned the Agent role, the same role cannot also be associated
with any other dependent; consult Chapter 8. We might also say that
agentive by is syntactically illicit in active clauses, with Bruening (2012).

In sum, the argument between ambiguity and nonambiguity theories is a draw. The debate is nonetheless interesting, in exercising many
of the basic assumptions that form our theory of argument structure.

7.3 PATIENT AND THEME

Andrews (1985) characterizes the **Patient** and **Theme** relations as in (31).
This reflects the tradition that stems from Gruber (1965), source of the
term "theme."

(31) a Patient: A participant which the verb characterizes as having something
      happen to it, and as being affected by what happens to it. Examples: objects
      of kill, eat, smash, but not those of watch, hear, and love.
      b Theme: A participant which is characterized as changing its position or con-
      dition, or as being in a state or position. Examples: object of give, hand,
      subject of walk, die.

The two terms are often collapsed into one. Something "which is char-
acterized as changing its position or condition" is presumably "characterize[d] as having something happen to it, and as being affected

---

[5] Schlesinger (1989:197) gives another account of why sentences like (15) would be
false. He says that an inanimate object counts as an agent only if it effects the
action without mediation, and stating the involvement of an instrument implies
mediation. Yet this at least suggests that the sentences in (1) below would have to
be false, which does not seem right.

(1) a The wind broke the window when it blew a rock into it.
     b The sun melted the chocolate when it shone through the lens on the shelf.

by what happens to it." Moreover, in practice, verb meanings are not often described as entailing both a theme and a patient participant at once.[6] The complementarity suggests that there may be no important distinction, and a single relation is sufficient. Authors differ over which term to use for that relation, Patient or Theme. I prefer Patient, but will vacillate.

In this section I will discuss the traditional Patient relation in two parts: patients of nonchanges in Section 7.3.1, where I focus on the obscurity of the notion, and patients of changes in Section 7.3.2, where I discuss their distribution. I then mention a proposed connection between telicity and thematic relations in Section 7.3.3.

7.3.1 Patients of nonchanges

Putting aside changes, patients or themes are said to come in either of two varieties, which I call **Holder** and **Happenee** in (32).

(32) a Patient as Holder
      "A participant which is characterized [...] as being in a state."
      b Patient as Happenee
      "A participant which the verb characterizes as having something happen to it."

But there is a worry about these. Typically, when a linguist proposes a thematic relation, or any theoretical primitive, his colleagues demand that its content be explicated. But what can be said about the general content of Holder(e, x) or Happenee(e, x), absent any particular description of e?

If Mo is warm, talented and Canadian, she allegedly bears Holder to various states. It is easy to say something about what these states consist in: Mo has a certain legal relation to Canada, for instance. But what exactly is *common* to the relations she has to these various states? Nothing at all really, except that she 'holds' them, whatever that means. We could stipulate a definition: maybe a state is a triple $\langle i, q, t \rangle$ of an individual, a quality and a time, and Holder$(\langle i, q, t \rangle) \equiv i$ (Kim 1976). But that won't advance understanding. So there are two choices. We can accept that our theoretical terms cannot always be explicated, and continue to use Patient in its Holder sense. Or we can insist on explication. In that case Holder is out, and we must instead use only more specific thematic relations such as $\lambda x \lambda e[\text{Warm}(e, x)]$, $\lambda x \lambda e[\text{Talented}(e, x)]$,

---

[6] Exceptions include sentences like *Al loaded the truck with the furniture*, which are sometimes described as having the truck as Patient and the furniture as Theme (Anderson 1971, Jackendoff 1990b). See Chapter 11.

or $\lambda x \lambda e$[Canadian(e, x)]. It seems to me that Parsons (1990) takes the former approach, while Kratzer (2003) inclines towards the latter. These are among the problems that lead Dowty (1991) to reject general thematic relations altogether (Chapter 6).

How about Happenee? What is it to be "[a] participant which the verb characterizes as having something happen to it?" There are common intuitions about what all happenees share: they are viewed as playing a 'passive' role, as simply receiving the 'transmission of force' exerted in the event (Croft 2012). Nonetheless, it is also clear that what counts as the happenee – that is, as the patient of a nonstative event that is not a change – again depends exquisitely on the verb. Suppose that Mo steals Lee's necklace, and that *in so doing* she disrespects Lee. The same stretch of history then verifies both sentences in (33).

(33)   a Mo stole Lee's necklace.
        b Mo disrespected Lee.

Something happened to the necklace in the stealing, and to Lee in the disrespecting. But something also happened to Lee in the stealing: she got robbed! Maybe something also happened to her necklace in the disrespecting, since the disrespecting consists at least partly in the theft; at least initially, it is as reasonable to say that the disrespecting *is* the theft, as it is to say that Mo is both a teacher and a woman. Despite this, (34a,b) are false.

(34)   a Mo stole Lee.
        b Mo disrespected Lee's necklace.

Maybe these are false because in fact the theft and the disrespecting are not identical, but two different events (Parsons 1990, Delancey 1991, Landman 2000). That does not much change the point, however: it is hard or impossible to say what counts as the happenee except relative to a description provided by a verb. The challenge sharpens with (33c), below.

(33)   c Mo robbed Lee.

Sentences (33a) and (33c) do seem like two ways of talking about the very same event; the same theft is both a robbing and a stealing. But then it cannot be that (33c) describes Lee as the patient of that event, since then it should entail (34a), a wrong result.

We have three ways out, prefigured in Chapter 6. One, deny that any of the sentences in (33) are made true by the very same event – contrary to conservative intuitions. Two, make Patient a three-place relation between an individual, an event, and a (perspective modified by a) verb-meaning – something of a semantic extravagance. Three, deny the root of the problem: the direct objects in (33) are not all interpreted by Patient. This lowers the theoretical utility of the predicate. But this may not matter, if the cost of keeping it is too high: the extreme generality of Patient mandates specificity elsewhere, either in the identity criteria of events, or in the logical form of the predicate. Uncomfortable with either result, some theorists (Dowty 1991, Kratzer 2003) prefer to eliminate the relation. More specific thematic relations (perhaps as specific as StealingOf) would not invite the same problems. Seeking to contain the damage, Kratzer argues that this problem with Patient or Theme is not shared equally by Agent. She writes (Kratzer 2003:4): "Themes lack the conceptual independence of agents. Theme arguments seem to be tightly linked to their verbs. Agents are different. Actions seem to have agents independently of how we describe them." That there is a contrast is clear. But for a critique of Kratzer's particular argument, see Williams (2009), which insists that all the highly general thematic relations are to an important extent dependent on the verb.

7.3.2 Patients of changes

At least superficially, change has a simple analysis: something changes just in case it is in state *s* after not being in *s* (von Wright 1968).[7] So, if we allow that there are events of change, in addition to the states between which they transit, we can stipulate that the patient (or theme) of a change is the thing that enters the state with which it ends. Parsons (1990) gives the meaning postulate for Become in (35), and events in the first term of a Become relation are changes.

(35) The Theme of [Become's] event is the same as the Theme of its Target state: $Become(e, s) \rightarrow [Theme(e, x) \equiv Theme(s, x)]$. (Parsons 1990:119)

This aspect of the traditional Patient or Theme relation, unlike Holder and Happenee, does admit of explication.

Of course it is not possible that every entailed change coincides with Patient or Theme in the meaning. Eaters get (at least briefly) fuller, and jumpers change their position. And anyhow, the entailments of an expression, on their own, *never* decide its semantic structure. They don't themselves announce which of them is strictly analytic. So we have a descriptive challenge. Given a sentence that entails a change, when should we say that a Patient relation to that change is explicit in its meaning?

---

[7] At the same time, change is among the most ancient problems of metaphysics, since it is not clear what it means for 'the same thing' to persist through changes.

In the literature this question has a special focus due largely to unaccusativity. An unaccusative is an intransitive clause whose surface subject behaves in some way like the direct object of a transitive (Chapter 11). Intransitives expressing changes are the most likely to exhibit other signs of unaccusativity (Sorace 2000). This has suggested that, in these intransitives, the undergoer of the clausal event is named by a direct object in 'underlying syntax' (Hall 1965, Perlmutter 1978, Burzio 1981). It is widely presumed that a direct object is never associated with Agent, but is often associated with Patient. This encourages the idea that, in a clause whose event is a change, a dependent naming the undergoer of that change never binds any thematic relation but Patient. I will now illustrate the issue with (36).[8] This discussion will be technical, but brisk; tired readers may prefer to skip ahead.

(36)   Syl ran to the club.

Sentence (36) entails a change in Syl: first he was not at the club, and then he was. On these grounds we might give it a meaning like (37), where To(e, the club) describes a change of which Syl is the theme. The unnamed relation R is meant to relate the traversal of a path to its means of movement.

(37) $\exists e[$ Theme(e, Syl) & To(e, the club) & $\exists e'[$ R(e, e') & Running(e') ...]]

This finds some support in facts of Dutch. There the analogue of (36) shows formal signs of unaccusativity (Zaenen 1988, 1993, Verkuyl 1993, van Hout 1996), suggesting that the subject on the surface is an object underlyingly. And an underlying direct object, it is widely assumed, is never interpreted by Agent, consistent with (37).

But there is a problem. Runners are agents of running; in this discussion let us take this as given. Consonant with this, the Dutch analogue of (38) shows signs of unergativity, suggesting that the subject here is not an object underlyingly.[9] Consequently it seems best to give (38) a meaning like (39).

(38)   Syl ran.
(39) $\exists e[$ Agent(e, Syl) & Running(e)]

---

[8] This section draws on many sources, including Jackendoff 1990, Dowty 1991, Verkuyl 1993, Goldberg 1995, Levin and Rappaport Hovov 1995, van Hout 1996, Schein 2002 and Borer 2005.

[9] Specifically, the Dutch versions of 'run' and 'run to the club' take different auxiliaries in the Perfect. The former takes hebben while the latter takes zijn. See Chapter 11.

But then why does (36), Syl ran to the club, entail (38)? As it stands, meaning (37) does not have meaning (39) as a provable consequence. So how does being the theme of running-to-the-club make Syl the agent of a running? Relatedly, why does (40a) entail (40b), as I think it does, if the event of Syl running to the club is not one of Syl running? And why can't (41) have the meaning in the gloss, escaping contradiction?

(40) a   Syl ran to the club quickly and backwards.
      b ⊨ Syl ran quickly and backwards.

(41) * Syl slowly ran to the club quickly but circuitously.
        'Syl got to the club slowly by running quickly but circuitously.'

There are three sorts of answer, abstracting from the compositional derivation. The first proposes a meaning like (42). From this, (39) follows analytically, by Conjunction Elimination. The apparent contradiction in (41) is also explained directly, if the same event cannot be quick and slow at once.

(42) $\exists e[$ Agent(e, Syl) & Running(e) & To$(e, \text{the club})$]

This is elegant. But it also implies that Dutch has been misanalyzed – the putative signs of unaccusativity in Dutch analogues of (36) must not show that the subject is an underlying object – and this is contentious. See Borer (2005) in opposition.

The two other sorts of answer hold fast to the analysis of Dutch, and to a Theme relation for Syl. They differ in what they add to (37). One adds explicitly that Syl is the agent of running, as in (43), filling in the earlier ellipsis. Now the entailment from (37) to (39) is provable again, a strict analyticity.

(43) $\exists e[$ Theme(e, Syl) & To$(e, \text{the club})$
        & $\exists e'[$ R(e, e') & Running(e') & Agent(e, Syl)]]

How does Syl, the subject of (36), come to bind two thematic relations in the meaning, both Theme and Agent? The answer will bear on many important issues.[10] But even with a satisfactory derivation of this, we

---

[10] Two representative options are sketched in (1) and (2) below.

(1) [Syl$_k$ [THEME [[ϵ_k run] [to the club]]]]

(2) [Syl [THEME [run [to the club]]]]

In (1), run has a local dependent, the empty category ϵ_k, which instantiates Agent relative to the running. This is in turn bound by the overt noun phrase Syl, whether by movement or local anaphora. In (2), on the other hand, there is no noun phrase argument specifically for the agent of running. Rather, we assume

would need still to explain the adverb facts in (40) and (41). If an event of running to the club is quick and backwards, why must the running also be so? Here we need to resort to a meaning postulate, concerning the relation R which relates the running to the traversal of the path.

The final option foreswears the challenges of assigning both Theme and Agent, adds nothing to (37), and is content with (44), where Syl binds no relation to the running at all.

(44)   ∃e[Theme(e, Syl) & To(e, the club) & ∃e′[R(e, e′) & Running(e′)]]

But now none of the entailments are formally provable. They must all be underwritten by postulate. The postulate in (45) gives one way of getting from (44) to (39) with a postulate about R. We'll need others for the adverb entailments in (40) and (41).

(45)   Necessarily, if R(e, e′) and Theme(e, x), then Agent(e′, x).

No postulates would be needed if R were just the identity relation. But this would imply that a runner can be either the agent or the theme of a running, just because he might run somewhere. This is unattractive (Dowty 1991), and contrary to our working assumption.

In sum, while 'patient of change' is an unobjectionable relation conceptually, there are difficulties in deciding where to deploy it.

7.3.3 Telicity and thematic relations

A change ends when its patient achieves its constitutive end state. Changes are among the sorts of events described by **telic sentences**. Whether a sentence is telic is often influenced by semantic properties of its direct object. Influentially, Krifka (1989, 1992) argued that this effect is mediated by a certain kind of thematic relation. The theory of telicity has therefore had some influence on the understanding of Patient or Theme. Here I briefly unpack this story, and indicate some problems.

A sentence is **telic** (Garey 1957) when it describes its event as having a particular point of completion, hence a non-arbitrary duration. As described by (46a), for example, Greg's drawing is complete when it has effected a complete circle.

---

that run has a functional semantic argument in this role, and it is inherited by run to the club, under Composition of the two predicates. This runner argument is then identified with that of THEME via a semantic operation that conjoins two-place relations, mapping f and g to λyλx[fxy & gxy]. Thus, where the first account relies on binding, the second relies on semantic 'inheritance' of arguments. This kind of choice has broad architectural consequences.

(46)   a Greg drew a circle.

Similarly, (46b) implies completion when all 500,000 visitors have seen the picture, (46c) (from Schein 2002) implies conclusion when the stated supply of concrete is exhausted, and (46d) implies completion when the cutlet is flat.

(46)   b 500,000 visitors saw this picture (in one afternoon).
     c Lefrak built condos out of 3,000 tons of concrete (in three months).
     d Al pounded the cutlet flat (in 10 seconds).

A standard diagnostic of telicity in English is the possibility of adding *in* X *time* to say that X time transpired from the start of the event to its conclusion. Only telic sentences allow this 'start-to-finish' interpretation for *in*-PPs. The sentences in (47) are *atelic*, in not implying a conclusion. As described by (47a) and (47d), for example, events of drawing circles or pounding the cutlet have no particular point of completion, and can continue indefinitely. Accordingly, these sentences do not accept *in* X *time* with a start-to-finish interpretation.

(47)   a Greg drew circles (*in 10 seconds).
     b Several visitors saw this picture (*in one afternoon).
     c Lefrak built condos out of concrete (*in three months).
     d Al pounded the cutlet (*in 10 seconds).

Now, telicity may depend on the meaning of a noun phrase dependent. Sentence (46a) is telic with the direct object *a circle*, but (47a) is atelic with *circles* in its place. We see the same shift from (46b) to (47b), and from (46c) to (47c). Krifka (1989, 1992) gives an account of this. He proposes that in cases like this the noun phrase binds a "gradual" thematic relation; this is *a thematic analysis of telicity*. A gradual relation ensures a correspondence between the part/whole structures of what it relates. If the relation between *draw* and *a circle* is gradual, the temporal parts of the drawing, and spatial parts of the circle, will correspond to one another. In particular, a complete circle will correspond to a complete drawing of one. In later work, this idea was importantly liberalized (Hay *et al.* 1999, Rothstein 2004, Wechsler 2005a). What matters may be, not the *spatial* parts of the NP, but some other scalar measure of it, decided by the predicate. Progress in pounding the cutlet flat, for example, is clearly measured, not by the total flatness of each bit of the cutlet, but by the whole cutlet's degree of flatness.

Krifka uses this "graduality" property to account for why *a circle* yields telicity in (46a), and *circles* yields atelicity in (47a). A proper part of a circle is not a circle, but among several circles there may still be circles. Given graduality, this mereological property is mirrored in the event: a proper part of drawing a circle will not be drawing a circle, but a proper part of drawing circles will sometimes be drawing of circles. And this sort of property, according to Krifka, contributes to explaining telicity.

Unfortunately, this cannot be what accounts for telicity in general, since telic sentences generally do not mandate the sort of incremental correspondence that Krifka discusses (Verkuyl 1993, Jackendoff 1996, Schein 2002, Rothstein 2004). The run-time of an event always moves forwards, but the relevant measure of its affected object may waver back and forth. It can be very frustrating to pound flat a highly elastic object, as its flatness both increases and then decreases cyclically, before the final victory. When one boils a beef tendon soft in exactly 5 hours, the first few hours will have the tendon getting harder, and yet those hours measure the time of boiling it soft. In these examples and countless others, the relation between the event and its participant is not in fact "gradual," and yet the sentence is nonetheless telic.

This does not eliminate the possibility that telicity is to be explained with some appeal to thematic relations (Tenny 1987, 1994, Borer 2005).[11] It just cannot be done by making these relations "gradual" (or, as in Krifka 1998, "incremental").

However, the examples in this section do raise a further challenge to any theory that would account for telicity via any one particular thematic relation, such as Patient or Theme. A noun phrase which impacts (a)telicity occurs as the direct object in (46a), as the subject in (46b), and as an oblique in (46c). It will not be easy to argue that the noun phrases in all these various positions bind the same thematic relation. I return to this point briefly in Chapter 11.

DISCUSSION POINTS

1 Is the subject of (1a) below interpreted as naming the agent of the swarming? How about in (1b)? Discuss this alternation in the terms of Dowty's Proto-Role theory. (See Chapter 11.)

(1) a Bees swarmed in the garden.
     b The garden swarmed with bees.

---

[11] For Borer 2005, the noun phrase that occasions telicity always binds a thematic relation she calls "subject-of-quantity," introduced by an interpretive rule. Borer characterizes this relation as "roughly subject-of-structured-change" (2005:72), which sounds like a version of the traditional patient-of-change relation.

2 As mentioned in this chapter, languages differ in whether or when they allow instrumental subjects. If you know a language other than English, compare it to English. When does it allow instrumental subjects? How should we think about this sort of cross-linguistic variation? How might children acquire this knowledge of when instrumental subjects are permitted? What kinds of errors would you expect them to make?

3 Discuss the judgments in (2) and (3). What do they show about the interpretation of subjects in transitive clauses that describe changes, and about *because* and *from*? (See Delancey 1984, Williams 2011.)

(2) Walt never smoked meth, but dealing it killed him.

    a ⊨ What killed Walt was meth.
    b ⊨ Walt died because of meth.
    c ⊨ Walt died from selling meth.
    d ⊭ Walt died from meth.

(3) Jesse blackened the pot by using dirty oil and cooking with fire.

    a ⊨ The fire / the oil / the fire and oil together blackened the pot.
    b ⊨ The pot blackened from the fire / the oil / the fire and the oil.
    c ⊨ The pot is black from the fire / the oil / the fire and the oil.
    d ⊭ The pot is black from Jesse.

4 Sentence (4) shows that the acceptability of in X time modifiers may depend on noun phrases in various positions, the direct object in (4a), or inside a PP in (4b) (Schein 2002). What would it take to argue that this is a surface effect, and that underlyingly the relevant dependent is always in the same syntactic position?

(4)   a Lefrak built *(the) condos in three months.
    b Lefrak built condos *(out of 3,000 tons of concrete) in three months.

5 We can use both (5a) and (5b) to talk about the same stretch of history. Plausibly, then, Lefrak build condos and Lefrak build the condos express predicates, LefrakBuildingCondos and Lefrak BuildingTheCondos, that can be true of the very same event. Let's say that they are in fact true of some one event, and give that event the name "Frak."

(5)   a Lefrak built condos for three months.
    b Lefrak built the condos in three months.

Now suppose that (5a) and (5b) have meanings with the form of (6a) and (6b), respectively. Then by assumption (7a) is true. This in turn has (7b) as a syntactic consequence. But wouldn't this be the meaning of the unacceptable (7b)? If so, why is this sentence acceptable? If not, why not?

(6) a   ∃e[LefrakBuildingCondos(e) & ForThreeMonths(e)]
     b   ∃e[LefrakBuildingTheCondos(e) & InThreeMonths(e)]

(7) a   LefrakBuildingCondos(Frak) & ForThreeMonths(Frak)
          & LefrakBuildingTheCondos(Frak) & InThreeMonths(Frak)]
     b ⊢ ∃e[LefrakBuildingTheCondos(e) & ForThreeMonths(e)
          & InThreeMonths(e)]

(8) # Lefrak built the condos for three months in three months.

6 Sentence (9a) implies (9b) (Williams 2009). Kratzer (2003) observes that (10a) does not imply (10b). What does this show us about the semantic relations bound by the direct objects in these sentences? How do they depend on the event description expressed by the verb? There seems to be a contrast between the objects and the subjects. Describe that contrast.

(9) a   Al wrote poems, and Bill drew pictures, jointly creating a book.
     b ⊨ Al and Bill created poems and pictures.

(10) a   Al dug a hole, and Bill stuck a bush in it, jointly planting a bush.
     b ⊭ Al and Bill planted a hole and flower.

7 Choose any predicate of English: man, chair, cat, apex, cut, drive, swim, touched the ceiling, fetched Paul Pietroski, on the mat, from the forest, American, transparent, poisonous, yellow – what have you. Do you think you could specify, for any conceivable circumstance, whether or not the predicate applies truly? If not, is there some information that would settle the matter? Are the challenges limited to vagueness, of the sort exhibited by tall?

Now ask the same question for harden the glass or plant the bush. Does any of this affect your view of whether we should use predicates like Agent or Patient in linguistic theory? Why or why not?

SUGGESTIONS FOR FURTHER READING

For a clear head on agency and actors, read Thomson 1977. Pietroski 2000 carries many of Thomson's thoughts into a linguistic context. Cruse 1973, Delancey 1984 and Van Valin and Wilkins 1996 illuminate many subtleties in the linguistic expression of agency and causation. Pylkkä-nen 2002 showed that agency and causation are separate even in the grammar. Kratzer 2003 is the rare, clear proposal about why (what we call) patients are special. Tenny 1994 and Borer 2005 underscore connections between patienthood and telicity, of the sort formalized in Krifka 1989.

8 Role iteration

8.1 INTRODUCTION

This chapter is about the observation in (1): in general, the semantic relation associated with one dependent cannot be repeated by another.

(1) Role Iteration Generalization (RIG)
Generally or always, two distinct dependents do not bind the exact same type of semantic relation.

Sentence (2a) reports some smacking, and what gets smacked there is the wall. That relation, of being what is smacked in this smacking, cannot be associated with a hypothetical second object, as in (2b). Were the smacking to be of several things, this would have to be conveyed via plurality or conjunction within a single dependent, as in (2c).

(2) a Nik smacked the wall.
    b * Nik smacked the wall the floor.
    c Nik smacked the wall and the floor.

I will sketch the broader pattern shortly, and also note some challenges. But my focus will be on how to explain the RIG, which I do believe to be fundamentally correct. What makes it impossible to assign the same relation-type twice? Is it the rules of building linguistic structure? Are dependents labeled with formal tags of their semantic roles, syntactic features like AGT and PAT, so that we can prevent the derivation of expressions which repeat a role label? Or, instead, are the meanings that would result in the general case incoherent? If they were, this might explain why languages don't have structures that violate RIG, without our needing Syntax to police against derivations that duplicate features. In short, is the pattern 'purely grammatical,' or is it at least partly semantic?

Historically, the purely grammatical response has been more common. Versions of it were influentially pursued (or at least implied) in Fillmore (1968), Bresnan (1980), Chomsky (1981) and elsewhere.

Chomsky's (1981) Theta Criterion is perhaps the principle most often invoked in this context (if often inappropriately). But there are good reasons, I believe, to prefer the partly semantic account of the pattern, exploiting what I will call *Role Exhaustion*. In this chapter I explain my preference.

I first define Role Exhaustion and describe its advantages over any purely grammatical account of the RIG (Section 8.2). I then discuss the relation between Role Exhaustion and event individuation (Section 8.3). The next two sections (8.4–8.5), both quite technical, confront two (of several) apparent challenges: temporal or locative adjuncts, (3), and comitative adjuncts, (4).

(3)   Al cooked sausages in Berlin at his apartment on Tuesday at 6.00 a.m.

(4)   Tony lifted the amp with Geezer.

Lastly I review two other principles that are meant in part to account for some of the RIG data: Chomsky's (1981) Theta Criterion (Section 8.6), and Heim and Kratzer's (1998) Principle of Interpretability (Section 8.7).

In the remainder of this introduction I will quickly fill out the data pattern. Let us return to Nik smacking the wall, (2). The lesson of (2b) is not just that *smack* abhors ditransitives, but something more general. Languages seem never to associate the same type of semantic relation with two distinct dependents. Thus, while it is possible for *yell* to inhabit a transitive clause, as in (5b), the subject and object will not both name yellers: (5c) can't mean (5d).

(5)   a   Lee yelled.
      b   Lee yelled slogans.
      c * Lee yelled Mo.
      d   Lee and Mo yelled.

Such facts have been familiar at least since Fillmore (1968). But the breadth of the pattern is often overlooked: it encompasses not only arguments but also adjuncts (Grimshaw 1990:148). With just a few possible exceptions, no pair of dependents, arguments or adjuncts, can share the same relation to the same event. Thus an argument cannot have its relation repeated by an adjunct, at least not in general. As shown in (6), for example, no adjunct can be added to (2a) to repeat the patient relation, with the meaning 'Nik smacked the wall and the floor.'

(6)   * Nik smacked the wall { at / of / to / for / with } the floor.
        'Nik smacked the wall and the floor.'

Neither can two adjuncts share the same relation, not in general. Grimshaw (1990:148) gives the example in (7), which is bad if meant to simply repeat the comitative role signaled by with.

(7)   * Pete destroyed the city with Joe with Sue.
       'Pete destroyed the city with Joe and with Sue.'

Further examples are given in (8–10). Sentence (8) says that the instrument of Al's cooking is a blowtorch, and its benefactor is Al's wife. And now, as (9) and (10) show, no adjuncts can state the same exact relations to distinct individuals. These sentences cannot mean what the glosses do. Of course the glosses themselves are fine sentences, but now we have conjuncts: with a blowtorch *and* a steamer, for his wife *and* his son.

(8)   Al cooked this for his wife with a blowtorch.

(9)   * Al cooked this with a blowtorch with a steamer.
        'Al cooked this with a blowtorch and (with) a steamer.'

(10)   * Al cooked this for his wife for his son.
        'Al cooked this for his wife and (for) his son.'

These facts match the contrast between (2b) and (2c), motivating the breadth of the RIG in (1), and making one thing clear at the outset. Whatever explains the RIG cannot be a restriction just on arguments, since the pattern governs adjuncts as well.

8.2   ROLE EXHAUSTION

There are good reasons to view the RIG as (in part) expressing what I will call **Role Exhaustion**, or sometimes just **Exhaustion**. I give a working statement in (11), aiming to generalize over variants in the literature.

(11)   Role Exhaustion
       When a dependent is assigned a relation to some (group of) event(s), it identifies *all and only* the individuals in that relation to that (those) event(s).

Role Exhaustion as a semantic principle was first discussed directly in Carlson (1984), who named it "Thematic Uniqueness," a term carried on in Kratzer (2003). It has also been discussed under several other names, including "Uniqueness of Role Bearer" (Dowty 1989), "Uniqueness of Objects" (Krifka 1992), the "Unique Role Requirement" (Landman 2000) and "Exhaustivity" (Schein 1993).

Let us work through this with example (2a), repeated as (12a). Here the direct object binds some relation R to a smacking; and whatever R is exactly, bearing R to a smacking entails getting smacked. Given Exhaustion, (12a) now requires that (12b) be true.

(12) a Nik smacked the wall.
    b There was smacking, and in it only the wall was smacked, and only Nik was
       a smacker.

Given this, it would be inconsistent to add that anything else, say the table, was smacked in the very same smacking. Were (13a) to assign R, the role assigned to the wall in (12a), to both of its objects, it would entail (13b), and this is inconsistent.

(13) a * Nik smacked the wall the floor.
    b There was smacking, and in it only the wall was smacked, only the floor
       was smacked, and only Nik was a smacker.

In (14a) the direct object is the wall and the floor. So here the wall and the floor must be the only things smacked in the reported smacking, as stated in (14b).

(14) a Nik smacked the wall and the floor.
    b There was smacking, and in it only the wall and the floor were smacked,
       and only Nik was a smacker.

On pain of inconsistency, we cannot say elsewhere that the very same smacking also involved the chair, for example, even if we were to do so *in a separate clause*.

Thus Role Exhaustion does not police against role repetition in the derivation. It neither governs how a verb takes its arguments (Bresnan 1980, Chomsky 1981), nor explicitly mandates that each dependent in a clause bind a different thematic relation (Fillmore 1968). It is a semantic principle, governing how any dependent is interpreted. For this reason it explains two further facts that a purely grammatical account cannot.

First, if the RIG expressed rules of sentence structure, its domain would be structurally bounded. But it isn't (Carlson 1984, Dowty 1989), as shown by (15).

(15) Kay killed Mo. Lee also killed Mo.

Saying (15), we cannot mean just that Kay and Lee killed Mo together, in the same event of killing.[1] But why? Not because of any clause-bounded constraint against assigning the same relation twice, since here we have two separate clauses. But there is an answer in Role Exhaustion. The

---

[1] Of course, (15) can be used to *correct* the statement that Kay killed Mo; or to call attention, metalinguistically, to the vagueness of agency; or to report two separate killings, interrupted by resurrection. It just can't be used to say, simply, that Kay and Lee killed Mo in the same killing.

first clause requires that Kay was the *only* killer in some event of killing Mo, and the second requires the same about Lee. But this is inconsistent if there was only one killing.

Example (16) pushes the same point further (Dowty 1989). This sentence cannot mean just that Kay and Lee attacked Mo together, with by Lee doubling the role of by Kay. It could only be used to discuss a situation where Lee acts on behalf of Kay, say as a lieutenant who is under Kay's command.

(16)   * The attack on Mo by Kay was made in part by Lee.
       'The attack on Mo was made by Kay and also Lee.'

But why? The two phrases, by Lee and by Kay, are not dependents of the same predicate. The latter is even embedded within the subject of the clause, the attack on Mo by Kay. Blocking their co-occurrence using principles of clause structure would require a derivational dependency between (i) an adjunct within the subject and (ii) an adjunct within the predicate. But on general grounds this is implausible. Furthermore, if the constraint were grammatical, it would presumably rule out (16) and (17) equally. Yet this seems wrong, since (17) immediately sounds better than (16), evidently because it is clear that the Germans include the Berliners.

(17)   The 1917 attack on Champagne by the Germans was made in part by Berliners.

Role Exhaustion again provides an account. We can say that (16) is derivable but inconsistent, unless we regard Kay as representing a broader group. In (17), on the other hand, there is no sense of contradiction, since even an attack that is wholly by Germans, we know, can be made in part by Berliners.

Second, Role Exhaustion also explains why (18) does not entail (19) (Schein 1993), something not at all addressed by a grammatical ban on role iteration.

(18)   Tony and Geezer lifted the amp and the organ.
(19)   ⊭ Tony lifted the amp.

For *reductio*, suppose that (19) meant merely that there was some lifting with Tony among the lifters and the amp among the lifted. Then (18) would be enough to make it true, since it reports some lifting that involves Tony and the amp, among others. But this is wrong. Sentence (18) doesn't even require that Tony ever touched the amp. So our supposition is wrong: (19) does *not* just say that Tony and the amp were among the lifters and the lifted in a lifting. It says more. Arguably it says there is a lifting in which Tony is the only lifter and the amp the only thing lifted, as required by Role Exhaustion. Sentence (18), meanwhile, requires that there was lifting whose lifters were just Tony and Geezer, and whose lifted were just the amp and the organ.

Of course, attribution of agency is always a delicate matter. We say that the farmer plowed his field, though he needed ten mules to do so. Likewise, under some circumstances, we might give Tony credit for lifting the amp even when he had several helpers. But surely we should not want that, under any circumstances whatsoever, (18) *entails* (19) as a matter of natural logic. Therefore we need Role Exhaustion independently of the RIG, just to explain why sentences with a plural dependent A don't always entail otherwise identical sentences where the same dependent names just a part of ⟦A⟧. Explaining the RIG comes at no extra cost, theoretically.

Role Exhaustion thus has two advantages over a purely grammatical restriction on role repetition. It covers more facts, such as those in (15) and (16); and it provides a deeper explanation, since some of the facts it covers, those in the family of (19), have nothing to do with role iteration. It is unclear whether any further, purely structural constraint is needed. We might make do just with Exhaustion plus the brute facts of a predicate's syntactic category. The verb smack has a category feature in virtue of which it occupies transitive clauses. This kind of syntactic stipulation is inevitable, regardless of how one explains the RIG.

If we now ask why there is not also a ditransitive structure with smack in it (or a ditransitive verb smack) that repeats Smackee role, we can float a nongrammatical answer. Given Exhaustion, this construction could, in the general case, only be used to state contradictions. It could only be used consistently when what it says is (partly or wholly) redundant, as in Nik smacked the table the table. And languages, we can reasonably conjecture, do not bother with such useless constructions.

Turning to technical matters, the most common way to implement Role Exhaustion (Krifka 1992, Landman 2000, Kratzer 2003) is by stipulating that thematic relations are *functions* from events to individuals. Thus any event bears a certain thematic relation to no more than one individual. Ancillary to this implementation is the assumption that plural noun phrases, whether simple or coordinate, stand for a single corporate individual comprising other individuals as parts (Link 1983). So when one uses (14a), one says that Nik smacked a single individual which has the wall and the floor as parts. There are other possible implementations (Schein 1993), sometimes with important differences. But I will not engage this issue here.

8.3 ROLE EXHAUSTION AND EVENTS

Carlson (1984, 1998) observes that Role Exhaustion is related to intuitions about event identity. Often enough, its consequences jibe with thoughts about when two descriptions can apply to a single event, or when they must apply to two.

If Lee stole a book and Lee stole a necklace, then we seem to have two events of stealing, one of the book and the other of the necklace – or also a third, comprising the first two put together. This suggests that stealings are individuated in part by what is stolen. If two distinct things are stolen, then there are at least two stealings. Events also seem to be distinguished by location.[2] If Lee stole something in Dresden and Lee stole something in Leipzig, there must again be two stealings.

Yet, importantly, not every relation to an event is like this. Stealings are not individuated by what they are *near*, for example. If Lee stole something near Dresden and near Leipzig, there may still be just one stealing, perhaps in Chemnitz, which is both near Dresden and near Leipzig.

Several philosophical proposals develop thoughts such as these. Kim (1976) defines events as "exemplifications by substances of properties at a time," where "substances" are "things like tables, chairs, ... bits of stuff like water and bronze, and the like." So if a property is exemplified at two separate times or by two individuals, there are two distinct events. Similarly Taylor (1985) defines events as a time, a verb sense, and a list of individuals, these last instantiating a distinguished set of participant roles. So again, if an event description gives two distinct times, or two distinct lists of participants, it describes two distinct events.

Thus Role Exhaustion may be motivated in part by our thoughts about event identity, or perhaps it partly explains them. But this goes only so far. Role Exhaustion imposes a restriction on sentence interpretation that has no logical or conceptual basis: it requires that a *single* dependent refer to the *entirety* of a given relatum. This restriction has two aspects that are worth separating.

First, a single dependent cannot refer to only a proper part of the relevant relatum. For this reason (20a) does not entail (20b), and (21a) does not entail (21b).

(20) a   Tony and Geezer lifted the amp and the organ.

      b ⊯ Tony lifted the amp.

---

[2] It is often difficult to say what the spatial location of an event is. See Dretske 1967 and Hacker 1982 for discussion.

(21)   a   Lee, Mo and 5,000 of their classmates surrounded the Forbidden City.
       b   ⊭ Lee and Mo surrounded the Forbidden City.

These entailments would hold if (20b) could mean that Tony is part of
the group who lifted a group containing the amp, or (21b) could mean
that Lee and Mo are part of the group that surrounded the Forbidden
City. There is nothing conceptually odd about those meanings, so conceptual oddity cannot be what explains their absence.

Second, according to Role Exhaustion, it must be just a single dependent that specifies the entirety of the relatum, and not several dependents acting in concert. Thus (22a) cannot mean, as (22b) in fact can,
that there was cooking with only the blowtorch and steamer as its
instruments

(22)   a * Al cooked this with a blowtorch with a steamer.
       b   Al cooked this with a blowtorch and a steamer.

There is nothing odd about (22b). The sentence might even concern
a single cooking, executed by steam from below and flame from
above. So there is nothing in our concept of events that would be
violated by interpreting (22a) like (22b). Nonetheless this would violate
Role Exhaustion.[3] And therefore Role Exhaustion is not wholly a
consequence of how we think of events and their criteria of identity. It
is at least in part a consequence of linguistic semantics.

8.4 TIME AND PLACE

For Role Exhaustion to be at all palatable, we have to think carefully
about modifiers of time and place. Sometimes, as in (23) and (24), these
can iterate within a single clause and in relation to the same event(s).
This would violate any simple restriction against repeating modifiers of
the same semantic class – itself an argument against a purely grammatical account of the RIG.

(23)   Al cooked cutlets on Tuesday after Mo arrived.

(24)   Al cooked cutlets in his Berlin apartment, in the kitchen.

But it would also violate Role Exhaustion – *if* we were to assume
that the adjunct expresses a relation to the event of the verb, following Davidson (1967b). To see this, suppose that in the kitchen

---

[3] It is a separate question whether the violation of Role Exhaustion is the sole reason
that (22a) is unacceptable.

expressed the 'In' relation between the kitchen and the cooking event, as in (25).

(25)   ∃e[AlCookingCutlets(*e*) & In(*e*, the kitchen) . . .]

Role Exhaustion would then require that no other thing has this same relation to the cooking. But this would make (24) inconsistent. The sentence would say that the cooking has the 'In' relation only to the kitchen, but then also to the Berlin apartment. This is impossible unless the kitchen is identical to the apartment.

In this exploratory section I would like to point towards a possible reconciliation of these facts with Exhaustion. The way is initially indicated by a notable semantic restriction on the iteration of Time and Place. Consider again (23) and (24). The first entails that the cooking of cutlets happened at a single time, which was both on Tuesday and after Mo arrived. The second entails that the cooking of cutlets happened at a single place, which was both in the Berlin apartment and in the kitchen. In contrast, the same is not so for (26) and (27) below.

(26)   Al cooked cutlets on Tuesday and after Mo arrived.

(27)   Al cooked cutlets in his Berlin apartment and in his kitchen.

Sentence (26) is consistent with Mo arriving on Wednesday, and so with Al cooking cutlets on two separate days. Likewise (27) allows for cooking at two separate locations, the Berlin apartment and a kitchen that is in a different place.

Thus, when temporal and locative modifiers iterate, the sentence can mean only that there is an event, or some events, at a time or place that is described by the conjunction of all the relevant modifiers. Consequently when two modifiers cannot consistently apply to a single time or place, the result is unacceptable. Under the relevant interpretations, (28) and (29) are unacceptable, while (30) and (31) are fine.

(28)   # Al cooked cutlets before Mo arrived, after Mo left.

(29)   # Al cooked cutlets in his Berlin apartment, in his London apartment.

(30)   Al cooked cutlets before Mo arrived and after Mo left.

(31)   Al cooked cutlets in his Berlin apartment and in his London apartment.

The reason (28) and (29) are inconsistent is because the mentioned intervals of time, or regions of space, do not overlap. The sentences in (32) are inconsistent for a different reason.

(32)   a # Al cooked cutlets in every room, in his kitchen.
       b # Al cooked cutlets throughout his house, in the kitchen.

Here the regions do overlap, if the kitchen is one of the rooms in the house. Still the sentences are inconsistent, because a location that is *in* the kitchen, inside of it, cannot also be in every room. Sentence (33), in contrast, is merely redundant.

(33) Al cooked cutlets in every room and in the kitchen.

Such facts suggest that we need to revise the logical form of temporal and locative modification. We need to reject Davidson's assumption, exemplified in (25) above, that such adjuncts are predicates of the event. Let us suppose instead that they are predicates of the event's time or place. Concretely, (23) and (24) then have logical forms something like (34) and (35), which I break into three segments for clarity. What is crucial is the introduction of a time, t, in (34), and a place, l, in (35).

(34) a $\exists e[$ AlCookingCutlets(e) &
      b $\exists t[$ Time(e, t) &
      c On$(t,$ Tuesday$)$ & Before$(t,$ Mo's arrival$)$ $]]$
(35) a $\exists e[$ AlCookingCutlets(e) &
      b $\exists l[$ Place(e, l) &
      c In$(l,$ Al's Berlin apartment$)$ & In$(l,$ the kitchen$)$ $]]$

Under this analysis the semantic job of the dependents – before Mo's arrival or in the kitchen – is not to identify the individual(s) in some thematic relation to the event of the verb. Consequently they are not restricted by Role Exhaustion, or so I suggest. As stated in (11), Exhaustion applies only to dependents of an event predicate which instantiate relations to its event. In our revised logical form, however, the temporal and locative adjuncts 'serve as modifiers.' Their semantic job is to give properties of the time or the place of the event. Such predicates, let us assume, are not governed by (any analogue of) Role Exhaustion. There is no requirement, for example, that a locative modifier of a location l name all and only the regions that l lies within. Conceptually this seems natural. Whereas an event is identified in part by its unique time or place, an interval of time or region of space is related to infinitely many others, past and future, here and there, no subset of which serves to define its identity. But while iterated modifiers of time or place are not governed by Exhaustion, they *are* predicated of the same variable, the t in (34c) and the l in (35c). Consequently the sentence will be inconsistent if any pair of modifiers is – that is, if they cannot jointly apply to a single time or place. My suggestion is that the unacceptability of examples such as (28), (29) and (32) registers this inconsistency.

Why inconsistency derived in this way registers, furthermore, as unacceptability is something I cannot explain. Certainly the false sentence Al is presently in Berlin and in London is not unacceptable in the same way. I can only suggest, without other justification, that inconsistencies which depend on implicit logical form, here the implicit introduction of a time or place variable, register as unacceptable.

It is instructive to distinguish this *modifier analysis* from another plausible proposal, call it the *reference analysis*. For Creary *et al.* (1989), locative PPs refer to a spatial region (Jackendoff 1983, Kracht 2002). In the kitchen, for example, stands for the region within the kitchen. There is a good reason for this: it explains why one can refer anaphorically to such regions with there (Jackendoff 1983). There in (36) may refer to the region behind the wall.

(36)   Al is not fixing drinks behind that wall, but Hal is still standing there.

The modifier analysis is not built to explain such anaphora. But I depart from Creary *et al.* because of their compositional semantics. They assume that locative adjuncts instantiate a relation to the event of the verb, call it the Within relation. In our terms we can render the proposed logical form of (37a) fairly as in (37b).

(37)   a Al cooked cutlets in the kitchen.
         b $\exists e$ [AlCookingCutlets(e) & Within(e, l) & $l =$ ⟦in the kitchen⟧]

But then locative adjuncts must be unusual, in that several can instantiate a single relation collectively. The semantics identifies the location term of the Within relation as the "intersection" of all those regions named by the locative PPs. So (38a) is treated roughly as in (38b), placing Al's cooking of cutlets within the region that is the "intersection" ($\sqcap$) of the apartment and the kitchen.

(38)   a Al cooked cutlets in his Berlin apartment in the kitchen.
         b $\exists e$ [AlCookingCutlets(e) & Within(e, l)
            & $l =$ ⟦in the kitchen⟧ $\sqcap$ ⟦in the apartment⟧]

I have two reservations about this. First, it goes against Role Exhaustion, which forbids collective instantiation of a relation; recall, this is meant to explain why Lee yelled Mo, for example, can't mean that Lee and Mo yelled, as it could if the yeller were identified as the mereological sum of Lee and Mo, provided collectively by the subject and object.[4] Second, I am concerned with examples like those in (32). The intersection of the regions denoted by throughout the house and in the kitchen is just

---

[4] Mereological summation is not the same thing as the intersection of regions. But a semantics which collects the referents of distinct dependents by intersection could equally do so by summation.

the region in the kitchen. Yet the examples in (32) are far worse than the merely redundant (33). This has some account if the adjuncts are predicates of the location, modifiers, but not if the location is identified with the intersection of the regions they denote. For these reasons I cautiously prefer the modifier analysis.

I think this is sufficient to keep our faith in Exhaustion. But, of course, problems remain. I bring up two in the discussion questions at the end of this chapter.

8.5 COMITATIVES

Example (39) includes a comitative adjunct, with Geezer. In using (39) one might mean to convey the thought expressed by (40). Call this the **collective** reading.

(39)   Tony lifted the amp with Geezer.

(40)   Tony and Geezer lifted the amp together.

The collective reading does not entail (41). And therefore if, on a particular use of (39), we think that the collective reading is intended, it would seem wrong to infer (41) from (39). In contrast there is no question about (42), where with is not comitative but instrumental: (42) does entail (41).

(41)   Tony lifted the amp.

(42)   Tony lifted the amp with a rope.

Now suppose that (39), after resolution of ambiguity, actually has the collective reading as a *meaning*, a meaning that does not entail (41). Then we have to ask, what is the logical form for this meaning? One idea is, Tony and Geezer are both assigned the same semantic relation, say Agent, in relation to exactly the same event. Were this correct, and only then, (39) would violate Exhaustion. For then the sentence would entail that the Agents include both Tony and Geezer, and yet on the surface these would not be identified by a single dependent.

There are three ways to defuse the challenge, other than by modifying Exhaustion. The first is to deny the presumed data. Maybe there is no collective meaning for (39), and the sentence in fact does entail (41). Maybe when we are unwilling to accept the inference from (39) to (41), it is just because we are assuming the speaker meant more than he said, the collective reading being some sort of pragmatic enrichment. If this seems strained for (39), it is less so for (43) and (44).

(43) a # Lee and Mo surrounded the Forbidden City with 5,000 of their classmates.
    b   Lee, Mo and 5,000 of their classmates surrounded the Forbidden City.

(44) a # In five minutes Al ate 500 hotdogs with his classmates.
    b   In five minutes Al and his classmates ate 500 hotdogs.

Sentences (43a) and (44a) are odd on the intended reading, while (43b) and (44b) are unremarkable. One way to explain this is by assuming that (43a) and (44a) entail that Lee and Mo surrounded the Forbidden City and Al ate 500 hotdogs. This would imply that there is no collective meaning for sentences with comitatives, only the possibility of using them to convey collective readings when the contribution of the accomplice, such as Geezer in (39), is relatively minor.

The second response is to accept both the collective meaning and its semantic analysis, but to revise the syntax. The violation of Role Exhaustion dissolves if (39) has more or less the same underlying syntax as (40), with Tony and Geezer separated by movement. Arguments for this position have been given in Zhang (2007); its plausibility is also boosted by data from Russian (McNally 1993, Dalrymple 1998) and Spanish (Camacho 2000), where verb agreement registers the contribution of the comitative.[5] At least for English, however, the position is not without complications. For instance, it must explain contrasts like (45) and (46), and also explain why (47a) is not synonymous with (47b) (Landman 2000).

(45) a # Tony both lifted the amp with Geezer.
    b   Tony and Geezer both lifted the amp.

(46) a # Together, Tony lifted the amp with Geezer.
    b   Together, Tony and Geezer lifted the amp.

(47) a   Tony carefully/intentionally lifted the amp with Geezer.
    b   Tony and Geezer carefully/intentionally lifted the amp.

The final response is to keep the apparent syntax, but to deny the assumed logical form. Landman (2000) suggests that the comitative has its own semantic relation, which I will call Accomplice, as in (48). The accomplice helps the agent, but does not keep him from qualifying as the agent.

(48)   Agent(e, Tony) & LiftingTheAmp(e) & Accomplice(e, Geezer)

In this way Exhaustion is satisfied: Tony is the sole agent and Geezer is his accomplice. However, it becomes necessary to deny that sentences with comitatives have a truly collective meaning, since (48) entails that

---

[5] See Stolz *et al.* 2006 for a cross-linguistic survey of comitatives.

Tony is the agent of an amp-lifting, validating the inference from (39) to (41). Schein (2002:331) proposes a different revision of the semantics, one that doesn't force us to deny the collective meaning. For Schein, in sentences with collective readings of comitatives, the subject names the agent, but not of the verb's event, e_2 in (49). It names the agent of another event, here e_1, that is related to that event by the meaning of with. The preposition expresses a three-place predicate that relates two events and an accomplice, here Geezer.

(49) $\lambda e_1 \exists e_2[$ Agent$(e_1,$ Tony$)$ & With$(e_1, e_2,$ Geezer$)$ & LiftingTheAmp(e_2) $]$

The formula in (49) does not entail that Tony is the agent of an amp-lifting. It says only that he is the agent of an event in a 'with Geezer' relation to an amp-lifting. Compositionally, this requires that the Agent relation is syntactically separated from the verb phrase (see Chapter 9), and that the structure introducing it joins the verb phrase only after the comitative adjunct. But it does not require that Tony and Geezer are born together in a single underlying subject constituent.

I will not decide which response is right. But I will say, again, that the apparent challenge to Role Exhaustion has some encouraging retorts.

8.6 THE THETA CRITERION

As discussed in Chapter 3, work in the tradition of GB (Chomsky 1981) assigns predicates a syntactic feature called the Θ-grid (Stowell 1981). This is an a-list whose members are called Θ-roles. When an expression with Θ-roles heads a phrase, its Θ-roles are paired off with dependents, according to the order of those roles in the grid. We then say that the head "assigns" a Θ-role to dependents, which then "bear" that role. Dependents that "bear" a Θ-role are ipso facto syntactic arguments.

The functional interpretation of the Θ-grid as a list of syntactic arguments is provided by (50), the "Theta Criterion" of Chomsky 1981. This stipulates that a dependent satisfies ("bears") just one Θ-role, and that each Θ-role must be satisfied ("assigned"). So the Θ-roles will match their satisfiers one-to-one (Bresnan 1980). In the terminology of Chapter 3, a head that *has* an argument must also *take* one.

(50) Each argument bears one and only one Θ-role, and each Θ-role is assigned to one and only one argument. (Chomsky 1981:36)

By assumption, the Θ-roles also correspond one-to-one to the semantic arguments of the predicate. So a dependent will bind a relation introduced semantically by the head if and only if it is syntactically assigned a Θ-role by that head. For this indirect reason, the Theta Criterion is relevant to the RIG. To see why, let us suppose that the verb smack in (51) has the Θ-grid in (52), with two members.

(51)   Nik smacked the wall.

(52)   smack:$\langle\langle\theta\rangle, \theta\rangle$

The Theta Criterion requires that this smack keep the company of exactly two dependents for its two Θ-roles. The smack of (52) therefore cannot occur in the intransitive (53), either failing to assign one of its roles or assigning both to the wall.

(53)   * The wall smacked.

Nor can the smack of (52) be the only Θ-role assigner in the ditransitive (54). Here the wall and the floor cannot both satisfy the same Θ-role of the smack from (52), and therefore cannot both instantiate the same semantic argument of that verb.

(54)   * Nik smacked the wall the floor.

The Theta Criterion therefore encodes the unacceptability of (53) and (54) – if we assume in addition that there are no other verbs pronounced "smack" which instead have either one Θ-role or three, and that (54) contains no additional Θ-role assigners. Given such assumptions, the Theta Criterion contributes to an account of the RIG. But it does so very modestly, just by assuring that an expression takes a syntactic argument for every one it has.

It is important to appreciate what the Theta Criterion does not do. The principle is easily taken to have either virtues or vices that it cannot possibly have. Here I will point to four explananda that are outside its scope.

First, it does not decide what the Θ-grid of predicate must be, given the concept it expresses. The verb smack expresses the concept of smacking. This concept applies to events with at least two participants: a smacker and thing smacked. But it is not the job of the Theta Criterion itself to say that smack therefore has a two-membered Θ-grid. The Theta Criterion does not decide what the lexical properties of a verb are, it only regulates how they are expressed in the derivation of the phrase it heads. Thus it is not the Theta Criterion alone that explains why there is no intransitive English sentence pronounced "the wall smacked" which means 'the wall underwent smacking.' To explain that, we have to explain why an English verb that expresses the concept of smacking cannot have a one-membered Θ-grid.[6]

Second, the Theta Criterion does not require that two members of a single Θ-grid are linked to two semantic relations with distinct content. It is consistent with the Theta Criterion on its own to have a ditransitive version of smack, call it schmack, where both arguments are interpreted as things smacked. This verb will have the Θ-grid in (55) and the meaning in (56), with both internal Θ-roles linking to a Patient relation. Sentence (54) could then mean Nik smacked the wall and the floor. Ruling this out will require a further principle, not the Theta Criterion itself.

(55)   schmack:$\langle\langle\theta,\theta\rangle,\theta\rangle$

(56) $[\![$schmack$]\!]$
       $= \lambda z \lambda y \lambda x \lambda e[$ Agent(e,x) & Smacking(e) & Patient(e,y) & Patient(e,z) $]$

Third, the Theta Criterion does not rule out the possibility that a predicate may occur in inaudible structure that itself introduces a dependent, where this dependent intantiates a relation to the same event. Thus the Theta Criterion does not on its own explain why (54) is unacceptable, even if the only English verb pronounced "smack" is the transitive smack of (52). To explain this, we must also say that English includes no VP context, separate from the verb, which itself introduces a second object argument, O2, and means 'the event of the verb was directed at the referent of O2.' Or in any case, if there is such a context, it cannot accommodate the verb smack.

Fourth, and expanding the second point, the Theta Criterion in no way restricts the content of the semantic roles to which Θ-roles are linked. It makes no claims about the satisfaction conditions of the semantic roles, or about the theoretical vocabulary in which they are described. For example, suppose we say that give in (57) has a Theta Grid with three Θ-roles, corresponding to what we can call the Giver, the Recipient and the Given.

(57)   Al gave Mo sausages.

Then (57) satisfies the Theta Criterion so long as Al, Mo and sausages are assigned those three Θ-roles, respectively. It does not matter at all how we describe the content of the relations to which those roles are linked

---

[6] This point is often missed in the literature on language acquisition, following an oversight in Gleitman 1990, who credits the Theta Criterion, incorrectly, with requiring that a verb with two *participant roles* occur in a transitive clause. The error is repeated in Lidz *et al.* 2003, for example.

in the meaning of (57), e.g., whether we describe the relation bound by AI as in (58a), (58b) or (58c).

(58)   a $\lambda x \lambda e$[Giver(e, x)]
     b $\lambda x \lambda e$[Agent(e, x)]
     c $\lambda x \lambda e$[Agent(e, x) & Source(e, x)]

The licit availability of (58c) in particular is worth emphasizing. This relation has a complex description. To say that it interprets the subject of (57) is therefore to invoke underived semantic decomposition (see Chapter 2). But it is not to split one Θ-role into two. Θ-roles are syntactic features that mark a syntactic argument as semantically interpreted. They are not themselves semantic relations, and there is no reason a single Θ-role cannot correspond to more than one predicate in the semantics, in any theory that allows for underived decomposition. So it is incorrect to claim, as has Jackendoff (1987, 1990b), that an analysis like (58c) contradicts the Theta Criterion by assigning two Θ-roles to a single dependent. The purpose of the Theta Criterion was never to rule out underived semantic decomposition of an argument relation.

8.7   THE PRINCIPLE OF INTERPRETABILITY

Heim and Kratzer (1998:49–58) wonder whether the Theta Criterion is necessary. Whatever work it does do, they contend, can be done by the semantics: if predicates have functions as semantic values, and we limit the rules of semantic combination to `Application` and `Conjunction`, then the most we need to assume in addition is the principle in (59), the **Principle of Interpretability**, henceforth PI.[7]

(59)   Principle of Interpretability (PI)
     Each syntactic part of a sentence must have a meaning; that is, "be in the domain of the interpretation function."

To an important extent this is correct. Assume that English has only one verb pronounced "laugh," and its semantic value is the one-place function in (60): this pairs those who laugh with True and everyone else with False.

(60) λx [True if x laughed and otherwise False]

---

[7] The complete statement of the PI is this: "All nodes in a phrase structure tree must be in the domain of the interpretation function, [[ ]]" (Heim and Kratzer 1998:49).

With this we can derive a meaning for (61) as in (62). We apply (60) to the value of Mo, yielding True just in case Mo laughed. PI is therefore satisfied.

(61)   Mo laughed.

(62)   ⟦ Mo laughed ⟧ = Application [⟦laughed⟧, ⟦Mo⟧]
       = True if Mo laughed and otherwise False

But with (60) alone, and just Application or Conjunction, we cannot derive a semantic value for (63).

(63)   * Lee laughed Mo.

Here we can treat the verb phrase, laughed Mo, exactly as we treated Mo laughed in (62). But then the semantic value of the verb phrase is a truth value, True if Mo laughed. Neither Application nor Conjunction can do anything with the pair of Lee and True, the values of the subject and predicate. Thus the sentence is not in the domain of the interpretation function, violating PI. We don't need the Theta Criterion to explain why it's bad.

Next assume that English has just one verb pronounced "slice," and it stands for the two-place function in (64), which maps x and y to True just in case x slices y.

(64) $\lambda y \lambda x$[True if x slices y and otherwise False]

Applying this function to Al yields the output in (65). This is 'to slice Al,' the same meaning we would assign the verb phrase in the sentence The knife sliced Al. So (66), with an expletive subject, while ungrammatical, accords with PI: it is interpretable, with (65) as its value.

(65) λx[True if x slices Al and otherwise False]

(66)   * There/it sliced Al.

Consequently, if slice is the only predicate in (66), if (64) is the sole semantic value for any verb pronounced "slice," and if Application and Conjunction are the only rules of semantic combination, it follows that (66) cannot have either meaning in (67). Therefore, as promised, we do not need the Theta Criterion to explain why (66) can't have either of these meanings.

(67)   a 'Al sliced himself.'
       b 'Something sliced Al.'

What remains for us to explain is why (66) is unacceptable with the interpretation that *is* derived, namely the function in (65), 'to slice Al.'

To say that the sentence is syntactically underivable with this interpretation would threaten to reintroduce the Theta Criterion. But perhaps a partly pragmatic explanation is available: maybe an expression is not judged acceptable *as a declarative sentence* unless its semantic value is a truth value.[8] This will also rule out (68), given the meaning for laugh in (60).

(68)   * There/it laughed.
         'to laugh'

However, it is still not the case that PI covers all of what the Theta Criterion covers, small as that jurisdiction might be. In particular, PI does not entail that a predicate whose value is a function must (in any sense) take an argument. The reason is, a function may itself be the argument to a higher-order function.

Imagine there were a word sumtimes, with the syntax of an adverb, but the meaning of the noun phrase someone, as in (69). It maps from one-place functions to truth values, yielding True for any f that is True on at least one member of its domain.

(69)   ⟦ sumtimes ⟧ $= \lambda f$⟦ True if and only if for at least one $x, f(x) =$ True ⟧

Then the pseudo-sentence in (70), with an expletive subject and our chimerical adverb, would satisfy PI even though laugh stands for a function. Yet (70) is something that would be ruled out by the Theta Criterion, since laugh does not assign its Θ-role.

(70)   There/it sumtimes laughed.
         'Someone laughed.'

So to match the coverage of the Theta Criterion, Heim and Kratzer need to rule out expressions like sumtimes. The restriction cannot be purely semantic, however, since sumtimes shares its meaning with the noun phrase someone, and arguably also with the passive morpheme.[9] Evidently the restriction must also refer to syntax: an expression with the semantics of a quantifier cannot be an *adverb*. Or perhaps the restriction

---

[8] What would not be reasonable would be to presume without argument that this postulate can itself be derived from the premise – let us take it to be a true premise – that the content of an assertion must be something with a truth value. For there do appear to be "nonsentential assertions" (Stainton 2006, Merchant 2010), direct speech acts with fully propositional content made in using nonsentential expressions, such as on the table, that do not stand for truth values.

[9] Passive The chair was carried has the truth conditions of 'someone carried the chair.'

is more general: an expression that maps from n-place function to an $(n - 1)$-place function cannot be syntactically an adjunct. Whether the required restriction is more or less attractive than the Theta Criterion depends on its final formulation. No matter what, however, the ambition of replacing the Theta Criterion with something *purely* semantic is plainly frustrated.

In my view this frustration should cause no worry, for two reasons. First, much or all of the data meant to be explained by either PI or the Theta Criterion is better explained by Role Exhaustion. Second, the hope of explaining the relative distribution of predicates and arguments just in terms of semantic types seems misplaced, for reasons Heim and Kratzer themselves point out: verbs are of the same semantic type as adjectives and nouns, but their argument structures are quite different. This point will be spotlighted in Chapter 11.

DISCUSSION POINTS

1 Might a syntactic principle like the Theta Criterion be justified, even on top of Role Exhaustion, or also the Principle of Interpretability? If so, why? It may help to recall our discussion in Section 3.7.

2 Does (1) below bear on the RIG? If so, how?

(1)   the black white adidas
      'the white adidas that somehow look black'
      *'the adidas that are black and white'

How about (2) and (3)? These look like violations of the RIG, but in relations to nouns, not verbs (Barker and Dowty 1993).

(2)   * the top of my house of the chimney
      'the top of my house and the chimney'

(3)   * the father of Peter of Greg of Bobby
      'the father of Peter and Greg and Bobby'

Is the RIG part of a much broader pattern? If so, does the broader pattern change our understanding of how the RIG is best explained? How?

3 In German (4), seiner Frau 'his wife' and den Rücken 'the back' are two separate dependents. But we understand that the man who massages his wife's back also massages her. Many languages have a construction like this. If you know such a language, can you reconcile this construction to the RIG? If so, how?

(4) Ein guter Ehemann massiert seiner Frau jeden Abend den
 a good husband massages his wife every evening the
 Rücken.
 back
 'A good husband massages his wife's back every night.'
 (Lee-Schoenfeld 2007)

4 I proposed in Section 8.4 that temporal and locative adjuncts serve as modifers of a time or place, not as predicates of the clausal event. It follows that something silent must introduce a time or place to be modified. How might this be done? In answering, consider (5), and make the assumption that "there" and "last week" pronounce the same expressions as they do in (6). Does your answer make my proposal more plausible? Less plausible?

(5) Al cooked there last week.

(6) a You should go there too.
 b Last week ruined me.

5 It is consistent to say that cooking which lasts all day also lasts all afternoon, or that cooking which happens throughout the house also happens in every hallway. So if that is what (7a) and (8a) meant, they should be consistent, just redundant. Yet they sound bad.

(7) a # Mo cooked sausage all day throughout the afternoon.
 b Mo cooked sausage all day and throughout the afternoon.

(8) a # Mo cooked sausage everywhere in her house in every hallway.
 b Mo cooked sausage everywhere in her apartment and in every hallway.

Can you reconcile this to the conclusions of Section 8.4? Notice that the modifers in (7) and (8) explicitly describe the *extent* of a time or space. Might such modifiers be interpreted in a way that makes them jointly inconsistent?

SUGGESTIONS FOR FURTHER READING

Carlson 1984 and Dowty 1989 are seminal works in this area, and they reward frequent reading; see also Lasersohn 1995 (e.g., Ch. 6). Fillmore 1968 and Bresnan 1980 provide an essential background. For more on the logic and compositional semantics of temporal and locative modifiers, see Francez and Steedman 2006.

9 Separation

9.1 INTRODUCTION

Because of the verb sing, (1) entails that there was a singing. It also entails that Ozzy was the singer, due in part to whatever relation R_s is bound by Ozzy in (1)'s derivation.

(1) Ozzy sings.

But in that derivation, is R_s introduced by sing itself? Is Ozzy a content argument of the verb, besides naming the singer? The answers "Yes" and "No" define the *projectionist* and *separationist* approaches, respectively, and this distinction is our topic in this chapter.

Say that some R is an entailed relation for a predicate V, as Singer or Agent are for sing. On a projectionist treatment, a dependent that binds R is also a content argument of V, which lexically has a semantic argument in that relation. Suppose that the meaning of sing is (2a); or maybe it is (3a), with lexical decomposition.

(2) a sing $\cong \lambda x \lambda e[$ SingingBy(e, x)]
     b [Ozzy sing] $\cong \exists e[$ SingingBy$(e, $Ozzy$)$]
(3) a sing $\cong \lambda x \exists e[$ Agent(e, x) & Singing(e)]
     b [Ozzy sing] $\cong \exists e[$ Agent$(e, $Ozzy$)$ & Singing(e)]

Combining sing with Ozzy by `Application` then yields (2b) or (3b). Either way, the relation that Ozzy binds, SingingBy in (2b) or Agent in (3b), comes from the verb sing. It therefore has a projectionist account, relative to sing.

A separationist treatment is simply not projectionist. The relevant dependent is not a content argument of V. It does bind a relation R that is entailed by V, but R is introduced by some other part of the derivation, not by V itself. Suppose that (1) has the syntax in (4), where AG is a silent lexical item (Krifka 1992, Kratzer 1996). Suppose also that AG and sing have the values in (5) and (6).

184

(4) [[Ozzy AG] sing]

(5) ⟦ AG ⟧ = λxλe[Agent(e, x)]

(6) ⟦ sing ⟧ = λe[Singing(e)]

AG will combine with Ozzy by `Application`. The result will combine with sing by `Conjunction` to yield (3b) as the meaning for (4). In this derivation, Ozzy is a content argument not of sing but of AG; indeed it is a functional argument of AG. For this reason the relation it instantiates has a separationist treatment vis-à-vis sing.

Here is a second separationist analysis. Suppose conservatively that Ozzy sings has no silent words, just Ozzy and sings. We might then introduce Agent with a rule of semantic combination, something like the `AgentRule` outlined in (7).

(7) If ⟦A⟧ is an individual and ⟦B⟧ is a predicate of events, then:
⟦ [A B] ⟧ = AgentRule(⟦A⟧,⟦B⟧) = λe[Agent(e,⟦A⟧) & ⟦B⟧(e)]

The combination of Ozzy and sings can then be interpreted by this rule, yielding the meaning in (3b) by a different route. This is still a separationist treatment, since the relation Ozzy instantiates does not come from sing. But now it comes from a rule and not a primitive of the derivation.

One last separationist option, analogous to both of the first two, is to introduce the Agent relation in a nonlexical primitive of the syntax (see Chapter 1). The relation between the dependent and the verb is then rendered as an unpronounced 'construction' (Goldberg 1995, Sag *et al.* 2012) which takes them both as functional arguments.

For any single relation between a dependent and a predicate, most linguists choose one or the other sort of treatment. But some blend the two approaches, treating the dependent as a content argument both of the verb and of something else (Goldberg 2006, Sag *et al.* 2012). The dependent binds both a highly specific relation from the verb and, redundantly, a more general relation from elsewhere. Call this *redundant separationism*, and let me illustrate with Ozzy sings. Sentence (8a) combines the projectionist sing of (2a) with the separationist AG of (5). By `Conjunction` and `Application`, (8a) means (8b). And now Ozzy is a content argument not only of AG but also of sing.[1]

(8) a [Ozzy [AG$_{(5)}$ sing$_{(2a)}$]]
b λe[Agent(e, Ozzy) & SingingBy(e, Ozzy)]

---

[1] My illustration uses AG, a lexical primitive that happens to be silent. Construction Grammarians would instead use a nonlexical primitive, but the difference doesn't matter here.

By design the more general relation is redundant with the more specific relation; the former is entailed by the latter. Consequently it is hard to distinguish redundant separationism from the projectionist alternative. For this reason I will not consider the view any further in this book; see Goldberg (2006) and Sag *et al.* (2012) for discussion. It is simpler to discuss only the two 'pure' approaches, unblended.

Historically, projectionism is the norm. At least three very general reasons for this are clear. First, the semantic relation between the verb and a subject or object often has no pronunciation separate from the verb itself. It may therefore seem simplest to avoid positing further meaningful parts that are silent, whether lexical items or rules of combination. Second, it relieves the syntactician and compositional semanticist of any need to account for the various relations a predicate may enter with its dependents, since these are already specified in the predicate's lexical properties. This may seem attractive when those relations are idiosyncratic to the predicate (Dowty 1989). Third, while a separationist analysis presupposes semantic decomposition (which it then resolves by syntactic derivation), a projectionist analysis does not. The projectionist can choose not to decompose the event predicate of the clause, and in that way avoid all of the questions that decomposition may raise, such as whether its primitives can be satisfactorily defined (Dowty 1991); see Chapters 6, 7 and 10.

In my own view, the best analysis is sometimes separationist and sometimes projectionist. But in this chapter I will take the position of a separationist partisan, as we will learn more this way. Clear arguments for separationism have less often had a fair hearing, and this book is an opportunity to give them one. More importantly, the pursuit of separationism is often analytically more fertile, even if it turns out to be wrong. The reason is, it takes semantic relations between a verb and its dependents to be forged in Syntax, where regularity is the norm. Projectionism, in contrast, takes such relations to be forged in Lexicon, where irregularity is no surprise. Pursuit of separationism therefore encourages us to find regularities and state them explicitly. This is valuable even to the committed projectionist, since a separationist analysis can be transposed into projectionist terms, just by reinterpreting the derivation as Lexical.

In Section 9.2, I consider in the abstract how separationist and projectionsist analyses might be distinguished empirically. This is a preface for the next seven sections, which present several arguments for separationism in the literature. I start with two of the best, if also the least familiar: Barry Schein's arguments from cumulative plurals (Section 9.3) and adnominal modals (Section 9.4). I then review arguments from complex predicates (Section 9.5), idioms (Section 9.6), argument structure alternations (Section 9.7), alternations across categories (Section 9.8) and, lastly, linking (Section 9.9). These are presented in what I view as descending order of strength. Finally, in Section 9.10, I outline the syntactic implementation of projectionist and separationist analyses, echoing the final section of Chapter 4.

9.2 DETECTING A DIFFERENCE

The difference between **projectionist** and **separationist** analyses is easily obscured, since in simple cases they yield the same meaning in the end. But there is a basic difference between the two sorts of treatments, and it is one that might express itself empirically, with the use of what I will call a **semantic wedge**.

A separationist treatment recognizes two parts of a meaning, P and Q, and links them to two distinct parts of a derivation. Since these two parts are separate, other material, other expressions, may in principle come between them. And this intervening material may treat the two differently. For example, an intervening operator may take P in its scope but not Q.

Nothing like this is possible within a projectionist regime, however. If the meaning does have two parts, P and Q, these are introduced together, in the meaning of a single lexical item. Standardly, semantic derivation is nontransformational (Chapter 2): meanings are opaque to rules of semantic derivation. So P and Q will 'project' together, as a unit, and cannot interact separately with the content of other expressions. It is not possible, for example, that P will fall in the scope of some operator without Q being there as well.

Thus consider our separationist account of Ozzy sings, using the AG and sing of (5) and (6), repeated here.

(5) $[\![\text{AG}]\!] = \lambda x \lambda e [\text{Agent}(e, x)]$
(6) $[\![\text{sing}]\!] = \lambda e [\text{Singing}(e)]$

Imagine that these lexical items find themselves in a syntactic context like (9). Here sing is distanced from [Ozzy AG] by a lexical item D, unlike in (4).

(9)

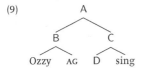

Now let D have the meaning in (10). It expresses a relation $\mathcal{D}$ between any event e_3 and some event e_2 described by its argument, P.

(10) $[\![\,D\,]\!] = \lambda P \lambda e_3 \exists e_2 [\ \mathcal{D}(e_3, e_2)\ \&\ P(e_2)\ ]$

D can then combine with sing using `Application`, yielding (11) as the meaning for C, the next node up.

(11) $[\![\,C\,]\!] = \lambda e_3 \exists e_2 [\ \mathcal{D}(e_3, e_2)\ \&\ \text{Singing}(e_2)\ ]$

Unlike sing itself, C is not a predicate of singings; it is a predicate of events related to a singing by $\mathcal{D}$, (11). This predicate then combines under `Conjunction` with B, a predicate of events that have Ozzy as their agent, (12). The result is (13).

(12) $[\![\,B\,]\!] = \lambda e_1 [\ \text{Agent}(e_1, \text{Ozzy})\ ]$

(13) $[\![\,A\,]\!] = \lambda e_1 [\ \text{Agent}(e_1, \text{Ozzy})\ \&\ \exists e_2 [\ \mathcal{D}(e_1, e_2)\ \&\ \text{Singing}(e_2)]\ ]$

Thus the whole expression, A, does not say that Ozzy is the agent of a singing. It says that he is the agent of an event related to a singing by $\mathcal{D}$. Because the argument to D includes sing but not AG, our two bits of meaning, Singing and Agent, apply to two different events. D drives a *semantic wedge* between them, to put it metaphorically. And this wedge can be driven in only because the two predicates are given a separationist treatment.

Nothing like this can happen with our projectionist account, whether (2a) or (3a). The latter, with decomposition, is repeated in (14). I switch into the notation of semantic congruence (Chapter 2), and use '$\cong$', to highlight semantic structure.

(14) $\text{sing} \cong \lambda x \exists e [\ \text{Agent}(e, x)\ \&\ \text{Singing}(e)\ ]$

Semantics is nontransformational, so no semantic wedge can penetrate a lexical meaning. Given (14), therefore, Agent cannot be separated from Singing in the course of deriving the clause. For example, suppose that this sing from (14) were to combine with the D from (10), repeated as (15). This can done by `Composition` to yield (16). Combining this with Ozzy by `Application` would then give (17).

(15) $D \cong \lambda P \lambda e_3 \exists e_2 [\ \mathcal{D}(e_3, e_2)\ \&\ P(e_2)\ ]$

(16) $D\ \text{sings} \cong \lambda x \lambda e_3 \exists e_2 [\ \mathcal{D}(e_3, e_2)\ \&\ \text{Agent}(e_2, x)\ \&\ \text{Singing}(e_2)\ ]$

(17) $[\ \text{Ozzy}\ [\ D\ \text{sings}\ ]\ ] \cong \lambda e_3 \exists e_2 [\ \mathcal{D}(e_3, e_2)\ \&\ \text{Agent}(e_2, \text{Ozzy})\ \&\ \text{Singing}(e_2)\ ]$

But this result of course preserves the initial relation between Agent and Singing established in the lexical meaning of sing. They remain conjunct predicates of one and the same event, a singing. Ozzy is therefore said to be the agent of a singing, not an event related to a singing by $\mathcal{D}$.

This difference between separationist and projectionist analyses relies only on the basic assumption of a nontransformational semantics. It will therefore support a very direct argument in favor of one sort of account or the other. If we find expressions that act as a semantic wedge between P and Q, like D in (9–13), this is direct evidence for separation – see Sections 9.3 and 9.4 just below. Arguments which rely on more controversial assumptions will be correspondingly less direct.

9.3 CUMULATIVE PLURALS

Schein (1993) uses sentences like (18) to motivate a separationist analysis for the thematic relation bound by subjects. To test for the separation of this relation, he employs the quantifier in the direct object as what I call a semantic wedge.

(18) Three coaches taught every quarterback (four new plays).

The jist of the argument is this. Sentences like (18) have one interpretation called the *cumulative* interpretation. This interpretation requires that the quantifier expressed by the direct object exclude from its scope the thematic relation associated with the subject. Thus in the cumulative interpretation of (18) every quarterback must exclude from its scope the thematic relation bound by three coaches. Of course the scope of the direct object quantifier must include the thematic relation associated with its own underlying position. Under ordinary assumptions, this is possible only if the two thematic relations, for the subject and for the object, are introduced at two separate nodes in the derivation. Therefore they cannot both be introduced by the verb. That is the argument. I will now recount it in more detail.[2]

Schein's sentences, such as (18), have a plural in the subject (three coaches) and a distributive quantifier (every quarterback) in the object. The relevant interpretation reads the plural subject as cumulative, not as collective or distributive. For (18) this means that each of three coaches did some teaching, and between them they taught all of the quarterbacks. To get a better grip on this, consider a scenario that verifies only the cumulative meaning, namely (19). Here Chuck, Dave, and Ed are the coaches; the quarterbacks are numbered 1–5.

(19) Chuck taught quarterbacks 1–3, Dave taught quarterback 2, Ed taught quarterbacks 4–5, and none of this was part of a single project.

[2] See also Kratzer 2000.

Each of the coaches taught one or more of the quarterbacks, though not together. Each of the quarterbacks was taught by one or more of the coaches. This verifies the cumulative interpretation. But it does not verify any of three stronger readings. The collective reading would require that the coaches work as a single corporate body. The distributive reading would require that each coach taught all five quarterbacks. One final reading, the inverse scope reading, would require that there were three coaches for each of the quarterbacks.

Why does Schein add the parenthesized portion of (18), about the four new plays? This is included to show that the cumulative reading does not depend on taking every quarterback to refer to a single corporate individual, a group comprising all the quarterbacks. It is available even with every quarterback understood as a genuine quantifier, with dependent expressions in its scope. So imagine that, in scenario (19), each of the quarterbacks learned four *different* plays. This would verify (18) only if every quarterback is a distributive quantifier with four new plays in its scope, the plays co-varying with the quarterbacks.

The descriptive challenge, then, is to assign sentences like these a meaning that supports this cumulative reading. Schein responds with an analysis in which the scope of the object quantifier excludes the thematic relation bound by the subject quantifier. He then argues that this is the only adequate sort of analysis. If he is right, it is a very strong argument for separation of the subject's thematic relation. For if the scope of the quantifier includes the relation of the object but excludes that of the subject, it has no plausible derivation in which these relations are introduced by the same lexical item.

Specifically, Schein proposes an analysis like (20). For readability I write this in prose and break it into semantically relevant segments. The formal version is provided in (21).

(20) a   'There are some events, the e's, such that ...'
      b   i 'there are coaches, three in number, such that...'
          ii 'they are the agents of the e's, ...'
      c   i 'and for each quarterback, there is an e' among the e's, such that ...'
          ii 'e' is a teaching of him'

(21) a $\exists e[$
      b   i $[\exists x : 3(x) \& \text{Coaches}(x)]$
          ii $(\text{Agent}(x, e))$
      c   i $\& [\forall y : \text{Quarterback}(y)][\exists e' : e' \leq e]$
          ii $(\text{teaching}(e') \& \text{Goal}(e', y))]$

Let's walk slowly through the parts of the analysis. First comes an initial quantifier, (21a), with two conjuncts in its scope, (21b) and (21c).

These two conjuncts give the interpretation of the subject and the verb phrase, respectively. Both the subject and verb phrase portions are then divided into two further parts: the quantifiers provided by the noun phrases, subject in (21b-i) and object in (21c-i), followed by the scope of that quantifier, (21b-ii) and (21c-ii).

What is important here is the subject and object quantifiers. Their scopes are independent. Each has in its scope only its own thematic relation, Agent for the subject and Goal for the object. The two conjunct statements are related, in that they both say something about the same events, *e*. Thus (20/21b) says roughly that three coaches are the Agents of some events, and every quarterback gets taught in one of these. An interpretation like this is consistent with the cumulative reading, but too weak to capture the collective or distributive readings: it does not require the coaches to work collectively and it does not require that each of them teach every quarterback. Schein (1993:70–84) then argues carefully that, in the general case, the cumulative interpretation simply cannot be captured if the object quantifier has the subject's thematic relation in its scope.[3] For this I refer the reader to Schein's original discussion.

What is plain is that (21) *can* be derived if the two thematic relations, informally 'get taught' and 'are the agents,' are introduced at separate nodes in the syntax. Here is one way this might proceed (I will ignore several others). The object quantifier combines with an expression interpreted as 'get taught.' The subject quantifier combines with an expression interpreted as 'are the agents.' The resulting predicates are conjoined and existentially closed, and we wind up with (21).

Now suppose to the contrary that the two thematic relations, 'get taught' and 'are the agents,' were introduced at the same node in the derivation. Then an object quantifier which binds the former will have the latter in its scope as well. Given the standard sort of quantification, this implies that the object quantifier will be involved in a scopal dependency with any quantifier that binds 'are the agents.' And this would not allow the cumulative interpretation, without further stipulation.

Thus Schein leverages separation to give an analysis of cumulative plurals, and, to the extent that the analysis succeeds, it provides excellent evidence for separation. Unfortunately, plurality is a very difficult topic. For opposition to Schein's treatment of it, see Link (1998), Yi (1999), Landman (2000), Oliver and Smiley (2001), Rayo (2002),

---

[3] Schein goes further, and argues that the observed readings cannot be captured with the use of branching quantifiers either (on which see Sher 1990).

Champollion (2010a), and Scha (2013); consult Schein (2006) and Zweig (2008) in response.

9.4 ADNOMINAL MODALS

Schein (1997) presents a second strong argument for separation, from sentences like (22), using the modal adverb possibly as a semantic wedge.

(22) The students and possibly the professors surrounded the manor.

Sentence (22) can be used to convey a thought like (23). So let us suppose, plausibly, that (22) has a meaning that entails (23).

(23) There are two possibilities: either the students surrounded the manor, or the students and the professors surrounded the manner.

In the meaning that entails (23), what is said to be possible? Certainly the right answer is not (24) or (25). Neither of these captures (23).

(24) Possibly: the students surrounded the manner and the professors surrounded the manor.

(25) The students surrounded the manor, and possibly: the professors surrounded the manor.

Here the statement that falls in the scope of possibly entails two propositions: that there was surrounding, and also that the surrounders were the professors. In Schein's diagnosis, this is the problem. He proposes to split up these two propositions and put only the latter in the scope of possibly: possibly, the professors were agents in some event. Thus Schein argues that the semantics must be along the lines of (26), ignoring for now some details that are important but not presently germane.

(26) 'There is an e that is a surrounding of the manor; the students are agents in e; and possibly the professors are agents in e as well.'

In (26) the scope of possibly includes a thematic relation, the relation bound by the subject, but excludes the predicate contributed by the verb. No plausible derivation will have this result unless these two predicates are introduced separately, at distinct nodes in the derivation. So if Schein is right, and (22) interpreted as (23) requires a semantics like (26), then this is strong evidence for a separationist analysis.

Schein observes that this argument extends to all thematic relations, not just those associated with subjects. For example, (27) can be used to convey a thought like (28). The same argument therefore suggests that the thematic relation associated with direct objects is also introduced separately from the verb (cf. Kratzer 2003).

(27) The cops gathered the students and possibly the professors.

(28) There are two possibilities: either the cops gathered the students, or the cops gathered the students and the professors.

9.5 COMPLEX PREDICATES

If thematic relations project from the verb, then the verb is the domain of generalizations about the distribution of dependents in those relations. The distribution of agent relations, for example, will be stated in terms of subcategories of *verbs* – lexical items. It will therefore be difficult to state any generalization that makes reference to a predicate that is syntactically complex, and not a lexical item. So if there are such generalizations – patterns where a certain thematic relation is licensed in relation to a syntactically complex predicate – then this is evidence for separation. In Chapter 13 I give an argument like this from resultatives in Igbo; see also the Discussion Points at the end of this chapter.

Here I present an influential argument by Borer (1994, 2003, 2005), to do with differences between unaccusative and unergative clauses. *Unaccusative clauses* are intransitives whose surface subject patterns like the direct object of a transitive clause, syntactically or semantically. *Unergative clauses* are the opposite, intransitives whose surface subject is like the subject of a transitive clause. Sometimes it is just the verb that decides whether a clause is unaccusative or unergative. But Borer observes that this is not always the case (Zaenen 1988). Sometimes it is the verb phrase as a whole that decides. In particular, the choice may depend on whether or not the entire verb phrase is a telic predicate (Garey 1957), one that implies an intrinsic point of conclusion for its event.

Borer discusses an example from Dutch. In Dutch the Perfect is formed either with hebben 'have' or with zijn 'be.' It is commonly said that intransitives with hebben are unergative, while those with zijn are unaccusative. By this standard (29) is unergative while (30) is unaccusative. But both clauses contain the same verb, springen 'jump.' The difference is just the presence of a dependent PP in the latter, in de sloot 'in the ditch.' This makes (30) telic – implying a conclusion to the jumping, namely when Jan reaches the ditch – and correspondingly unaccusative.

(29) Jan heeft gesprongen.
      Jan has   jumped
      'Jan jumped.'

(30) Jan is   in   de   sloot gesprongen.
      J   has   in   the   ditch jumped
      'Jan jumped into the ditch.'

Now suppose that the distinction between unergative and unaccusative clauses implies a difference in what semantic relation is
borne by the surface subject. Suppose the subject bears relation A
in an unergative, but relation T in an unaccusative (evoking Agent
and Theme, but noncommitally). In that case the choice of A or T also
depends on the whole verb phrase, and not just on its verb. With
separation, stating a pattern like this is straightforward. Relations A
and T are introduced separately from the verb, by a structure that
keeps the company of a verb *phrase*. We just say directly what sorts of
verb phrases the thematic structure goes with – phrases of class 1 for
structure that introduces A, and phrases of class 2 for structure that
introduces T. The class of a verb phrase is in turn determined jointly
('compositionally') by its various elements. For example, an adjunct
expressing a path with an endpoint will put its VP into class 2, even
if its verb is in class 1. When the verb phrase is simple, comprising
only the verb, we merely reach the limiting case, where the class of the
phrase is decided solely by its head.

Things will be much less simple, however, if the thematic relations project from the verb. Then we will need to recognize two
homophonous verbs with the same basic meaning, except that one
projects an A argument while the other projects a T argument. Worse,
each verb will have to somehow be restricted to occur only in appropriate contexts: unergative contexts for verb with an A argument, and
unaccusative contexts for a verb with a T argument. Technically, this
will not be a trivial matter. Whether it is even possible is not clear, since
sometimes unaccusativity seems to depend on *adjuncts*. By definition,
an adjunct cannot be specified in the lexical properties of the verb. So
if appearances are real, and an adjunct effects unaccusativity, it cannot
be that unaccusativity projects from the verb. Thus, on the face of it,
the separationist approach of Borer seems simpler.

9.6 IDIOMS

Kratzer (1996) proposes to "sever the external argument from the verb."
That is, in a clause that describes an action, the verb does not have the
subject as an argument. That privilege belongs to AG, a lexical item

with the value in (31), audible in some languages but silent in many others.

(31) $[\![\text{AG}]\!] = \lambda x \lambda e[\text{Agent}(e, x)]$

Kratzer takes AG to occupy structures like (33), her analysis for (32). It has category v and combines with a VP complement.

(32) Val killed the boar.

(33) [$_{vP}$ Val [$_{\bar{v}}$ [$_v$ AG] [$_{VP}$ kill the boar]]]

Semantically the VP is taken to be just a predicate of events, as in (34).

(34) $[\![$ [$_{VP}$ kill the boar] $]\!] = \lambda e[$ KillingOf(e, the boar)]

The combination of the VP with AG is interpreted as in (35), using a rule called "Event Identification", defined in (36). This rule combines the semantic effects of function conjunction and function composition.

(35) $[\![$ [$_{\bar{v}}$ [$_v$ AG] [$_{VP}$ kill the boar]]] $]\!]$
     $= \text{EventIdentification}([\![\text{AG}]\!], [\![\text{kill the boar}]\!])$
     $= \lambda x \lambda e[$ Agent(e, x) & KillingOf(e, the boar)]

(36) $\text{EventIdentification}(\alpha, \beta) \equiv \lambda x \lambda e[$ $\alpha(x)(e)$ & $\beta(e)$]

The result is a predicate true of the agent of the VP event, which yields (37) when applied to [[Val]], the final step in interpreting (33).

(37) $[\![(33)]\!] = \lambda e[$ Agent(e, Val) & KillingOf(e, the boar)]

Thus the object but not the subject is a content argument of kill.

In this section we will review the main part of Kratzer's argument for this conclusion, which concerns what I will call *dependent-triggered idioms*. Such idioms are exemplified by the sentences in (38).

(38) a Val killed three long evenings.
      b Val killed three bottles of wine.

In these a certain dependent has its ordinary meaning, but triggers a special meaning for the verb. Killing an evening and killing a bottle involve an evening and a bottle, but neither involves ending a life, as killing a boar does. In addition, while the killing of (38a) involves only time spans, and that of (38b) involves only drinks, it is not clear that this is part of the sentence's truth-conditional content, i.e., of what one uses the sentence to assert. If it were, one could use (39) to correctly deny that the boar is a time span that Val wasted, or a drink that she finished, and it is not clear that one can. The assumption that one cannot is, let us say, the *trigger assumption*.

(39) Val did not kill the boar.

Marantz (1984:23–31) makes a generalization about idioms like these. Many depend on a direct object but not the subject, as in (38). But when the sentence describes an action, very few depend just on the subject to the exclusion of the object (Marantz 1997). Cases like the fictional (40) are very rare. Here greet is supposed to have a special meaning just when the subject refers to food, as in (40b).

(40)   a { Ignacio / Olivia / ... } greeted *x*.
          '{ Ignacio / Olivia / ... } welcomed *x* politely.'
       b The { nachos / olives / ... } greeted *x*.
          'The { nachos / olives / ... } upset *x*'s stomach.'

Call this the *(idiom) asymmetry generalization*. There is some question about its strength (Bresnan 1982a, Nunberg *et al.* 1994, Lidz 2000, Borer 2010). But to understand Kratzer's discussion, we need to take it for granted.

Kratzer argues that this generalization supports her separationist proposal: in a clause that describes an action, the object but not the subject is a content argument of the verb. Her reasoning is based on one way of encoding dependent-triggered idioms.[4] Kratzer treats the verb as naming a function over the relevant dependent, and then partitions its domain (Marantz 1984:26). So kill names a function over the direct object, and its domain divides into the time spans, the drinks and so forth. Arguments drawn from different subdomains may then map to event predicates with different truth conditions.[5] ⟦Kill⟧ maps a time span *x* to 'waste *x*,' but a drink *y* to 'finish *y*,' and any organism *z* to 'end the life of *z*.' This might all be the work of a single lexical item kill, expressing a function that is defined over every subdomain, including the time spans, drinks and organisms. But Kratzer also allows that there might instead be several homophonous verbs. Each names a partial function, defined over just one of the relevant subdomains: one kill for time spans, another kill for drinks. This second option is arguably the right one, *pace* Marantz (1984:25).[6] On this view (38a) involves a verb $kill_2$

---

[4] Kratzer (1996:114) is explicit in regarding the nonidiomaticity of the object to be important: "What is interesting and highly relevant about the data [in (38)] is that the phrases listed there do not involve completely frozen idiom chunks."

[5] The theory itself makes no distinction between 'normal' and 'special' meanings here. For Kratzer there is no theoretical difference between the 'waste time' and 'make dead' meanings of kill.

[6] Evidence for ambiguity comes from the status of examples like (1) below. These have the feeling of wordplay, as does (2), which plays on the clear ambiguity of "decline." The silliness of (3) is likewise evidence that cut class and cut hair feature distinct but homophonous verbs (Searle 1980:222).

meaning (41). The notation "$\lambda y : \Phi(y)[P(y)]$" means that the function is defined only over those values for y that meet condition Φ.

(41) $[\![kill_2]\!] = \lambda y : y$ is a time span $[\lambda e [e$ is an event of wasting $y]]$

Thus Kratzer takes dependent-triggered idioms to be cases where a verb-form has as one of its semantic values a partial function from a certain subset of the domain to a 'special' predicate of events. A dependent that triggers such an idiom must therefore be an argument. And this gives Kratzer an account of the asymmetry generalization. Typically with verbs of action, an object will be an argument of the verb but a subject will not be, and so typically a subject cannot trigger an idiom.

Wechsler (2005b) has an informative objection to this conclusion. He contends that Kratzer's assumptions are not enough to explain the asymmetry generalization, since they do not rule out, for example, a verb like the fictional greet$_2$ of (42), alongside the familiar greet$_1$ of (43).

(42) $[\![greet_2]\!] = \lambda y [\lambda e : e$ has an agent that is food $[$ True iff e is an event of some food upsetting y's stomach $]]$

(43) $[\![greet_1]\!] = \lambda y [\lambda e [$ True iff e is an event of somebody welcoming $y]]$

This greet$_2$ has only the 'greeted' as an argument, not the 'greeter.' But given any 'greeted' argument it returns an event predicate that is defined only over events with an agent that is food. Wechsler objects that this would make for a subject-triggered idiom, since the special meaning implies a semantic restriction on the subject.

But this objection misses its mark if we stick fast to the trigger assumption. That assumption says that the special meaning is available only with the right sort of dependent; and meanings like (42) for greet

(1) a # We could kill this bottle faster than we ever could a boar.
    b # The bottle took longer to kill than the boar did.
    c # We killed the weekend before we could the keg.

(2) # He declined that noun faster than I could the wine he had offered me.
    'He listed the forms of that noun faster than I could refuse the wine he had offered me.'

(3) # The math class was harder to cut than your hair was.

These all contrast with cases like (4), which seem quite normal, even though the activity of cutting cake is in fact quite different from that of cutting hair (*ibid.*).

(4) a We could cut Lee's hair faster than we ever could this cake.
    b Lee's cake took longer to cut than her hair did.

will not give us that. To see this, consider (44), where the subject names a person, not food.

(44) Ignacio greeted Olivia.

With greet$_2$ as its verb this will still be a meaningful sentence with a truth value. Its Kratzerian vP will have the meaning in (45), a partial function we can call F for short. In turn the whole sentence will mean (46).

(45) λe : e has an agent that is food [True iff Ignacio is the agent of e and e is an event of some food upsetting Val's stomach]

(46) $\exists e[F(e)]$

F is defined only for events with an agent that is food; no such event can have Ignacio as its agent. Consequently $F(e)$ can be True for no e at all, and (46) is necessarily false. But it is nevertheless meaningful, and meaningful with the 'upset stomach' meaning of "greet." It is just always false, wherever defined. By the criterion implied by the trigger assumption, therefore, (42) does not count as a subject-triggered idiom. This is just a case of ambiguity where one meaning for "greet" can be true only if the subject names food. By hypothesis it is therefore not something that Kratzer needs to rule out.

Given the trigger assumption, therefore, dependent-triggered idioms do in fact support Kratzer's separationist proposal.

Importantly, however, her proposal receives no further support from any other sorts of idioms, a fact that is easily overlooked. Take idioms like (47a) and (47b).

(47) a Val bit the bullet.
      b Val pulled some strings.

These concern neither biting nor bullets, neither pulling nor strings. So neither the verb nor its object has its ordinary meaning, and the idiom is conditioned symmetrically by the two in tandem. Let us call these *symmetrical verbal idioms*. Here Kratzer's treatment of idioms has no very clear application. It is stated over the semantic values of a head and its arguments. But in symmetrical idioms neither verb nor object has a value that is generally available outside the collocation. Notionally one might decompose pull strings into 'exert' plus 'influence,' but neither of these notional meanings is independently available, as shown in (48).[7]

---

[7] Nunberg *et al.* 1994 refer to idioms that are at least notionally decomposable, such as bite the bullet or pull strings, as "idiomatic combinations." They observe that, in the context of the collocation, the parts behave as if they each had a special

(48)   a   # Val does not like to pull her influence at the company.
       b   # Most people don't have strings at the company.

More importantly, even when pull and string are together, no notional components of the resulting meaning are straightforwardly available as referents for subsequent ellipses or pronouns, as suggested by (49).

(49)   a   # Val does not like to pull strings at the company, nor Mo, her influence in the extended family.
       b   # Val does not like to pull strings at the company, because not everybody has them.

So it is not clear that the parts of the idiom even have semantic values, let alone that ⟦pull⟧ is a function with ⟦some strings⟧ as its argument. And in that case no proposal about the semantic values of verbs, Kratzer's or any other, will explain the asymmetry generalization in the domain of symmetrical verbal idioms. This limits the force of Kratzer's separationist conclusion, since we will need an independent account for these other kinds of idioms. I bring up an additional challenge in the Discussion Points at the end of this chapter, from Marantz (1997).[8]

9.7 ARGUMENT STRUCTURE ALTERNATIONS

Separation and projection permit different responses to *alternations*. In alternations we find a word in different constellations of arguments, contributing the same sound and the same nugget of meaning. Item (50) is an example. Each sentence here has one more argument than the one below it, and assigns one more thematic relation. But they all say something about a kick, and this is in virtue of including a word pronounced "kick." Item (51) is a second example.

(50)   a Mo kicked somebody something.
       b Mo kicked something.
       c Mo kicked.

meaning. One can say things like I have so many huge bullets to bite this year. Here I add only the point that the special meaning is not available outside the collocation. Clearly one cannot use I have so many huge bullets this year to talk about a mess of very difficult decisions.

[8] Unlike Kratzer, Marantz 1997 rejects the assumption that the domain for stating idiomatic dependencies is lexical items. For Marantz the domain is, more broadly, expressions in Syntax, as large as an entire verb phrase. To account for the asymmetry generalization, he proposes that the domain for "special meanings" is bounded by AG: an expression outside the sister of this *v* cannot be the context for a special meaning within it.

(51) a Mo ate something.
      b Mo ate.

Semantically a pair of alternates may be in one of two relations, abstracting from the contribution of their arguments. Either their content is the same, supporting all the same entailments, or it is different. Let us say that alternates with the same content are *s-synonymous*, while those with different content are *s-heteronymous*. All the sentences in (50) are s-heteronymous. Sentence (50a) entails that the kicking is *to* something, but (50b) does not, while (50a) and (50b) both entail that the kicking is *of* something, but (50c) does not. On the other hand, (51a) and (51b) are arguably s-synonymous. Both entail that the eating was *by* something and *of* something. And perhaps any differences there may be between them can regarded as differences in conditions on usage, not narrow semantic content – though this is easily disputed.

The treatment of alternations differs in two ways between separationist and projectionist approaches. I will first quickly say what they are, and then describe them in more detail, using our examples. The first difference is this. For the separationist, the addition of a dependent in the syntax corresponds to the addition of a predicate in the meaning (Carlson 1984). For the projectionist, on the other hand, the removal of dependents in the syntax corresponds to the semantic addition of an existential quantifier (Dowty 1981, Gillon 2012). The second difference is expressed only when the alternates are s-heteronymous, as in (50). In such cases a separationist analysis allows us to say without error that the alternates include exactly the same verb. A projectionist analysis does not (Parsons 1990). For (50), our example with "kick," it will require three distinct verbs, though these may be related in Lexicon. All else being equal, these two differences favor the separationist approach on meta-theoretical grounds. But the advantage is not overwhelming.

These points can be confusing, so I will use the rest of this section to unfurl them more fully. Expert readers should skip ahead to the final paragraph.

Consider again our example of the s-synonymous alternates in (51). The separationist can say that both alternates, transitive and intransitive, involve the verb in (52). This contributes just the information that its event is an eating.

(52) $[\![\text{eat}]\!] = \lambda e[\text{ Eating}(e)\ ]$

Thematic relations for the subject or object are then contributed by structure in which this eat occurs, whether by silent lexical items or by rules of combination. The transitive context in (51a) will add both

Agent and Theme, yielding the meaning in (53). The intransitive context in (51b) will only add the former, yielding (54). Here there is an attractive symmetry between structure in the syntax and structure in the semantics.

(53)　$[\![$ Mo ate something $]\!] = \exists e[$ Eating(e) & Agent(e, Mo) & $\exists y[$Theme$(e, y)]$ $]$

(54)　$[\![$ Mo ate $]\!] = \exists e[$ Eating(e) & Agent(e, Mo) $]$

The formula in (54) does not have (53) as a syntactic consequence. Still we can underwrite the observed entailment from the intransitive to the transitive by meaning postulate, stipulating that every eating in fact has a theme (Dowty 1989, Parsons 1990).

Under a projectionist approach our options are different. If both alternates are to involve the same verb, we have to generalize to the most expansive case, as in (55), giving eat both the eater and the eaten as arguments.

(55)　$[\![$ eat $]\!] = \lambda y \lambda x \lambda e[$ Agent(e, x) & Eating(e) & Theme(e, y) $]$

In the transitive context of (51a), both arguments will be saturated by overt dependents, returning the value in (56).

(56)　$[\![$ Mo ate something $]\!] = \exists y \lambda e[$ Agent(e, Mo) & Eating(e) & Theme(e, y) $]$

But in the intransitive context of (51b) something inaudible must provide an existential quantifier to bind the role of Theme (Gillon 2012). The question then arises, why does the absence of an overt dependent correspond to the presence of an existential quantifier? This must simply be stipulated; and this is a stipulation that is obviated under the separationist approach (Carlson 1984). To skirt this particular problem, the projectionist can of course retreat, and say that the alternates do not involve the same verb. Rather, transitive (51a) has the two-argument eat from (55), while intransitive (51b) has the new one-argument eat in (57). But certainly the postulation of (57) does not *add* to the attractions of the theory.

(57)　$[\![$ eat$_2$ $]\!] = \lambda y \lambda e[$ Agent(e, Mo) & Eating(e) $]$

The second difference between separationist and projectionist treatments is one that *forces* the latter to multiply verbs. A projectionist account requires distinct verbs in s-heteronymous alternates; using the same verb will produce incorrect entailments. To see this, consider again the s-heteronymous alternates in the kick alternation from (50). The separationist, remember, can use the same verb in all three, namely (58).

(58)　$[\![$ kick $]\!] = \lambda e[$ Kicking(e) $]$

This verb contributes to each sentence just the information that its event is a kicking. The relations bound by Mo, somebody and something – let us assume they are Agent, Goal and Theme – are introduced by other bits of structure, silent in these sentences, that license the occurrence of the added dependents. In the end we get meanings for sentences (50a–c) along the lines of (59a–c), respectively.

(59)   a ∃e[Kicking(e) & Agent(e, Mo) & ∃x[Theme(e, x)] & ∃y[Goal(e, y)]]
       b ∃e[Kicking(e) & Agent(e, Mo) & ∃x[Theme(e, x)]]
       c ∃e[Kicking(e) & Agent(e, Mo)]

And now observe the logic of these three meanings. Rules of deduction do not support an inference from (59c) to (59b), or from the latter to (59a). These are not provable consequences, since the conclusion includes a conjunct that is not shared by the premise. And this is as it should be, since the corresponding pairs of English sentences in (50) don't even entail each other: (50c) does not entail (50b), nor (50b), (50a). This is why the alternates are s-heteronymous. Thus we avoid an incorrect entailment by not having the verb carry the same thematic predicates into every alternate (Parsons 1990). And just so, the same result is unattainable within a projectionist approach, since there the verb *would* carry the same predicates into every alternate. Suppose we had the same kick in all three sentences of (50). Within a projectionist approach, we would have to generalize to the most expansive case. The verb would need a meaning like (60), with three semantic arguments, corresponding to Agent, Theme and Goal.

(60)   ⟦ kick ⟧ = λzλyλxλe[Agent(e, x) & Kicking(e) & Theme(e, y)
         & Goal(e, z)]

The first two arguments of this kick, corresponding to the Theme and the Goal, are both optional. When they are not bound by an overt argument, they will have to be interpreted as existentially bound. But then as a result, all three of our alternates will have exactly the same meaning, namely (61). This is unacceptable, as the sentences in (50) are not s-synonymous.

(61)   ∃z∃yλe[Agent(e, Mo) & Kicking(e) & Theme(e, y) & Goal(e, z)]

Avoiding this problem requires that the verbs be distinct. With the three kick's in (62), for example, there would be no inappropriate entailments. The truth conditions for our three sentences would be exactly those of (59), the meanings that were assigned under the separationist theory.

(62)   a $[\![$ kick$_{(50a)}$ $]\!]$ $= \lambda z \lambda y \lambda x \lambda e[$ Agent(e, x) & Kicking(e) & Theme(e, y)
        & Goal(e, z)]

     b $[\![$ kick$_{(50b)}$ $]\!]$ $= \lambda y \lambda x \lambda e[$ Agent(e, x) & Kicking(e) & Theme(e, y)]

     c $[\![$ kick$_{(50c)}$ $]\!]$ $= \lambda x \lambda e[$ Agent(e, x) & Kicking(e)]

Thus to avoid incorrect entailments, the projectionist theory requires distinct verbs in s-heteronymous alternates.

The depth of this problem should not be overstated, however. The projectionist can still recognize a relation between his three kick's in Lexicon, provided that there is such a thing (for skepticism, see Marantz 1997 and Fodor and Lepore 1998). Whatever structure the separationist puts in Syntax can be transposed wholesale into Lexicon, simply swapping lexical for prelexical items, and syntactic for lexical derivations.[9] So the projectionist, like the separationist, is able to generalize across alternate occurrences of kick. The difference is just in where the generalization is stated: over primitives of Lexicon, or over primitives of Syntax. The issue is therefore whether there is any reason that such generalizations must be stated at one or the other level – a subtle and difficult question.

9.8   ALTERNATIONS ACROSS CATEGORIES

Alternations can cross categories. A predicate that occurs in verbal contexts, such as kick or sneeze, may also occur in nominal or other contexts, if often with an affix. These alternations are especially telling when the range of meanings found in verbal contexts is not matched in the others. In this section I will quickly discuss one sort of example, involving nominalization.

---

[9]   Suppose the separationist has the verb kick in (1) below. It has the sound [kɪk], the category V[*], and the meaning $\lambda e[$Kicking$(e)]$. To derive kick something, there will need to be some structure to introduce the Theme relation. Suppose this is the lexical item in (2), a silent morpheme with category v[*] and meaning $\lambda x \lambda e[$Theme$(e, x)]$. Finally suppose that (3) is a licit derivation in Syntax, interpreted by Kratzer's rule of Event Identification so as to output (4).

(1) $\langle$ [kɪk], V[*], λe.Kicking(e) $\rangle$

(2) $\langle$ [ϵ], v[*], $\lambda x \lambda e$.Theme(e, x) $\rangle$

(3)   [v[*] V[*]]

(4) $\lambda x \lambda e[$Kicking(e) & Theme$(e, x)]$

Then the projectionist can transpose this analysis wholesale into Lexicon. He need only say that (1) and (2) are not two lexical items, but two prelexical items, which can enter the lexical derivation in (3). Adding structure which introduces the agent will then output the transitive verb kick with the meaning in (62b).

Consider sneeze. As a verb one normally finds it in intransitive clauses such as (63). But it may also occur in clauses like (64) with a direct object and an oblique naming a path (64) (Goldberg 1995).

(63) Mo sneezed.

(64) Mo sneezed the tissue across the room.

Now, in (64) does the verb have the object and the oblique as semantic arguments? The discussion in Section 9.7 gives us one reason to say "No": (63) and (64) are s-heteronymous; the latter entails that someone sneezed something somewhere, but the former does not; so if the object and oblique were semantic arguments of the verb in (64), this could not be the same sneeze as that of (63). But this sort of argumentation is weak. If there is a Lexicon, why not have two related sneeze's?

A stronger reason comes from adding a third alternate to the mix, (65). Here sneeze occurs in a nominal context.

(65) Lee witnessed a sneeze.

Semantically this sneeze is like (63) and unlike (64). Sentence (65) does not entail that somebody sneezed something somewhere. This would be surprising if the verb in (64) had the object and the oblique as arguments semantically. For then there would be a verb that means 'to sneeze something somewhere,' and why couldn't this verb occur in nominal(izing) contexts? The answer may be: that's just the way it is. But the facts would receive an explanation if there were no such verb. And if there is no such verb, the direct object and PP in (64) are not arguments of the verb.

Marantz (1997), developing Chomsky (1970), gives this kind of argument for grow. As a verb, grow can occur in both intransitive (66) and transitive (67).

(66) The tomatoes grew.

(67) Mo grew the tomatoes.

The question now is about the subject of the transitive: is it an argument of the verb? Marantz answers No, because of the noun growth.

Growth is a nominal form of intransitive, and not transitive grow, as shown by (68). (68) is like (66) and unlike (67); it has no use which entails that somebody grew something. To see this, notice that if Lee witnessed the tomatoes growing, we can only use (68b) to say something false; in particular, we will speak falsely even if Lee failed to see the tomatoes being grown *by somebody*. Thus growth is the noun form only of the grow in (66), which does not entail a grower.

(68) a Lee witnessed the growth (of the tomatoes).
　　　b Lee did not witness the growth (of the tomatoes).

If there were a verb grow that meant 'to grow something,' it would be a lexical accident that this cannot be nominalized as growth. But this would have an explanation if there were no such verb, no verb with an argument interpreted as the grower. To achieve this apparent advantage, Marantz concludes that indeed there is no such verb, and consequently that Mo in (67) must be an argument of structure that is separate from the verb, namely Kratzer's AG.[10]

Of course this argument is quite limited in scope. It does not apply directly to all verbs which occur in transitive clauses. It does not apply directly to destroy, for instance, since this has no nominal form that fails to entail a destroyer: if Jalal witnessed the 1221 CE destruction of Merv, then necessarily he witnessed the 1221 CE destruction of Merv by Tolui and the Mongols. Nonetheless, Marantz proposes to project the conclusion he derives from grow to the general case, so that no verb in a transitive clause describing an action has the subject as an argument. For resistance to this, see Wechsler (2008), who builds on Smith (1972).

9.9 LINKING

There are regular correspondences between grammatical and semantic relations, at least at a level of 'underlying' grammatical relations (Chapter 11). In transitive clauses that describe an action, for example, the subject normally names its agent.

Sometimes the existence of such regularities is cited as evidence for separationism (Goldberg 1995, Kako and Wagner 2001, among others). The reason is, the regularities are captured if the grammatical relations are themselves associated with the matching semantic relations, independently of the verb – for example, if the direct object relation itself is interpreted by the Patient relation, separately from the verb. We then expect the observed correspondence.

True enough. But this is not an argument *against* projectionism, since the projectionist simply transposes the separationist's derivation into Lexicon, swapping its primitives and rules for prelexical analogues.

---

[10] The argument I present in this paragraph is a simplification of the one actually given in Marantz 1997. Marantz concerns himself with the fact that the possessor can be understood as the agent when the noun is destruction (Tolui's destruction of Merv), but not when the noun is growth (John's growth of tomatoes).

Where the separationist has a silent v for the Agent relation, plus a V pronounced "sing" for the property of being a singing, the projectionist can have exactly the same predicates as *pre*-lexical items, giving them prelexical categories ʌ and Λ.[11] The regularities that the separationist captures in Syntax are then captured in Lexicon.

So there is no question that the projectionist is *able* to state the observed correspondences, given Lexicon as a level of analysis. The question is just whether it is better to state them in one place or the other, and this is not answered by the mere existence of the correlations. Nor does their mere existence demonstrate that there is no Lexicon in which the projectionist can do his work. The argument against such a Lexicon cannot be quite that easy (Sproat 1985, Goldberg 1995, Marantz 1997, Fodor and Lepore 1998, Embick and Noyer 2007).

9.10 SYNTACTIC IMPLEMENTATION

In our initial example, (1), Ozzy names a participant relative to sing. On a projectionist account, Ozzy is also a content argument of sing semantically, but on a separationist account it is not. In this section I quickly describe what each sort of account would (most likely) say about the syntax of clauses with sing.

(1) Ozzy sings.

The projectionist treatment of (1) gives sing the singer as a functional argument.

(69) $[\![\mathrm{sing}]\!] = \lambda x \lambda e [\ \mathrm{SingingBy}(e, x)\ ]$

As noted in Chapter 4, linguists most often assume that functional arguments coincide with syntactic arguments. So if sing has a meaning like (69), it will usually be given a syntactic category like (70). Here $\langle\langle\rangle, \mathrm{N}\rangle$ is an a-list calling for an external argument of category N.

(70) sing:V[$\langle\langle\rangle, \mathrm{N}\rangle$]

Jointly, (69) and (70) ensure that a lexical item with sound "sing" and meaning 'sing' may occur with a dependent naming the singer. It takes more to guarantee that any such lexical item, at least when serving as the predicate of a tensed active clause, *must* occur with a singer

---

[11] The inversion of the category labels here alludes to Dowty's 1979 theory of Lexicon as "upside-down Generative Semantics."

dependent. To do that, one must require that no verb meaning 'sing' fails to have an argument for the singer, and that a verb which has an argument must also take an argument in Syntax; see Chapters 3 and 11. Now compare the separationist alternative in (71). Here the semantic value of sing is just the event predicate in (71a), and the singer is a content argument of a silent lexical item AG with the value in (71b).

(71)   a $[\![\text{sing}]\!] = \lambda e[\ \text{Singing}(e)\ ]$
       b $[\![\text{AG}]\!] = \lambda x \lambda e[\ \text{Agent}(e, x)\ ]$

To ensure that sing clauses may or must have a dependent naming the singer, one now has to fix the syntactic categories of sing and AG so that they may or must go together. I will discuss two ways to do this. One says that AG has both Ozzy and sing as arguments in syntax, while sing has no arguments at all. The other says that sing, though it has no arguments in the semantics, does have the complex of AG and Ozzy as an argument in the syntax. This is less orthodox, because it gives the verb a syntactic argument with no semantic correlate.

The first approach is illustrated in derivation (72).

(72)   Ozzy sing:v

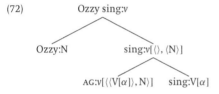

Here sing has the minor category feature α. This is not a contextual feature; it just puts sing in a certain minor category of verbs. Meanwhile AG has the major category v and the contextual feature $\langle \langle V[\alpha] \rangle, N \rangle$, an argument-list. With this a-list, AG has an internal argument of category $V[\alpha]$ and also external argument of category N. In (72), it thus takes sing and Ozzy as syntactic arguments. Semantically, AG combines with sing by Kratzer's rule of EventIdentification, defined above in Section 9.6. The result combines with Ozzy by Application to yield (73).

(73) $[\![(72)]\!] = \lambda e[\ \text{Agent}(e, \text{Ozzy})\ \&\ \text{Singing}(e)\ ]$

All of this ensures that sing may occur with a noun phrase naming the singer. To guarantee that it must, at least in tensed active clauses, we need two further stipulations. One, every tensed active clause must have a predicate of category v, and not just a V phrase. Two, it must be that AG is the only v that selects verb phrases of class α. Notice, these stipulations echo what is required by the projectionist to achieve the same effect.

The second separationist syntax I will discuss is (74), which echoes ideas in Krifka (1992) and Hornstein (2002).[12]

(74)

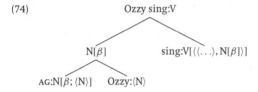

This preserves the meanings for sing and AG in (71), so sing has no arguments semantically. But with the a-list $\langle\langle\ldots\rangle, N[\beta]\rangle$, it does give sing an external argument of category $N[\beta]$. Meanwhile, AG is itself an N of subclass β, which also has the a-list $\langle\langle N\rangle\rangle$. It thus takes Ozzy as an internal argument, and returns the $N[\beta]$ that sing is to take as its argument. Semantically this is interpreted by applying $[\![AG]\!]$ to $[\![Ozzy]\!]$, as in (75a), and conjoining the result with $[\![sing]\!]$, as in (75b).

(75) a Application($[\![AG]\!]$, $[\![Ozzy]\!]$) $= \lambda e[$ Agent(e, Ozzy) $]$
      b Conjunction($[\![sing]\!]$, $[\![AG\ Ozzy]\!]$) $= \lambda e[$ Agent(e, Ozzy) & Singing(e) $]$

Under this analysis, Ozzy is a syntactic argument of AG, and then the resulting complex of the two is a syntactic argument of sing. So sing has an argument in its syntax that does not correspond to a functional argument in its semantics. This makes AG something like a semantically interpreted but inaudible marker of case, marking the underlying subject relation between the verb and its external argument.

This comparison of projectionist and separationist approaches makes clear that separationism demands that more work be done in Syntax. But this is work that can be done: by separating an argument from the verb, we do not lose the power to restrict the verb's distribution relative to that argument. If sing occurs only with a singer, the separationist must ensure that sing always occurs with AG. The projectionist is relieved of this task in Syntax, but he has an exactly analogous job in Lexicon. He still has to ensure that the sing with a singer argument is the only "sing" there is; and technically this is just like requiring that the only v which selects sing is AG.

In short, a verb that lacks semantic arguments is not therefore permitted to occur wherever it likes. I have often heard the opposite, but this is simply an error.

---

[12] For a related alternative, see Hunter 2011, who develops Pietroski 2005a. Hunter uses a rule of interpretation, defined over the local grammatical relations of first and second argument, to introduce thematic relations.

DISCUSSION POINTS

1 Do you find it attractive to presume, absent powerful evidence to the contrary, that two synonymous alternates, as in (1) below, have exactly the same lexical item as their predicate? Why or why not?

(1) a Mo ate something.
　　 b Mo ate.

2 Igbo (2) has the complex predicate sọ ji 'poke snap' in either a transitive (a) or intransitive (b) clause. The intransitive subject has the interpretation of the transitive object.

(2) a Ọ　sọ　ji　　-ri　osisi　m.
　　　　3sS　poke　snap　-FACT　wood　my
　　　　'S/he made my stick snap from poking.'
　　 b Osisi　m　sọ　ji　　-ri　asọji.
　　　　wood　my　poke　snap　-FACT　BVC
　　　　'My stick snapped from poking.'

But neither part of sọ ji 'poke snap' has the same privileges. Sọ 'poke' but not ji 'snap' goes in transitives, (3a), and vice versa for intransitives, (3b). How might this be used to argue for the separationist conclusion that sọ 'poke' does not have the poker as a lexical argument? (Williams 2005, 2014a)

(3) a Ọ　sọ　　/　*ji　-rọ/ri　osisi　m.
　　　　3sS　poke　/　snap　-FACT　wood　my
　　　　'S/he poked/*snapped my stick.'
　　 b Osisi　m　ji　　/　*sọ　-ri/rọ　eji/asọ.
　　　　wood　my　snap　/　poke　-FACT　BVC
　　　　'There was a snapping/*poking of my stick.'

3 Consider (4) and (5). How might you capture these patterns in a projectionist theory? And in a separationist theory? Be explicit about both the syntax and the semantics.

(4) a I stuffed the chicken with rice.
　　 b ⊨ I stuffed the chicken.
(5) a I stuffed rice into the chicken.
　　 b ⊭ I stuffed rice.

In (6) and (7), stuffed occurs in an adjectival context, and describes a state that results from stuffing. Sentence (7) is bad without into the chicken. How might these facts bear on your analyses of (4) and (5)? How would you extend your analyes to these data?

(6) The chicken stayed quite stuffed (with rice).

(7) The rice stayed quite stuffed ?*(into the chicken).

4 According to Marantz (1997:209), there are "idioms with [a]
causative [morpheme] and [a] lower non-agentive verb," such
as (8a), but none "with [a] causative morpheme and [a] lower
agentive verb," such as the hypothetical (8b).

(8) a make ends meet
     b* make dogs fight
        'to engage in a heated argument just out of boredom'

Marantz sees this as an extension of the *asymmetry generalization*,
discussed in Section 9.6, and endeavors to explain it in the same
terms. Is this extension possible given Kratzer's view of idioms,
as cases where the value of some head is a function with a parti-
tioned domain? Why or why not?

5 Are idioms like The shit hit the fan or The roof caved in on *x* consistent with the idiom asymmetry generalization? Explain why or
why not.

6 Suppose we take the data in (63) and (64), repeated here, to provide
an argument for a separationist treatment of thematic relations.
How would you then account for the oddity of (9) and (10), without
giving up the separationist hypothesis?

(63)   Mo sneezed.

(64)   Mo sneezed the tissue across the room.

 (9)   # Mo shattered the tissue across the room.

(10)   # Mo witnessed the tissue across the room.

7 At the end of this chapter I said: "a verb that lacks semantic arguments is not therefore permitted to occur wherever it likes. I have
often heard the opposite, but this is simply an error." Explain this
quotation in your own words. What assumptions about grammar
underlie the claim that verbs with no semantic arguments are
syntactically unrestricted?

8 As mentioned in Section 9.10, Krifka (1992) has thematic relations
introduced separately with each individual DP. Thus, in (11), the
DPs Tony and Geezer have the values in (a) and (b). In a system like
this, could we implement the principle of Role Exhaustion from
Chapter 8? How?

(11) Tony and Geezer sang.

      a $[\![[_{DP} \text{ Tony}]]\!] = \lambda e[\text{Agent}(e, \text{Tony})]$
      b $[\![[_{DP} \text{ Geezer}]]\!] = \lambda e[\text{Agent}(e, \text{Geezer})]$

9 As discussed in Section 9.4, Schein (1997) argues from sentences like (24), repeated below, that thematic relations are introduced by structure separate from the verb. Specifically some part of (24)'s derivation means 'the professors are agents of event e.'

(24) The students and possibly the professors surrounded the manor.

Does the unacceptability of (12) create a problem for this view? If so, how might the problem be resolved?

(12) *Not the professors surrounded the manor.

SUGGESTIONS FOR FURTHER READING

On separation, read Fillmore 1968, Carlson 1984, Dowty 1989, Schein 1993, 1997, 2002, 2012, Kratzer 1996, 2000, 2002, 2003, Marantz 1997, Borer 2003 and Pietroski 2005a, to appear b.

10 Event structure

10.1 INTRODUCTION

Abstracting from its noun phrases, a clause is semantically a predicate of events, (1). Call this the **main event** of the clause.

(1) $\lambda e[\, P(e)\,]$

P might relate the main event to others, as in (2), which cashes out P as a predicate of events that bear R to some other event. R might be Cause, for example.

(2) $\lambda e[\, \exists e'[R(e')](e)\,]$

A semantic analysis like this is called an **event structure**. The events to which the main event is related are called **subevents** of the clause. Sometimes subevents might *be parts of* the main event (Schein 1993, Rothstein 2004).

An event structure is **complex** when it includes more than one predicate of events. When a clause with a single audible predicate is given a complex event structure, this is a claim of semantic decomposition. I assume by default that decomposition is strict, in the sense of Chapter 2, but will sometimes consider alternatives.

This chapter is about a much-used class of event-structural decompositions that derive from sources including Lakoff (1965, 1971), McCawley (1971), Ross (1972) and Dowty (1972). These works advance analyses like (3–6), with (b) giving the meaning of (a).

(3) a The glass is hard.
     b Hard(the glass)
(4) a Floyd viewed the glass.
     b $\mathrm{Do}_p\langle\text{Floyd}, \text{View(Floyd, the glass)}\rangle$
(5) a The glass hardened.
     b $\mathrm{Become}_p\langle\text{Hard(the glass)}\rangle$
(6) a Floyd hardened the glass.
     b $\mathrm{Cause}_p\langle\, \exists\phi[\mathrm{Do}_p\langle\text{Floyd}, \phi\rangle],\ \mathrm{Become}_p\langle\text{Hard(the glass)}\rangle\,\rangle$

Here Do_p, $Become_p$ and $Cause_p$ are propositional operators. Event structures are often written in this format. Yet they are usually talked about as relations over events, and we can rewrite them explicitly in those terms. One possible revision is given in (7–10), roughly following Parsons (1990).[1] For expository clarity I mark the main event as e_1 and leave it bound only by a lambda; the meaning of the complete sentence would have this variable existentially quantified.

(7)   a The glass is hard.
      b $\lambda e_1[\ \text{Hard}(e_1, \text{the glass})\ ]$
(8)   a Floyd viewed the glass.
      b $\lambda e_1[\ \text{Do}\langle e_1, \text{Floyd}\rangle\ \&\ \text{Viewing}(e_1, \text{the glass})\ ]$
(9)   a The glass hardened.
      b $\lambda e_1[\ \exists e_2[\ \text{Become}\langle e_1, e_2\rangle\ \&\ \text{Hard}(e_2, \text{the glass})\ ]]$
(10) a Floyd hardened the glass.
      b $\lambda e_1[\ \text{Do}\langle e_1, \text{Floyd}\rangle\ \&\ \exists e_2[\ \text{Cause}\langle e_1, e_2\rangle\ \&$
         $\&\ \exists e_3[\ \text{Become}\langle e_2, e_3\rangle\ \&\ \text{Hard}(e_3, \text{the glass})\ ]]]$

I will first discuss general motivations for these decompositions (Section 10.2), and then (Section 10.3) counter the suggestion that they "embody a hypothesis about possible versus impossible [...] meanings" (Dowty 1979:125). Section 10.4 observes that event-structural decompositions may or may not be syntactically derived, and Section 10.5 concerns the relevance of adverbs to this choice. I then (Section 10.6) argue against the very common semantics implied by (10), according to which the main event of a transitive clause describing a change is one that *causes* a change of state. And finally (Section 10.7), I review how event structures have been used to revise traditional inventories of thematic relations.

10.2 GENERAL MOTIVATIONS

Event-structural decomposition is in the first place encouraged by the semantic correlates of formal paradigms such as (11) (Hall 1965, Lakoff 1965).

(11) a The glass is hard.
      b The glass hardened.
      c Floyd hardened the glass.

---

[1] This eventish translation is unfaithful only in its treatment of Do. In the original (Dowty 1972) and also in some recent adaptations (Van Valin 2004), Do_p relates an individual x to a proposition $P(...)(x)$, where P is stative. This suggests a translation of $\text{Do}(e_1, e_2, x)\ \&\ P(...)(x)(e_2)$. But following Parsons 1990 I simplify this to: $\text{Do}(e, x)\ \&\ P(...)(x)(e)$.

The differences in meaning here coincide with differences in formal structure: the presence or absence of -en, transitive or intransitive syntax. So it is reasonable to infer that the meanings of (11b) and (11c) have derived structure, plausibly analyzed in terms of Become, Cause and Do.

But the semantic decomposition has some motives that persist even in the absence of obvious morphological support – for example, in analyzing kill and die, or melt and liquid. Event structures put clauses and their verbs into broad semantic classes. Given (10), for example, transitive clauses with harden are in the class of sentences whose meanings involve (or are described as involving) Cause and Become. The classification is empirically motivated if it permits the statement of general patterns. Of central interest are general patterns in inferential relations, or in the distribution of verbs relative to arguments and modifiers.

For instance, suppose that all clauses claimed to mean $\text{Cause}_p(\phi, \psi)$ entail ψ, regardless of their particular verb. One instance of this would be the entailment in (12), paired with the semantic analyses in (6) and (5), respectively.

(12)   a   Floyd hardened the glass.
      b ⊨ The glass hardened.

Another would be (13), if we assign these sentences the meanings in (14).

(13)   a   Al killed the ewe.
      b ⊨ The ewe died.
(14)   a $\text{Cause}_p \langle\ \exists\phi[\text{Do}_p\langle\text{Al}, \phi\rangle], \text{Become}_p\langle\text{Dead(the ewe)}\rangle\ \rangle$
      b $\text{Become}_p\langle\text{Dead(the ewe)}\rangle$

Then we can capture all of these entailments, for all the various verbs, with a single meaning postulate for Cause_p: we stipulate that, for any ϕ and ψ, if $\text{Cause}_p(\phi, \psi)$ is true, then ψ is true as well (Dowty 1979). Without the event structural analysis, or something comparable, we would need a distinct meaning postulate for each individual verb, missing a generalization.

We can do still better with (10b), our eventish translation. Formula (10b) has (9b) and (7b) as provable syntactic consequences, by Conjunction Elimination in the scope of an existential quantifier. So if (10b) gives the meaning of (10a), the entailment from (10a) to (9a) and (7a) requires no postulates about the meanings of Cause or Become: it is a strict analyticity, underwritten by logical form alone. And that is entirely impossible without some semantic decomposition. The decomposition provides structure over which patterns of inference can be defined.

The same point applies, *mutatis mutandis*, to the inferences in (15) and (16) as a justification for semantic decomposition in terms of Become.

(15) a   The glass hardened (at noon).
    b ⊨ The glass was hard (at noon).
(16) a   The ewe died (at noon).
    b ⊨ The ewe was dead (at noon).

Turning to patterns in syntax, suppose that all clauses with Cause or $Cause_p$ in their meaning are transitive. Then we need just a single grammatical principle that links $Cause_{(p)}$ meanings to transitive syntax. Without the event structural analysis, there would again be a loss of generality, as we would need a distinct linking principle for every verb individually. So the event structure isolates semantic distinctions that are grammatically relevant (Rappaport Hovav and Levin 1998).

Dowty (1979) argues that the fourfold paradigm of event structures in (3–6) is justified in particular by the independent *aspectual classes* of Vendler (1957). Vendler discerns four semantic classes of sentences: states, activities, achievements and accomplishments.[2] The division manifests itself in what temporal modifiers the various classes accept, and in what temporal inferences they license. For example, while the addition of in 10 minutes to an achievement or accomplishment sentence can straightforwardly describe the duration of its main event, as in (17), the semantic effect of the same addition to a state or activity sentence is different, as in (18). The sentences in (17) concern a two-minute hardening, but those in (18) do not entail that there were two minutes of hardness or viewing.

(17) a   The glass hardened in two minutes.
    b   Floyd hardened the glass in two minutes.
(18) a   The glass was hard in two minutes.
    b ? Floyd viewed the glass in two minutes.

Or also, if a state or activity sentence is true over a time interval, then in general it is true over any part of that interval. For example, if it is true all day Monday that the glass is hard or Floyd viewed the glass, then the same is true all Monday morning. But this is not so for achievement

---

[2] Vendler's 1957 observations echo or develop thoughts in Aristotle's *Metaphysics* and in Ryle 1949. Published in the same year was Garey 1957, a study on perfective and imperfective in French, which introduced the terms "telic" and "atelic." Achievement and accomplishment sentences are telic, while state and activity sentences are atelic.

and accomplishment sentences. If it is true of Monday in its entirety that Floyd hardened the glass, for instance, the same need not be true of Monday morning. For extensive discussion of aspectual classification, see Comrie (1976), Klein (1994) and Smith (1997).

According to Dowty, this classification suggests that verbs in general have one of the four event structures in (3–6). Stative clauses, like the glass is hard, have a simple event structure, a single unanalyzed predicate of states, whose content is specific to the adjective or verb. The other classes are derived by various additions of Do, Become and Cause. Activity sentences, like Floyd viewed the glass, add Do to a stative predication; achievement sentences, like the glass hardened, derive from statives with addition of Become; and accomplishment sentences, like Floyd hardened the glass, in turn derive from achievements with addition of Cause, and (perhaps) also Do. A decomposition along other lines, using different constellations of relations, might not coincide with the Vendler classes at all. And to that extent, this event-structural decomposition has a specific empirical motivation.

One last kind of argument for event-structural decomposition is explicitly psychological. If semantic values are mental concepts, and event structures give the structure of a clause's semantic value, then tokening the clause means tokening mental concepts that are the values of predicates in the event structure. The first-blush plausibility of an event-structural decomposition is therefore increased if its primitives, such as Do or Cause, stand for concepts that seem to play an important role in our conceptual or perceptual repertoire (Jackendoff 1990b). But of course an argument for plausibility goes only so far. It would be no small feat to demonstrate empirically that tokening Floyd hardened the glass, for example, consists in tokening the concept Cause. Semantic decompositions have in general found little support from experimental psychology (Fodor et al. 1975) – though for promising recent thoughts on this, see Lidz et al. (2011) and Pietroski et al. (2011).

10.3 IMPOSSIBLE MEANINGS?

Event-structural analysis affords semantic structure over which general patterns of inference or grammar can be stated. Sometimes it is taken to do more, and "embody a hypothesis about possible versus impossible [...] meanings" (Dowty 1979:125) for verbs or their clauses. Certainly this is true if "meaning" is identified with semantic structure; but then the point is definitional. For it to be substantive, "meaning" must be not structure but content, something like entailments or satisfaction conditions. But in that case the promise is deeply misguided, as emphasized by Dowty himself (*ibid.*). In this section I will say why.

Event-structural analysis recognizes a few general predicates, such as Do, Cause and Become, that are shared by clauses with many different verbs. The remainder are predicates more particular to the verb, perhaps even unique to it. Many verbs occupy clauses with Become in their meaning, but far fewer contribute Hard to the mix. The verb-specific contribution is sometimes called the *root*, after Pesetsky (1995).

For Dowty (1979) and some others, restrictions on the interpretation of these general predicates are a central concern of the theory of event structure: these are meant to underwrite general patterns of inference in the manner of logical constants, in the logic of the theorist's metalanguage.[3] But even for Dowty, the event-structural analysis as such says nothing about the more specific predicates. Restrictions on their interpretation are the domain of a different theory. For example, nothing in the theory of event structure rules out a stative predicate *schard*, where the schard are those who stand a good chance of undergoing something unpleasant late at night as a result of someone else's reckless daytime actions – a meaning whose explication is rather complex, involving modality, causation, subtle subcategories of action, and so forth. The theory says only that, given this predicate, there can be a clause Tim schardened Jay, with the semantic structure: Tim caused Jay to become schard.

Because of this, the theory of event structure itself puts few or no restrictions on what content a sentence might have – that is, on what one might entail or on what would make it true. As Dowty writes in making this point:

> [To] say that a possible sentence meaning is any proposition
> expressible by a sentence formed out of stative predicates plus
> aspectual operators CAUSE, BECOME, DO, etc. is not really to exclude
> any proposition (set of [worlds]) as impossible, nor is it to exclude
> any function [from individuals to truth values] as an impossible
> intransitive-verb meaning, etc. No real limitation is being made [...]
> as long as we do not limit the interpretation of the primitive (stative)
> predicates. (1979:125–126)

---

[3] Here it is again important that, for Dowty, the decomposition is metasemantic. Therefore Dowty's only claim is that relevant inferences are valid in the logical metalanguage of the theorist. There is no *direct* claim that they are valid in some sort of logic in which the object language is itself embedded, much less that the inferences are *perceived* as valid by anyone competent in the language.

An analogy to logic may be useful. With the rule that ⌜Φ & Ψ⌝ entails ⌜Ψ⌝, we can treat many entailments as instances of a general pattern. But this puts no restrictions at all on what truth conditions an arbitrary formula, ⌜Φ⌝ or ⌜Ψ⌝, and hence ⌜Φ & Ψ⌝, might have. Content is never determined entirely by logical form, or by the meanings of a few special constants.

So only a theory of the specific primitives, our analogues of nonlogical constants, will limit what can be expressed. But, despite important observations here and there, and ambitious efforts in roughly the spirit of Carnap (1928),[4] we have no substantial account of what kinds of states can be described by natural predicates. Evidently we tend not to have words like grue, a predicate that is true of things that are green and observed before 2017, or otherwise blue (Goodman 1955), as Dowty (1979:128) notes. Yet grue is no harder to define, or more removed from concepts that seem perceptually or otherwise 'basic' to us, than are the words chair, vegetable, money, nerd, flaw, rainbow, vitamin, illegitimate, poisonous, ashamed, opalescent, porous, virtuous, Jewish, able, offend or pollard. It just isn't as useful for making generalizations. Prospects for a genuine and comprehensive theory of primitive meanings look slim; and in any case, it is hard to imagine why this should be part of linguistic theory.

What event-structural analysis does do, like any semantic decomposition, is *classify* meanings, and recognize some facts as instances of general patterns that are governed by that classification. It embodies hypotheses about what inferences are analytic and which semantic classes are relevant vis-à-vis arguments and modifiers. For the mentalist it also embodies a claim about what concepts are tokened by an expression. But it embodies no hypotheses about limits on possible content.

10.4 PROJECTION AND SEPARATION

How does a complex event structure relate to the parts of the derivation? As with thematic relations, discussed in the previous chapter, there are two approaches, projectionist and separationist. On a projectionist approach, the entire event structure comes from the verb. According to (19), for example, all the predicates in (10b) – not only Hard, but Do, Cause and Become, project from the verb harden.

---

[4] Dowty himself wagers a few guesses about the inventory of basic statives (1979: 126–129). But these have not been carried forward in subsequent work.

(19) harden $\cong \lambda y \lambda x \lambda e_1 [\exists e_2 [\text{Do} \langle e_1, e_2, x \rangle \, \& \, \exists e_3 [\text{Cause} \langle e_1, e_3 \rangle \, \&$
      $\& \, \exists e_4 [\text{Become} \langle e_3, e_4 \rangle \, \& \, \text{Hard}(e_4, y) \,]]]]$

The separationist says instead that the event structural decomposition is syntactically derived. The various predicates come from distinct parts of the derivation (Lakoff 1965, 1970, von Stechow 1995). For example, (10) may have a syntax like (20), where DO, CAUSE and -en are lexical items that mean Do, Cause and Become. The semantic contribution of hard, the verb stem here, is just the stative predicate Hard.

(20) [[Floyd DO] [[CAUSE [-en [[the glass] hard]]]]]

Only the first, projectionist option puts structure in the meaning of a lexical item, a claim of lexical semantic decomposition. Recall from Chapter 2 that this can be taken in various ways. If the decomposition is strict, (19) may mean that harden has a semantic value with underived structure. Or it may mean that harden is derived in Lexicon out of prelexical parts whose meanings are Do, Cause, Become and Hard. This is particularly plausible for harden, since the predicates Hard and Become coincide with the stem hard and its -en suffix. As usual, the theoretical options are multiplied further by metasemantic and representational views of decomposition, both of which are very well attested among proponents of event-structural analysis.

In the next section, I will discuss the use of adverbs, the adverb again in particular, to distinguish separationist from projectionist analyses empirically.

10.5 ADVERBS

Debates over event structure often depend on adverbs, since these may serve as what I called a *semantic wedge* in Chapter 9. I will discuss the relevance of adverbs first to separationist and then to projectionist theories.

Before that we need a distinction between modifying and describing. A modifier *modifies* what it combines with. In (21) the adjectives blond and illegitimate syntactically modify child and semantically modify its meaning.

(21) a blond child
      b illegitimate child

A modifier may also *describe* certain things, implying that they have particular properties. In (21a) blond describes the individuals that satisfy blond child, since these are entailed to have golden hair. But it also describes the hair of those children, since their hair is entailed to be golden. Similarly the adjective in illegitimate child describes the child in virtue of describing its parents, who are implied to have been unmarried at its birth.

Thus a modifier may describe not only the satisfiers of a predicate it modifies, but also other things to which these are related, including their own parts. Given this, an adverb that modifies a predicate of changes might well describe the change in virtue of describing its end state, as blond describes a part of what it modifies; and an adverb that modifies a predicate of states might describe the state in virtue of describing its cause, as the origins of what is modified are described by illegitimate.

10.5.1 Adverbs and separated event structures

On a separationist view, the parts of a complex event structure come from distinct parts of the clause. So the clause will have parts whose meaning contains no more than a part of the total event structure. If (22a) means (22b), for example, its syntax will have a part, call it E, that just means 'be shut.'

(22) a Syl closed the window.
      b $\lambda e_1[\text{Do}\langle e_1 \text{Syl}\rangle$ & $\exists e_2[\text{Cause}\langle e_1, e_2\rangle$ &
         & $\exists e_3[\text{Become}\langle e_2, e_3\rangle$ & BeingShut$(e_3, \text{the window})$]]]

Syntax permitting, such a part can be modified by an adverb, and in that case the adverb is guaranteed to describe a subevent of the event structure. Whether it describes other events to which that subevent is related (as illegitimate describes people to whom the child is related) will depend on its specific meaning. For example, if the syntax permits an adverb to modify the hypothetical part E of (22a), that adverb is guaranteed to describe the state of being shut (e_3); but it may not describe the events of becoming shut (e_2) or causing to become shut (e_1). So if in fact an adverb in a transitive clause with close can describe just the state of being shut, this is good initial evidence for the separationist analysis. It is not decisive, however, since an adverb may well describe a proper part of the event denoted by the expression it modifies, just as blond describes a proper part of the child when it modifies child.

Sometimes an adverb does seem to describe just part of a complex event structure. Many speakers find an ambiguity in sentences like (23), with a verb of change and again. The adverb describes either the closing itself, or the end state of the window being shut (Morgan 1969, McCawley 1971:24, Dowty 1979:251, von Stechow 1996, Beck and

Johnson 2004, Beck 2005). The first, *repetitive* interpretation implies that someone had previously closed the window. The second, *restitutive* interpretation implies only that it had previously been in a shut state.

(23)   Syl closed the window again.

Item (24) sketches a separationist analysis that allows this directly (McCawley 1971, von Stechow 1996). According to (24a) the state of the window being shut is expressed by close the window on its own. So if again is permitted to modify this constituent, as in (25), the result will say just that a state of this sort once obtained before.[5]

(24)   a $[\![$ [close the window] $]\!] = \lambda e[$ BeingShut$(e,$ the window$)$]
       b $[\![$ [BECOME [close the window]] $]\!]$
           $= \lambda e_2[$ $\exists e_3[$ Become$\langle e_2, e_3 \rangle$ & BeingShut$(e_3,$ the window$)$]]
       c $[\![$ [CAUSE [BECOME [close the window]]] $]\!]$
           $= \lambda e_1[$ $\exists e_2[$ Cause$\langle e_1, e_2 \rangle$ &
           $\exists e_3[$ Become$\langle e_2, e_3 \rangle$ & BeingShut$(e_3,$ the window$)$]]]

(25)   [CAUSE [BECOME [[close the window] again]]]

On the other hand, if again modifies a larger constituent, as in (26), it will describe (at least) the making-shut, the main event of closing the window. The separationist analysis therefore allows for ambiguities of attachment.

(26)   [CAUSE [BECOME [[close the window]]] again]

However, things are not always this way. In general an adverb *cannot* describe only a subevent of the predicate it modifies, as stressed in Fodor (1970). The sentences in (27), for example, cannot have the given interpretations, where the adverb is meant to target the result state of being cool. Here even modification by again, in (27c), is unnatural: if a soup made of cool raw cucumbers warms up near the stove, and Dirk brings it back to room temperature, he has not cooled it *again*. Chierchia and McConnell-Ginet (1990:359) make the same point with (28).

(27)   a   * Dirk very cooled the cucumber soup.
               'Dirk made the cucumber soup be very cool.'
       b   * Dirk cooled the cucumber soup on Saturday.
               'Dirk made the cucumber soup be cool on Saturday.'
       c   * Dirk cooled the cucumber soup again.
               'Disk made the cucumber soup again be cool.'

---

[5] Here I am cavalier about the semantics; for a careful discussion see Beck and Johnson 2004.

(28)   * John cleaned the jacket again.
       'John made the jacket again be clean.'

To explain this, the separationist must rely on syntax: the syntax must forbid adverbs from modifying the relevant constituent. This is not unreasonable, as there do seem to be such restrictions: not every expression with a verb in it can be modified by an adverb. Consider (29).

(29)   Al quickly pounded the cutlet flat (#slowly).

Without the addition of slowly, this can mean that Al flattened the cutlet quickly with his pounding, but it cannot mean just that the pounding was quick (Rappaport Hovav and Levin 2001, Williams 2009). If it could, then, contrary to fact, the addition of slowly would be acceptable, with the meaning that Al flattened the cutlet slowly by pounding it very quickly. This observation implies that the smallest part of (29) that accepts adverbs is a predicate of flattenings, and not merely of poundings. Yet plausibly the verb pound in this sentence is itself a predicate of poundings; and if this is correct,[6] it must be that quickly simply cannot modify pound on its own. For some reason the syntax forbids it: perhaps adverbs can only modify full phrases, for instance, and the smallest phrase containing pound is already a predicate of flattenings, not poundings. The separationist partisan will have to invoke similar restrictions for cases like (27); he must insist that, while transitive sentences with cool do have a part that is a predicate of cool states, this part cannot accommodate adverbs.

But then why can (23), Syl closed the window again, be true even when Syl has never before touched the window? Most likely the sentence does not differ relevantly from (27) in its syntax. And absent such a difference, the separationist must argue that here the adverb describes an event other than (just) the event of the predicate it modifies. Exactly this claim must also be made under a projectionist regime.

10.5.2 Adverbs and projected event structures

On a projectionist analysis, the entirety of a complex event structure projects from the verb. Consequently, it is the entirety of the event structure that will be modified by any VP adverb. Given that semantics is nontransformational (Chapter 2), it follows further that the semantic

---

[6] On some views, such as that of Simpson 1983, this would not be correct. The verb pound in pound flat would not be the ordinary pound, but rather a homophone that means 'to cause Px to come about by pounding x,' in which case it is a predicate of causings. See Chapter 13.

output of modification cannot compose the adverb meaning with just part of the event structure, to the exclusion of the remainder.

Correspondingly what is described by a VP adverb will be at least the main event. It may furthermore describe some subevent, or it may not. This will depend on the exact meaning of the adverb in question, just as it depends on the exact meaning of blond that it describes a person's hair. Facts like those in (27), partly repeated here, are therefore no surprise.

(27) b * Dirk cooled the cucumber soup on Saturday.
         'Dirk made the cucumber soup be cool on Saturday.'

Necessarily the adverbs in (27) describe the event of Dirk cooling the soup. It may be that this description entails something about the end state of the cooling: for example it is certainly true that if Dirk cools the soup on Saturday, it must also be true that on Saturday the soup is cool (Fodor 1970, Thomson 1971b). But for a cooling of the soup to satisfy on Saturday, or again or very, it is evidently not enough that these modifiers be satisfied by its end state alone. If the soup ends up cool on Saturday, that doesn't make it true that on Saturday Dirk cooled the soup.

What then of cases like (23), repeated here? How come the adverb may (by assumption) describe just the end state of the closing? And how come it may also describe the closing itself?

(23) Syl closed the window again.

On a projectionist account there can be no syntactic ambiguity in what constituent the adverb modifies; and given a nontransformational semantics, there is no possibility of its being interpreted in relation to different parts of the verb's meaning. Thus the ambiguity must be in the adverb itself. There must be two again's, as argued in Dowty (1979).[7] For one of them, to close the window again is to again make the window be shut, but for the other, it is to make the window again be shut. Dowty (1979:265) describes the second again, in relation to the first, as follows:[8] "[A]n individual x stands in the again$_2$ relation to the property of bringing it about that p by doing P, if and only if x brings

---

[7] Alternatively the ambiguity might be in the semantic rule for interpreting phrases with again. But this is even less attractive.

[8] Formally, the meaning postulate is as follows (Dowty 1979:265), broken up for readability:

(1) a $\forall x \forall P \forall p \Box [$
     b $\text{again}_2(\lambda y[\text{CAUSE}\langle Py, \text{BECOME}\langle^\vee p\rangle\rangle])(x)$
     c $\leftrightarrow \text{CAUSE}\langle Px, \text{BECOME}\langle \text{again}_1(p)\rangle\rangle$]

it about that again$_1$ p by doing P." Thus for Dowty the second again describes an event to which the main event of the verb is related, just as blond and illegitimate in illegitimate blond child describe other things to which the child is related.

But this much can be said without any strict event-structural decomposition of verb meaning. Nobody suggests that child must be decomposed to allow for adjectives like blond or illegitimate, and neither is it necessary to decompose the meaning of close to allow for description of its end state by again. We stipulate that blond is true of individuals whose hair is golden, that illegitimate is true of individuals whose parents are unmarried at the birth, and that again is true of events that cause a becoming which ends with an event of a previously instantiated type. Thus the adverb facts cannot, even in principle, justify a claim of strict lexical decomposition – more precisely, a claim that the semantic value of a verb is either structured or derived.

Even if the semantic values of verbs are not themselves structured, however, one might use complex event-structural *representations* of their values in characterizing the meanings of adverbs. In particular one might stipulate that the meaning of an adverb may refer to an event only in the terms of some canonical event-structural representation.[9] Then if, for example, the canonical representation of hardenings were in terms of Cause and Become, any adverb which modifies harden could describe only the causing, the caused event, or the end state of the becoming. But of course this extravagance would need to be justified. We don't need a structured semantic representation of child to explain the meaning of blond, and we don't need event-structural representations to tell us that events have causes

---

[9] Perhaps this is what Beavers and Koontz-Garboden (2012:355) have in mind when they write:

> In lexical theories of event structure (Dowty 1979: ch.5), some additional machinery (e.g., meaning postulates) is needed to ensure that when again modifies a predicate headed by a verb associated with the appropriate event structure, the interpretation is such that it takes scope semantically over only the result root or some larger event, though again *this builds on the hierarchical structure* [my italics] and in principle any bracketed element can be targeted by again.

As a matter of fact the meaning postulate does not require hierarchical structure in the semantics of any verb, any more than the definition of blond requires structure in the meaning of any noun. It is enough that *events* should have structure – for example, that hardenings have an end – just like it is enough that children have hair.

and effects, or that changes have ends. So why exactly do we need structured semantic representations to explain the meaning of *again*? To be justified, the representational format would have to explain restrictions on adverb meaning that cannot be explained otherwise, for instance, just by how we tend to think about events – say as spatio-temporal particulars, with causes and effects, beginnings and ends, run-times and participants, satisfying a definitive sortal. But such justification is hardly something we can take for granted, or for which there is very much evidence at all.

In broad outlines, then, the choice between separationist and projectionist treatments comes to this. The separationist will need to carefully restrict the syntactic privileges of adverbs, while the projectionist will need to posit surprising ambiguities. Neither position scores a clear victory here.

10.6 *CONTRA CAUSE*

As we have seen, clauses like those in (30) are often assigned a **causing event semantics** like (31). Here they are rendered as predicates of a **causing event**, true of one event e_1 that causes another e_2.

(30) a Floyd hardened the glass.
      b Syl closed the window.
      c Nora melted the candy.

(31) $\lambda e_1[\ R_s(e_1, \llbracket \text{Subject} \rrbracket) \ \& \ \exists e_2[\ \text{Cause}\langle e_1, e_2 \rangle \ \& \ \exists e_3[\ \text{Become}\langle e_2, e_3 \rangle$
      $\& \ R_0(e_{2/3}, \llbracket \text{Object} \rrbracket) \dots]]]$

On this semantics the subject instantiates some relation R_s, maybe Agent or Do, to the causing event e_1. The object instantiates some relation R_0 to a different event, and here there are two separate options. The classic analysis makes R_0 a relation to the end state e_3 of a caused becoming; that is, to the second term e_3 in a Become relation whose first term is the caused event e_2. For our example (30a), R_0 would be the Hard relation to e_3, as in (32), while for (30c) it would be the Liquid relation.

(32) $\lambda e_1[\ \text{Do}\langle e_1, \text{Floyd} \rangle \ \& \ \exists e_2[\ \text{Cause}\langle e_1, e_2 \rangle \ \& \ \exists e_3[\ \text{Become}\langle e_2, e_3 \rangle$
      $\& \ \text{Hard}(e_3, \text{the glass}) \ ]]]$

Parsons (1990), however, argues otherwise. For him R_0 is a Theme relation directly to the becoming event e_2, rather than to the terminal state, e_3, with which it ends. Thus he analyzes (30a) roughly as in (33).

(33) $\lambda e_1[\ \text{Agent}(e_1, \text{Floyd}) \ \& \ \exists e_2[\ \text{Cause}\langle e_1, e_2 \rangle \ \& \ \exists e_3[\ \text{Become}\langle e_2, e_3 \rangle$
      $\& \ \text{Theme}(e_2, \text{the glass}) \ \& \ \text{Hardness}(e_3) \ ]]]$

Parsons then gives a reasonable meaning postulate: the Theme of a becoming is also the Theme of its terminal state (1990:158). To be the theme of a becoming that ends in hardness, for example, is to be the theme of the hardness. Thus for Parsons the entailment from Floyd hardened the glass to The glass hardened is a syntactic consequence, but the entailment to The glass was hard is secured by postulate.

Notably, what no version of the causing event semantics can say is that the subject and object both name participants in one and the same event. Floyd may harden the glass just by pushing a button on a cooling device. In that case the glass is related to the button pushing, since it becomes hard as a result of it. But certainly it is not a participant in the pushing, along with Floyd and the button.

The causing event semantics has as its main motivation the fact that sentences like those in (30) generally entail similar sentences with the English verb cause. Sentence (30c) entails (34), for example.

(34)   Nora caused the candy to melt.

But, as we discussed in Chapter 7, Cause clearly cannot mean what cause does, since the converse is not guaranteed to be true: (34) does not entail (30c) (Hall 1965, Fodor 1970). If Nora does aerobics she may warm up her room and cause the candy to melt. But in this scenario (30c) seems wrong. It is therefore common to say that transitives like (30) differ from sentences with cause in requiring what is often called "direct" causation (Fodor 1970, Shibatani 1976, McCawley 1978, Delancey 1984, Bittner 1999, Wolff 2003), a relation labeled DirectlyCause in (35).

(35) $\lambda e_1[\ R_S(e_1, [\![\text{Subject}]\!]) \ \& \ \exists e_2[\ \text{DirectlyCause}\langle e_1, e_2\rangle$
          $\& \ \exists e_3[\ \text{Become}\langle e_2, e_3\rangle \ldots \& \ R_0(e_{2/3}, [\![\text{Object}]\!])\ ]]]$

I will not ask again, as I did in Chapter 6, what it is to cause something directly, since there is a simpler problem for the causing event semantics, even with the revision in (35). It gets the adverb facts wrong.[10] For if sentences like (30) have meanings like (31) or (35), VP adverbs should describe a causing event. And yet in general they do not and cannot, pace Parsons (1990) (Pietroski 2000, 2005a).

(36)   a Nora melted the candy quickly.
          b Nora melted the candy with her left hand.
          c Nora melted the candy on Saturday.

The sentences in (36) cannot mean that Nora's immediate action, the one that caused the candy to melt, was done quickly, with her left hand,

---

[10] The rest of this section simply reports the discussion in Pietroski (2005a:178–189).

or on Saturday. If Nora melts the candy by rubbing it quickly, this is not enough to verify (36a). If she melts it by moving around a lens with her left hand, this is not enough for (36b). And (36c) is not true if Nora sets a fire on Saturday that does not melt the candy until Sunday. Rather, in each case the adverb has to describe Nora's melting the candy per se, and not just acts she performed in its service.

This urges a rejection of the causing event semantics. If transitives like (30) have a semantics something like (37), the C here cannot be Cause, DirectlyCause or anything similar. The e_1 term in C cannot be a causing event, an event by which Nora brought about the melting or Floyd effected the hardening.

(37) $\lambda e_1[\, R_s(e_1, [\![\text{Sbj}]\!]) \,\&\, \exists e_2[\, C\langle e_1, e_2\rangle \,\&\, \text{Become}\langle e_2, e_3\rangle \,\&\, R_0(e_3, [\![\text{Obj}]\!])\,]\,]$

Rather, as argued by Pietroski (2005a:180) following Lombard (1985), C must be more like the relation between a process and its end state. This relation is not in any normal sense causation, since processes include their ends but do not *cause* them.

With this amendment, the adverb facts make sense. Sentence (30c) will mean something like (38), with End in place of C.[11] Here I analyze the candy's melting as its becoming liquid, but this is not presently important.

(38) $\lambda e_1[\, \text{Agent}(e_1, \text{Nora}) \,\&\, \exists e_2[\, \text{End}\langle e_1, e_2\rangle \,\&\, \text{Patient}(e_1, \text{the candy}) \\ \&\, \exists e_3[\, \text{Become}\langle e_2, e_3\rangle \,\&\, \text{Liquid}(e_3)\,]\,]\,]$

Formula (38) is a predicate not of causing events, but of processes that end with the candy melting (becoming liquid). So a modifier of the VP must be true of this process. And for a process to be quick, or with the left hand, it is not enough that some part of it be, even if that part contributes causally to its success. Similarly, recall, the quick pounding doesn't make for a quick flattening, even if the flattening is achieved by pounding. This is a virtue of this semantics, and I will later make use of it (Chapter 13) in analyzing resulatives like pound flat.

This **process semantics** also changes what we say about the inter-pretation of subject and object. The subject now names the agent of a process, not a causing event. Surely the agent of a process must be involved in an event which starts off the process and is among the causes of its end (Pietroski 2000). But this is no reason to *identify* the process with any such event (Thomson 1971a, *contra* Davidson 1969).

---

[11] Pietroski 2005a labels the relation "Terminater," following Lombard 1985.

Turning to the direct object, we are now able to say that it binds a relation to the same event as the subject does, namely the main event of the clause. They are the agent and patient of the process that ends with the melting. This is very attractive, for two reasons. First, it gives clauses like Nora melted the candy the same thematic structure as transitives with a simpler, 'one event' event structure, such as Nora rubbed the candy, allowing us to generalize naturally over both types (see Chapter 11). Second, as suggested by Pietroski (2005a:188), it may help underwrite our intuitions about causal "directness." Individuals viewed as coparticipants in the same event are viewed as more directly related than are those participating in distinct events.

So the candy undergoes a process that ends with melting. But we have not yet said that it melts. It seems natural to stipulate, with Lombard 1985 and Pietroski (2005a:181), that the patient of a process (or if you prefer, its theme) is the patient of its end, (39).

(39)   End Patient Postulate
         $End(e_1, e_3)$ & $Patient(e_1, x) \vDash Patient(e_3, x)$

The candy is then the patient of melting. Given that meltings themselves end in liquidity (Parsons 1990:119), and that a patient (or theme) of liquidity is liquid (Chapter 7), we get the right result. I reprise these points in Chapter 13.

In sum, the causing event semantics, while widely endorsed, has problems that do not afflict a semantics in which the main event of the clause is a process, its agent and patient named by the subject and object.

10.7 EVENT STRUCTURE AND THEMATIC RELATIONS

Event structures may commingle with thematic relations. The formula in (40b) is our event-theoretic rendering of Dowty's semantics for (40a), repeated from above. This involves not only the inter-event relations Cause and Become, but also two thematic relations, the highly general Do and the very specific Hard. In place of Do we might also find Act or Agent with similar meaning.

(40)   a Floyd hardened the glass.
         b $\lambda e_1[Do(e_1, Floyd)$ & $\exists e_2[Cause\langle e_1, e_2 \rangle$
            & $\exists e_3[Become\langle e_2, e_3 \rangle$ & $Hard(e_3, the glass)]]]$

At the same time, many linguists have suggested, consonant with suggestions in Jackendoff (1976 and 1987), or also Dowty (1979), that event-structural analysis eliminates the motives for some of the traditional thematic relations, such as Agent and Patient (e.g., Levin and Rappaport Hovav 1995, Van Valin 2004, Schein 2012). Typically the elimination is meant to replace the traditional relation with a conjunction of relations that are descriptively more useful, or analytically less obscure, yielding what can loosely be called **event-structural thematic relations**. We can distinguish between two different cases.

First, some of the traditional relations might be defined as the composition of a relation between events with a still more general thematic relation, as in (41) for example. This decomposition may permit additional generalizations, by recognizing commonalities in verbs that the traditional thematic taxonomy puts into nonoverlapping categories (Jackendoff 1987).[12]

(41) $\lambda x \lambda e[$ Causer(e, x) $] =_{\text{def}} \lambda x \lambda e[$ $\exists e'[$ Do$\langle e', x \rangle$ & Cause$\langle e', e \rangle$ $]]$

Second, generalizations afforded by the traditional thematic analysis may in some cases be captured more cleanly in terms of event relations plus a highly specific thematic relation. For example, rather than generalize over transitive harden, melt and kill by saying that their direct objects are all interpreted by the Patient relation, as in (42), we can say instead that their meanings all involve Become plus the highly specific thematic relations Hard, Liquid and Dead, as in (43).

(42) a $\lambda e_1[$ Hardening(e_1) & Patient(e_1, x) $]$
      b $\lambda e_1[$ Melting(e_1) & Patient(e_1, x) $]$
      c $\lambda e_1[$ Killing(e_1) & Patient(e_1, x) $]$
(43) a $\lambda e_1 \exists e_2[$ Become(e_1, e_2) & Hard(e_2, x) $]$
      b $\lambda e_1 \exists e_2[$ Become(e_1, e_2) & Liquid(e_2, x) $]$
      c $\lambda e_1 \exists e_2[$ Become(e_1, e_2) & Dead(e_2, x) $]$

This is attractive inasmuch as Become is easier to define than Patient, which it certainly is if Patient is meant to generalize not only over things that get hardened, melted or killed, but also over things that get kissed, kicked or criticized, events that do not involve changes.

---

[12] For cases like this, Jackendoff (1987:378) writes that the traditional thematic relations "are to be reduced to structural configurations in conceptual structure; the names for them are just convenient mnemonics for particularly prominent configurations." Jackendoff's semantics is mentalist and takes "conceptual structures" as its semantic values. So for the mentalist who uses traditional thematic relations, the point of this quote is just that many of them can be analyzed in terms of certain other relations, and that this should be done at the level of semantic values.

A radical version of the eliminativist project, in the first of the two styles, is defended in Schein (2012), though for different reasons. In order to account for certain interpretations of plurals, Schein proposes that all arguments are interpreted by the same thematic relation, namely the maximally general relation of "Participant." Schein would give (44a) the meaning in (44b), where both Lee and Mo instantiate the Participant relation to two different events. What roles Lee and Mo actually play is informed by the Cause relation, and the sortal applied to the caused event.

(44) a Lee humiliated Mo.
      b $\exists e_1 \exists e_2 [$ Participant$\langle e_1, Lee\rangle$ & Cause$\langle e_1, e_2 \rangle$
         & UndergoingHumiliation(e_2) & Participant$\langle e_2, Mo\rangle$]

I refer the reader to Schein's paper for his arguments. Here I bring up the proposal for cautionary purposes. There is a problem with thinning the semantics of the subject to this degree: it predicts that swapping participants will always preserve truth. Suppose that Lee stole Mo's necklace, causing Mo to feel foolish and ashamed. Then (44a) is true, and for Schein it is true because it means that Lee participated in an event which caused Mo to be ashamed. But certainly one such event was the theft of the necklace. Since the participants in that theft include not only Lee but the necklace and Mo, the sentences in (45) should also be true in this scenario. But they aren't. So the use of an overly general thematic relation can sometimes cause problems.

(45) a The necklace humiliated Mo.
      b Mo humiliated herself.

DISCUSSION POINTS

1 Suppose a neurolinguistic study gave evidence that sentences like those in (1) below evoke one kind of response pattern in the brain, while those like (2) evoke another. What would this show? Would it be evidence for a hypothesis of strict semantic decomposition, whereby the sentences in (1) but not (2) have Cause as part of their meaning? Why or why not?

(1) a Al melted the cheese.
     b Mo boiled the potatoes.
     c Lee closed the lid.
(2) a Al slept.
     b Mo cried.
     c Bo ran.

2 Consider (3), and the two possible semantic descriptions of it in (4) and (5)? Does one description allow generalizations or insights that the other does not?

(3) Rip slept.

(4) $\lambda e \exists e_1 [\, \text{Do}\langle e_1, x \rangle \,\&\, R(e_1, e_2) \,\&\, \text{Sleeping}(e_2) \,]$

(5) $\lambda e \exists e [\, \text{Agent}(e_1, x) \,\&\, \text{Sleeping}(e_1) \,]$

3 What does (6) show us about the sentence Al upset his wife, and the possibility of decomposing its meaning in terms of relations between events, or also thematic relations?

(6) a Al drank rum again. This upset his wife.
     b $\nvDash$ Al upset his wife again.

4 Many speakers agree with the inference in (7). This is the restitutive reading of again, on which it describes the end state of the clause's main event.

(7) After the door closed, Mo opened it.
     Therefore Mo opened the door again.

In Mo opened it, the predicate is simple, with just the verb open. According to Beck (2005), restitutive again is available with simple predicates only in languages that productively have complex, resultative predicates, like English pull open in (8). If Beck is correct, what might explain this generalization?

(8) Mo pulled the door (as) open (as it has ever been).

Notice that, in a resultative, the end of the main event is described by a separate predicate: pulling the door open ends with the door being open, and this event is separately modified by open, a predicate that can even host clausal modifiers.

5 Events are different from objects. For instance, events often have durations, with beginnings and ends, like your life does; meanwhile objects often have sizes and surfaces, like you do. Or anyway, this is a natural way of thinking.

Adjectives and nouns are normally satisfied by objects, while verbs and adverbs are normally satisfied by events. For this reason alone, predicates in the two classes will tend to differ in their content. Verbs and adverbs may often make reference to ends, for instance, or also to agents and so forth.

But are there differences between the meanings of predicates in these two classes, that are not explained by the nature of their satisfiers, or by nonlinguistic facets of human experience? Are there any limits on verb meaning that we need a linguistic

theory of event structure to explain? Or limits on adjective meaning, for which we need a linguistic theory of object structure? Can
you think of any examples?

In reflecting on this, don't forget the richness of examples like
illegitimate blond Australian child, where the adjectives describe the
hair, nation and parents of the child – the last, specifically at the
event of the child's birth.

SUGGESTIONS FOR FURTHER READING

For work on event structure in the vein of Davidson 1967b, see Lombard
1985, Parsons 1990, Pietroski 2005a and Schein 2012, as well as the
overview in Maienborn 2011. Jackendoff 1983, 1990b, Talmy 2004 and
Croft 2012 have a more cognitive focus, as well as fantastic descriptive
detail. Van Valin and LaPolla 1997 serves as a bridge between the
two traditions, building on Dowty 1979. Tenny and Pustejovsky 2000,
Maienborn and Wöllstein 2005 and Dölling et al. 2008 collect many
interesting papers in the area. Borer 2005 and Ramchand 2008 derive
event structural decomposition syntactically, with an emphasis on
relations between syntax and telicity. The many genres of lexical
decomposition receive a useful survey in Engelberg 2011.

11 Linking and framing

11.1 INTRODUCTION

A dependent occupies a syntactic relation, and binds a semantic relation. We say the one relation *links* to the other. In a transitive clause with smack, subject and object link to relations under the rubrics of "Agent" and "Patient," for instance. Meanwhile a predicate occurs in some *frames* but not others, a frame being a particular constellation of dependents. Smack can occur in a transitive frame with an Agent subject and a Patient object, for example, but not in an intransitive frame with just a subject naming what got smacked. Generalizations about patterns in linking (Section 11.2) and framing (Section 11.3) are the topic of this chapter.

11.2 LINKING

11.2.1 Introduction

Linking generalizations (Carter 1976) say what sorts of semantic relations go with what sorts of syntactic relations. All the sentences in (1) report on some kind of striking, and in each it is the subject that names the striker, and the object that names the struck. Beginning here, and throughout the remaining chapters, I will for convenience refer to these surface relations, subject and object, with the abbreviations S and O.

(1) a Nik smacked the table.
     b The mule kicked Otis.
     c Rocky punched the beef.

In English we do not find the reverse, active transitive clauses whose event is a striking, but where O names the striker and S names the struck. These would look like the items in (2), imagining these to be synonymous with their counterparts in (1).

(2) a * The table schmacked Nik.
     b * Otis schkicked the mule.
     c * The beef schpunched Rocky.

Only rarely does any language even seem to exhibit the **linking** in (2) –
these being the apparently "deep ergative" languages such as Dyirbal
(Dixon 1994) – and the analysis of such languages is in every case highly
controversial. More importantly, I know of no language where some
verbs of striking exhibit pattern (1), and others, pattern (2).[1]

Such regularities are not limited to verbs of striking. Routinely we
find verbs like lick, move, hurl, slice or break, but nothing like the imag-
inary inverses of schlick, schmove, schurl, schlice or schpreak in (3), again
taking X schverbed Y to mean 'Y verbed X.' Nor do we find verbs with
meanings like describe, yell or know but with the grammar of schtescribe,
schyell or schnow in (4).

(3) a * The kitten schlicked its mother.
     b * The beetle schmoved the kitten.
     c * The javelin schurled Jan.
     d * Salami schliced Al.
     e * The computer schproke the flood.
(4) a * The landscape schtescribed Mo.
     b * Several words schyelled Lee.
     c * That the Earth is round schnows Al.

Such facts are not to be explained piecemeal. There are generalizations
to be had. Within a language, there are surely many. Encouraged
by the cross-linguistic stability of linking patterns, Perlmutter and
Postal (1984) go still further, with the **Universal Alignment Hypothesis**
in (5).

(5) Universal Alignment Hypothesis
     There exist principles of U[niversal]G[rammar] which predict the initial [syntac-
     tic] relation borne by each nominal in a given clause from the meaning of the
     clause. (Perlmutter and Postal 1984:97)

Any such theory has a foundation with three parts: the semantic analysis, the syntactic analysis, and the format for stating relations between
them. In this section I start with the semantics (Section 11.2.2), and
then the format for stating linking relations (Section 11.2.3). The next
two subsections (Section 11.2.4–11.2.5) describe ways of responding to
empirical challenges, with revisions either to the semantics or to the

---

[1] There is variation in the realization of what is struck, however, which is often
  identified by an oblique or prepositional phrase. See Levin 2012 for a review.

syntax. The latter (Section 11.2.5) concerns the challenge of unaccusativity in particular. I conclude by quickly distinguishing projectionist and separationist perspectives in this area (Section 11.2.6).

11.2.2 Semantics for linking

To state our linking generalizations we need a general way of distinguishing the smackers, kickers, punchers, lickers, movers, hurlers, slicers, breakers, describers, yellers and knowers on the one hand from the smacked, kicked, punched, licked and so forth on the other. This is a challenge. It is not easy to say what is common to all these specific relations, or even to various groups into which they might be sorted, without relying on jargon that itself resists explication. As we have seen (Chapter 6), there are two common ways of responding to this challenge: decomposition in terms of general relations, or comparative sorting of specific relations around some opposition.

On the first, decompositional response, we claim that each verb-specific thematic relation, such as Kicker or Describer, corresponds uniquely to some highly general relation in a structured description of the clause's meaning. The general relation may be a primitive of the analysis, like the Agent relation in (6). Or it may be complex, as in (7) or (8) (Jackendoff 1987, Levin and Rappaport Hovav 1995, Van Valin and LaPolla 1997). Such choices were discussed in Chapters 6 and 10.

(6) $\lambda x \lambda e[$ Agent(e, x)]

(7) $\lambda x \lambda e[$ Do(e, x) & $\exists e'[$ Cause(e, e')]]

(8) $\lambda x \lambda e[$ Source(e, x) & $\exists e'[$ Goal(e', x)]]

The linking rules are then stated in these terms. Perhaps what is common to kickers, describers and so forth, and what distinguishes them from the kicked and the described, is their being *agents*, as per (6). Then we can state a broad generalization: in a basic transitive clause describing an action, S binds Agent.

The second response is to sort the specific relations for each verb in comparison to one other, around some opposition. For Dowty (1991) what matters is the relative proximity of the roles to either of two prototypes, "Proto-Agent" and "Proto-Patient." The ranking can then be used in linking generalizations, such as Dowty's (9).

(9) In predicates with grammatical subject and object, the argument for which the predicate entails the greatest number of Proto-Agent properties will be lexicalized as the subject of the predicate; the argument having the greatest number of Proto-Patient entailments will be lexicalized as the direct object. (Dowty 1991:576)

For instance, if a hurler has more "Proto-Agent" properties than what she hurls, Hurler will link to the subject in a transitive clause with hurl. Beavers (2006a,b) defends a further generalization that is similarly comparative: the relation linked to an oblique is less specific than one linked to a direct object. Importantly, no such approach requires a unique and exhaustive classification of all verb-specific relations in terms of more general predicates in a semantic decomposition.

For brevity, I will henceforth presuppose the decompositional approach, and talk mainly in terms of 'traditional' thematic relations, such as Agent and Patient. But I will not presuppose that the decomposition is strict. This is important. Structure in the semantic description used by a linking theory need not indicate structure in the meaning or value of the expression itself. It may serve no role at all outside of the linking theory; it may be purely representational (Chapter 2). We can say that Ss name agents, without saying that any part of the clause, or any prelexical part of its verb, has Agent as (part of) its meaning. Likewise we can say why blond child is better than blond diameter, without saying that child but not diameter has a part that means 'hair.' It is a common mistake to think otherwise.

Now, theories of linking differ variously in their choice of semantic analysis. In Chapters 6, 7 and 10, we discussed some of the choices. According to Jackendoff (1987), relations bound by arguments may be structured concepts – as he puts it, a single argument may bind several thematic relations – such as the conjunction of the Source and Goal concepts in (8). In turn, linking for Jackendoff may refer to the parts of these complex concepts, cross-classifying the arguments semantically. Wechsler (1995) argues that the best theory of linking refers not to Agent, Patient and so forth, but rather to three broad categories of relations: Notion, Nuclear, and Part. Another idea is that the relations relevant to linking are "aspectual" (Tenny 1987, 1994, Rosen 1996, van Hout 1996, Borer 2005, Ramchand 2008). In particular, the direct object links to a homomorphic function Θ from intervals on some scalar measure of x to the temporal intervals of event e (Chapter 7). Thus every increase in the measure of x corresponds to an increase in the runtime of e, in this sense "measuring" or "delimiting" the event (Krifka 1989, 1992, 1998, Dowty 1991, Jackendoff 1996, Rothstein 2004, Wechsler 2005a). In Nora melts the candy, the candy binds a relation that maps every increase in the candy's liquidity to progress in the time of the event; see Schein (2002) for objections, as well as Section 7.3.3.

Among the broadest choices, however, is this: does linking refer only to thematic relations or also, perhaps instead, to event structure? Thematic relations relate an event to an individual. Event structure includes relations among events, such as Cause or Become. Linking theories that refer to event structure are developed by a wide variety of linguists, including Foley and Van Valin (1984), Jackendoff (1987), Grimshaw (1990), Van Valin and LaPolla (1997), Croft (1998), Rappaport Hovav and Levin (1998), Ritter and Rosen (1998), Borer (2005), and Schein (2012). I will illustrate with a common example, familiar from Chapter 10. Suppose that the meanings of transitive clauses with verbs of change, such as harden or melt, can be described as in (10). Here *P* is a stative predicate specified by the verb.[2]

(10) $\lambda e_1[$ Do$\langle e_1, x \rangle$ & $\exists e_2[$ Cause$\langle e_1, e_2 \rangle$ & $\exists e_3[$ Become$\langle e_2, e_3 \rangle$ & $P(e_3, y)$]]]

For Floyd hardened the glass this gives us (11).

(11) $\lambda e_1[$ Do$\langle e_1, \text{Floyd} \rangle$ & $\exists e_2[$ Cause$\langle e_1, e_2 \rangle$
         & $\exists e_3[$ Become$\langle e_2, e_3 \rangle$ & Hard$(e_3, \text{the glass})$]]]

Here there are two thematic relations, Do and Hard, and two relations among events, Cause and Become. To predict from this whether it is S or O that links to *x* or *y* in (10), it is sufficient to mention only the event relations. As stated in (12), the subject but not the object binds a relation to the causing event, the first term in the Cause relation (Grimshaw 1990). (Note, this allows that O's referent may be related to the causing event out in the world; the linking rule only requires that no such relation be stated in the sentence meaning.)

(12)   Causing Event Linking Rule (hypothetical)
       In a clause with meaning $\lambda e_1 \exists e_2[\text{Cause}\langle e_1, e_2 \rangle \ldots]$, the subject must bind a relation to e_1, and the object must not.

Alternatively, if the Cause relation is introduced by a silent lexical item, CAUSE, separate from the verb, we can ensure the same result by stipulating the order of its arguments, as in (13): its first argument must be the caused event, its second, the causing event. Thematic relations to the caused and causing events will then have to be introduced below and above CAUSE, respectively.

(13)   CAUSE Argument Order Rule (hypothetical)
       A lexical item CAUSE that expresses the Cause relation may have the meaning $\lambda e_2 \lambda e_1[\text{Cause}\langle e_1, e_2 \rangle]$, but not $\lambda e_1 \lambda e_2[\text{Cause}\langle e_1, e_2 \rangle]$.

---

[2] In Section 10.6, I argued that this decomposition, if understood strictly, is incorrect: clauses with a verb of change are not predicates of a causing event. But here we need only read the decomposition representationally, in order to understand a general point about linking.

Either way, we state a very general linking rule solely in terms of Cause, a relation thought to be less obscure than Agent or Theme.

Generalizing away from thematic relations may also be useful descriptively. Suppose that in some language we find a single clause, with a seemingly simple verb that means 'x did something that caused y to do a dance.' Then x and y are both doers in their respective events. Nevertheless, (12) and (13) imply an asymmetry. Both require the causing event to be 'higher,' the main event of the clause, and so both will link x and not y to the subject.

This route is attractive, if indeed the inter-eventive relations are less obscure or more natural. But even then, theories of linking that refer *only* to inter-eventive relations stand to miss generalizations that cut across different kinds of event structure. To see this, continue to suppose that Floyd hardened the glass is described by (11). On the face of it, the same event structure is not plausible for Floyd pounded the glass, since pounding is not a change. Here we seem to need a 'simpler' meaning like (14).

(14) $\lambda e_1 [\text{Do}\langle e_1, \text{Floyd}\rangle \ \& \ \text{Pounding}(e_1, \text{the glass})]$

Unlike (10), (14) does not involve Cause, so the Causing Event Linking Rule cannot apply here. But aren't hardeners and pounders named by subjects for the very same reason? Shouldn't the same linking principle govern both of these cases?

If so, there are two options. We can maintain the event-structural distinction between harden and pound. But then the linking principles must refer to Do, a thematic relation that (10) and (14) share in spite of their differences (cf. Van Valin 2004), diminishing the descriptive utility of the Cause relation.[3] The second option is to save the purely event-structural theory by insisting, with Schein (2012), that even a verb like pound has a causative analysis, something like (15).

(15) $\exists e_1 \exists e_2 [\text{Participant}\langle e_1, \text{Floyd}\rangle \ \& \ \text{Cause}\langle e_1, e_2\rangle$
          $\& \ \text{HavingBeenPounded}(e_2, \text{the glass})]$

But this is a failure, if we want the virtue of generality without the vice of obscurity. Now our use of "Cause" is more obscure than ever. By assumption, it is *only* in pounding the glass that one can "Cause" the state of its having been pounded. There is no other way. So this so-called

---

[3] In response to this observation, one might say that Doers of a pounding have something in common with participants in a causing event, and this is why these two roles are linked in the same way. That may be, but this explanatory supplement is not represented explicitly in the theory itself.

"Cause" is a notion far more subtle and particular than even 'direct causation.' It is at best a new name for Agent, a predicate whose obscurity we tried to avoid. To me it is not clear, therefore, that on either way of generalizing over both harden and pound, the event-structural relations do any more explanatory work than do traditional thematic relations.

11.2.3 Linking functions

In many developments of the Universal Alignment Hypothesis, but not all (see below), the promised prediction takes the general form of a function. Each input to the function is a set of semantic relations, such as {Agent, Patient}, {Agent, Goal, Theme}, or {Patient}, comprising all the roles for a given clause. Each such set is mapped to exactly one pairing of its members with grammatical relations, such as {⟨Agent, Subject⟩, ⟨Patient, Object⟩}. One classic source of this perspective is Fillmore (1968), which describes data like (16) with the linking function in (17). Sentence (16b) is described by (17b), for example, which maps from {Instrument, Patient} to a pairing of Instrument with Subject and Patient with Object.

(16) a Mo opened the front door with the blue key.
      b The blue key opened the front door.
      c The front door opened.

(17) a i   {Agent, Patient, Instrument}
          ii ↦ {⟨Agent, Subject⟩, ⟨Patient, Object⟩, ⟨Instrument, Oblique⟩}
      b i   {Instrument, Patient}
          ii ↦ {⟨Instrument, Subject⟩, ⟨Patient, Object⟩}
      c i   {Patient}
          ii ↦ {⟨Patient, Subject⟩}

On this most general view, each set of semantic relations in the domain maps to a unique pairing in the range. But an individual semantic relation, such as Instrument, needn't always have the same partner in syntax. That will depend on its cohort in the input set. In (17), Instrument is paired sometimes with Subject and sometimes with Oblique, depending on whether Agent is in its cohort (Fillmore 1968:33). Similarly, Patient links to Object, except in the absence of Agent or Instrument.

This general theory is often made stronger. The most common way of doing so is by requiring that linking be order-preserving. Specifically, it is assumed that both the semantic and the syntactic relations are ordered, on the **Thematic** (Jackendoff 1972) and **Obliqueness Hierarchies** (Sag 1985), respectively. The correct Thematic Hierarchy is a matter of much dispute, but one option is (18).

(18)   Thematic Hierarchy (Larson 1988)
       Agent < Patient/Theme < Goal < Instrument/Manner/Location/Time/...

On the other hand, an Obliqueness Hierarchy that amounts to (19) is widely taken for granted. Theories do differ, however, on whether "Subject," "Object" and "Oblique" are theoretical primitives. For some they are, but many others use these terms merely as shorthand for common combinations of basic properties, not all of which matter to linking. On many of the latter accounts, notably Larson (1988), the Obliqueness Hierarchy reduces to asymmetrical c-command: for two expressions A and B, A<B on the Obliqueness Hierarchy just in case the initial position of A c-commands that of B and not vice versa. This is what I will assume by default.

(19)   Obliqueness Hierarchy (Sag 1985)
       Subject < Object < Obliques

The linking function is then required to preserve the ordering of its input in its output. If $p < q$ on the Thematic Hierarchy, and the linking function maps $\{p, q\}$ to $\{\langle p, 1 \rangle, \langle q, 2 \rangle\}$, then it must be that $1 < 2$ on the Obliqueness Hierarchy.

   Consider Fillmore's (17) in light of this restriction. According to (19), Subject < Object, and Object < Oblique. Thus (17a) preserves order only if Agent < Patient, and Patient < Instrument. But this contradicts (17b), which requires that Instrument < Patient. So if linking preserves order, and the Obliqueness Hierarchy is held fixed, one of two things must be wrong, either Fillmore's (17) or the Thematic Hierarchy in (18).

   Baker (1988) proposes a still more restrictive theory, with the **Uniformity of Theta Assignment Hypothesis** in (20). For consistency, let us read Baker's "structural relationships between [...] items at the level of d-structure" as homologues of Perlmutter and Postal's "initial relations," or more generically of the 'underlying grammatical relations' between a dependent and its verb in the syntactic derivation.

(20)   Uniformity of Theta Assignment Hypothesis (UTAH)   ·
       Identical thematic relationships between items are represented by identical
       structural relationships between those items at the level of d-structure. (Baker
       1997)

In practice, UTAH is taken to mean that the sets in the domain of the linking function are singletons, as in (21). Equivalently, linking is taken to be a function directly from thematic to syntactic relations. In (21) I use "Subject" and "Object" as nicknames for the relevant relations at d-structure, perhaps Specifier-of-V and Complement-of-V, where Specifiers asymmetrically c-command Complements.

(21) a i   {Agent}
          ii ↦ {⟨Agent, Subject⟩}
      b i   {Patient}
          ii ↦ {⟨Patient, Object⟩}

Under UTAH, a given thematic relation is always paired with the same grammatical relation. Baker (1997) does not insist, however, that the linking function be one-to-one. He allows that a single "structural relation at the level of d-structure" may be interpreted by a variety of thematic relations, given different verbs. We can still say that Al has the same d-structural relation to the verb in both (22a) and (22b), for example, even if it binds different thematic relations, Agent in the one and Experiencer in the other. This is fortunate, since it seems that some thematic distinctions have no syntactic correlate.

(22) a Al sliced salami.
      b Al loves salami.

Perhaps the main virtue of UTAH, in comparison to weaker hypotheses, is its greater potential utility in language acquisition. Given UTAH, a child's guess about the thematic relation bound by a dependent would unambiguously decide its underlying syntactic relation (Section 11.3.4). In the reverse direction, a guess about the underlying syntactic relation would be more informative as to the thematic relation than it would be in weaker theories.

The cost of UTAH is a more frequent disjunction between surface and underlying relations, and hence a greater reliance on movement – or, if not on movement, then on reference to some other structure that is not manifest in surface relations, perhaps in the a-list of the verb, or in some kind of semantic representation. Suppose that the candy is interpreted by the same thematic relation in (23b) as it is in (23a).

(23) a Nora melted the candy.
      b The candy melted.

Then, by UTAH, it must have the same d-structural relation to the verb in both, call it the underlying object relation. Consequently in (23b) it must undergo movement, as shown in (24), or whatever one uses to relate surface (final, s-structure) positions (relations) to distinct underlying (initial, d-structure) positions (relations).

(24) [[the candy]$_k$ [melted t_k]]

These commitments make UTAH an attractively strong theory, prone to falsification. Its plausibility depends on whether there is other evidence against the underlying syntactic positions it postulates, and the movements they require. We will discuss some challenges in the next two subsections (11.2.4–11.2.5).

Not all linking theories state their rules as functions, mapping to a *unique* pairing of relations. Some allow for ties, with more than one permissible pairing. This is common in theories that sort semantic relations comparatively, following Dowty (1991). Recall Dowty's (9) (Section 11.2.2). This links the more agent-like of two relations to S, and the more patient-like to O. When two relations are equally agent-like, or equally patient-like, either one can link to S, or to O, respectively. This is how Dowty (1991:579) describes the alternation in (25), or also (30) in the next subsection.

(25)   a Mo rented it from Lee.
       b Lee rented it to Mo.

11.2.4 Responding to challenges

Generally it seems right to say that transitive clauses with action verbs have subjects that name agents. This seems fair for (26) and (27).

(26)   Nora melted the candy.

(27)   Mo opened the front door.

But (28) is a problem if the candy is in every sense the subject of this clause, since the candy is not the agent of its melting; and (29) may be a problem, if its subject binds the Instrument relation, as Fillmore (1968) claimed.

(28)   The candy melted.

(29)   The blue key opened the front door.

Faced with such challenges, we must revise the syntax or revise the semantics, if we want to keep the linking rule. Perhaps in (28), the candy is underlyingly a direct object, and a subject only at the surface. Our generalization is then saved if it governs not surface but underlying relations. I will discuss this further in Section 11.2.5. Meanwhile, maybe we should bring (29) into line with a different semantics. Perhaps the blue key here counts as the agent of the opening (Chapter 7).

Much of the literature explores which sort of revision is right for a particular challenge, if either. The sentences in (30) and (31) are among the commonly disputed cases.

(30)   a Al likes arguments.
       b Arguments please Al.

(31) a Lee gave the necklace to Mo.
      b Lee gave Mo the necklace.

Both sentences in (30) imply that Al gets pleasure from arguments, and both in (31) imply that someone got the necklace. But the surface positions of Al, or of the necklace, differ across the two alternates. So if the two alternates are to be subsumed under a single rule of linking, and this rule determines a *unique* linking, we will need one of our two revisions. Either the two surface positions relate to a single underlying position, or the dependents bind different semantic relations, though the results overlap in entailments. Concerning (30), see Belletti and Rizzi (1988), Grimshaw (1990), Dowty (1991), and Pesetsky (1995). For (31), see Chomsky (1975), Oehrle (1976), Larson (1988), Jackendoff (1990a), Dowty (1991), Pesetsky (1995), Baker (1997), Harley (2002), and Pylkkänen (2002).

Here I will briefly review another illustrative case, (32), one instance of the *locative alternation* (Hall 1965, Anderson 1971, Chomsky 1971, Fillmore 1971a, Dowty 1991, Arad 2006).

(32) a Kay loaded the truck (with the furniture).
      b Kay loaded the furniture onto the truck.

Sentences (32a) and (32b) can be verified by the same stretch of history. They both imply that Kay put the furniture on the truck. So maybe the truck and the furniture bind the same semantic relations in both, let's say Goal and Theme, respectively. But in that case, the same set of semantic relations has different linkings in the two alternates. If we suppose that linking rules are functions, this is impossible.

To address this, we might revise the syntax. In accord with UTAH, we can have Goal and Theme link to the same underlying positions across the two alternates. Then we must argue that independent differences in syntax, such as the availability of case, lead to two different surface forms, as a result of movement and morphological processes. This approach goes back to Hall (1965).

The alternative is to say that the two alternates differ not only in syntax but also in meaning, in the strict sense of the term. In support of this, observe that a speaker of (32b) but not (32a) can continue with (33) (Anderson 1971).

(33) But there's still tons of room for the bicycles and mattresses.

Thus (32a) but not (32b) implies that the furniture fills the truck, or is distributed throughout it, to the relevant standard of fullness. This is known as the "holistic" (Anderson 1971) or "distributive" (Jackendoff

1990b) effect on the referent of O. Plausibly, therefore, O in (32a) but not (32b) binds the role of Patient to an event that ends with the fullness of its patient. About (32b) we can say that O names the Patient of a different sort of event, one of moving its patient to a goal. Thus O links to Patient in both alternates, and we regain our generalization.

The cost is an ambiguity. If O binds the same *type* of thematic relation in both (32a) and (32b), say Patient, then this relation cannot be to the same sort of event in the two cases, since then (34) should be acceptable.

(34)   * Kay and Lee loaded the truck and the furniture, respectively.
'Kay loaded the truck, and Lee loaded something with the furniture.'

So we must say that the two clauses have different sorts of events. One is a transition to fullness, call it a *floading*, the other a directed movement, call it a *mloading*. If in both cases the sole contribution of the verb is a predicate of the clausal event, it follows that we have a lexical ambiguity in "load." This pronounces two different verbs, satisfied by two different events, floadings and mloadings (Pinker 1989, Jackendoff 1990b, Dowty 1991, Levin and Rappaport Hovav 1995).[4] Contrapositively, if there is just a single verb load, it cannot provide, both in (32a) and in (32b), only a predicate of the clause's event. Either (32a) or (32b), or both, must have a part, call it L, that is a predicate of a different event, not the event of the clause; and it must be L that hosts the event predicate contributed by load, call it Loading. The syntactic context of L then has a meaning that relates the loading to the event of the clause, either a floading or a mloading. In short, if there is just one load, there must be a structural ambiguity in its context; for versions of this view, see Goldberg (1995) and Arad (2006).[5]

11.2.5 Unaccusativity

Sometimes an intransitive S displays some privilege of a transitive O. This is a **sign of unaccusativity**. The S of an intransitive clause with freeze, for example, can control a resultative secondary predicate (Levin and Rappaport Hovav 1995), as in (35). Transitive clauses generally limit

---

[4] Proponents of lexical ambiguity often relate the two verbs in Lexicon, with derivations that share a common prelexical source LOAD (Pinker 1989, Jackendoff 1990b).

[5] These comments are easily transposed into the framework of Distributed Morphology (Halle and Marantz 1993, Marantz 1997, Embick and Noyer 2007). In that framework, a single phonological word ω may be the phonetic value of a complex syntactic structure, only a subpart of which is semantically modified by the syntactic primitive ('root') that is among the conditions for ω.

this privilege to their object, as shown by (36), which lacks an otherwise plausible ambiguity (Chapter 13).

(35) The beef froze solid.

(36) Rocky's fists pounded the frozen beef bloody.
'Rocky's fists made the frozen beef bloody in pounding it.'
*'Rocky's fists became bloody in pounding the frozen beef.'

Consider also (37). The past participle of *freeze* serves adjectivally to describe things in the role bound by the intransitive S. For transitives this privilege generally goes to the object role, as shown by the nonambiguity of (38).

(37) ten frozen sides of beef
'ten sides of beef that froze'

(38) one bloodied boxer
'one boxer who was bloodied'
*'one boxer who bloodied somebody'

Not all intransitive clauses show signs of unaccusativity. It depends on the predicate, sometimes just on the verb. With *scream*, S cannot control a resultative predicate, (39), and its past participle cannot describe a screamer, (40). So there is no sign of unaccusativity with *scream*.

(39) * The chefs screamed hoarse.
'The chefs got hoarse from screaming.'

(40) * ten screamed chefs
'ten chefs who screamed'

In Hebrew, a 'possessor dative' headed by *le* in a transitive clause can indicate the possessor of O but not of S, as shown in (41), from Borer and Grodzinsky (1986).

(41) Le-mi   ha-yeladim   xatxu 'et   ha-gader.
     to-who   the-boys   cut   ACC   the-fence
'Whose fence did the boys cut?'
*'Whose boys cut the fence?'

And in intransitive clauses, *le* can associate with the surface S, (42), but not always, (43) (Borer and Grodzinsky 1986, Borer 2005). So we have a sign of unaccusativity in clauses with *nafla* 'fell' but not *yilelu* 'whine.'

(42) Le-mi   ha-mitriya   nafla.
     to-who   the-umbrella fell
'Whose umbrella fell?'

(43) * Le-mi   ha-xatulim   yilelu.
       to-who   the-cats   whined
'Whose cats whined?'

See Chapter 9 (Section 9.2.5) for cases where what matters is more than just the verb.

What explains such signs?

Perlmutter (1978) wagers one answer. The clause may be **deeply unaccusative**, in having a surface subject that is an object underlyingly (Hall 1965, Burzio 1981). Specifically, in such cases, S's 'initial' relation in the syntactic derivation is equivalent to that of O in a transitive clause. There are many ways to formalize this equivalence. For Perlmutter himself, underlying objects have the "2" property at the "initial stratum" of Syntax. In many GB theories, they are the "Complement" of the verb at "d-structure," or also satisfy an "internal argument" of it. In many analyses after Chomsky (1995), Kratzer (1996) and Marantz (1997), they are arguments of the verb root itself, as opposed to arguments of a v that has the verb's phrase as its complement. On any of these implementations, the signs of unaccusativity are explained directly, if we assume that these respond to initial, underlying relations in the syntactic derivation.

Deep unaccusativity promises to simplify the linking rules, provided that S binds the sorts of semantic relations that are otherwise associated with Os – for example, if it binds Theme but not Agent. Very often this seems right. The beef that freezes and the umbrella that falls are not actors, but maybe the chefs who scream and the cat that whines are. In European languages, some of the verbs that regularly induce signs of unaccusativity are verbs meaning 'arrive,' 'decay,' 'die,' 'remain' and 'break' (Sorace 2000), and none of these, it seems fair to say, describe their event as having an agent.

But things are not always so clear (Rosen 1984). Often enough, the event of a formally unaccusative clause seems to be agentive, or (perhaps more often) the event of a formally unergative clause does not. In Mandan (Siouan, USA), intransitives with unergative subject-agreement permit verbs meaning 'enter' and 'arrive' (Dixon 1994), whereas in many languages such meanings go with unaccusative clauses. In Tolai (Austronesian, Papua New Guinea), intransitives with unergative subject/verb word order include verbs meaning 'be cold' and 'be sick,' while 'be nice' occurs with unaccusative order (Dixon 1994). Surely being cold or sick is not more agentive than being nice. Thus the formal and semantic signs seem not to align with each other. And in such cases, the formal signs cannot be used as independent evidence for a strict theory of linking.

How else might signs of unaccusativity be explained, if not by deep unaccusativity?

Van Valin (1990) preserves the idea that the signs refer in some sense to 'underlying relations,' but interprets this differently, in the service of a nontransformational syntax. For Perlmutter (1978), Burzio (1981) or Baker (1988), the relations expressed by signs of unaccusativity are in the syntactic derivation – specifically, in its "initial stratum" or "d-structure." For Van Valin, they are only in a grammatical feature that he calls "LS." The LS is (in the strict sense, Chapter 2) a semantic representation. Specifically it is a formula whose structure matches a description of the verb's meaning, more or less as this is given in Dowty (1979). Relevant examples are given in (44) (Van Valin 1990:224,228). Italics and bold-face distinguish two classes of predicate-names, the "activity" and "state" classes respectively.

(44) a LS for intransitive run: *run*(x)
       b LS for intransitive break: BECOME **broken**(x)
       c LS for transitive break: [DO(x)] CAUSE [BECOME **broken**(y)]

The formulas in (44b) and (44c) share formal properties that (44a) lacks: BECOME, and a predicate-name in the state class. Rules that refer to these parts will therefore neutralize the distinction between transitive and intransitive break, distinguishing both from *run*. This neutralization may yield a sign of unaccusativity, without there being any further equivalence between the unaccusative S and transitive O in the syntactic derivation.

One last possibility is that some signs of unaccusativity do not index 'underlying relations' at all, not in d-structure, not in LS, not in anything similar. Instead, they respond to surface configurations that, for independent reasons, *correlate* with distinctions in meaning or argument structure. In the remainder of this section, I will examine a possible example of this, the clitic ne in Italian. Since Burzio (1981), this has been among the signs of unaccusativity most often discussed.[6]

Ne pronominalizes the restriction of a quantifier in an argument position. In transitive clauses, the associated quantifier can be in O, (45a), but not S, (45b).

(45) a Ne   ho   mangiati due.
          of.them have.1s eaten   two
          'I ate two of them.'   (Calabrese and Maling 2009)
       b * Ne   hanno mangiato molti (la   torta), in questo bar.
          of.them have   eaten   many (the cake) in this   café
          'In this café, many of them ate (the cake).'   (*ibid.*)

In intransitive clauses, ne can associate with a postverbal S, but only sometimes. It can in (46) with sono arrivati 'arrived,' but it can't in (47) with hanno parlato 'spoke.'

---

[6] For critical questions about the possessor dative in Hebrew, see Landau 1999 and Gafter 2014.

(46)   Ne   sono   arrivati   tre.
       of.them   are   arrived   three
       'Three of them arrived.'

(47)   * Ne   hanno   parlato   tre.
         of.them   have   spoken   three
       'Three of them spoke.'

So there are signs of unaccusativity with arrivare 'arrive,' but not with parlare 'speak,' and also not with mangiare 'eat' in the variant of (45b) that drops la torta 'the cake.' The distinction is supported by a correlated difference in the Perfect auxiliary: arrivare takes essere 'be,' while parlare and mangiare take avere 'have.'[7]

The full picture, however, is more complicated. Outside of the Perfect, ne is possible with parlare and many other verbs that take avere (Lonzi 1986, Saccòn 1993, Levin and Rappaport Hovav 1995, Calabrese and Maling 2009). Sentence (48) is an example.

(48)   Anche oggi   ne   parleranno tre,   al   convegno.
       also today   of.them   speak.FUT   three at.the   meeting
       'Today too, three will speak at the meeting.'
       (Calabrese and Maling 2009, adapting Saccòn 1993)

It would be odd to say that, in clauses with parlare, S is an underlying O except in the avere-Perfect. And therefore it would also be odd to assume, in light of (48), that ne is an unequivocal sign of deep unaccusativity. It would be no less odd to say that the verb has different LSs in the two cases. But then what is going on?

Two things are certain about ne, besides the S/O contrast in transitive clauses, on display in (45). First, its associated quantifier must be postverbal, unless it is focus-fronted or wh-fronted (Cinque 1990). It can neither be right-dislocated nor in a non-focussed preverbal position (Calabrese and Maling 2009). Second, the understood restriction of that quantifier must be topical. Both properties strongly constrain the discourse contexts that will allow use of an intransitive with ne. And we have good reason to expect that these constraints, whatever exactly they are, will interact differently with different verb-meanings, or different aspects, perhaps even in a way that distinguishes intransitives from transitives. Our reasons come from contrasts like those in (49), noticed by Bolinger (1961, 1972). Stress on mother marks full-sentence focus in (49a), but narrow focus on mother in (49b). As a result, (49a) is felicitous discourse-initially, while (49b) requires a relevant set

---

[7] See Sorace 2000 on this correlation across European languages.

of acquaintances who fell down or worked hard, other than your mother.[8]

(49) What happened?

    a   Your MOTHER arrived / called.

    b ? Your MOTHER fell down / worked hard.

This contrast has to do with the content of these sentences, including the content of the verb, relative to ordinary conversational expectations.[9] It does not have to do with argument structure, since (49a) and (49b) both have one verb that is typically unaccusative (arrive, fall), and one that is typically unergative (call, work). Still, there is a substantial correlation. Many of the verbs in class (49a) are typically unaccusative, like arrive and die, while many in class (49b) are typically unergative, like work and scream. This correlation might be mistaken for causation. The retracted placement of stress in (49a) might be mistaken for a sign of a deeply unaccusative clause. And it is possible that a similar mistake has been made in understanding the facts of Italian. Clearly *ne* is sensitive to the surface position of the quantifier. But its seeming dependence on argument structure may be mediated by an interaction between information structure and the meaning of the predicate. See Calabrese and Maling (2009) for a different but similar view.

11.2.6 Projection and separation

Linking generalizations take on a different cast in projectionist and separationist theories. It is worth being clear about how.

On a projectionist view, linking rules generalize over individual lexical items, verbs in particular. We say things like: any verb implying participants that can be classified as an agent and a patient will have an external argument for the former, and an internal argument for the latter. This does not require that Agent and Patient predicates are in any *other* way active in the grammar. In particular, it does not require that the verb have prelexical parts with these relations as their meanings.

---

[8] Ordinarily, full-sentence focus in English exhibits roughly sentence-final stress, whether with intransitives ("Your mother FELL DOWN") or otherwise ("Your mother greeted some GUESTS").

[9] According to Calabrese and Maling 2009, who report Lonzi 1986 and Saccòn 1993, (48) serves to make the point that there will be three episodes of speaking by the topical group, and not to add a comment about the speakers. Other felicitous cases are arguably similar. As with the use of impersonal passives in Germanic, the conversational point is to say that certain events happened, and not to comment on their agents.

A separationist view commits to a stronger hypothesis. The derivation of the clause has parts, separate from the verb, that do have meanings like Agent or Patient. The linking rules are generalizations over syntactic derivations that involve these parts, governing their distribution relative to certain classes of verbs. Suppose, for concreteness, that Agent and Patient are introduced by lexical items named AG and PT. Derivation (50a) is then possible, but (50b) is not, and the syntactic categories of AG and PT must be arranged to ensure this.

(50)   a   [Al [AG [salami [PT slice]]]]
        b * [salami [PT [Al [AG slice]]]]

In particular, the contextual features of PT must be such that it cannot have a phrase headed by AG as its sister. How this might be done was discussed briefly in the final section of Chapter 9. Abstractly, the task is no different from ensuring the right ordering of auxiliary have and be in English, so as to permit (51a) but forbid (51b).

(51)   a   Al has been slicing the salami.
        b * Al is having sliced the salami.

Similar comments apply no matter which genre of semantics is used in the linking theory. For example, suppose we give a separationist treatment of event-structural decomposition, as in (52). Then we must arrange the syntactic category of DO, BECOME, CAUSE and hard so as to prevent (53), for example, from having exactly the meaning of (52).

(52)   [Floyd [DO [CAUSE [BECOME [[the glass] hard]]]]]
        'λe_1[Do$\langle e_1, x \rangle$ & $\exists e_2$[Cause$\langle e_1, e_2 \rangle$ & $\exists e_3$[Become$\langle e_2, e_3 \rangle$ & $V(e_3, y)$]]]'
(53)   * [[[the glass] hard] [BECOME [CAUSE [Floyd DO]]]]

Finally, it should again be noted that any analysis the separationist uses in Syntax can be transposed into Lexicon by the projectionist, swapping lexical for prelexical items. The choice between the separationist and projectionist versions must be decided on independent grounds (Chapter 9).

11.3 FRAMING

11.3.1 Frames and semantic classification

A **frame** is a predicate and its satellites, viewed in abstraction from the words. The *basic transitive frame* in (54) is a transitive clause with S interpreted by Agent, and O by Theme. The verb hit can occur in this frame, replacing Verb and *Verbing* in (54) with "hit" and Hitting in (55).

(54) a NP$_1$ Verb NP$_2$.

    b ∃e[Agent(e, [[NP$_1$]]) & *Verbing*(e) & Theme(e, [[NP$_2$]])]

(55) a John hit the fence.

    b ∃e[Agent(e, [[John]]) & *Hitting*(e) & Theme(e, [[the fence]])]

From a separationist perspective, a frame does not project from the verb. From a projectionist perspective, it does, though its structure may be derived in Lexicon.

Usually a verb will occur in more than one frame. As observed in Fillmore (1977), hit can occur not only in the basic transitive frame, but also in the *instrument-path frame* of (56). Here O names the instrument of the action, wielded along a path described by the prepositional phrase that follows.[10] Significantly, (56) entails that John hit the fence with the stick.

(56)   John hit the stick against the fence.

A verb will also be excluded from some frames. Hit cannot occur in the *unaccusative frame* of (57) (Fillmore 1970), an intransitive clause where, putting it simply, S names the patient of the event.

(57)   * The fence hit.

       'There was an event of hitting in which the fence was hit.'

So frames are selective: they accept some verbs but not others. Fillmore (1970, 1977) contrasts hit with break. Like hit, break can occur in the basic transitive frame, (58). But, unlike hit, it is excluded from the instrument–path frame – (59) cannot have the meaning in the gloss – and is accepted in the unaccusative frame, (60).

(58)   John broke the fence.

(59)   * John broke the stick against the fence.

       'John broke the fence by wielding the stick against it.'

(60)   The fence broke.

Importantly, verbs with similar frame-distributions are generally satisfied by similar sorts of events. Verbs that pattern with hit include poke and smack, for example, while burst and crack pattern with break. Similarity in distribution coincides with similarity in the events. So what are the relevant dimensions of similarity on either dimension, and how do they relate? What are the *framing generalizations*?

---

[10] The instrument–path frame is one half of what Levin 1993 calls the "with/against alternation." Note, however, that against is not the only preposition that occurs here. If John pokes the dog with a stick, for example, he pokes the stick *into* the dog.

Verbs with the distribution of break, observed Fillmore, describe a substantive change, whether in material integrity, function or position. These seem to be categorically excluded from the instrument–path frame. Meanwhile, verbs that are permitted in the unaccusative frame (in English but not all languages) describe events that we can view as spontaneous. As we normally view the world, a thing may break or crack or burst on its own, without anything breaking, cracking or bursting it. But neither characteristic holds of hit, smack or poke. These all describe events of motion ending in contact (Levin 1993), and we view such events as involving both of the things that come into contact. We don't view strikings in abstraction from the striker, and in this (extended) sense we don't view them as possibly spontaneous. Accordingly, such verbs are generally excluded from the unaccusative frame in English.[11] They are not excluded from the instrument–path frame, however, because they do not describe changes. What is struck need not change any of its intrinsic properties.[12] So there is a broad correspondence between the semantic and distributional classifications. In English, only verbs that do not imply a real change go in the instrument–path frame, and only verbs whose event we can view as spontaneous go in the unaccusative frame.

There are dozens of further cases, many uncovered or catalogued in Levin (1993). Here are two. Zwicky (1971) observes a regular difference between verbs that describe the physical manner of speech, such as mutter or shriek, and those that classify the illocutionary act, such as claim or state. The two sorts of verb can both occupy the frame in (61a), but they differ in (61b–c).

(61) a Mo muttered / claimed that locusts were swarming.
      b Mo muttered / *claimed (at me).
      c Mo muttered / *claimed for me to bring a flyswatter.

Second, the *conative frame* in (62), which accepts (e.g.) cut, kick and eat, but not touch, smack, or smash (Guerssel *et al.* 1985, Laughren 1988,

---

[11] There are exceptions like (1) below, however. But these are acceptable only when what is struck is understood from context.

(1) The meteor struck at midnight.

[12] Of course, what is struck does change in entering the state of having been in the Strike relation to something. But on this weak notion of change, known as a "Cambridge change" after Geach 1969 (pp. 71–2), any one thing undergoes infinitely many changes at every moment, since it is related in varying ways to infinitely many others. Therefore we generally focus on changes that are somehow 'intrinsic' or 'natural.' These include changes in some relational properties – including weight, location, and many social or family relations – but not all.

Pinker 1989, Levin 1993, Goldberg 1995, van der Leek 1996, Beavers 2006a, Vincent 2013). The contrast, many have suggested, is in whether the verb describes some characteristic activity of the agent leading up to the typical final effect on, or contact with, the patient. By hypothesis, cut, eat and kick do, but touch, smack and smash do not. The latter verbs describe the contact or effect, but not the action that precedes it.

(62) Mo cut / kicked / ate / *touched / *smashed at the melon.

One aspect of framing (or also linking) is the relation between a dependent's syntactic category, and the 'kind' of thing that satisfies the semantic relation it binds. This is the relation between *c(ategory)-selection* and *s(emantic)-selection* (Pesetsky 1982). Grimshaw (1979) put cases like (63) in the spotlight.

(63) a   Val wonders who Hal is.
      b   * Val wonders Hal's identity.
      c   * Val wonders that Hal is somebody.

Wonder goes only in a frame where O has the category of an interrogative clause. Semantically, O gives the content of the wondering. What *kind* of thing is that? Intuitively, it is a question. The content of Val's wonder is not a fact (Hal being Al's twin), a property (being Al's twin) or a material object (Hal), but a question (Who is Hal?). So wonder **c-selects** an interrogative and **s-selects** a question; it goes in frames with an interrogative O, and describes events related (by the Content relation) to a question. Now compare know and believe, (64).

(64) a   Val { knows / *believes } who Hal is.
          'Val has { knowledge of / a belief about } who Hal is.'
      b   Val { knows / *believes } Hal's identity.
          'Val has { knowledge of / a belief about } who Hal is.'
      c   Val { knows / believes } that Hal is Al's twin.

These verbs differ in distribution both from wonder and from each other. There is an attendant difference in the events. Neither believing nor knowing has as its content a question. The content of belief is a proposition, let's say. The content of knowledge is a true proposition, or a fact. These s-selectional properties appear to condition the c-selectional patterns – though not fully determine them (Grimshaw 1979, Pollard and Sag 1987, Chomsky and Lasnik 1993, Odijk 1997). The observed patterns constitute framing generalizations. See Lahiri (2002), Égré (2008), Moulton (2009) and White *et al.* (2014) for more recent work in this area.

In the rest of this section, I describe three of the simplest and most stable patterns of framing cross-linguistically (Section 11.3.2), and broach the topic of how framing generalizations might be explained (Section 11.3.3). The final subsection (Section 11.3.4) concerns the utility of framing generalizations in language acquisition. For a monographic treatment of these very rich topics, see Levin and Rappaport Hovav (2005).

11.3.2 Three stable patterns

The simplest framing generalizations have to do just with whether or not the frame realizes a certain role – that is, provides a dependent to bind it. The three generalizations in (65–67) are perhaps the most stable across languages. I list them in what seems to me decreasing order of robustness.

(65) Role Realization Generalization
      A basic clause realizes some participant in its event.

(66) Change Realization Generalization
      In general a basic clause whose event is a change realizes its patient.

(67) Agent Realization Generalization
      Typically a basic clause whose event is an action realizes its agent.

In this subsection I will expand these slogans somewhat. To begin, the notion of 'basic clause.' This is a useful descriptive rubric. It might even play a role in language acquisition. But I do not presuppose that it has any place in the language acquired, or that it has a proper definition. Here I will just wave towards two of its aspects. First, a basic clause is of a type that is highly independent. There are few conditions on the contexts of its use, whether syntactic, semantic or pragmatic, beyond knowing the values of its referring expressions and unbound variables. In this way the (a) cases in (68–70) are more independent than the (b) cases.

(68) a Bill would like for Al to slice salami.
      b for Al to slice salami

(69) a Any salami that Al ever sliced turned out very thin.
      b Al ever sliced salami

(70) a It's easy to slice salami.
      b Salami, it's easy to slice.

Second, a basic clause is maximally 'unmarked' in form, relative to the resources of the language. In English, I take passive clauses to be more 'marked' than active clauses in form, since they require an auxiliary verb, and use by where actives do not. What counts as more or less 'marked' in general is a difficult question, to which there may be no categorical answer. But this is enough for our purposes.

Now to (65), the Role Realization Generalization. If the main event of a basic clause has participant roles implied by its predicate, then at least one of those roles will be bound by a dependent. The situation in (71) is representative. The event of (71a) is one of laughing, and here the subject binds the role of Laugher. In (71b) there is no dependent binding that role, and the result is ungrammatical.

(71)　a　Someone laughed loudly just now.
　　　b　* There/it laughed loudly just now.
　　　　　'There was loud laughing just now.'

Realization of a participant is not necessary in clause types fairly classed as nonbasic, such as the German passive in (72), formed with the past participle plus an auxiliary use of 'become' (Chapter 12).

(72)　Dann　wurde　laut　gelacht.
　　　then　became　loudly　laugh.PPL
　　　'Then people laughed loudly.'

Nor is it necessary in (73), an existential sentence with a nominalization of the verb. This sentence rejects adverbs that can describe laughings, such as *loudly* in (74). Thus the event of (73) is evidently not one that satisfies *laugh*, a laughing, but rather something like the state of there being laughter. Such a state does not itself have a laugher, any more than there are stripes on the state of there being tigers in the zoo.

(73)　There was loud laughter just now.

(74)　* There was laughter loudly just now.

But I know of no language where a basic clause whose event has participants nevertheless has no dependents that realize one. And, importantly, this is not something that follows from the pragmatics of conversation. Sentences (72) and (73) are fine ways to begin a discussion, and they convey no less information than does (71a). Certainly we have communicative motives for introducing event participants into conversation. But these motives needn't be served with basic clauses; nonbasic clauses would work just as well. In this sense, the absence of basic clauses like (71b) is a synchronically irreducible fact about argument structure in natural languages, reminiscent of the ancient observation that sentences tend to divide into predicate and subject (Strawson 1959).

The second stable pattern is (66), the Change Realization Generalization. This concerns basic clauses whose main event is one of change, like a melting, bending, cutting, cracking or killing. In general, such clauses will have a mandatory dependent that binds the patient (or undergoer) of the change. For example, both clauses in (75) say what was melted, and removal of the patient in (76) is unacceptable.

(75) a The heat melted the candy.
      b The candy melted.
(76) a * The heat melted.
         'The heat melted stuff.'
      b * There/it melted.
         'There was melting.'

Naturally there are nonbasic cases. Goldberg (2001:506) discusses (77).

(77) Tigers only kill at night.

But the general pattern is without question robust, evidently across languages (Levin to appear). There is also evidence that children are aware of this pattern by the age of two.[13]

Of course verbs of change are not alone in preferring the company of their patients. Verbs of striking or contact, with meanings like 'strike' or 'touch,' are saliently similar. But here the preference is not quite as strong. As suggested by (78), verbs that describe a characteristic motion that precedes or accompanies the contact are often acceptable in an intransitive frame with S naming the 'agent,' given a durative or pluractional interpretation. See Levin (to appear) for extensive discussion.

(78) Rocky punched / rubbed / ?*struck / *touched for hours.

The third major pattern, the Agent Realization Generalization of (67), governs basic clauses that describe their event as not being spontaneous, but rather as having an agent – as usual in the very loose sense of the term, whereby a book that strikes the floor is called the agent of the striking. In many languages, such a clause will include a mandatory dependent to bind the agent role. English is again illustrative. The verbs punch and cut entail a puncher and a cutter, roles we can classify as agents. These verbs can occur in transitives like (79), but neither can occur in a basic unaccusative frame, (80), without a subject to bind the agent role.

[13] See Naigles 1990, 1996, Fisher 1996, Brandone *et al.* 2006, Arunachalam and Waxman 2010, Fisher *et al.* 2010, Yuan and Fisher 2009, Yuan *et al.* 2012. These studies suggest that two-year-olds do not expect that speakers will use an intransitive clause to describe a caused change, wherein one creature forcibly changes the condition of something else. For instance, they do not expect that The duck is gorping will be used to describe a scene where the duck changes the posture of a companion, hence is 'gorping somebody.' See Section 11.3.4.

(79) a Rocky punched the wall.
     b Rocky cut this bread.

(80) a * The wall punched.
     b * This bread cut.

These verbs can occur without mention of the puncher or cutter only in contexts that are fairly called nonbasic, such as passives, (81a), and middles, (81b).[14]

(81) a This bread was cut too sloppily.
     b This bread cuts too sloppily with that knife.

The agent is also unnecessary when punch and cut do not occur 'as verbs,' but rather occupy contexts for adjectives or nouns, as in (82).

(82) a This bread is cut.
     b This cut is sloppy.

But abstracting from these epicycles as usual, we can say that agentive verbs occur only in those basic clauses that realize the agent, in many different languages.

But not all. Agents are not as tenacious as are patients of change, as we might recall from our discussion of Fijian (Chapter 5). In St'át'imcets, a Salish language of British Columbia, quite nearly every verb in the language can occupy an eventive unaccusative clause, even if it entails an agent (Davis 2000, 2010, Davis and Demirdache 2000). This includes sek 'whip,' mets 'write,' and ats'x 'see,' which entail whippers, writers and viewers. Sentence (83) has qámt, which means 'to hit with a thrown object,' similar to American English bean. In (83) this occupies an unaccusative clause whose only dependent names the person who got beaned.

(83) Qámt k^w꞊ s꞊ K^wímčxen.
     bean DET꞊ NOMZ꞊ K.
     'There was a beaning, and K^wímčxen was the beaned.'

This deserves to be called a basic clause. Semantically it is eventive, not stative, so its meaning directly expresses the meaning of the verb. Formally, the verb is bare, unaffixed. In contrast, in transitives the verb requires a derivational suffix, (84).

---

[14] The middle is nonbasic at least inasmuch as it generally takes a modifier, (1a), and resists the Perfect, (1b).

(1) a The bread cut ??(sloppily).
     b ?? The bread will have cut sloppily with that knife.

(84) Qám̀t -š̌   -áš̌   kᵂ⁼ s⁼   Kᵂímč̌xen ta⁼ twə́ww̌ət ⁼a.
     bean -TRANS -3S.ERG DET⁼ NOMZ⁼ K.   DET boy   ⁼EXIST
     'The boy beaned Kᵂimč̌xen.'

St'át'imcets also has a passive, (85), built on the complex transitive
stem. The simple intransitive, (83), and the passive, (85), differ in ways I
discuss in Chapter 12, but they do not differ in the meaning of the root.

(85) Qám̀t -š̌   -túm   kᵂ⁼ s⁼   Kᵂímč̌xen (ʔə⁼ta twə́ww̌ət⁼a).
     bean -TRANS -3S.PASS DET⁼ NOMZ⁼ K.   (OBL⁼DET boy⁼EXIST)
     'Kᵂímč̌xen got beaned (by a boy).'

Also, in Igbo, predicates that entail an agent may inhabit unaccusative
clauses, but not freely. Unaccusatives reject ₋agentive predicates that
do not describe a change, such as kụ 'strike' in (86), but accept some
predicates that do, such as kụ wa 'strike split' in (87) (Nwachukwu 1987).

(86) * Ọba ahụ kụ   -rụ   akụ.
       gourd that strike -FACT BVC
       'That gourd was the patient of a striking.'

(87)   Ọba ahụ kụ   wa   -ra   akụwa.
       gourd that strike split -FACT BVC
       'That gourd split from [something] striking [it].'

Some agent-entailing predicates that describe a change still cannot
occupy unaccusatives, witness (88), which replaces the kụ 'strike' of (87)
with zọ 'tread on' (Hale et al. 1995). The relevant difference is not clear,
but I have suggested (Williams 2005, 2014a) that it pertains somehow
to animacy. Many predicates that are 'defined' by features of animate
creatures, like mobile legs, are excluded from unaccusatives.

(88) * Ọba ahụ zọ   wa   -ra   azọwa.
       gourd that tread split -FACT BVC
       'That gourd split from [something] treading on [it].' (Hale et al. 1995)

Thus the conditions on when an agentive verb can occur in a basic
unaccusative clause vary across languages. English is perhaps the average case, but it is also at the extreme, with verbs that imply an agent
semantically demanding one in the syntax.

These deviations from the putatively average case serve to amplify
a point made earlier. On its own, the content of a verb entails nothing whatsoever about its distribution. Logic gives no reason that an
event predicate has to occur in the company of a participant argument,
and there is no pragmatic reason that one must use a basic clause to
talk about an event's participants. Yes, the facts of English do reflect
a very common pattern, one that may express some broad functional

tendency – hence our generalization. But they do not reflect common sense, conceptual necessity or even, I am suggesting, a universal grammatical requirement.

Lastly, note the combined effect of the Change Realization and Agent Realization Generalizations. A basic clause whose event is a change wrought by an agent – a killing, for example – will tend strongly to realize both the agent and the undergoer of the change, hence to be transitive. See Hopper and Thompson (1980).

11.3.3 Explaining framing generalizations

In general it is easy to implement a framing generalization formally. To a certain class of lexical (or prelexical) items, we assign a category feature that is compatible with some syntactic (or prelexical) frames and not others. Let all unaccusative clauses be built around a *v* that selects VPs with feature [−A], for example. Then we can describe English by giving all and only the verbs whose event is not viewed as spontaneous the conflicting feature [+A], and describe Igbo by assigning [+A] to just a certain subset of these verbs (Williams 2005, 2014a).

But what explains the generalization in the first place? *Why* does a frame exclude the verbs it excludes?

Sometimes the exclusion seems to reflect semantic inconsistency. The combination of predicate and frame yields an event description that cannot be true. No state has an agent, for example, and no state is a motion. So a stative verb, such as know or resemble, if placed in a frame with a dependent for an agent or a path of motion, would yield an event description that cannot be true. Such inconsistency might register directly in judgments of acceptability. Or maybe it is also 'grammaticized,' and the incompatible verbs have a syntactic feature that keeps them out of the frame.

An account like this might be offered for the instrument–path frame. Recall that this accepts verbs of motion ending in contact, (89a), but not verbs of change, (89b).

(89)　a　John poked the needle into the balloon.
　　　b　* John burst the needle into the balloon.

The pattern in (89) would be predicted given three suppositions. The event of the clause is a directed motion, one whose path is given by the PP; the verb modifies that event; and pokings are directed motions (that end in contact), but burstings are not (Levin 1993). This is reasonable – but not indubitable. The latter two suppositions need a defense. Why assume that the PP and the verb describe the same event? And why not assume, with Davidson (1970), that the motion of a needle into a balloon can also be a bursting of it? Our account of (89) is superficial, unless these issues are addressed.

Dowty (2001) gives a (weaker sort of) consistency account of the *swarm-with frame* in (90) (Fillmore 1968, Anderson 1971, Chomsky 1971, Levin 1993).

(90) a The garden swarmed with bees.
      b The wall crawled with roaches.
      c The church echoed with the voices of the choristers.

Contrasting (90) with (91), among other examples, Dowty observes, following Salkoff (1983), that this frame only accepts verbs "that refer to 'small' movements, simple light emissions, simple sounds, or smells."

(91) a * The field grazed with cows.
      b * The sky flew with birds
      c * The church harmonized with the voices of the choristers.

Dowty then suggests that only such verbs are compatible – this is a matter of conceptual or practical compatibility, not logical consistency – with the meaning of the frame, which he introduces in a rule of lexical derivation, and describes as (92).

(92) [S Vs with X] describes the property a location [S] has when the kind of activity denoted by [V] is being performed in most/all (very small) subparts of location [S], by some instance of [X] in each case.

The frame describes a state that is related to activities "distributed throughout all small regions" of the location named by the subject. The compatible verbs must therefore describe events that *can* be so distributed; and these events, suggests Dowty, are only the "simple, small" ones. (On uses of *swarm* or *crawl* in their 'normal' frame, see the Discussion Points at the end of this chapter.)

In any case, explanations based on consistency are limited in two ways. First, they cannot explain why we have only the frames and verbs that we do. Consistency might explain why the intrument–path frame does not itself accept burst; but it will not explain why there is no 'result–instrument–path frame' like (93), or why there is no second verb burst$_2$, satisfied by directed movements that end with a burst, that might go in the instrument–path frame. Either possibility would permit (94), exactly what we were trying to rule out with the consistency account.

(93) NP1 Verb NP2 Prep NP3
      'In moving NP2 along path Prep NP3, NP1 caused NP3 to Verb.'

(94)   * John burst the needle into the balloon.
       'In moving the needle into the balloon, John made the balloon burst.'

According to Rappaport Hovav and Levin (2010), no verb carries information both about the manner of an action and about a change it brings about. Our hypothetical burst$_2$ would be excluded, if this generalization were true; but Beavers and Koontz-Garboden (2012) give good evidence against it. Nor does there seem to be a ban on single-clause constructions that describe both the manner and a result of an action, given resultatives such as the familiar (95).

(95)   Rocky's fists pounded the frozen beef bloody.

Second, as a matter of fact, semantic consistency will not explain every framing pattern. The frame in (96) accepts eat but not melt.

(96)   Nora ate / *melted.
       'Nora ate / melted stuff.'

The rejection of melt is an instance of the Change Realization Generalization in (66). This is a robust generalization, maybe even a consequence of human nature. Still, consistency does not explain (96), since it is not inconsistent to say that Nora melted stuff. Or consider (97), from Hale and Keyser (1997).

(97)   Mud splashed / *smeared on the wall.

One can say that there was smearing of mud, without mention of smearers. So, as I stressed in discussing the Agent Realization Generalization (Section 11.3.2), (97) expresses a grammatical requirement that cannot follow from semantic consistency.

In discussing (97), Hale and Keyser (1997) propose to *deduce* this requirement, with reference to a derivation in Lexicon. They derive smear from at least two separate prelexical items, call them $\Lambda 1$ and $\Lambda 2$, using the inverted "V" as a prelexical category label. $\Lambda 1$ describes qualities of, or effects on, what is smeared. $\Lambda 2$ describes the actions of the smearer. The latter, they assume, in turn mandates an argument for the agent whose actions are described. The derived verb smear inherits this argument for a smearer, and therefore cannot inhabit an unaccusative frame, where its argument would not be satisfied. So instead of saying just that smear has an agent argument, Hale and Keyser deduce this by saying that a prelexical part of it does. This stipulation, along with the lexical decomposition of smear, may interact fruitfully with other parts of their theory, and so be justified by its downstream effects. But on its own it is unmotivated. There is no independent reason a predicate describing an action, their $\Lambda 2$, needs an argument for the entailed actor. Nor of course is there any reason a verb satisfied by smearings must be derived, with separate prelexical parts for its 'manner' and 'result.' Brunettes are people with brown hair, but it doesn't follow that brunette has prelexical parts that mean 'person,' 'brown' and 'hair.' So while this derivation of smear's requirements might explain other facts, it gives no account of the requirement itself.

A framing pattern with no semantic explanation may be synchronically arbitrary, lacking any grammatical explanation. Or it may yet be explained by independent syntactic or phonological properties of the verb or frame. Here are two examples. First, bleed on things, (98), but not bleed, (99), can occur in the passive frame. This is explained by the independent syntactic fact that English does not freely allow expletive subjects. I repeat this example in Chapter 12.

(98)   In hospitals things are often bled on.

(99)   * In hospitals there/it is often bled.

Second, some frames tend to exclude Latinate verbs in favor of native stock. The double object construction in (100) permits give, send and show, but not donate, transfer or demonstrate (Pinker 1989, Grimshaw 2005). The proclivities of the resultative construction in (101) are similarly Anglo-Saxon (Green 1972, Harley 2011).

(100)   Lee gave/sent/showed/*donated/*transferred/*demonstrated Mo $100.

(101)   a The doctor cut/?incised the scar open.
         b The pudding froze/?congealed solid.

The exclusion of these verbs cannot be explained by what sorts of events they describe. Show patterns with give and not demonstrate, even though showings are more like demonstrations than like givings. So if the pattern is to have a synchronic explanation, it must appeal to the phonology of these verbs, their morphology, or some independent aspect of their syntax. The question is pursued in Gropen et al. (1989), Pinker (1989), Grimshaw (2005), Coppock (2009), and Harley (2011). On the history of the double object construction in English, see Allen (1995) and McFadden (2002).

Finally, allow me to repeat an alarm already sounded in Chapters 3 and 8. Sometimes Chomsky's (1981) Theta Criterion is mistaken for a principle of framing, something that relates the distribution of a verb, at d-structure,[15] to the sort of event it describes.[16] Specifically,

---

[15] The "Projection Principle" (Chomsky 1981) then requires that arguments licensed at d-structure are preserved at other levels of representation.

[16] This error is found even in otherwise excellent work, such as Gleitman 1990 and Lidz et al. 2003.

it is mistaken for a principle requiring that every notional participant in a verb's event must be realized by an argument at d-structure (Section 11.3.4). But the Theta Criterion is a syntactic principle. It serves only to functionally define certain syntactic features, the Θ-roles, as obligatory syntactic arguments (Chapter 3). This provides a mechanism for implementing a framing pattern in Syntax, since the Θ-roles are presumed to coincide with semantic arguments in participant roles. But it does nothing to explain any particular pattern, since it is not the job of the Theta Criterion to decide what Θ-roles a lexical item has in the first place (Chapter 8).

11.3.4 Framing and language acquisition

As we have seen in this chapter, syntactic categories often have semantic correlates. Most generally, verbs express event sortals, nouns express object sortals, adjectives express qualities, determiners express relations over cardinalities, prepositions express spatial relations, and so forth. A learner who knows any such correlation has a good basis for inference. Given information about the syntactic category of a word, she can infer something about its meaning: this is **syntactic bootstrapping** (Landau and Gleitman 1985, Gleitman 1990). Given information about its semantic class, she can infer something about its syntax: that is **semantic bootstrapping** (Pinker 1979, 1984, 1987, Grimshaw 1981, Wexler and Culicover 1981).

Here is an example with a fictional word, loesst. Suppose a child understands that this means 'having windblown hair,' an object quality, and knows that in general only adjectives express such qualities. Then if she knows the characteristic distribution of adjectives, in distinction to nouns and determiners, she can infer that (102a) is acceptable, but (102b) and (102c) most likely are not.

(102)   a They look so loesst!
       b See the many loessts?
       c Loesst of the dogs are thirsty.

Conversely, if the child has no prior idea what loesst means, she can infer that it expresses a quality – or an object sortal, or a quantifier, as the case may be – depending on whether she hears it in (102a), (102b) or (102c). It has been shown that children as young as 14 months are sensitive to the semantic correlates of nounhood, but not adjectivehood (Waxman 1998, Waxman and Markow 1998, Booth and Waxman 2003, 2009). Sensitivity to the semantics of adjectives is active by the age of four, however, as is the distinction between adjective- and determiner-meanings (Gagliardi *et al.* 2012, Wellwood *et al.* 2014a).

Framing generalizations about minor categories (subcategories) can be used in the same way. Suppose that clauses with the shape of (103a) – where MainS is the class of strings than can themselves serve as a main, nonsubordinate clause – generally have a verb with the semantic outlines of (103b) (Bolinger 1968), and also conversely.

(103)   a NP VERB MainS
        b VERB is true of an event in which someone [named by NP] represents things as being a certain way [as given by MainS]

A learner who knows this has a good basis for inference (Gleitman 1990, Fisher et al. 1991, de Villiers and de Villiers 2000, White et al. 2014). If she encounters a new verb in context (103a), she can guess that its meaning is like (103b), and have a good chance of being right. Two examples consistent with this are (104a) and (104b), with the verbs think and say, which here both concern representation.

(104)   a Val thinks that Hal arrived.
        b Val said that Hal arrived.

Or imagine a child who grasps what her father wants to convey when he utters What does Mama think? or Mama thinks so. She knows that these strings are used to talk about how her mother represents a certain situation. So if she can also recognize think as a verb here, (103) will allow her to guess correctly that (104a) is a possible sentence, and one which implies that according to Val, Hal arrived.

The general question, then, is this. Which correspondences actually do guide children at which ages, and how do they come to 'know' these correspondences? The literature is full of suggestions, especially after Grimshaw (1981), Pinker (1984) and Landau and Gleitman (1985). In the remainder of this section, I will concentrate on one idea, pursued in much work after Gleitman (1990) and Naigles (1990), and particularly pertinent in this chapter.[17] The idea is that, by around the age of two, children's acquisition of verbs is guided by (105), which I call **Participant-to-Argument Matching**, or **PAM**. This says that the NP arguments in a clause exactly match the participants implied by its verb, one-to-one.

(105)   Participant-to-Argument Matching (PAM)
        In basic clauses, the nominal satellites of a verb (subject, object, indirect object, …) correspond exactly to its participants, one-to-one.

---

[17] Fisher 1996, 2002, Hirsh-Pasek et al. 1996, Naigles 1996, Lidz et al. 2003, Brandone et al. 2006, Yuan and Fisher 2009, Arunachalam and Waxman 2010, 2011, Fisher et al. 2010, Noble et al. 2011 and Yuan et al. 2012.

Thus toddlers are said to presume that a transitive clause has a verb with two participant roles, while the verb in an intransitive clause has only one. This is sometimes called the "one-to-one mapping" hypothesis (e.g., Brandone *et al.* 2006).

Many experiments have aimed to test this, in children between 18 and 40 months. The experiments are mostly variations on the same theme. A child is presented with a novel verb, like dax or gorp, in either an intransitive or a transitive clause. Yuan *et al.* (2012) use the stimuli in (106).

(106) a He is gorping.
       b He is gorping him.

Using metrics such as duration of eye gaze, one then measures differences in the child's response to the display of two scenes, as a function of whether they hear the transitive or intransitive clause. The two scenes differ in the number of participants, two or one, implied by what seems to the experimenter like their most natural description. For example, the 2-participant scene might have one person causing another to lean over by pushing against his back, while the 1-participant scene just has people waving their arms, or leaning over (Naigles 1990, Yuan *et al.* 2012). Which scene is the child more likely to regard as verifying the given sentence?

The child guided by PAM, if she perceives the scenes under the intended descriptions, will assume that the transitive clause cannot be verified by the 1-participant scene. It has more arguments than the scene, as we view it, has participants. Nearly all experimental results are consistent with this prediction.[18] But despite what is often supposed, this is not distinctively supportive of the PAM hypothesis. The same behavior would follow from something much weaker than PAM. Suppose instead that the child is guided by just the assumption that *Arguments Name Participants* (ANP): any NP satellite binds some participant role implied by the verb. In other words, there must be some role for every NP argument in a clause, and none are pleonastic. The observed fact then follows: a transitive clause cannot be verified by a 1-participant scene. But it follows from something much harder to imagine being false, and therefore less interesting.

What is special to PAM is its prediction about the child's view of the *intransitive* clause. The child guided by PAM, and not just ANP, will

---

[18] Naigles 1990, Fisher 1996, 2002, Brandone *et al.* 2006, Fisher *et al.* 2010, Arunachalam and Waxman 2010, 2011, Noble *et al.* 2011, Yuan *et al.* 2012.

associate an intransitive clause only with a 1-participant scene, and not a 2-participant scene, if the scenes are perceived as intended. In the seminal study of Naigles (1990), this expectation is supported, but only very weakly; and, since then, it has not found robust support. In Yuan *et al.* (2012), the 19- and 21-month-olds presented with the intransitive clause He gorped did not look longer at a 1-participant scene than they did in a control condition. In Arunachalam and Waxman (2010), 27-month-olds presented with The boy and the girl are going to moop were no more likely to point at a 1-participant scene than would be expected by chance. According to Noble, Rowland and Pine (2011) which reviews twenty years of literature, these are representative results. One must therefore conclude that PAM, while it has not been falsified, has not been supported in distinction to the ANP, itself an almost trivial hypothesis.

This may seem disappointing, but there is reason to be happy. Were children in fact guided by PAM, this would sometimes cause big problems – or so one expects given intuitions about participanthood (Williams 2005, He *et al.* 2013). Consider the verb steal, for example (Goldberg 1995). It can occur in transitive clauses, such as (107).

(107)   The boy stole the toy.

Here S and O identify the thief and the loot in the stealing. PAM will therefore tell the child that stealings have only two participants. But this seems wrong. Doesn't steal also have Victim as a participant role? It is odd to suggest that the victim in a stealing has the same status as its Place or Time, roles that are entailed, but not explicit constituents of the 'event sketch' (Chapter 4). In addition, there is experimental evidence that both adults and very young children do view scenes of theft *as* involving the victim, in addition to the thief and the loot (He *et al.* 2013, Wellwood *et al.* 2014b, building on Gordon 2003). If this is right, then PAM will give toddlers the wrong advice in cases like these – and steal is just one of many examples. This bad advice should make learning difficult, if PAM is indeed strong enough to be useful as a learning bias.

Worse problems arise in languages where the counterparts of English transitive verbs need not occur in transitive clauses. Recall the extreme example of St'át'imcets (Section 11.3.2). In this language, nearly every verb can occur in an unaccusative frame, including qám̓t 'to hit with a thrown object.' Surely this verb does not have *only* the thing hit as a participant role. And, more than likely, when we see someone throw a rock and hit something, the rock is explicitly represented in our view (Wellwood *et al.* 2014b). Therefore the child who hears qáṁt in an intransitive clause will get the wrong advice from PAM. Similar comments can be made about Fijian, Igbo, Hindi and Mandarin, among other languages.

The response to problems like these cannot be that toddlers are just as happy to view a theft as involving two rather than three, participants – that is, to view a theft under a concept truth-conditionally equivalent to English steal, but without the victim as an explicit consituent – and will readily do so whenever they are confident that an observed theft verifies a transitive clause. This would utterly void the bootstrapping hypothesis of any predictive force. Syntactic bootstrapping is useful only if it narrows the range of scenes, as naturally viewed, that might verify the sentence. PAM will effect no narrowing at all if every scene that is most naturally viewed under an n-participant perspective is equally liable to be viewed under an $(n - m)$-participant perspective. As emphasized in Gordon (2003), bootstrapping requires that the child's *nonlinguistic* perspective on the world is stable and consistent with our own. For example, unless toddlers are overwhelmingly likely to view scenes of giving under a 3-participant concept, rather than a 2-participant concept with the same satisfaction conditions, the fact that we use give in clauses with three NPs cannot help them pick out which it describes in the observed scene.

Two other responses are more sensible. First, perhaps the child learning St'át'imcets, Igbo, Mandarin or Fijian, for example, learns very quickly that PAM is not useful for her language. But if a child can learn to back off of PAM by the age of two, it must be a rather weak bias; and the weaker it is, the less useful it will be for learning. The last hypothesis is that children are quick to exclude sentences that conflict with PAM as non-basic or exceptional cases. Something like this is required even in English, just to deal with passives, for example. But English passives have special morphology. There is no independendent evidence that English clauses with steal, or St'át'imcets unaccusatives with qaṁt, are in any way exceptional or non-basic.

In my own judgment, therefore, PAM-based bootstrapping is both experimentally unsupported and theoretically unhelpful. I expect that the child is instead guided both by more trivial principles, such as the ANP, and by much more *specific* framing generalizations, such as the Change Realization Generalization in (66) – and, most importantly, by a nonlinguistic perspective on the world that is substantially shared.

DISCUSSION POINTS

1 Alongside (1a) below, we have (1b). Is this alternation a problem for linking theories? That is, are these two synonymous clauses, with exactly the same thematic relations, that nevertheless show two different patterns of linking?

(1)   a   The wall is crawling (*quickly) with roaches.
      b   Roaches are crawling (quickly) on the wall.

Specifically, should we assume that roaches and the wall each bind the same relation in both alternates? Are these two clauses satisfied by exactly the same *sort* of event? How does the contrasting acceptability of quickly matter to your answer? In answering, think carefully about the semantic characterization Dowty gives (1a), quoted in (92) above.

2 One can clear a table by pushing the plates off of it. But clear and push have different distributions, as shown by (2) and (3).

(2)   a   Al cleared the plates from the table.
          ⊨ Al cleared the plates.
          ⊭Al cleared the table.
      b   Al cleared the table of plates.
(3)   a   Al pushed the plates off the table.
          ⊨Al pushed the plates.
          ⊭Al pushed the table.
      b   * Al pushed the table of plates.

Which other verbs behave like clear, and which like push? Do the verbs in each class have something in common, semantically? If so, can you carefully describe what it is? Can you state a framing generalization?

3 Do you know a language with signs of unaccusativity in intransitive clauses? Describe what those signs are. Can you argue for or against the hypothesis that these signs are explained by deep unaccusativity?

4 Would it be useful for the child acquiring her first language to distinguish between 'basic' and 'non-basic' clause types? If so, how exactly would this be useful? How might a child acquiring a language be able to make this distinction, at least roughly? And how would they come to have this ability?

5 Many languages divide their nouns into classes, sometimes called genders. These classes typically display some commonalities among their members. For example, in Tsez (Nakh-Dagestanian), class 1 nouns include all and only male humans; class 2 nouns

include all female humans, plus many other things; class 3 nouns include all nonhuman animates, plus many other things; and class 4 nouns include only inanimates (Gagliardi 2012).

Does the existence of these noun classes require that each noun includes features for human, animate, etc., as part of its linguistic representation? Does it require that these properties are furthermore parts of the noun's *meaning*, in the strict sense? The majority of nouns referring to things made out of paper fall into class 2. Does this fact change your answer?

Now, in what way are noun classes like and unlike generalizations about the mapping of verbs to particular syntactic frames?

6 In clauses with win, an overt direct object may name either a contest or a prize. But when there is no overt object, the unrealized role ranges only over contests. To see this, imagine using (4a) when you have no knowledge of a contest in which Ron might have participated. Then (4b-i) will be an infelicitous response. It cannot be used, as (4b-ii) can, to say that Ron won the bear.

(4) a   There is a teddy bear on the sofa.
     b i # Ron won.
        ii   Ron won it. [=the teddy bear]

As an exercise, describe this pattern with win in terms of s-selection and c-selection. Next, do the same for notice, using the facts below.

(5) a   Lee broke Mo's nose.
     b i   I noticed that it was broken.
        ii   I noticed it, but was it broken?
        iii # I noticed, but was it broken?

Is there some similarity between the cases of win and notice? Is the unrealized role always a certain *kind* of thing? Try to construct further paradigms with other similar verbs, such as forget, which allow two interpretations of an overt object, but only one for their definite unrealized role. Then ask again: is there some correspondence between c-selecting a definite null object, and s-selecting a certain kind of semantic relatum? If so, can you account for the correspondence?

7 Consider two event concepts, GIV and KIV. Both are satisfied only by all and only events of giving. However, GIV but not KIV represents the given explicitly, in addition to the giver and recipient. In this way KIV is like ☺: the drawing needn't represent the nose explicitly to be a drawing of a human face. Suppose we had

similar doublets for all events that entail at least three roles, such as sendings, bettings, buyings, stealings, beanings and so forth. Now imagine that toddlers were equally likely to view givings under either concept, GIV or KIV. How would this weaken the utility of syntactic bootstrapping that relies on PAM? That is, explain the following remark from the main text:

> "[u]nless toddlers are overwhelmingly likely to view scenes of giving under a 3-participant concept, rather than a 2-participant concept with the same satisfaction conditions, the fact that we use give in clauses with three NPs cannot help them pick out which event it describes in the observed scene."

SUGGESTIONS FOR FURTHER READING

Among the classic works on linking are Gruber 1965, Fillmore 1968, Jackendoff 1972, 1990b, Carter 1976, Perlmutter 1978, Baker 1988, Dowty 1991, and Levin and Rappaport Hovav 1995. Fillmore 1970 remains a source of inspiration on framing, as is Grimshaw 1979. Levin and Rappaport Hovav 2005 is a signature overview of both linking and framing. On the use of framing generalizations in language acqustion, see Pinker 1979, 1984, 1989, Grimshaw 1981, Landau and Gleitman 1985, Gleitman 1990, as well as the retrospective in Fisher *et al.* 2010.

Part IV
Case studies

12 Passives

12.1 INTRODUCTION

This chapter is about the demoted deep-subject role in passives. In (1) this is the Stealer role bound by Lee. In (2) the same role is unrealized.

(1) The necklace was recently stolen by Lee.

(2) The necklace was recently stolen.

My focus will be on the common view that this role is linked to an argument, realized by the by-phrase in (1), silent but grammatically present in (2). In Section 12.4, I discuss the mechanics of this view, as executed in several different analyses; I also sketch the opposing view, and bolster it against some initial objections. Section 12.5 is then an extended critique of the best justification for the standard view, namely that we need an implicit syntactic argument to explain data like (3), discussed in Roeper (1987). Relying in part on new observations, and agreeing with Landau (2000), I will conclude that this justification is much weaker than it has seemed.

(3) The ship was sunk to collect the insurance.
    'The ship was sunk so that its sinker might collect the insurance.'

But before this case study of implicit argumenthood, I would first like to say more about the terms "demotion" and "passive" (Section 12.2), and then consider a traditional question of framing (Section 12.3): what sorts of predicates occur in passive clauses?

12.2 PASSIVES AND DEMOTION

Passives and actives are satisfied by the same sorts of events. Passive (1) and (2) above, like the active (4), are all satisfied by stealings. Stealings involve a thief, so this role is entailed by all three sentences, as "entail" was defined in Chapter 2.

(4) Lee recently stole the necklace.

The role bound by S in an ordinary active clause is the **deep-subject role**, or **deep-S role**, for its verb.[1] In any kind of **passive**, this role is assigned to neither S nor O. In a **long passive**, such as (1), it is realized by some other dependent, like the by-phrase in English. In a **short passive**, such as (2), it is unrealized and existential (Chapter 5).[2] We see that the UR is existential, because (2) can be used without some potential thief being topical; because (5a) must mean (5b); and because (6a) cannot mean what (6b) can, with the thieves matching the formerly generous boyfriends.

(5) a The necklace was not recently stolen.
     b The necklace was not recently stolen by anybody.
(6) a No necklace given to Mo by a boyfriend was later stolen from her.
     b No necklace given to Mo by a friend was later stolen from her by him.

Let us refer to this relation between two clauses as **demotion** of the deep-S role, not committing to any analysis. Clauses related in this way have predicates that describe the same sorts of events, but differ in how they realize the role. It is S in one clause, but neither S nor O in the other, and if unrealized it is existential.

Demotion relates (4) to both (1) and (2). It does not relate (4) to (7), however, since in (7) the predicate is satisfied, not by stealings, but by states that result from a stealing. Stealings have agents, but states of being stolen do not.

(7) The necklace is clearly stolen.

Nor does demotion relate (8) to (9), since (9) but not (8) is consistent with (10). This would not be so, if the two entailed the same roles.

(8) Something hoarsened his throat.

[1] This characterization leaves room for what counts as *ordinary*. For example, we might say that (1a) below is an ordinary active clause, but (1b) is not. And then we would not say that S in the latter binds the deep-S role. Such decisions will not matter much to our discussion, however.

(1) a Al bought a lot of lard.
     b $20 buys a lot of lard.

[2] According to Keenan and Dryer (2007:329), every language with a passive has a short passive, but only some of these have a long passive. Dryer (1994:69) reports that in the passives of Kutenai (a language isolate of Idaho, Montana and British Columbia) the deep-S role cannot be realized.

(9)   His throat hoarsened.

(10) But nothing hoarsened it.

I will use "passive" only for clauses related to the active by demotion. Thus neither (7) nor (9) is a passive. With Deo (2012), I would call (7) a *result stative*, avoiding the term "adjectival passive" for clarity; see also Embick (2004a). As for (9), this is just an intransitive clause whose event does not involve an agent. Since its event is a change, it is more specifically an *inchoative*. Sentence (9) also differs sharply from the English passive in form, and in what dependents it allows: its verb is not participial, and it permits neither a by-phrase nor an instrumental with-phrase. But these are correlates of the passive in English, and not definitive of passive more broadly.

Passives are not the only sort of clause with demotion of the deep-S role. Relative to active (11a), for example, there is demotion not only in passive (11b), but also (one might say) in (11c), a so-called '*middle*'. The English middle is distinguished from the passive both in form and in what dependents it admits (Section 12.5).

(11) a Hunters carry this pistol.

      b This pistol is carried by hunters.

      c "[A] Ruger 7-1/2" .44 Magnum carries easily while hunting."[3]

In St'át'imcets, demotion relates active (12) not only to "passive" (13), but also to the "patient oriented intransitive" in (14) (Davis 2010). The verb here is qámt 'to hit with a thrown object' or, roughly, 'bean.'

(12) Qámt -š   -áš   kᵂ⁼ s⁼   Kᵂímčxen ta⁼ twáwẃẁət ⁼a.
      bean -TRANS -3S.ERG DET⁼ NOMZ⁼ K.   DET boy   ⁼EXIST
      'The boy beaned Kwímčxen.'

(13) Qámt -š   -túm   kᵂ⁼ s⁼   Kᵂímčxen (ʔə⁼ta   twáwẃẁət=a).
      bean -TRANS -3S.PASS DET⁼ NOMZ⁼ K.   (OBL⁼DET boy⁼EXIST)
      'Kᵂímčxen got beaned (by a boy).'

(14) Qámt kᵂ⁼ s⁼   Kᵂímčxen.
      bean DET⁼ NOMZ⁼ K.
      'There was a beaning, and Kᵂímčxen was the beaned.'

When any of these three sentences is true, there is an airborn projectile. The role of its thrower is demoted in both passive (13) and intransitive (14). But the two constructions differ both in form and in argument structure. Sentence (14) has the verb in its bare form, but (13) adds "passive" -túm to the "transitive" stem in -š. And (13) but not (14) allows the thrower to be identified with an oblique headed by ʔə.

---

[3] *Guns Magazine* February 1, 2011 (Davies 2008–).

Those clause types singled out as passive tend to have further qualities in common. Most important for us, their demoted role tends to be viewed as an implicit argument (Chapter 5), in being relevant to some pattern in the language. When the demoted role is not in any way active, grammatically, pragmatically, or psychologically, a construction is usually not called *passive*. In St'át'imcets, for example, an oblique can bind the agent role in (13) but not (14), and Davis (2010) calls only the. former a passive.

Sometimes when a role is demoted, another role is **promoted**: S binds a relation other than the deep-S role. In (1) and (2) above, with steal, S binds the role of Loot. This is promoted while Thief is demoted. Going from active (15a) to passive (15b) in German, the role of Laughed-at is promoted, while Laugher is demoted.

(15) a Oft   hat   sie   Axel   ausgelacht.
         often has   she   A.   out laugh.PPL
         'She laughed at Axel often.'
     b Oft   wurde Axel ausgelacht.
         often became A.   out laugh.PPL
         'Axel was laughed at often.'

But compare German (16). Sentence (16b) has the same verbal morphology as (15b), and Laugher is again demoted in relation to active (16a). But now no role at all is promoted. If the clause has an S, it must be a silent expletive pronoun (Safir 1985).

(16) a Oft   hat   Helga gelacht.
         often has   H.   laugh.PPL
         'Helga laughed often.'
     b Oft   wurde gelacht.
         often became laugh.PPL
         'There was often laughter.'

Adapting Blevins (2003, 2006), let us use the term *S-less* for clauses with no thematic, nonexpletive S. Sometimes an S-less clause also has an *impersonal* meaning: the deep-S role is understood as if it were filled by a potentially plural indefinite, such as indefinite one, people or they in English. German (16b) is both S-less and impersonal. It also has the verbal morphology of a passive. English in general forbids S-less passives, as seen in (17).

(17) a * Rarely was there/it laughed (by anybody).
           'People rarely laughed.'
     b * Mo broke her nose, but there/it was never noticed (by anybody).
           'Mo broke her nose, but people never noticed that she had.'
     c * There/it was never noticed Mo's nose (by anybody).
           'People never noticed Mo's nose.'

There is one exception. S in an English passive may be the expletive *it* when the verb has a clausal argument, as in (18), just as in actives such as (19).

(18)   It was noticed (by nobody) that Mo broke her nose.
(19)   It bothered nobody that Mo broke her nose.

I will not discuss promotion in passives, or the relation between promotion and demotion (Perlmutter 1978, Burzio 1981). The reason is this. Promotion is an alternation in surface syntactic position, a kind of movement, in transformational theories. But it sometimes targets a phrase that is not obviously an argument, or even a dependent, in relation to the predicate that is 'passivized.' Examples include Ron in (20) and *things* in (25) below.

(20)   a Many expect Ron to have won.
       b Ron is expected by many to have won.

Demotion of the deep-S role, however, always targets an argument. So for us it is the more central topic, since our interest is in predicates and their arguments.[4]

12.3 FRAMING

Not every active clause has a passive counterpart. Some examples are given in (21–24).

(21)   a   In hospitals people often bleed.
       b * In hospitals there/it is often bled.
(22)   a   That necklace would suit Lee.
       b * Lee would be suited by that necklace.
(23)   a   The remaining $20 bought a lot of lard.
       b * A lot of lard was bought by the remaining $20.
(24)   a   Our plans depend on Mo.
       b * Mo is depended on by our plans.

This poses a question of framing. What sorts of predicates occur in passive contexts?

Sometimes the answer is purely syntactic, implying nothing about what sort of event the predicate describes, or about the involvement of

---

[4] One need not apply the term "passive" to every construction with a demoted deep-S role that is an implicit argument. A language may distinguish S-less transitives from passives with O promotion, for example, even if the deep-S role is somehow or other an implicit argument in both. See Maling and Sigurjónsdóttir 2002 on Icelandic, or Lavine 2013 on Slavic.

the participants in its event. In English, for example, S-less passives are mostly impossible, a blunt fact of syntax. As a consequence, an active will have a passive only if the active includes, in addition to its subject, a promotable DP or clause within its predicate. Thus, while (21) shows that People bleed lacks a passive, (25a) has the passive in (25b).

(25) a In hospitals people often bleed on things.
     b In hospitals things are often bled on.

However, many restrictions on passive do have a semantic aspect. When a passive is forbidden, the participants in the demoted or promoted roles often lack some typical property of an agent (such as volition) or a patient (such as affectedness), respectively. Which properties matter differs somewhat among different passive constructions; but there are strong regularities. Most likely to have a passive is a transitive clause like Lee crushed the basket, with a human actor in the S role and a thing changed for the worse in the O role. At the other end of the spectrum are cases like suit in (22) above, or cost in (26) below, with verbs that are both stative and nonpsychological. The necklace and the lard are neither active nor sentient, and nothing happens to Lee or the price.

(26) a The lard cost $20.
     b * $20 was cost by the lard.

Perlmutter and Postal (1984) observe facts like (23) above, where S with buy names the price and not the purchaser. Bach (1980) notes (27). Here again the involvement of the participant named by S in the active is not typically agentive (Siewierska 1984:209ff.). $20 and 1943 are not actors in the buying and the finding.

(27) a 1943 found Ezra Pound in Italy.
     b * Ezra Pound was found in Italy by 1943.

The contrast between (24b) and (28) teaches a similar lesson. Plans that depend on Mo cannot act in service of this dependence, unlike the family that depends on her.

(28) Mo is depended on by our family.

In many South Asian languages, a passive is possible only when when its event has a volitional actor (Pandharipande 1981), as in Marathi (29).

(29) a Ram -kadun zada todli zatat.
        R.   -by   trees broke go
        'The trees were broken by the Ram.'   (Pandharipande 1981:170)

b * Varya -kadun zada todli zatat.
wind -by trees broke go
'The trees were broken by the wind.' *(ibid.)*

The participant in the promoted role may also be relevant. For many verbs in Central Gur languages, including Ditammari, the satisfier of a patient role promoted to S must be inanimate (Reinecke and Miehe 2007). According to Aze (1973), cited in (Shibatani 1998), the passive in Parengi (Munda) allows a verb only if the undergoer of its event is "affected," exhibiting a significant change: it allows di? 'finish' but not po? 'stab,' for example. In English, prepositional passives often suggest that the event has a relevant effect on the promoted participant (Tuyn 1970, Bolinger 1977, Davison 1980), making (30a) more normal than (30b) in an average situation.

(30) a   This blanket was recently slept on.
     b   ? This tree was recently slept near.

Unfortunately, such generalizations are often quite porous. While some statives resist the passive in English, like cost in (26b), many others allow it, as in (31).

(31) a   Navin was not loved by his dog.
     b   The dog was owned by Navin.

The unacceptability of (24b) seems to reflect a lack of agency in its demoted role, and yet, in the acceptable (32), the intersecting lines are surely not portrayed as actors.

(32)   "[T]ypically only a small fraction of pixels is intersected by any line[.]"[5]

So there is still some arbitrariness in whether a predicate can occur in the passive. This will have to be encoded in the syntactic category of the predicate, if it is to be represented in the narrow grammar at all. The depend of (24b) or the cost of (26b) will have to have category features that exclude them from passive contexts.

Things seem less arbitrary, and thus more interesting, among S-less or impersonal passives, such as Dutch (33) from Perlmutter (1978).

(33) Er   wordt   heer veel   geskied.
     EXPL   becomes here much   ski.PPL
     'People ski a lot here.'

According to Perlmutter and Postal (1984:107), "[n]o impersonal Passive clause in any language can be based on an unaccusative predicate."

---

[5] Gabor T. Herman. 2009. *Fundamentals of computerized tomography*. Dordrecht: Springer.

Given the common correlates of unaccusativity, this implies that, in general, intransitive verbs occur in passives only if their deep-S role is agentive. Perlmutter and Postal adduce much data to support this, mainly from Dutch. Sentence (33) is acceptable, with the agentive and unergative verb ski 'ski,' but (34) is bad, with nonagentive and unaccusative bleven 'stay.'

(34) * Er   werd   door   de   kinderen   in   Amsterdam   gebleven.
     EXPL   became   through   the   children   in   Amsterdam   stay.PPL
     'The kids stayed in Amsterdam.'

When a verb that can occur in unaccusative clauses does occur acceptably in a passive, Perlmutter and Postal say that the clause describes a deliberate action, and so that it is in this case unergative. They contrast (35a) with (35b) (1984:110).

(35) a   In   het   tweede   bedrij   werd   er   door   de   nieuwe
         in   the   second   act   became   EXPL   through   the   new
         acteur   op   het   juiste   ogenblik   gevallen.
         actor   on   the   right   moment   fall.PPL
         'The new actor fell at the right moment in the second act.'
     b * Er   werd   door   twee   mensen   uit   de   venster   van
         EXPL   became   through   two   people   out   the   window   from
         de   tweed   verdieping   gevallen.
         the second   story   fall.PPL
         'Two people fell out of a second-story window.'

However, as documented in Primus (2011) with found data and acceptability surveys, the facts are not so simple. Nonagentive, possibly unaccusative intransitives do occur in passives, not describing deliberate actions, and without wordplay or metaphor. The sentences in (36) are Dutch, and those in (37) are German.

(36) a   [D]an   spoeden   wij   ons   tuinwaarts   om   te   zien   hoe
         then   hurry   we   ourselves   garden-wards   in.order   to   see   how
         schitterend   er   ook   zonder   onze   aanwezigheid   gegroeid   en
         wonderfully   EXPL   even   without   our   presence   grow.PPL   and
         gebloeid   wordt.
         blossom.PPL   becomes
         '[T]hen we hurry toward the garden to see how wonderfully things are growing and blooming even in our absence.'   (Primus 2011, corpus data)
     b   Merkt   men   dat   er   tijdens   de   behandeling   meer   dan
         notice.PRES.3s one   that EXPL   during   the   treatment   more   than
         normaal   getranspireerd   wordt,   ...
         normal   perspire.PPL   becomes,
         'If one notices that there is more sweating than normally during the treatment, ...'   (ibid.)

c Deze zullen via   Rhenen nog worden uitgebreid, zodat
these will   through Rhenen still become extend.PPL, so.that
moe maar zeker   voldaan in Veenendaal wordt
tired but   certainly satisfied in Veenedaal   becomes
aangekomen.
arrived
'These will be extended through Rhenen, so that people arrive in Veenendaal
tired but definitely satisfied.'   (*ibid.*)

(37) a |G|eblüht   wird   nur, wenn die Pflanze auch etwas
blossom.PPL becomes on   when the plant   also somewhat
älter ist.
older is
'There is blossoming only when the plant is a bit older.'   (*ibid.*)

b sodass im Ernstfall   dann gefroren   wird
so.that in emergency then freeze.PPL becomes
'consequently in emergencies people will freeze'   (*ibid.*)

c In Bosnien wird   weiter   gestorben.
in Bosnia   becomes further die.PPL
'People continue to die in Bosnia.'   (Rapp 1997)

These clauses appear to be passive. Perhaps this is misleading, and they differ from ordinary passives in a relevant way, as Maling and Sigurjónsdóttir (2003) claim for the "new passive" in Icelandic. But if they are indeed passive, Perlmutter and Postal's conjecture is incorrect: a passive clause may describe a nonagentive event, and its verb may be unaccusative. In such cases, passive cannot be described as demotion of an 'agentive' role, linked to an 'external argument' in the active. For example, in such cases one cannot say, with Embick (2004b) or Bruening (2012), that passives differ from actives just in the formal realization of the "Agent" or "Initiator" role. Rather, passive will have to be described as demotion of whichever role is bound by S in the active. Moreover, when a passive with an unaccusative verb is unacceptable, as in (34), this cannot be explained on categorical syntactic grounds. For thoughts on what does explain it, see Primus (2011) and Kiparsky (2013).

12.4 REPRESENTING THE DEEP-SUBJECT ROLE

This section introduces the common analyses of long and short passives, focussing on the representation of the demoted role. Our main examples will be (38) and (39).

(38) The chair was carried by Navin.

(39) The chair was carried.

I will presume that the by-phrase comprises only by and a DP sister,[6] and will refer to the expression it attaches to as the *host*. Section 12.4.1 surveys analyses within the standard genre, on which even the short passive has an argument in the deep-S role. Section 12.4.2 then assesses the opposite position.

12.4.1 Base Argument Theories

Most theories of passive make the assumption in (40). Some syntactic part of a short passive clause, this says, and also some part of the host in a long passive, has a functional semantic argument in the deep-S role.

(40) Base Argument Theory
       Some syntactic part of a short passive clause, and some part of the host in a
       long passive, has a functional semantic argument in the deep-S role.

Let us refer to the largest part of the clause with this semantic argument as the *passive base*, and to any theory that assumes (40) as a **Base Argument Theory** or **BAT**. For (38) and (39), the BAT means that some part of The chair was carried has a meaning like (41), with an argument in the Carrier role.

(41) $\lambda x \ldots \lambda e[\text{Carrier}(e, x) \ldots]$

On some accounts, this argument of the base projects from the verb (Bach 1980, Bresnan 1982, Baker *et al.* 1989, Grimshaw 1990). On others it comes from elsewhere, such as a silent lexical item of category v with the VP as its complement (Davis 2000, Embick 2004b, Bruening 2012). But on nearly all, the base has a corresponding *syntactic* argument as well. Putting it generally, it has an a-list like (42), specifying an argument with some feature [F]. This feature may be particular to by, or common to any DP, depending on the analysis.

(42) $\langle [\text{F}], \ldots \rangle$

BATs then divide into three varieties, differing in what happens to this argument: it is satisfied by a silent pronoun; optionally satisfied by the by-phrase; or eliminated by a special passive morpheme. I will now discuss these variants in turn, in three rather dense subsections.

---

[6] See Collins 2005 for an alternative, where by has the entire verb phrase as its complement, all silent but for the by-DP. Collins's analysis has some similarities to Huang's (1999) treatment of the passive-like bei-construction in Mandarin.

12.4.1.1 Pronominal varieties

In **pronominal varieties** of the BAT (Fukui and Speas 1986, Baker
et al. 1989), both long and short passives contain an expression with
the meaning of a pronoun, call it *pro-ps*. Pro-ps is generated in the same
position as S is in the active, (43), satisfying both the syntactic and the
semantic argument of the base.

(43) [[[$_{DP}$ pro-ps]$_k$ [carry the chair]]] [by Navin]$_k$]

According to Baker *et al.* (1989), pro-ps in English surfaces on the verb as
the participial suffix -en.

This has a motive in UTAH.[7] Given pro-ps, the deep-S role is linked
to the same position in both passives and actives. Accordingly the by-
phrase must be some sort of adjunct, not selected by the base, and
irrelevant to compliance with UTAH. That it includes by in particular
must therefore follow from other grammatical principles. For Baker
et al. (1989), by is like a case prefix, the morphological reflex of a special
grammatical relation, one that links the by-DP to pro-ps.

Semantically, the value of pro-ps in long passives is determined by
an endophoric link to the by-DP. Baker *et al.* (1989) compare the link to
clitic-doubling. But the analogy isn't perfect. In general, clitic-doubling
is selective about what kinds of DPs can be doubled.[8] Long passives, in

---

[7] Baker *et al.* 1989 advertise a second motive for the pronominal BAT. Pro-ps c-
commands the underlying direct object. Thus it cannot be coindexed with the
object, without violating either Principle B or C of the Binding Theory. Consistent
with this, the two sentences in (1) below are not synonymous, though of course
there are situations that verify both.

(1) Mo was soundly criticized. $\neq$ Mo was soundly criticized by herself.

Baker *et al.* present this as strong evidence for the pronominal theory of passive. But
it is not. Surely we should not treat every fact in (2) as a Condition B effect, positing
a silent argument for essay, rant and stuff. Rather, the antireflexive message is just
a common pragmatic enrichment, signaled by choosing not to make the stronger
reflexive statement. The same account is plausible for (2).

(2) a Lee wrote an essay. $\neq$ Lee wrote an essay about herself.
     b Ron ranted. $\neq$ Ron ranted about himself.
     c Mo stuffed the duvet cover. $\neq$ Mo stuffed the duvet cover with herself.

[8] See Rizzi 1986b, Anagnostopoulou and Giannakidou 1996, Gutiérrez-Rexach 1999
and Arregi 2003. There are a few cases where the doubled DP is unrestricted, such
as the doubling of datives in Spanish.

contrast, are never selective about the by-DP, certainly not in English, as shown in (44).[9]

(44) They were criticized soundly by {nobody/few students/somebody/at least eight students/between 3 and 7 of their students/way too many students/every third student/themselves/each other}.

In long passives, therefore, pro-ps seems initially like an ordinary bound variable, just one that must be bound by a by-DP. But then what binds it in a short passive? Short passives will have to contain a second silent pronoun to bind it, call it *pro-imp*, in the position of a by-phrase (Baker *et al.* 1989). This pro-imp is neutral as to person or number, and cannot introduce an ordinary discourse referent, (45a), or license reflexives in a controlled adjunct (45b) (Koenig and Mauner 2000, Landau 2010).

(45) a * The chair was carried, but he/one dropped it.
       'The chair was carried, but the carrier dropped it.'
     b * That chair was carried just to make himself/oneself happy.
       'That chair was carried just to make the carrier happy.'

If this seems extravagant, the alternative is to treat pro-ps as a chimera: it is necessarily bound *only* in long passives, and has the meaning of pro-imp when free (Koenig and Mauner 2000). But this will be the more attractive analysis only if such chimerical pronouns are otherwise motivated, outside of passives.

One last feature of pronominal BATs is that they require the underlying O to leap-frog over pro-ps on its way to the surface S position, as in (46). As stressed in Collins (2005), this may be a problem, since leap-frogging seems to violate minimality, the leap-frogged expression being the closer potential mover.

(46) [[the chair]$_j$ [was ... [[[$_{DP}$ pro-ps]$_k$ [carried t_j]] [by Navin]$_k$]]]

12.4.1.2 Argument-by varieties

On **argument-by varieties** of the BAT, the syntactic argument of the base is satisfied by the by-phrase itself. Concurrently the host takes the by-phrase as a functional argument semantically. By is treated as vacuous, so that ⟦by Navin⟧ is Navin, and combining the host with by Navin under Application yields (47), as desired.

(47) ... λe[Carrier(e, Navin) ...]

---

[9] Baker *et al.* 1989 claim that by-DPs cannot be reflexive, following Lees and Klima 1963 and Postal 1971. But I know no-one else who rejects themselves or each other in (44).

On many accounts, the base furthermore specifies that its argument is oblique, and has by as its head (Bresnan 1982, Grimshaw 1990, Sag and Wasow 1999).[10] For instance, our [F] may be more specifically a feature [BY], particular to by. The base is therefore a predicate that is specific to passives, and is not found in actives. The relation between the passive and active predicates is captured by deriving one from the other. Typically the derivation is in Lexicon: there is a rule of lexical derivation that maps a verb to a passive alternate with an oblique argument in the deep-S role (Bresnan 1982, Grimshaw 1990, Sag and Wasow 1999). Bresnan (1982b:9) gives the lexical rule in (48), for any lexical item 'L'. Here the colons pair the name of a grammatical relation with the name of its associated semantic relation.

(48) $L[(\text{SUBJ}):\text{agent}, (\text{OBJ}):\text{theme}] \mapsto L[(\text{BY OBJ})/\emptyset:\text{agent}, (\text{SUBJ}):\text{theme}]$

Bach (1980), however, derives one from the other in Syntax, following Thomason (1976). He gives a rule of syntactic derivation which, simplified somewhat and rewritten as unary, is (49). The rule adds passive morphology, and reverses the order of semantic arguments.

(49)   LongPassive (after Bach 1980)

$$\begin{bmatrix} \text{Category} : \text{TransVP} \\ \text{A-List} : \langle [\text{N}], [\text{N}] \rangle \\ \text{Sound} : /\text{V}/ \text{ , Value} : \lambda y \lambda x [fyx] \end{bmatrix} \mapsto \begin{bmatrix} \text{Category} : \text{PassVP} \\ \text{A-List} : \langle [\text{N}], [\text{N}] \rangle \\ \text{Sound} : /\text{Ved by}/ \text{ , Value} : \lambda x \lambda y [fyx] \end{bmatrix}$$

To allow for short passives, the argument in the deep-S role must be 'optional,' and interpreted existentially when unrealized. For Bach, this means a second rule of derivation, (50), which eliminates the relevant argument of the passive base.

(50)   ShortPassive (after Bach 1980)

$$\begin{bmatrix} \text{Category} : \text{TransVP} \\ \text{A-List} : \langle [\text{N}], [\text{N}] \rangle \\ \text{Sound} : /\text{V}/ \text{ , Value} : \lambda y \lambda x [fyx] \end{bmatrix} \mapsto \begin{bmatrix} \text{Category} : \text{PassVP} \\ \text{A-List} : \langle [\text{N}] \rangle \\ \text{Sound} : /\text{Ved}/ \text{ , Value} : \lambda y \exists x [fyx] \end{bmatrix}$$

This differs little from Bresnan's later (48), except that it applies in Syntax.

---

[10] For Grimshaw 1990, the by-phrase is an "argument adjunct" because it satisfies a "suppressed a-structure position" of its host (1990:107). Such positions are special members of an a-list. They are satisfied only optionally, and (in the clausal context) by an oblique dependent, neither S nor O. Moreover, any expression whose a-list has a "suppressed position" is derived from a synonymous expression with an obligatory, nonoblique argument in the same semantic role. Thus "suppression" is a lexicalist encoding of the demotion relation, and "argument adjuncts" remain a kind of syntactic argument (Chapter 3).

This first type of argument-by theory disagrees with UTAH. The deep-S role is aligned with S in actives but an oblique in long passives. Some supporters of UTAH therefore pursue a second kind of argument-by theory, where the argument structure of the passive differs in no way from that of the active (Mahajan 1995, Goodall 1997, Collins 2005). The by-phrase, or at least its DP, has the same underlying position as S in the active; it surfaces with by for some independent reason, perhaps related to the participial form of the verb. As on pronominal theories, the underlying O then raises to S, leap-frogging over the by-DP. See the cited works for further details.

12.4.1.3 Adjunct-by varieties

The last sort of BAT is the **adjunct-by variety**. Here the base takes neither the by-DP nor a pro-ps as an argument. Its syntactic argument is never, strictly speaking, satisfied by an expression matching on [F], not even in a long passive. Instead it is eliminated by a special lexical item (or rule) that I will call PASS. PASS takes the base (or its verb) as its complement (or operand), and yields a result that lacks the deep-S argument. Accordingly, on any adjunct-by BAT, the by-phrase is treated as a pure syntactic adjunct, not selected syntactically by its host.

In Bruening (2012), PASS is a lexical item with category "Pass[S:Voice (S:N)]." Syntactically it selects an argument of category "Voice(S:N)," which is a "Voice" phrase with a syntactic argument of category N. (This happens to be the unsatisfied argument in the deep-S role.) The combination then returns an expression of category "Pass" with no syntactic arguments, as in (51).

(51)

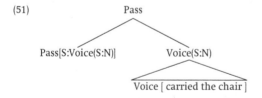

In a short passive, the semantic effect of PASS is existential quantification, (52).

(52) $[\![$ PASS carry the chair $]\!] = \lambda e \exists x [\ [\![$ carry the chair $]\!](x)(e)\ ]$

For Landman (2000), the same is true in long passives. Again PASS binds the deep-S role, leaving the host with no semantic argument: the host to by Navin has the meaning in (52). Accordingly, the role bound by the by-DP comes, not from the base, but from by itself. The preposition "adds whatever role is appropriate for the verbal head, usually an agent" (Landman 2000:68), as in (53).

(53) $⟦$ by Navin $⟧ = \lambda e[$ Agent$(e,$ Navin$)$ $]$

I discuss semantic challenges to this view in Section 12.4.2. But, compositionally, (53) combines with (52) by `Conjunction` to yield (54).

(54) $⟦$ PASS carry the chair by Navin $⟧$
  $= \lambda e \exists x[$ CarryingOf$(e,$ the chair$)$ & Agent(e, x) & Agent$(e,$ Navin$)$ $]$
  $= \lambda e[$ CarryingOf$(e,$ the chair$)$ & Agent$(e,$ Navin$)$ $]$

Bruening's (2012) analysis of the by-phrase is different. It has the by-phrase adjoin to the Voice(S:N) expression, below PASS. It requires a host of exactly this category, a Voice phrase with an N argument. Semantically, by has no thematic content. It just lifts the type of its DP, so that by Navin has the value in (55), a function over properties.

(55) $⟦$ by Navin $⟧ = \lambda f[$ $f($Navin$)$ $]$

The host is (56). Applying (55) to (56) then yields (57).

(56) $⟦$ [Voice [carried the chair]] $⟧$
  $= \lambda x \lambda e[$ Agent(e, x) & CarryingOf$(e,$ the chair$)$ $]$
(57) $⟦$ [[Voice [carried the chair]][by Navin]] $⟧$
  $=$ `Application`$[(55), (56)]$
  $= \lambda e[$ Agent$(e,$ Navin$)$ & CarryingOf$(e,$ the chair$)$ $]$

The deep-S role having been instantiated by Navin, there is nothing left for PASS to do in the long passive. Thus Bruening treats PASS as ambiguous. In short passives it existentially quantifies over the deep-S role, but in long passives it is vacuous, (58). This is an ambiguity that Landman (2000) designs his theory to avoid.

(58) $⟦$ PASS$_{\text{long}}$ X $⟧ = ⟦$ X $⟧$

Why do passives go specifically with by? For Bruening, by happens to be the only vacuous preposition to require a host of category Voice(S:N), a phrase with an unsatisfied syntactic argument of category N.

Bruening's account is interesting in making two deeply uncommon assumptions. First, the by-phrase is an adjunct, yet it requires a host with arguments. Second, while the by-DP is neither a syntactic nor a functional argument of the passive host, it is nonetheless a content argument (Chapter 4) in relation to the head of its host, namely the Voice head, instantiating the Agent role that this Voice head introduces. Besides this, Bruening's account also disregards UTAH – but in this it is like most theories of passive.

12.4.2 No Base Argument Theories

No Base Argument Theories (NoBATs) deny the Base Argument Theory. Even the host in a long passive, they say, has no argument in the deep-S role (Chomsky 1981). No part of passive carried the chair has a semantic argument in the role of Carrier, (59), not even the verb, (60). Nor does any part of the host select syntactically for a by-phrase.

(59) [[carried the chair]] = λe[CarryingOf(e, the chair)]

(60) [[carried]] = $\lambda x \lambda e$[CarryingOf(e, x)]

Instead, by itself introduces the thematic relation bound by its DP complement: "[i]t adds whatever role is appropriate for the verbal head, usually an agent" (Landman 2000:68), as in (53) above. Syntactically the by-phrase is either an adjunct (Bruening 2012), or a head that takes the passive VP as its complement.

Very few linguists have embraced this view. Most have charged that there must be an argument in short passives, so as to license and properly interpret certain dependents, not only the by-phrase, but also those in (61) for example, namely on purpose and to collect the insurance:.

(61) a The table was moved on purpose.
      b The ship was sunk to collect the insurance.

I discuss these challenges at length in Section 12.5. Here I first address three general semantic objections to the suggestion that by has thematic content.[11]

If by has content, why is it in every case synonymous with the subject relation in some corresponding active? Any role associated with the by-DP – such as Carrier, Repeller, Facer, Intersecter, Owner, Hater or Believer in (62) – may also be bound by S in an active clause with the same verb form. This cannot be an accident.

(62) a The chair was carried by Navin.
      b The ball was repelled by a magnet.
      c This problem is faced by many working mothers.
      d "This road is intersected by potentially dangerous avalanche paths."[12]
      e The dog was owned by Navin.
      f Navin was hated by his dog.
      g That was believed by very few people.

The most sensible explanation would be allomorphy. "By" must be an allomorph of whatever introduces S's thematic relation in ordinary

---

[11] This section owes a special debt to Bruening 2012.

[12] US Department of Agriculture, trail guide for White River National Forest, Colorado. www.fs.usda.gov/Internet/FSE_DOCUMENTS/stelprdb5186855.pdf.

actives, a primitive that is silent in actives but pronounced "by" in passives. There should be just one such primitive, call it AG, the same throughout (62). There should not be several, each with a different meaning (say, Agent for one and Experiencer for another) since distinct items cannot plausibly share the same pattern of allomorphy. But then this AG must be either highly polysemous or extraordinarily general. It must range over relations as diverse as Carrier, Intersecter, Owner and Believer, relations both to actions and to states. Some theorists (Parsons 1990, Baker 1997, Embick 2004b, Borer 2005, Ramchand 2008, Bruening 2012) accept that there might be such an indeterminate predicate; whether or not by has content is then to be decided on other grounds. But many others find this indeterminacy implausible, in agreement with Dowty (1991) (Chapter 6). In part for this reason, NoBATs are far less common than BATs.

The second objection to giving by content is based on by in certain noun phrases. In some kinds of deverbal nominals, a by-phrase corresponds to the deep-S role of the associated verb. The by-phrase realizes the deep-S role in nominals (63a) and (64a), just as it does in clauses (63b) and (64b).

(63)   a   the destruction of Merv by Tolui
       b   Merv was destroyed by Tolui.
(64)   a   the singing of the intro by Ozzy
       b   The intro was sung by Ozzy.

Not every nominal that describes an event allows this, however. The phrases in (65a,b) appear to describe events of sight and fear, and yet by is unacceptable (Jackendoff 1977, Culicover and Jackendoff 2005).

(65)   a   the frequent sight of ewes (*by wolves)
       b   the constant fear of wolves (*by ewes)

This is said to show that, with at least some noun phrases, but never in the passive, by stands for a thematic relation, call it "Affector" (Fox and Grodzinsky 1998), whose domain excludes such events as seeings or fearings. Accordingly, by in (65) is taken to induce a category error or presupposition failure: the by-phrase is a predicate that simply 'cannot' apply to the events that satisfy the noun. The noun phrases therefore lack a semantic value, and are judged unacceptable.[13]

---

[13] The literature is not clear on whether the putative category error is furthermore syntacticized, with nouns whose event lacks an affector having a formal feature that cannot cohabit with N-by.

On this account of (65), the good noun phrases in (66) below must involve a different word by, not the one that means Affector. If events of fear or sight do not have affectors, then neither do events of anticipation or perception (Bruening 2012). Presumably, therefore, the by in (66) is the by that otherwise occurs in passive clauses. Call this V-by, distinguishing it from the hypothetical N-by that means Affector.

(66)   a the perception of ewes by wolves
       b the anticipation of wolves by ewes

By assumption, N-by cannot occur with sight and fear. But now, why can't these nouns tolerate V-by? The answer cannot be that V-by expresses a relation that is undefined over fearings or seeings, when its domain does include events of anticipation and perception. The answer must be grammatical: V-by must conflict with either the syntactic category or the semantic type of phrases with sight and fear.[14] But then, if V-by is grammatically incompatible with sight and fear, we lose our motive for N-by. Our question was: why can't by ewes accompany frequent sight of wolves? And the answer is, because V-by is grammatically incompatible with sight. There is no reason to imagine a second by meaning Affector. Note, the objection is not that we must avoid ambiguity; surely "by" is multiply ambiguous, at least as between the V-by of (66), the by of means in (67), the by of authorship in (68) and the spatial by in (69).

(67)   Al flattened the cutlet by pounding it.

(68)   a bicycle wheel by Duchamp

(69)   Val is over by Hal.

But to explain (65), we do not need a fifth by that means Affector, when the grammar already keeps V-by away from sight and fear. Thus the argument from nominals against a thematic by is unsound.

Third, it is sometimes objected that if by can mean 'Agent,' and by-phrases are adjuncts, then they should be compatible with any predicate whose event has an agent. But they aren't, witness (70) and (71).

(70)   a The cheese sliced easily with a butter knife (*only by me).
       b The house sold (*by Ben).
       c The remaining $20 bought a lot of lard (*by Al).

(71)   The crook sank the ship (*by his accomplices).

---

[14] Maybe V-by must adjoin to a phrase with a feature [A], that phrases with sight or fear don't have (Bruening 2012). Or maybe sight of wolves is a function from events to truth values (type $\langle v, t \rangle$), while by ewes stands for ewes (type e), and the two cannot compose.

But this objection is weak. It presumes that an adjunct will go wherever its meaning is sensible, without any syntactic restrictions. Yet surely syntax does play a role in the placement of adjuncts, since adverbs are incompatible with nouns: *quickly argument. So it is reasonable to suppose that by is incompatible with actives just for reasons of syntax. They clash in syntactic features. Going further, perhaps by even selects for a syntactic feature of passives, as suggested in different ways by Collins (2005) and Bruening (2012). I raise further concerns about objections to NoBATs from the distribution of the by-phrase in the Discussion Points at the end of this chapter.

For these reasons, NoBATs are not dead in the water, as is often presumed. I will now argue further that the best evidence for BATs is weaker than it has seemed.

12.5 IMPLICIT CONTROL OF ADJUNCTS

In short passives the deep-S role is unrealized and existential. In general, existential URs are pragmatically and grammatically inactive (Chapter 5). They don't require any potential satisfier of the role to be topical or relevant; they cannot be bound; and they cannot on their own antecede a pronoun. Yet the unrealized deep-S role in a short passive is often regarded as exceptional, the rare case of an existential UR that is an implicit argument in the narrow sense. This section is a study of the strongest motive for that claim: certain adjuncts can be construed as predicates of the individuals who in fact satisfy the deep-S role. In (72) the relevant purposes can be those of the table-mover, and in (73) the collector of insurance can be the ship-sinker.

(72)   The table was moved on purpose / intentionally.

(73)   The ship was sunk to collect the insurance.

Section 12.5.1 deals quickly with (72). The rest of the section concerns (73). After setting out some basic facts and terminology (Sections 12.5.2–12.5.3), I will introduce (Section 12.5.4) and then oppose (Sections 12.5.5–12.5.8) the common account of (73), according to which the sentence, along with others like it, shows that short passives have a syntactically represented argument in the deep-S role, as per the BAT (Section 12.4.1).

12.5.1 Adverbs about agents

Using (72), a speaker may mean for the adverb, on purpose or intentionally, to describe the intentions of the mover, the agent of the clausal event. Some conclude from this that the clause must have an argument for this agent (Lasnik and Fiengo 1974, Fox and Grodzinsky 1998, Alexiadou and Schäfer 2013). But this is too quick. Again, one does not conclude from blond child that child has an argument for hair.

The conclusion is warranted only if this construal of the adverb requires more than just a clause whose event has an agent.[15] The question is whether some such clauses forbid this construal, for no evident pragmatic or conceptual reason, and, therefore, whether the clauses that allow it must be distinguished grammatically. Fox and Grodzinsky (1998) say that passives with get are exactly such a case: they judge that get-passives do not allow on purpose to describe the intentions of the entailed agent. Yet everyone I have asked can use (74) to say that someone chose to move the table, and (75) was in fact used to ask whether people chose to bury the story.

(74) The table got moved on purpose.

---

[15] Certainly on purpose and intentionally do not themselves require their host to describe an event with an agent. They occur naturally with statives, as in (1) and (2), to convey that the state results from some design or intention.

(1) a "Your back is curved on purpose."
        http://adjusthealth.info/index.php?option=com_content&view=article&id=
        66%3Adriving-without-back-pain&catid=60&Itemid=80
     b "[Y]ou're saying now that [New Orleans] was disproportionately black
        on purpose?"
        Media Rediscovers the Other America; Emotional Coverage of Katrina;
        Roberts on the Hot Seat, 9/18/2005, CNN. From Davies 2008–.

(2) a "As with most CIA safe houses, this one was intentionally bland."
        Vince Flynn. 2012. Kill Shot: An American Assassin Thriller. New York: Pochet
        Books.
     b "The woodblock medium changed the intentionally bland brushwork of
        the Chinese style into a stronger two-dimensional design."
        www.worcesterart.org/Collection/Japanese/1961.7.html

They are normally odd with eventive and nongeneric clauses that do not entail an agent, like (3). But this may have a simple account. Use of such sentences ordinarily suggests that the event was spontaneous; and yet the adverb implies, contrarily, that it was brought about by design. Thus they are sensible only when we understood that a seemingly spontaneous event is actually controlled, as in (4).

(3) ? The table moved on purpose.

(4) "I'm still holding firm that his voice cracked on purpose during that
      second catch (as in, it was a conscious directorial choice [...])[.]"
      http://obsessivedilettante.tumblr.com/post/76320584412/im-still-holding-
      firm-that-his-voice-cracked-on

(75) "[D]id the story get buried on purpose?"[16]

Another test case might be middles such as (76). This sentence is odd, if one means to describe the intentions of the slicer, and not the cheese-maker.

(76) ?# The cheese sliced easily on purpose.

But then, this may have the same pragmatic account as passive (77), namely: on purpose has easily in its scope, and one doubts that the agent's intentions can make it easy to slice the cheese or move the table.

(77) ?# The table was moved easily on purpose.

In my view, therefore, these adverbs do not make a very strong case for an implicit argument. The stronger case is made by reason clauses, to which we now turn.

12.5.2 Reason clauses

Sentences (78) and (79) are examples of **reason clauses**. They are also called **rationale clauses**, after Faraci (1974) and Jones (1985).[17]

(78) Sam sank the ship to collect the insurance.
    'Sam sank the ship because he might collect the insurance.'
(79) Grass is green to promote photosynthesis. (Williams 1974)
    'Grass is green because this might promote photosynthesis.'

A reason clause is a nonfinite clause construed as offering a teleological explanation.[18] It expresses some fact, *the reason*. A second clause, the **target clause**, expresses some other fact, **the target**. The constellation

---

[16] Alan Colmes, Hannity & Colmes, Fox News Channel, 6/15/2007. From Davies 2008– .

[17] I prefer "reason" to "rationale," since the latter suggests intention, planning or justification, inappropriately. Reason clauses need not specify plans or intended goals, witness (79). Promotion of photosynthesis may be the *reason* grass is green, but I find it odd to say that this is its *rationale*.

[18] Jones 1985 carefully distinguishes reason (rationale) clauses, both syntactically and semantically, from two kinds of "purpose clause" (Williams 1980, Bach 1982). The first kind, as in (1), has a non-subject gap within it. The second kind, as in (2), is controlled by an object in the host clause, not the subject.

(1) The pencil$_k$ is here to write with ϵ_k.
(2) They$_j$ brought Dolkun$_k$ along just ϵ_k to translate for them$_j$.

I will take Jones's conclusions for granted, as is standard. But I will add to them a less familiar distinction between reason clauses and the second sort of purpose clause. The distinction comes out in (3–5), where control crosses distinct sentences, a possibility that is the topic of Section 12.5.5.

of the two implies that the reason explains the target, because it is a possible consequence of it, lawful or intended. Why did Sam sink the ship? According to (78), because an intended consequence of that fact was Sam's collecting the insurance. Why is grass green? According to (79), because the promotion of photosynthesis is a lawful consequence of grass being green.

A reason clause has no overt subject. But semantically the subject role may be construed anaphorically. In (78) the understood collector of insurance is Sam, the referent of the subject in the target clause. In (79) the understood promoter of photosynthesis seems to be the fact that the target clause expresses, namely the fact that grass is green.

Let us say that the reason clauses in (78) and (79) are *controlled* by Sam and the greenness of grass, respectively. Here I stretch the jargon. On my use, control is not a grammatical dependency, but a relation between an individual, a clause, and a thought that the speaker means to communicate in using that clause. An individual x **controls** an infinitival reason clause C with meaning P just in case, in using C, the speaker means to give Px as the reason for the target fact. It will also be convenient to say that a *role* controls a reason clause C when the satisfier of that role controls C. So in (78), control is by the sinker or the sinker role. Finally, I will say that an expression *antecedes* a reason clause when its referent controls that clause.

In (78) above, the reason clause is anteceded by the subject of the target clause, Sam, which here fills the deep-S role of sink. In (79) it is anteceded by the target clause itself, Grass is green. Sentences (80) and (81), below, illustrate two further possibilities.

(80)   The ship was sunk by Sam to collect the insurance.

(81)   Sam was arrested by the police, just to seem like a radical.

In (80) the controller is the deep-S role, here associated with a by-phrase, not S. In (81) on the other hand, the controller is again given by the

(3)   They$_j$ brought Dolkun$_k$ along. His only job was ε_k to translate for them$_j$.

(4)   * They$_j$ brought Dolkun$_k$ along. The only motive/purpose/reason/goal was ε_j to translate for them$_j$.

(5)   They$_j$ brought Dolkun$_k$ along. The only motive/purpose/reason/goal was ε_k to have him$_k$ translate for them$_j$.

Discourses (3) and (4) are like Jones's purpose construction in (2): control of to translate in the second clause is by the object in the first, Dolkun. This is acceptable in (3), which explicitly specifies the *function* or the *job* of the intended controller. But it is quite unacceptable in (4), which specifies the motive or reason for the fact expressed by the first sentence. In contrast, as shown by (5), the latter construction, involving "remote control" of a reason clause (Section 12.5.5), does allow control by the subject of the first sentence, they.

surface subject, but now this does not bind the deep-S role. Here we must understand, however, that Sam was in some way responsible for bringing about her own arrest. As Zubizaretta (1982) put it, she must be the "secondary agent" of her arrest.

Thus, when a reason clause has an overt antecedent, it must fall into at least one of three formal categories. An overt antecedent must be either:

    1 the target clause;
    2 the subject of the target clause; or
    3 a dependent in the target clause that is assigned its deep-S role.

Antecedence by an overt expression in any other grammatical relation is impossible. Thus (82a) is fine but (82b) is not.[19]

(82)   a   Mo walked the dog to make herself thinner.
       b   * Mo walked the dog to make itself thinner.

And while (83a) can be used to say that sharks have their gills cleaned by parasites, (83b) cannot. Sentence (83b) implies that there are parasites with gills.

(83)   a   These sharks cover themselves with parasites to have their gills kept clean.
       b   Parasites cover these sharks to have their gills kept clean.

Roeper (1987:299) observes that (18a) cannot be used to convey the gloss, even though "it is quite natural that Mary might go to John to make a good impression."

(84)   * John received Mary to make a good impression.
       'John received Mary so that Mary might make a good impression.'

Thus overt antecedence of reason clauses is restricted in ways that *can* be described syntactically. At least in general, it is restricted to just those dependents that are 'subjects' at some level of analysis, surface or deep, except when the controller is the target clause itself.

As we will now see, this generalization motivates the claim that the deep-S role in a short passive, when unrealized, is in the narrow sense an implicit argument.

12.5.3 Passives and reason clauses

The deep-S role of a short passive can sometimes control a reason clause (Keyser and Roeper 1984, Roeper 1987). Sentence (85), like (86), can be

---

[19] This generalization rests on the distinction between reason clauses and purpose clauses in footnote 18.

used to convey the message in the gloss, where the recipient of blessings is the killer of the ewe.

(85)   The ewe was killed to gain the blessings of Apollo.
       'The ewe was killed so that the killer might gain the blessings of Apollo.'

(86)   The ewe was killed by someone to gain the blessings of Apollo.

This is special, since in general a UR cannot control a reason clause. Stealings have victims, but one cannot use (87) to tell the story about insurance fraud in the gloss.

(87)   * A hired crook stole the ship to collect the insurance.
       'A hired crook stole the ship so that *the victim of the theft* might collect the insurance.'

And, famously, there is a minimal contrast between passives and middles. A middle with an agentive verb, such as (88), entails an unrealized agent; the example expresses a generalization over events that involve killers. Yet the entailed killers cannot control a subsequent reason clause (Keyser and Roeper 1984, Roeper 1987), as shown in (89).

(88)   Ewes kill easily.

(89)   * Ewes kill easily to survive the winter.
       'Ewes are easily killed so that the killers might survive the winter.'

Example (89) is, moreover, representative. The deep-S role in a middle can never control a reason clause.[20] This is not because middles are always bad with reason clauses. Sentences (90) and (91) are acceptable examples.

(90)   Ewes kill easily, to ensure the survival of the local predators.
       'Ewes kill easily, because this ensures the survival of the local predators.'

(91)   "The shoulder harness adjusts easily up and down to fit a wide range of torsos."[21]
       'The shoulder harness adjusts easily, so that it might fit a range of torsos.'

But in cases such as these, the reason clause is anteceded by the target clause or by its subject. It is not controlled by the deep-S role of that clause. The controller is not the entailed killers in (90), but rather the fact that ewes kill easily. In (91), it is not the entailed adjustors of the harness, but rather the shoulder harness itself.

The UR in a short passive is therefore an exception to the apparent rule. Normally, the controller of a reason clause cannot be unrealized.

---

[20] Mauner and Koenig 2000 support this conclusion with evidence from behavioral studies.

[21] J. Harlin, "A tent for stargazers," *Backpacker* 25(4):118, 1997. From Davies 2008– .

And when the reason clause has an overt antecedent, it is either the target clause itself, its subject, or a dependent that realizes the deep-S role. In this way the deep-S role in a short passive has some properties of an overt dependent, either a subject or a by-phrase, making it an implicit argument in the narrow sense (Chapter 5).

Still open, however, is the question of what explains these facts. What exactly is the grammatical status of the implicit argument? And what mediates the control relation? I will now present the standard answer (Section 12.5.4), and then pave the way (Sections 12.5.5–12.5.7) for an alternative (Section 12.5.8).

12.5.4 The A-theory of reason control

The facts of Section 12.5.3 are most commonly explained with two assumptions. First, the *grammatical theory* of how reason clauses are controlled. This says that control here is mediated by a syntactic dependency between the reason clause and the target clause, and decided with reference to a syntactic representation of argument structure, such as an a-list (Roeper 1987, Koenig and Mauner 2000). Specifically, when control is not by (the fact expressed by) the host clause, it is by (a role linked to) a syntactically encoded argument, either the surface-S argument or the deep-S argument. Second, the *argument theory* of the contrast between passives and middles, according to which the deep-S role corresponds to an argument *only* in the former. Jointly, these assumptions make what I will call the **A-theory**. The A-theory can be implemented using any version of the Base Argument Theory (Section 12.4.1).

We will now see some new facts with no account under the A-theory (Sections 12.5.5–12.5.7). I will then suggest (Section 12.5.8) that the best account of these facts leaves nothing for the A-theory to do. If that is correct, then the construal of reason clauses does not on its own support any claims about argument structure.

12.5.5 Remote control

Reason clauses can occur, not only as adjuncts, but also as the complement to a copula, as in (92–94).

(92) "I have only purchased one Manilow album in my life: 1984's *2:00 AM Paradise Café*. The reason was to hear the song 'When October Goes.'"[22]

---

[22] Erik Haagensen, "Manilow on Broadway brings Vegas to the Great White Way," www.backstage.com. From Davies 2008– .

(93) "There's a great deal of distortion and deception within the Roman Catholic church, at least there was, and the reason for it was to protect the reputation of the institution."[23]

(94) "The new colony was a private enterprise funded by a group of venture capitalists called the Virginia Company. Much like investors in today's dot-com start-ups, the backers wanted a quick return. They believed, incorrectly, that the Chesapeake Bay region was laden, like Mexico and Peru, with vast stores of gold and silver. The goal was to acquire these precious metals as expeditiously as possible."[24]

Here the syntactic host to the reason clause does not itself express the target fact. In (94), for example, the target is the funding of Jamestown, a fact expressed by previous sentences. Instead, the target fact is alluded to by the subject of the host clause, as the goal in (94) alludes to the funding of Jamestown.

Moreover, the controller of the reason clause is plainly not associated with an argument in its syntactic host. In (93) and (94), for example, those who protect the church or acquire precious metals do not satisfy any argument in the host clause, a copular sentence. And this would be so even if those clauses covertly had the structure in (95), since the Virginia Company and the Catholic Church still aren't arguments here.[25]

(95) a The goal of the Virginia Company was to aquire these precious metals.
      b The reason for the deception by the Catholic Church was to protect the reputation of the institution.

Thus the control relation is (92–94) is not mediated by a grammatical dependency. It spans distinct sentences. Call this **remote control**. Remote control shows that control of reason clauses need not be mediated by a syntactic relation to a clause with the controller as an argument. Sometimes it is mediated by processes of construal that are not in the sentence-internal grammar: 'by discourse.'[26]

And now here is the crucial point: the contrast between passives and middles is sustained even in remote control. The passive in (96) is much

[23] Bill Manseau, 'Priest Bill Manseau and his wife Mary, a former nun, talk about their lives in the church and about their son's new book, *Vows: The Story of a Priest, a Nun, and Their Son'*, FreshAir, NPR. 10/25/05. From Davies 2008– .

[24] Charles Mann, "Creating America (Jamestown)," *National Geographic* 211(5), 2007. From Davies 2008– .

[25] See Discussion Point 2 for a comparison with connectivity in specificational sentences.

[26] McCourt *et al.* 2014 report a self-paced reading-time study of remote control with passive antecedents. Reason clauses are read no more slowly when the controller is "remote" than when it is "local," regardless of whether the controller is the overt S or the unrealized deep-S role.

better than the middle in (97), with the readings given. And (97) is impossible even though middles can antecede reason clauses, as in (98).

(96)   The ewe was killed. And the reason was to win the favors of Apollo.
       '...the reason was, that way the killers might win the favors of Apollo.'

(97)   * Ewes kill easily. And the reason is to survive the winter.
       '...the reason is, that way the killers might survive the winter.'

(98)   Ewes kill easily. The reason is to ensure the survival of the local predators.
       'Ewes kill easily, as this ensures the survival of the local predators.'

Consequently, what distinguishes passives from middles cannot just be a difference in argument structure, or in any other aspect of sentence-internal grammar. No such difference on its own has the distinction in remote control as a consequence. There must also be a distinction in their effects on the common ground or the discourse model. I will now introduce some new facts that hint at what this might be.

12.5.6 Passives without control

Not every combination of a short passive and a reason clause permits control by the deep-S role (Williams 1974, Lasnik 1988). For instance, Lasnik observes that the combination in (99) is unacceptable on the given reading.[27]

(99)   # The ship was sunk to become a hero.
       'The ship was sunk so that the sinker might become a hero.'

For us it is important that the acceptability of such control can be affected by *additions* to the passive clause. In (100), for example, it is easy to construe the survivors of the winter as the killers of the ewes, but in (101), significantly, it is not. The difference is a shift from *were killed* to *are easily killed*.

(100)   Several ewes were killed. And the reason was to survive the winter.

(101)   # Ewes are easily killed. And the reason is to survive the winter.
        '...And the reason is, that way the killers might survive the winter.'

Example (102) is much better than (101), even though it expresses a thought very similar to the intended message of (101).

---

[27] While (99) is bad, sentence (1) below is much better (Alexis Wellwood, p.c.), evidently because acquiring notoriety is viewed as more 'active' than is becoming famous. See Clark 1990 and Landau 2000 for discussion.

(1)   The king's ship was sunk just to acquire notoriety.
      'The king's ship was sunk just so that the sinker might acquire notoriety.'

(102) Ewes are easily killed. And the reason is to ensure that the local predators
      survive.
      '...And the reason is, this may ensure that the local predators survive.'

So the problem is not that the intended message of (101) is nonsense. It
is just that the shift from were killed to are easily killed forbids control
by the deep-S role. In (102) this is not a problem, since the deep-S role
is not meant to be the controller. In (102) what is understood to ensure
that the killers can survive is, rather, the fact that ewes are easily killed.

If the entailed agent is an "argument" in both (100) and (101), why
can it control the remote reason clause only in the former? There is no
answer in the A-theory, which simply says that control is by (deep or
surface) subject arguments. In Section 12.5.8, however, I will suggest
my own answer, developing a proposal in Landau (2000), and building
on one last fact.

12.5.7 Absent secondary agents

Lasnik (1988:10) observes that we can use (103) to talk about a situation in which "it is the agent of the sinking that intended to prove a
point." By "the agent of the sinking," Lasnik means the party responsible for the fact that a torpedo sank the ship, perhaps the launcher of the
torpedo.

(103) The ship was sunk by a torpedo to prove a point.

And yet it is not the launcher of the torpedo that fills the deep-S role
of sink. That role is filled by the torpedo.[28] So Lasnik suggests that the
actual antecedent for the reason clause in (103) is the target clause
itself: what is said to prove a point is the fact that the ship was sunk
by a torpedo. This is reasonable (Williams 1985, Grimshaw 1990), since
one can say (104) and still think that the point proven by the sinking is
a point that was *intended* by those who launched the torpedo.

(104) The ship's being sunk by a torpedo proved a valuable point.

In this way Lasnik preserves the assumption that the controller is
always given either by an argument in the target clause or by the target

---

[28] That the deep-S role in (103) is bound by a torpedo is demonstrated by the
unacceptability of (1), as observed by Lasnik 1988. This is not just the repetition of
by, as shown by (2). It is rather that the Sinker role, once bound by one dependent,
cannot also be bound by another.

(1) * The ship was sunk by a torpedo by the navy.

(2) * the navy's sinking of the ship by a torpedo
     'the sinking of the ship by the navy and a torpedo'

clause itself. But Lasnik's example inspires others for which this is less plausible. One is (105).

(105) The ribbon was cut by a young girl just to acquire the support of female voters.

We can use (105) to talk about the motives of the group who organized the ribbon-cutting, and so to say what we could say more explicitly with (106).

(106) The group who organized the ceremony had the ribbon cut by a young girl just to acquire the support of female voters.

It is then the organizing group that is meant to acquire the support of female voters, not the young girl, and certainly not the fact that she cut the ribbon.

So it is simply not true that the controller is always given by the target clause, when it is not given by an argument in that clause. Sometimes the controller is the party responsible for the target fact even when that responsible party is not associated with an argument in the target clause, overt or implicit. That is, there is control by total nonarguments, when they are what Zubizaretta (1982) calls a "secondary agent" in relation to the target fact. The A-theory has no way to explain this.

12.5.8 Reasons and responsibility

Given (107), it is fair to say that the killers are responsible for the fact that the sentence expresses. But this is not so for (108).

(107) Several ewes were killed.

(108) Ewes are easily killed.

Sentence (108) generalizes over killings. The killers are responsible for each of those killings; that is why they are the killers. But it is not equally fair to say that they are responsible for the fact that ewes are killed easily. Surely the ewes also matter to this. It is their properties, if in relation to their would-be predators, that *explain* why they are easy to kill.

Similarly, it has often been remarked that, in middles, the referent of S must be "responsible" (van Oosten 1977, 1986, Fagan 1992). Consider (109). The killers are not solely responsible for the fact this reports, which is not explained by their properties alone. It has largely to do with the ewes, if in relation to their would-be predators.

(109) Ewes kill easily.

As Ackema and Schoorlemmer (2006) put it, "the grammatical subject of a middle (if present) must have properties such that it can be understood to be responsible for the action expressed by the predicate." More precisely, I would say, it must be their properties that explain the target *fact*, which may be a generalization over actions.

I suggest that this notion of "responsibility" matters to the construal of reason clauses.[29] When control is not by the target fact, it is by the party that is explanatorily responsible for that fact. Presumably this relates ultimately to the function of reason clauses, which is to offer a teleological explanation on the basis of laws or intentions. Landau (2000:181), responding also to Farkas (1988), anticipates this. He says that reason clauses are controlled by the "purposeful" or "intentional causer" of the target. My suggestion is a bit broader. As some of our examples will show, controllers needn't be purposive or intentional; they need only be explanatorily responsible for the target.

This **responsibility theory**, while still vague, already gives us some purchase on our contrasts. Example (110) permits the entailed killers to control the reason clause, because they are viewed as responsible for the fact that several ewes were killed.

(110)   Several ewes were killed. And the reason was to survive the winter.

But the party viewed as responsible for the fact that ewes *are killed easily*, (108), or *kill easily*, (109), is not the killers alone. Therefore these killers will not serve as good controllers, whether the target clause is passive or middle, as we saw in (101) and (89), respectively. It is entirely moot whether the unrealized role of Killer is furthermore linked to an argument, as the A-theory requires.

In a middle, the responsible party is regularly named by S, the subject. If a shoulder harness adjusts easily, this is because of the harness itself, albeit in relation to its would-be adjusters. Accordingly, control of a reason clause by S in a middle is possible, as in (91): "The shoulder harness adjusts easily up and down to fit a wide range of torsos."

In an active transitive clause, the subject often names the responsible party. When the wolf kills the ewe, he is most likely responsible for that fact. But if we make clear that he is not, as in (111), the wolf is no longer a good controller.

(111)   # The wolf inadvertently killed a ewe. The reason was to survive the winter.

---

[29] Farkas 1988 suggests that control of infinitival adjuncts is in general sensitive to responsibility. My own suggestion is specific to reason clauses, and connected to their function in explanation.

(112) is better, and for a telling reason. Unconscious actions, unlike inadvertent ones, may still be explained by the goal of survival, perhaps via the sensation of hunger.

(112) ? The wolf unconsciously killed a ewe. The reason was to survive the winter.

One last advantage of the responsibility theory emerges when we consider other sorts of S-oriented nonfinite adjuncts, like *while* hunting or *without* studying. Under the A-theory, we expect by default that passives and middles should again differ here. Only the passive, with its putative argument, should have a capacity for control. Under the responsibility theory, however, we have no reason to expect a difference. By hypothesis, responsibility is pertinent only for reason adjuncts, since only these invoke explanation in virtue of intentions. So, what are the facts? Consonant with the responsibility theory, there is no categorical contrast. Normally, adjuncts with *while* or *without* cannot be controlled by the deep-S role of either a middle or a short passive. But for both, they sometimes they can be, especially when the host expresses a modal generalization (Bhatt and Izvorski 1998, Williams 2013). Middle (113) is an attested example, cited above in (11c); see also Vinet (1987) and Iwata (1999). Passive (114), with the modal *can*, is discussed in Chomsky (1982) and Williams (1985).

(113) "[A] Ruger 7-1/2" .44 Magnum carries easily while hunting."
(114) The books can be sold without reading them.

Thus the responsibility theory promises to cover data that the A-theory cannot.

Implementationally, I suggest that the reason clause has an unbound PRO subject, interpreted as a variable which, in this context, can be restricted to range just over parties responsible for the target fact. Compare the examples in (115).[30]

(115) a At the gold medal fight, the Russian did not vote for the Russian.
　　　b Take the thing out of the hat.
　　　c Mo put chips on 17 and won.

Such examples show, as Evans observed (1982:312, fn.), that "[o]ften the predicate does more to narrow down the range of possible interpretations of the referring expression than does the referring expression

---

[30] Example (115a) is adapted from Neale 2004, who responds to McCawley 1979 and Westerståhl 1985. Example (115b) is adapted from Stone and Webber 1998, who respond to Dale and Haddock 1991. Example (115c) is adapted from Condoravdi and Gawron 1996, after Partee 1989. See Williams 2012 for discussion.

itself." In (115a), S and O will find values only if restricted to range over judges and boxers, respectively. Sentence (115b) can be used felicitously even in a context with many things and many hats, provided there is just one thing *in* a hat that may be taken out. And (115c) allows the definite UR of *win* to range just over contests involving Mo (Chapter 5), even though none have been referred to explicitly. I take the construal of PRO in reason clauses to work similarly. If Φ is the target fact, and P is the property expressed by the infinitival clause, the construction means roughly: 'Φ, because Φ makes Px more likely.' This semantic context for x, I suggest, narrows its domain to just would-be satisfiers of P among parties viewed as responsible for Φ.

One problem is still glaring, for both theories. Recall our examples of sharks and parasites in (83), transposed to remote control in (116).

(116) a   These sharks$_k$ cover themselves with parasites. And the reason is, to have
            their$_k$ gills kept clean.
       b * Parasites cover these sharks$_k$. And the reason is, to have their$_k$ gills kept
            clean.

We still cannot use (116b) to say what we say with (116a). So control by overt *non*-subjects remains impossible, even across discourse. This fact needs an account.

I don't have one. I can only assert that the referent of an overt dependent, unless it is the subject or fills the deep-S role, is never viewed as the responsible party.[31] This is not an attractive claim. But, notice, it puts the responsibility theory at no disadvantage vis-à-vis the A-theory. The fact that these sharks is not the subject of the first clause in (116b) is a syntactic fact which, as such, does not persist through discourse. Consequently the A-theory cannot use it to explain the contrast between (116b) and (116a). So the stipulated account offered in the terms of the responsibility theory is as yet in competition with no account at all.

DISCUSSION POINTS

1 Do you know a language with a passive, other than English? If so, which predicates does it allow and forbid in the passive frame? Is the framing pattern different from English? Does the language have a long passive? If so, is the form of the oblique dependent specific to the passive?

---

[31] Roeper 1987:299 makes a related observation: "secondary agents are limited to subject position."

2 Sentence (1) below is excerpted from (93). Explain why, here, the understood controller of the reason clause is not an argument in the host clause (that is, in the clause where the reason clause is a dependent). Should sentences like (2) change our perspective on this? (See Heycock and Kroch 1999.)

(1) The reason for it was to protect the reputation of the institution.

(2) The main problem I think the church$_k$ has is itself$_k$.

3 As we saw, Bresnan (1982) and Bach (1980) use very similar rules to derive passives. For Bresnan this rule applies in Lexicon, while for Bach it applies in Syntax. Can you provide an argument that favors one approach over the other?

4 In English, prepositional phrases with *from* can be used to name the cause of some state or event, as in (3). (The distribution of this *from* is subtle: Delancey 1984, Williams 2011.) Does this show that the predicates in (3) have an implicit argument in the role of Cause? Why or why not?

(3) a The pot is black from the dirty oil.
    b The pot blackened from the fire.
    c Al was screaming from the pain.

How could you tell whether, in a given language, a certain oblique dependent is like the English *from*-phrase, or like the English *by*-phrase?

5 Sometimes data like (71) are taken to suggest that the *by*-phrase realizes an argument of its passive host. Why would that be? Are there good reasons for this conclusion? How is this position affected by (4) and (5), which illustrated the Role Iteration Generalization (RIG) discussed in Chapter 8?

(4) The ship was sunk by the crook (*by his accomplices).

(5) Al cooked this for his wife (*for his son).

6 How might the ungrammatical sentences in item (70) of the main text themselves be explained as instances of the RIG? Do you think it would be plausible to explain them in that way?

7 As shown by (6) and (7), predicates that do not entail an agent cannot host a *by*-phrase. Does this by itself show that short passives have an argument in the deep-S role? In this connection, consider your thoughts about (3) above, as well as the difference between blond child and blond diameter.

(6) a The ship sank ⊭ Something sank the ship.
    b * The ship sank by the explosion.

(7)   a   The pot is black ⊭ Something blackened the pot.
      b * The pot is black by the fire.

8 Imagine that the *responsibility theory* is correct for cases of Remote Control. Does this require that it is also correct for the 'traditional' cases of Local Control, where the controller is an argument in the syntactic host to the reason clause? Should we prefer a uniform account?

SUGGESTIONS FOR FURTHER READING

To get a grip on the data that go under the heading of "passive," it is helpful to read Perlmutter and Postal 1983, Siewierska 1984, Keenan and Dryer 2007, and Kiparsky 2013. Bresnan 1982 and Baker *et al.* 1989 seem still to represent the two most common analytical perspectives. Collins 2005 and Bruening 2012 are more recent challenges to some aspects of the orthodoxy. On the semantic status of the unrealized deep-subject role in short passives, read Roeper 1987 and Koenig and Mauner 2000.

13 Resultatives

13.1 INTRODUCTION

We have focussed on clauses whose predicate is simple, comprising no more than a verb. But a theory of argument structure must generalize to clauses whose predicate is complex, with more than one part. How do arguments then relate to the parts of the complex predicate, and how do the parts relate to each other? What we say here should be a natural extension of what we say for simple predicates. This chapter treats a test case: clauses with resultative complex predicates, like (1) or (2).

(1) Al pounded the cutlet flat.

(2) Ozzy sang his throat hoarse.

These have long been fertile pasture for theories of argument structure.[1] The goal is to relate (1) and (2), for example, to such kindred sentences as those in (3) and (4), in terms that permit useful generalizations.

(3) a Al pounded the cutlet.
    b Al flattened the cutlet.
    c The cutlet was flat.

(4) a Ozzy sang *Paranoid*.
    b Ozzy hoarsened his throat.
    c Ozzy's throat was hoarse.

This will require the full battery of analytical tools reviewed in this book, and so provides a good exercise to conclude. Resultatives cast an

---

[1] McCawley 1971, Dowty 1972, Green 1972, Thompson 1973, Williams 1980, Rothstein 1983, 2001, 2004, Simpson 1983, Kayne 1985, Hoekstra 1988, Jackendoff 1990b, Li 1990, 1995, 1999, Larson 1991, Carrier and Randall 1992, Huang 1992, Hale and Keyser 1993, Goldberg 1995, Levin and Rappaport 1995, Washio 1997, Wechsler 1997, 2005a, Bittner 1999, Rappaport Hovav and Levin 2001, Goldberg and Jackendoff 2004, Kratzer 2005, Williams 2005, 2009, accepted.

exceptionally bright light on our most basic assumptions about argument structure and event structure, in both their semantic and syntactic aspects. Here we will bask briefly in that light. For an excellent contemporary review of the topic, see Beavers (2012).

I begin with the terms of discussion (Section 13.2), and the division of labor between Lexicon and Syntax in building resultatives (Section 13.3). I then examine the event structure of resultatives (Section 13.4), laying the foundation for the rest of the chapter. The remaining sections concern thematic relations between these events and the referents of S or O. Relations to the result event are the topic of Section 13.5, which reviews accounts of the Direct Object Restriction. Section 13.6 discusses apparent sharing of an argument, where S or O appears to name a participant in two different events. I finish with a diagnostic use of resultatives, in the choice between projectionist and separationist theories of argument structure (Section 13.7).

13.2 *TALKING ABOUT RESULTATIVES*

A **resultative** is a single clause comprising two overt predicates, a *means predicate* **M**, and a *result predicate* **R**, neither one introduced by a conjunction or adposition. In (5) M is pound and R is flat. The smallest constituent containing both M and R, I will refer to with the abbreviation **MR**. In Igbo (6), M is kụ 'strike' and R is wa 'split.' These are both verbs, and are always adjacent on the surface.

(5) Al pounded the cutlet flat.

(6) Eze kụ   wa   -ra   ọba   ahụ.
     E.   strike split -FACT gourd that
     'Eze made that gourd split from [his] striking [it].'

I gloss all resultatives with an unidiomatic but usefully neutral formula, either "S made O R from M'ing" or "S got R from M'ing."

No audible morphemes signal the meaning of the construction. But a resultative clause entails that there was a process (or change) that ended with the event of R, and was achieved by means of the M event. For example, (5) entails that there was a process that ends with flatness, and is achieved by means of pounding. In general this entails that the M event caused that of R.

A speaker of (5) may mean that the reported pounding was not only by Al but also of the cutlet, just as in (7).

(7) Al pounded the cutlet.

S and O in (5) then name the same participants in the pounding as they do in (7). On this understanding of (5), S and O are therefore, let us say, *selected*. In contrast, O is *unselected* on the normal understanding of (8), since this does not imply that Ozzy's throat got sung, even though, in (9), O must name what is sung.

(8)   Ozzy sang his throat hoarse.

(9)   Ozzy sang *Paranoid*.

I use the term "selected" to describe the meaning intended by a speaker. Often it is an open question whether the relation we notionally associate with a selected S or O is moreover entailed by the sentence (Hoekstra 1988, Sybesma 1999, Kratzer 2005, Williams 2005) – and a still further question whether this relation is assigned to S or O in the derivation, or is just an implicit consequence of an explicit relation to a different event. These issues will be relevant at several points in this chapter.

In the process described by a resultative, some individual changes, entering the result condition implied by R. The overt phrase that identifies this individual **controls** R. In (5), flat is controlled by the cutlet, the surface direct object of the clause, since (5) entails that the cutlet wound up flat. This is an *O-control* resultative. In (10), it is the surface subject that controls R, since the sentence entails that the lake wound up solid. This is an *S-control* resultative.

(10)   The lake froze solid.

O-control resultatives are transitive clauses, with both a subject and an object. S-control resultatives are typically (but perhaps not always) intransitive clauses, with a surface subject and no surface object. The transitivity of the clause should not be confounded, however, with the category of the verb in M. There are transitive clauses with a resultative predicate whose M verb is intransitive, such as (8). Since O in (8) is unselected, the verb in M is presumably the intransitive sing of Ozzy will sing. And in such cases we have to speak carefully: the resultative clause is transitive, with both a subject and an object, but we need not say the same for the verb M.

In English an intransitive S-control resultative never has a transitive verb in M. Sentence (11) is representative. Unergative verbs such as sing are also excluded, (12), in general and perhaps always (Levin and Rappaport Hovav 1995).

(11)   * The cutlet pounded flat.
       'The cutlet got flat from [someone] pounding [it].'

(12) * Ozzy's throat sang hoarse.
       'Ozzy's throat got hoarse from [Ozzy] singing.'

This is not true universally, however. Igbo (13a) has a resultative predicate, kụ wa 'strike split,' in an intransitive clause. But the verb in M, kụ 'strike,' is transitive: on its own it cannot exhaust the predicate in an intransitive clause, as shown in (13b).

(13) a   Ọba   ahụ   kụ   wa   -ra   akụwa.
          gourd   that   strike   split   -FACT   BVC
          'That gourd split from striking.'   (Hale *et al.* 1995)

      b * Ọba   ahụ   kụ   -rụ   akụ.
          gourd   that   strike   -FACT   BVC
          'That gourd suffered a strike.'   (*ibid.*)

Such patterns will be relevant in Section 13.7.

13.3 LEXICON VERSUS SYNTAX

There are three views about where the resultative predicate is assembled: the fully syntactic, partly lexical, and fully lexical views. Again I will discuss these using (14).

(14) Al pounded the cutlet flat.

The *fully syntactic view* makes two claims. First, a resultative clause has M and R as distinct syntactic parts. "Pound" and "flat" pronounce distinct parts of (14)'s derivation, for instance. Second, the resultative meaning does not come from the lexical head of either M or R. It comes from something that is separate from both, either a silent syntactic primitive (Goldberg 1995, Kratzer 2005) or a rule of interpretation (Dowty 1979, Bittner 1999, Rothstein 2001).[2] Jointly, the two parts of the fully syntactic view imply that the heads of M and R are lexical items that are also found outside of resultatives. For example, "pound"

---

[2] Here are two examples. Kratzer (2005) proposes a silent syntactic affix CAUSE, with the value in (1) below. It takes R as an argument and yields a predicate true of events that "Cause" an R state. Rothstein (2001) gives a semantic rule called "Resultative Conjunction," defined in (2). This combines M and R, summing their events, identifying their arguments, and requiring that the 'culmination' of the M event is part of R event.

(1) $[\![\text{CAUSE}]\!] = \lambda P \lambda e \exists s [$ State(s) & Event(e) & $P(s)$ & Cause$(s)(e)$ $]$

(2) ResultativeConjunction(M,R)
     $\equiv \lambda y \lambda e \exists e_1 \exists e_2 [(e = e_1 \sqcup e_2)$ & M(e_1, y) & R(e_2, y) & (Culmination$(e_1) \sqsubseteq e_2)$ $]$

and "flat" pronounce exactly the same lexical items in (14) as they do in (15).

(15)   Al pounded the cutlet and now the cutlet is flat.

The *partly lexical view* shares the first part of the fully syntactic view. Again M and R are syntactically separate. But it does not share the second. Resultative meaning projects from one of the two overt predicates, and not from their environment. The predicate that projects resultative meaning then has the other as an argument, in one or another sense. According to Simpson (1983), for example, "pound" in (14) has a meaning like (16): 'to cause y to become P by pounding.' This then takes flat as a functional semantic argument (Müller 2006, Steedman and Baldridge 2011).

(16) $[\![\text{pound}_2]\!] = \lambda P \lambda y \ldots [\text{CauseToBecome}(e_1, e_2) \ \& \ \text{PoundingOf}(e_1, y) \ \& \ P(e_2, y) \ldots]$

On the partly lexical view, therefore, "pound" pronounces two different lexical items in (14) and (15), with related but very different meanings.

Finally, on the *fully lexical view* M and R are not syntactically separate. MR is a single lexical item. For example, according to Thompson (1973) and Li (1990), Mandarin za ping 'pound flat' is itself a primitive in the derivation of (17). The sentence itself does not have za 'pound' or ping 'flat' as parts, though these are prelexical parts of za ping's derivation in Lexicon.

(17)   ta   za   ping -le   nakuai   rou.
       3s   pound   level -PFV   that   meat
       'S/he pounded that meat flat.'

This is meant to explain why neither M nor R can separately accommodate adverbs, (18a), and why they cannot be separated by suffixes or enclitics, (18b). See Williams (2014b) for more detail.

(18)   a * ta   za   hen   ping -le   nakuai   rou.
             3s   pound   very level -PFV   that   meat
             'S/he pounded that meat very flat.'

       b * ta   za   -le   ping   nakuai   rou.
             3s   pound   -PFV   level that   meat
             'S/he pounded that meat flat.'

To understand this three-way distinction, let's consider each option for pound flat. Here the fully lexical view is implausible, since M and R can be separately targeted by affixes and adverbs. Past tense -ed attaches to M, not MR as a whole; assuming that -ed is a syntactic suffix (and not a prelexical infix) this implies that M is separate from R in Syntax. More decisively, adverbs can modify R independently of M or MR, even clause-sized adverbs, as in (19).

(19)   a Al pounded the cutlet very flat.
        b Al pounded the cutlet as flat as anything Mo had ever seen.

This leaves us with either the partly lexical or fully syntactic views. One thing we have to explain now is (20) (Rappaport Hovav and Levin 2001).

(20)   * Al very rapidly pounded the cutlet flat quite slowly.
        'Al quite slowly flattened the cutlet by pounding it very rapidly.'

This shows that a pound flat clause has no part that is both a predicate of poundings, and can furthermore accommodate an adverb. On the fully syntactic view, such a clause does have a part that is a predicate of poundings, namely the verb pound; therefore on this view we need to conclude that M cannot accommodate an adverb syntactically (Section 13.4). On the partly lexical view, there is also a second possibility. We can say that "pound" in pound flat pronounces a verb that is satisified, not by poundings, but by processes achieved by pounding. Given this, no adverb could modify a predicate of poundings, since there is no such predicate in a pound flat clause.

Thus both the fully syntactic and partly lexical view have some way of accounting for (20). There are other facts, however, that favor the former. Compare (21) to (22).

(21)   # The slow pounding (of the cutlet) was achieved by striking it very rapidly with a mallet.

(22)   The slow transformation / flattening / pounding flat (of the cutlet) was achieved by striking it very rapidly with a mallet.

The first sentence sounds contradictory, unlike the second. This should not be so on the partly lexical view. It posits a verb pound with resultative meaning. Since verbs in general can form gerunds, there should be a gerund pronounced "pounding" that describes processes achieved by means of pounding. And if there were, (21) could say something sensible. Sentence (23) too could escape contradiction, with the meaning that there were no processes achieved by pounding, even though Al banged cutlets all day.

(23)   # There was no pounding, though Al did spend the whole day banging very tough cutlets with a mallet.

These facts imply that resultative meaning does not come from M. Judging by (24), it also doesn't come from R, since (24a) cannot mean (24b).

R maintains the usual meaning of its head, along with its adjectival form.[3]

(24) a # Al cut the bone methodically/loudly open.
      b Al methodically/loudly cut the bone open.

Thus, resultative meaning evidently comes from the structural context of both M and R, via silent primitives or semantic rules, as implied only on the fully syntactic view.

Sometimes this view is resisted on grounds of irregularity: many combinations of M and R sound odd for no clear reason. Sentence (25) sounds bad (Green 1972:84), for example, but there is no settled account of why, when shoot dead and punch bloody are fine (though see Goldberg 1995:195). This sort of irregularity, it is suggested, should not be available to structures built in Syntax (Boas 2003).

(25) # She shot him lame.

But the premise about irregularity is tendentious (Marantz 1997). Arguments that rely on it must yield to more direct kinds of evidence. If there is a verb pound with resultative meaning, it should form a gerund; and if there is a verb pound flat, its prelexical parts cannot be affixed to or modified in Syntax. Cross-linguistically, moreover, irregularity in resultatives does not seem to track their syntactic complexity. In Igbo and Mandarin, a fully lexical analysis is at least initially plausible, since neither M nor R can host suffixes or adverbs individually, unlike in English. And yet the resultative in these languages is less irregular and more productive than it is in English, where the lexical view is, I have argued, directly contradicted.

In what follows I will generally presuppose the fully syntactic view, for every language I discuss. This will simplify exposition, even if it is wrong. The reader curious about the alternative views is encouraged to transpose syntactic into lexical derivations, and assess the resulting theory.

13.4 EVENT STRUCTURE AND ADVERBS

Resultatives imply a causal relation between the M and R events. But this description is preliminary. It decides neither the logical form of

---

[3] Importantly, facts like (24) also show that no consituent containing R but not M is a predicate of the means event, or the event of the clause (*pace* Kratzer 2005).

resultatives nor the exact content of the relation between their events. This relation must imply causation, but it need not be causation, and almost certainly it isn't. Here I give initial evidence for the semantic structure of resultatives, mainly from the interpretation of adverbs.

The most common semantics for resultatives, rendered in eventish form, is (26). This says that the M event causes an event of becoming R, following McCawley (1971), Dowty (1972), Parsons (1990) and many others. I assume that on this semantics the event of the clause (e_1) is that of M, so that pound flat is a predicate satisfied by certain poundings, namely those related to an event of becoming flat.

(26)   MR $\cong \ldots \lambda e_1 \exists e_2 \exists e_3 [$ Cause(e_1, e_2) & Become(e_2, e_3)
        & $[\![M]\!](\ldots)(e_1)$ & $[\![R]\!](\ldots)(e_3) \ldots]$

This semantics for resultatives is an elaboration of what I have called the causing event semantics for simple causatives such as (27), discussed in earlier chapters and applied to flatten in (28). There is just one difference. With pound flat but not flatten, the causing event (e_1) receives an explicit description, provided by pound.

(27)   Al flattened the cutlet.

(28)   flatten $\cong \ldots \lambda e_1 \exists e_2 \exists e_3 [$ Cause(e_1, e_2) & Become(e_2, e_3)
        & $[\![\text{flat}]\!](\ldots)(e_3) \ldots]$

In Chapter 10 we saw two problems for this semantics, and both arise again here. First, "Cause" must be a relation much narrower than merely causation. If Mo punches Lee, causing Lee to stumble across the room, hit her head on a cabinet and black out, we can say that the punch caused the blackout, as we can say that a rainstorm caused a crop failure. But we cannot say that Mo punched Lee unconscious. For this reason it is common to say that resultatives (Bittner 1999), like single verb causatives (Shibatani 1976, Talmy 1976, McCawley 1978, Wolff 2003), imply 'direct' causation. But the new name doesn't illuminate much (Shibatani 2002, Pietroski 2005a; compare Kratzer 2005).

The bigger problem concerns VP adverbs, and what events they *cannot* describe. Unsurprisingly, such adverbs cannot describe the R state, as shown in (29).

(29)   * Al very pounded the cutlet flat.
        'Al pounded the cutlet very flat.'

Remarkably, however, they cannot freely describe the means event either (Rappaport Hovav and Levin 2001, Williams 2009). For example in (30a), which repeats (20), very rapidly cannot describe the M event. If it could, it would escape inconsistency, since it could be used to say (30b).

(30) a # Al very rapidly pounded the cutlet flat quite slowly.
      b   Al quite slowly flattened the cutlet by pounding it very rapidly.

Thus (31a) has no analysis that entails (31b), showing that the adverb cannot modify M on its own.

(31) a   Al very rapidly pounded the cutlet flat.
      b ⊭ Al very rapidly pounded the cutlet.

The adverb in (31a) can only describe a process to which the pounding is related, a process that may be rapid, even when the pounding is slow, or also slow, when the pounding is rapid. This has an important consequence for argument structure: the phrase modified by the adverb, namely MR, must be a predicate of this process and not of the pounding. MR must have a meaning like (32).

(32) Process Semantics for Resultatives
      MR $\cong \lambda e_1 \exists e_2 \exists e_3 \lfloor K(e_1, e_2, e_3)$ & $[\![M]\!](\ldots)(e_2)$ & $[\![R]\!](\ldots)(e_3) \ldots \rfloor$

Here K relates a process e_1 to its end e_3, and also to an event e_2 by means of which it is achieved. In addition, the event of MR need not itself satisfy the description provided by M, as stated in (33). Were the MR event instead to always satisfy M, the pounding flat would itself be a pounding, and (31a) would wrongly entail (31b).

(33) **Process/Means Distinctness**
      $\exists e [[\![MR]\!](\ldots)(e)] \not\models \exists e [[\![M]\!](\ldots)(e)]$

Of course, there are examples where an adverb does seem to describe the means event. (34) suggests that the pounding was loud, for example.

(34) Al loudly pounded the cutlet flat.

But in light of (30a), it is best to see this as pragmatic. The sentence itself means only that there was a loud process of flattening achieved by means of pounding. The process may be loud because of the pounding, just as a child is blond because of his hair. But it does not follow that the process has all of the qualities of the pounding, any more than the blond child has all the qualities of his hair.

I said that $K(e_1, e_2, e_3)$ is true just in case e_1 is a process that ends with e_3 and is achieved by means of e_2. Thus it is equivalent to the conjunction of two other relations, called Means(e_1, e_2) and End(e_1, e_3) in (35).

(35) $K(e_1, e_2, e_3) \equiv$ Means(e_1, e_2) & End(e_1, e_3)

Means and End are no less natural than Cause or Become as primitives of semantic analysis. But I do not offer (35) as a claim of semantic decomposition. There is no clear evidence (from adverbs, for example) for separation in Syntax; relations of the process to its means and result events do not seem to be introduced by distinct parts of the derivation. And this removes the best motive we might have for decomposing K in the semantics.

Nonetheless, to distinguish the present account from the causing event semantics, I ought to clarify why $\text{Means}(e_1, e_2)$ and $\text{End}(e_1, e_3)$ are not simply different names for $\text{Cause}(e_2, e_1)$ and $\text{Become}(e_1, e_3)$, respectively. There are two reasons. First, when e_2 is the means of e_1, it does not always seem right to say that e_2 causes e_1. Causes precede effects, but a means event may be concurrent with its process, and need not precede it. Second, while $\text{Become}(e, s)$ surely entails $\text{End}(e, s)$ – an event of becoming e ends with what Parsons (1990) calls its "target state" s – the reverse does not seem right. Not every event with an end is a becoming. Some processes have agents, but no event with an agent is a becoming, by assumption. This will matter in Section 13.5, where I will suggest that the process of flattening a cutlet has an agent.

Now let me draw out two implications of the Process Semantics, as given by (32) and (33), for syntax and argument structure.

The first concerns the syntax of M. The means event, we just saw, cannot in general be described by adverbs. If M is a predicate of the means event, as we decided in Section 13.3, it follows that M cannot host an adverb syntactically. In any such case I infer that M also does not contain any arguments, based on the presumption in (36). For brevity: M is then *not phrasal*. This is in agreement with nearly all syntactic analyses of resultatives (Hoekstra 1988, Larson 1991, Rothstein 2001, Kratzer 2005).[4]

(36) No Adverbs No Arguments
     When M cannot be adverbially modified, it contains no dependent phrases.

But why presume (36)? If M were to contain dependents, it would have all the structure of a full verb phrase, and we would expect it to tolerate adjuncts as well. But if M is not an ordinary verb phrase we have no such expectation, and are therefore free to stipulate (pending an explanation) that it cannot host adjuncts. To this I add the further premise in (37), common but usually implicit.[5]

---

[4] The rare exceptions to this rule include Déchaine 1993 and Nishiyama 1998, who have the M verb combine with O before the result combines with R. Carrier and Randall 1992 have a ternary structure where M and R are *both* sisters to O.

[5] This is a subcase of the broader premise, common to nearly all work in the Chomskyan tradition, that *any* head with arguments also takes those arguments immediately.

(37) Functional Heads Take Arguments Immediately
   Functional heads that introduce arguments take these arguments immediately, within the phrase they project.

Jointly, (36) and (37) now imply that, when M cannot host adverbs, it contains nothing beyond the verb, neither dependent phrases nor silent argument-introducing heads. This will be important to several points in later sections.

The second consequence of the Process Semantics concerns thematic relations. Sentence (38a) entails (38b); or in any case, so it appears.

(38)   a   Al pounded the cutlet flat.
       b $\models$ Al pounded the cutlet.

This is explained if S and O in (38a) bind relations to the pounding, as in (39).

(39) $\lambda e_1 \exists e_2 \exists e_3 [\ldots \text{Agent}(e_2, [\![S]\!]) \, \& \, [\![M]\!](e_2) \, \& \, \text{Patient}(e_2, [\![O]\!]) \ldots]$

But given our semantics, (32), the means event is not the event of the clause. So now we have a question. If S and O bind relations to the M event, do they *also* bind relations to the event of MR, as in (40)?

(40) $\lambda e_1 \exists e_2 \exists e_3 [\ldots \text{Agent}(e_1, [\![S]\!]) \, \& \, [\![MR]\!](e_1) \, \& \, \text{Patient}(e_1, [\![O]\!]) \ldots]$

Imagine first that they don't. Then (38a), with pound flat, and (38b), with just pound, will differ in argument structure: only in the latter will S or O bind a relation to the event of the clause. As a result, we stand to lose attractive generalizations: those governing simple predicates may fail to extend to resultatives. We will be unable to say, for example, that S and O are assigned Agent and Patient roles to the event of a transitive clause, whether the predicate is pound flat or pound. In Section 13.5 below, I will argue that this generalization is essential to explaining control of R.

In the interests of explanatory generality, therefore, we may want to insist on (40), so that in resultatives too, S and O bind relations to the event of the clause. But this attraction comes at a cost. It will make the derivation more complex, if we continue to assume (39). For S and O will bind relations *both* to MR *and* to M, and we will need a grammatical account of how this comes about, of how MR comes to 'share' an argument with M. I discuss this briefly in Section 13.6.

13.5 THE DIRECT OBJECT RESTRICTION

In the first *Rocky* movie, Rocky's fists become bloody from pounding some frozen beef. But this cannot be conveyed with (41), which means (41a) and not (41b). O controls R, and S cannot.

(41) Rocky's fists pounded the frozen beef bloody.

    a 'In pounding the frozen beef, Rocky's fists made it bloody.'
    b * 'In pounding the frozen beef, Rocky's fists got bloody.'

Similarly, if (42) is read as resultative, hoarse must be controlled by O. The sentence means (42a), and not the more sensible (42b).

(42) Ozzy sang *Paranoid* hoarse.

    a 'In singing *Paranoid*, Ozzy made it hoarse.'
    b * 'In singing *Paranoid*, Ozzy got hoarse.'

Sentences (41) and (42) are therefore among the sentences that fall under the **Direct Object Restriction**, or DOR, in (43) (Williams 1980, Simpson 1983, Levin and Rappaport Hovav 1995).

(43) Direct Object Restriction
    R in a resultative is controlled by the underlying direct object.

Limiting the DOR to "underlying" objects is important. In (44) R is controlled by S on the surface. But this complies with (43) if this S is a direct object underlyingly.

(44) The beef froze solid.

This may mean that (44) is deeply unaccusative, and the beef moves to S from a position occupied by O in transitive clauses (Chapter 11). Or, in nontransformational theories, it might mean only that (44) has no dependent naming the agent of its event. Either account is plausible for sentences like (44), so the DOR remains viable. I will mention a further challenge at the end of this section. But our focus will be on how to explain the DOR, for the large class of data it governs unambiguously.[6]

When a phrase controls R, there is an entailed relation between its referent and the result event. Standard theories of the DOR give this relation an *explicit account*. They represent it as an explicit part of the sentence meaning, so that our pound flat clause has a meaning like (45).

(45) $\lambda e_1 \exists e_2 \exists e_3 [\ldots \& \text{FlatnessOf}(e_3, \text{the cutlet})]$

---

[6] This section summarizes Williams, accepted.

Thus the relation to the R event must be assigned to the controller in the semantic derivation, or to an empty category whose reference it determines. Syntactically there are two routes to this end, (46) and (47). In (46) there is a DP inside of R, binding a relation to the event of its sister. This DP is either the overt O, (46a), or it is an empty category bound by O from outside of R, (46b). The empty category may be either an anaphor (say, PRO) or a trace of O's movement.

(46)   a $[^{MR} [^M$ pound $] [^R [^O$ the cutlet $]$ flat $]]$
       b $[[^O$ the cutlet $]_k [^{MR} [^M$ pound $] [^R \epsilon_k$ flat $]]]$

The second route, (47), has no DP inside of R. Instead, R has an unsatisfied argument that it passes upwards to MR; technically, this requires a semantic rule something like `Composition`.[7]

(47) $[[^O$ the cutlet $] [^{MR} [^M$ pound $] [^R$ flat $]]$

Pound flat will therefore have a meaning like (48), with a functional argument (λy) in the role of 'flat thing.' This argument is satisifed by O, the cutlet.

(48) $[\![[$ pound flat $]]\!] = \lambda y \ldots \lambda e_1 \exists e_2 \exists e_3 [K(e_1, e_2, e_3)$
       $\& \ldots \& \text{FlatnessOf}(e_3, y)]$

These two analyses, (46) and (47), have less common rivals that do not share their starting point, namely the presumed meaning in (45). These rivals contend that the entailed relation to the R event need not be explicit, since in any case it has an *implicit account*. By hypothesis it is a nonanalytic, purely semantic consequence of an explicit relation to a different event, either the means event or the resultative process. Given this, an explicit relation to the R event would add nothing to the truth conditions. The decision of whether to state such a relation explicitly in the meaning, and hence whether to give R an argument, must therefore be made solely on grammatical grounds, and not on the basis of truth conditions.

This idea comes in two quite different varieties. One relies on the postulate in (49), versions of which are suggested in Rappaport Hovav and Levin (2001), Rothstein (2004), and elsewhere. This says that the means and the end of a process have the same theme. Control of R will therefore be a semantic consequence of a Theme relation to the M event, voiding the need for an explicit relation to the R event.

---

[7] See Dowty 1988, Jacobson 1990, and Steedman 1996 for uses of `Composition` in Syntax. By definition: `Composition`$[f, g] \equiv \lambda x[f(gx)]$

(49) Means Theme Postulate
     In the event described by a resultative, the theme (or patient) of the result event
     is also the theme (or patient) of the means event:
     $[\![MR]\!](e_1, e_2, e_3)$ & $Theme(e_3, x) \vDash Theme(e_2, x)$

But (49) has problems. The domain that it governs must be gerryman-
dered to exclude all cases of unselected Os, such as English (50), or Igbo
(51) from Williams (2008a).

(50) Ozzy sang his throat hoarse.

(51) Eze bi   kpụ -rụ   mma ahụ.
      E.   cut dull -FACT   knife that
      'Eze made his knife dull from cutting.'

Here (49) would tell us that what Ozzy sang became hoarse, and that
what Eze cut became dull, incorrectly. So, unless the exclusion of these
data can be explained, an approach to the DOR based on (49) is unattractive (Williams, accepted).

The second variety is proposed in Williams (2005, accepted), following Parsons's (1990) treatment of inchoatives, and Pietroski's (2005a)
treatment of causatives. It relies first on (52). S and O in a resultative are
assigned thematic relations to the event of the clause, perhaps among
other events, as in (53), a slight variant of (40).

(52) Outside Relations (OR) Semantics for resultatives
      S and O in a resultative are assigned thematic relations at least to the event of
      the clause.

(53) $\lambda e_1 \exists e_2 \exists e_3 [\ldots Agent(e_1, [\![S]\!]) \ \& \ [\![MR]\!](\ldots)(e_1) \ \& \ Theme(e_1, [\![O]\!]) \ldots]$

The event of a resultative clause, e_1 in (53), is a process with an end.
Suppose that the theme of a process is the theme of its end, as in (54),
familiar from Chapter 10. (In chapter 10 I had "Patient" for "Theme"; in
this context it makes no difference.)

(54) End Theme Postulate
      $End(e_1, e_3)$ & $Theme(e_1, x) \vDash Theme(e_3, x)$

This echoes (55) from Pietroski (2005), swapping "Terminater" for "End."
Postulate (54) also entails the postulate in (35) from Parsons (1990), if
events of becoming are processes ended by their "target state."

(55) [T]he Theme of a process is also the Theme of any Terminater of that process.
      (Pietroski 2005:181).

(56) The Theme of [Become's] event is the same as the Theme of its Target state.
      (Parsons 1990:119).

And now, given (54), control of R follows from naming the Theme of
the MR process. Since this process is the event of the resultative clause,

the OR semantics in (52) renders the DOR a subcase of a far broader generalization: an underlying O names the theme of its clause's event.[8] In our sentence about Rocky's fists, for example, R is controlled by O and not S for *exactly* the same reason that O but not S names what is pounded in Rocky's fists pounded the beef. In a transitive clause it is O and not S that names the theme of the clausal event. This assimilation of the DOR to a more general pattern is attractive. It also counts as explanatory, if we regard the End Theme Postulate in (54) as a natural one, following Parsons and Pietroski.

Compare this to the explicit accounts of R-control in (46) or (47). In my view, these fail to provide an equal explanation. S controls hoarse on the subject-depictive analysis of (57), on which it means (57a). So why can't S control hoarse on a resultative analysis of (57), with the result in (57b)? Why should the difference between 'while' in (57a) and 'from' in (57b) matter to the control of secondary predicates?

(57) Ozzy sang *Paranoid* hoarse.

    a   'Ozzy was hoarse while singing *Paranoid*.'
    b * 'Ozzy got hoarse from singing *Paranoid*.'

The two analyses do differ in syntax, witness (58).

(58) a   Ozzy sang his throat hoarse naked.

      b * Ozzy sang his throat naked hoarse.

So perhaps their secondary predicates live in different places, the former below O and the latter above it (Rothstein 1983, 2001). But that does not answer our question, which asks why things cannot be otherwise. Why *not* have a resultative predicate that attaches above O? The resulting meaning, (57b), would be both sensible and easy to derive compositionally. So why is it unavailable? I believe there is no answer, so long as we identify control of R with binding an explicit relation to the R event. Yet it does have an answer, I have argued (Williams, accepted), if we assume that S and O bind Agent and Patient relations to the event of the resultative clause. Also see Williams (2008b) for an

---

[8] Parsons gives a similar account of why (1) below entails that the cutlet was flat. His meaning for (1) is (2), which does not say explicitly that the cutlet is flat. But it does say that the cutlet is the theme of e_2, an event related to the flatness by Become, thus a change that ends in flatness. The postulate in (35) therefore ensures that the flatness too has the cutlet as its theme.

  (1)   Al flattened the cutlet.

  (2) $\lambda e_1 \exists e_2 \exists e_3 [\text{ Agent}(e_1, \text{Al}) \ \& \ \text{Cause}(e_1, e_2)$
          $\& \ \text{Become}(e_2, e_3) \ \& \ \text{Theme}(e_2, \text{the cutlet}) \ \& \ \text{Flatness}(e_3)]$

argument that only this semantics allows us to explain cross-linguistic patterns in the word order of resultatives.

Before leaving this section, let me mention one challenge to the DOR. Some linguists take sentences like those in (59) to contradict the DOR (Verspoor 1997, Wechsler 1997, Rappaport Hovav and Levin 2001).

(59) a The wise men followed the star to Bethlehem.
      b Mary danced across the room.
      c Bruce wriggled free.

Each of these entails that the referent of S traverses a path described by the secondary predicate, and winds up at its terminus: Bethlehem, the other side of the room, or freedom. In this sense S controls that predicate. And yet here, unlike in (44), it is not plausible that S is an O underlyingly. The sentences in (59) would therefore contradict the DOR, were we to assume that they are in fact resultatives, with the same semantic structure as clauses with punch bloody or sing hoarse.

Initially it is reasonable to say that they are, since they do entail that the path is traversed *by means of* a movement that is described by the verb: following, dancing, wriggling. But it is also reasonable to question this, since a shared entailment is on its own a very weak criterion. One also wants evidence that, in the strict sense, the meanings of these sentences share the same structure, and the same relations among their subevents. Some linguists have argued they do not: instead (59) exemplifies a different construction, dedicated to directed movements (Goldberg 1995, Rothstein 2004). There is no reason this construction should also evince the DOR, the objection continues, since it differs from punch bloody or sing hoarse in its meaning and its syntax. For example, in the one construction but not the other, an adverb immediately preceding the secondary predicate can describe the event of the verb, or perhaps also process of movement or change, as shown in (60) (Williams, accepted).

(60) a   Mary danced loudly / gracefully across the room.
      b # Al pounded the cutlet loudly / gracefully flat.

13.6 ARGUMENT SHARING

Most analyses of our pound flat example would assign it a meaning like (61). O binds two distinct relations, one to the pounding and one to the flatness. In some sense, therefore, O is an argument that is shared by both M and R.

(61) ... $\exists e_2 \exists e_3$[... PoundingOf(e_2, the cutlet) & FlatnessOf(e_3, the cutlet)]

How to encode apparent **argument sharing** is a major topic in the theory of argument structure (e.g., Baker 1989). In this section we will therefore suppose that (61) is correct, ignoring various important alternatives, so as to see what it would require of the grammar.

Given our background assumptions, any relation an argument binds must come from a predicate that it c-commands, at some interpreted stage of the derivation.[9] More parochially, I argued in Section 13.3 that resultative meaning does not come from (the lexical heads of) either M or R. Pound and flat in pound flat are satisfied by any pounding or flatness at all, not just those serving as the means or end in a process. Therefore, if O is to bind relations to both the means and the result events, it cannot c-command just M or just R. It must c-command both, as in (62). This is the **Outside Object syntax for resultatives**.

(62) $[\,[^O$ the cutlet $][\ldots[^{MR}$ pound $\ldots$ flat $]\,]]$

Ruled out is (63), the **Small Clause syntax** of Kayne (1985), Hoekstra (1988), Sybesma (1999), Kratzer (2005) and others. Here O forms a constituent with R, to the exclusion of M. (We might call this an 'inside object' syntax.) Given our assumptions, all quite standard, this will not allow O to bind any relation to the M event; I will come back to this shortly.

(63) $[^{MR}\,[^M$ pound $]\,[\ldots[^R\,[^O$ the cutlet $]$ flat $]]\,]$

One final constraint is supplied by a specific conclusion from Section 13.3. There I argued that M contains no more than the verb, a widely agreed conclusion. Consequently it contains no empty category whose referent might be determined by O, neither a trace nor an anaphor. In addition we established in Section 13.3 that MR and M are predicates of different events. So if O is to bind a relation to the means event from outside of MR, the complex predicate must inherit an unsatisfied argument from M. The verb pound must have what is pounded as a semantic argument, as in (64), and pound must transmit this argument to pound flat, yielding (65).

(64) $[\![$ pound $]\!] = \lambda y \ldots \lambda e[\,\text{PoundingOf}(e, y) \ldots]$

(65) $[\![$ pound flat $]\!] = \lambda y \ldots \lambda e_1 \exists e_2 \exists e_3[\,K(e_1, e_2, e_3)\,\&\,\text{PoundingOf}(e_2, y) \ldots]$

This then leaves two options for deriving (61): (66) and (69). In (66), MR contains no noun phrase dependents, neither in M nor in R. Semantically it inherits and identifies the functional arguments of

---

[9] The relevant assumptions are that semantics is nontransformational (Chapter 2), and that there is no Sidewards Movement (Chapter 1).

both its parts, M and R, so that pound flat in (66d) has an argument, marked by λy, that relates both to the pounding and to the flatness.

(66) a $[[^O$ the cutlet $][\ldots[^{MR}$ pound flat $]]]$
     b $[\![\,M\,]\!] = \lambda y \ldots \lambda e[$ PoundingOf$(e, y) \ldots]$
     c $[\![\,R\,]\!] = \lambda y \lambda e[$ FlatnessOf$(e, y)]$
     d $[\![\,MR\,]\!] = \lambda y \ldots \lambda e_1 \exists e_2 \exists e_3[K(e_1, e_2, e_3)$ & PoundingOf(e_2, y)
        & FlatnessOf$(e_3, y) \ldots]$

This derivation has semantic effects similar to those of Conjunction (Bittner 1999, Rothstein 2001). Just as black ewe holds only of something that is both black and a ewe, pound flat on this analysis holds only of something that is both pounded and flat. One way to reach this end technically is by combining M and R under the operation called Konjunction in (67); compare Rothstein (2001:158).

(67) Konjunction(M,R) $\equiv \lambda y \lambda e_1 \exists e_2 \exists e_3[K(e_1, e_2, e_3)$ & $[\![M]\!](y)(e_2)$
     & $[\![R]\!](y)(e_3)]$

Like what I call VP-Conjunction in (68), Konjunction abstracts over the first argument of both its operands, and binds their events existentially. It differs only in introducing the resultative event, e_1, and the eponymous K along with it.[10]

(68) VP-Conjunction(laugh, cry) $\equiv \lambda y \exists e_2 \exists e_3[[\![laugh]\!](y)(e_2)$ & $[\![cry]\!](y)(e_3)]$

For simplicity I ignore in (67) the possibility that M (or R) may have more than one argument, such as an argument for an agent.

Our second live option is (69). Here R includes a silent argument for its head, ϵ_k, either an anaphor or a trace of movement, to be bound eventually by O.

(69) a $[[^O$ the cutlet $]_k [^{MR} [^M$ pound $] [^R \epsilon_k$ flat $]]]$
     b $[\![\,M\,]\!] = \lambda y \ldots \lambda e[$ PoundingOf$(e, y) \ldots]$
     c $[\![\,R\,]\!] = \lambda e[$ FlatnessOf$(e, x)]$
     d $[\![[^{MR} [^M$ pound $] [^R \epsilon_k$ flat $]]\,]\!] = \lambda y \ldots \lambda e_1 \exists e_2 \exists e_3[K(e_1, e_2, e_3)$
        & PoundingOf(e_2, y) & FlatnessOf(e_3, x) & $\ldots]$

The resulting R phrase, $[\, \epsilon_k$ flat $]$, does not itself have an argument. Its meaning, (69c), just includes a free variable, restricted (by movement or anaphora) to have the same value as the cutlet.[11] Therefore the

---

[10] Of course what we do in (67) with a rule of derivation might instead be done with a silent derivational primitive, lexical or nonlexical.

[11] The formal implementation of pronoun binding is not trivial, but I will not discuss this here. See Büring 2004.

derivation of MR need not identify two arguments, as was necessary in (66). MR will only need to inherit the argument of M, as it does under what I call the Komposition operation in (70).

(70) Komposition(M,R) $\equiv \lambda y \lambda e_1 \exists e_2 \exists e_3 [\ [\![M]\!](y)(e_2) \ \& \ [\![R]\!](e_3)$
      $\& \ K(e_1, e_2, e_3) \ ]$

Both (66) and (69) involve some complexity. They require the inheritance (or, inversely, transmission) and identification of unsatisfied arguments. Is such complexity necessary? Some linguists would like to say No, and to that end deny one of our background assumptions.

Most often targeted is the initial premise that, in deriving the meaning of a resultative, O may bind an explicit relation to the means event. This is denied by every proponent of the Small Clause syntax in (63), for example. Absent this premise, there is no object-sharing in any resultative, and no need to account for it. But the simplification comes at a cost. It leaves us with no good account for (71) and (72).

(71)   Al cut the bone open, so Al cut the bone.

(72)   * Al cut the knife dull.

For those who deny that the bone in cut the bone open binds a relation to the cutting, the inference in (71) is not strictly analytic. So what explains its force? If we say it is pragmatic and defeasible (Hoekstra 1988, Sybesma 1999, Kratzer 2005), we cannot explain why English (72) is unacceptable. For it is fine to say that Al dulled his knife in cutting the bone, where the effect on the knife is surely direct. Indeed in Igbo we can even express this with a resultative, as we saw above in (51), repeated here.

(51)   Eze   bi   kpụ -rụ   mma ahụ.
       E.   cut dull -FACT   knife that
       'Eze made his knife dull from cutting.'

So we should prefer to say that (71) does indeed express an entailment, if not an analyticity. But without an explicit semantic relation between O and M, this will require a meaning postulate. We need to stipulate that, when $K(e_1, e_2, e_3)$, events e_2 and e_3 have the same theme. This will account for both (71) and (72). But as already noted in Section 13.5, this stipulation is unattractive in the face of unselected objects, as in Igbo (51), or in our sing hoarse example. Furthermore, the valid inference in (73) will pose an additional challenge.

(73)   Al cut the bone open, so Al cut something.

Plausibly, the base position of AI, the subject, is outside of MR. For if it were inside of M, it would be hard to explain why M cannot accommodate adverbs (Section 13.4). Outside of MR, AI can bind a relation to the event of the clause, without difficulty. But it can bind a relation to the M event, the cutting, only if MR inherits an argument from M. So without rules of argument inheritance, (73) will mandate yet another postulate for K: when $K(e_1, e_2, e_3)$, events e_1 and e_2, the process and its means, have the same agent. This is not wholly unreasonable; see Williams (2014a) for discussion in a cross-linguistic setting. But it certainly adds to the cost of keeping the derivation simple by forbidding inheritance of arguments. If MR cannot inherit an argument from M, entailed relations to the means event must either be secured by postulates of little generality, or go entirely without account.

In Sections 13.4 and 13.5 I endorsed the Outside Relations Semantics for resultatives, whereby S and O are assigned Agent and Patient relations to the process described by MR. If this is correct, and if M also has arguments, there will be a different sort of argument sharing: M may share S or O *with* MR. Grammatically, this might involve any of the mechanisms already discussed. I leave consideration of the various possibilities to the reader, and illustrate just one (perhaps the simplest) in (75). Here sharing of O is implemented by the conjunction operation defined in (74).

(74) $\text{Conjunction}^e_V[f, g] \equiv \lambda x \lambda e[f(x)(e) \ \& \ g(x)(e)]$

(75) a $[\![\text{pound flat}]\!] = \lambda y \lambda e_1 \exists e_2 \exists e_3 [\ K(e_1, e_2, e_3) \ \& \ \text{PoundingOf}(e_2, y) \ \& \ \text{Flatness}(e_3) \ ]$

　　　b $[\![\text{PT}]\!] = \lambda y \lambda e [\ \text{Patient}(e, y) \ ]$

　　　c $[\![\ [\text{PT} [\text{pound flat}]] \ ]\!] = \text{Conjunction}^e_V[(75a), (75b)]$
　　　　　$= \lambda y \lambda e_1 \exists e_2 \exists e_3 [\ K(e_1, e_2, e_3) \ \& \ \text{PoundingOf}(e_2, y) \ \& \ \text{Flatness}(e_3) \ \& \ \text{Patient}(e_1, y) \ ]$

　　　d $[\![\ [\text{the cutlet} [\text{PT} [\text{pound flat}]]] \ ]\!] = \text{Application}[(75c), [\![\text{the cutlet}]\!]]$
　　　　　$= \lambda y \lambda e_1 \exists e_2 \exists e_3 [\ K(e_1, e_2, e_3) \ \& \ \text{PoundingOf}(e_2, \text{the cutlet}) \ \& \ \text{Flatness}(e_3) \ \& \ \text{Patient}(e_1, \text{the cutlet}) \ ]$

In (75a), pound flat has an argument for what is pounded. This is identified with the Patient argument of PT, along with the event arguments of the two predicates, in deriving (75c) under Conjunction^e_V. Application then combines O with the result.

13.7 PROJECTION, SEPARATION AND M

When M contains no more than the verb, resultatives distinguish between projectionist and separationist encodings of arguments

(Williams 2005, 2008a). The addition of resultative structure, hence the event to which the events of M and R are related, then serves as what in Chapter 9 I called a *semantic wedge*. It allows us to tell whether or not the verb in M has arguments.

The outline of the reasoning is this. In English and many other languages, a verb in M enters the same pattern of argument dependencies as it does in basic, nonresultative clauses. This is expected if those relations project from the verb, and is otherwise hard to explain. But not every language is like English. In Igbo and Mandarin, unlike in English, resultatives do not inherit the argument structure that the verb in M inhabits when solo. For these languages, this contributes to a case against projection and for separation of the argument relations from the verb.

Let me now unravel this, beginning with English. Here verbs generally enter the same patterns of argument relations in M as they do in simple nonresultative clauses. Take cut and sing, for example. On their own, both verbs occur in an active clause only if S names the agent of their event. In (76a) S names the cutter of the bones, while (76b) and (76c) are unacceptable. Similarly in (77) S must name the singer.

(76) a Lee cut the bones.
    b * The bones cut Lee.
       'Lee cut the bones.'
    c * The bones cut.
       'The bones got cut.'

(77) a Mo sang (the intro).
    b * The intro sang Mo.
       'Mo sang the intro.'
    c * The intro sang.
       'The intro got sung.'

The data in (78) and (79) now show that this same pattern is expressed when these verbs occupy M in a resultative clause. Here too S always names the agent of their event.

(78) a Lee cut the bones open.
    b * The bones cut the knife dull.
       'The bones made the knife dull from [its] cutting [them].'
    c * The bones cut open.
       'The bones came open from [something] cutting [them].'

(79) a Mo sang her throat hoarse.
    b * The intro sang Mo hoarse.
       'The intro made Mo hoarse from [her] singing [it].'
    c * Mo's throat sang hoarse.
       'Mo's throat got hoarse from [her] singing.'

Likewise, the transitivity of the verb is expressed equally in simple and resultative clauses. That is, to whatever extent the verb on its own must occupy a clause whose O names the patient or theme of the verb's event, the same is true in resultatives. Cut is highly transitive. In general it occurs in an active clause only if that clause has an O that names what is cut. So, except in special circumstances – for example, where the chore of cutting some relevant stuff is topical – (80) is unacceptable.

(80)   * Lee cut.
       'Lee cut [something].'

And now again when cut is in a resultative, O must name what is cut, except in those same special circumstances. Sentences like (81) are in general unacceptable (Dowty 1979:222, Carrier and Randall 1992:187, Levin and Rappaport Hovav 1995:39, but compare Boas 2003:113, Williams 2005:102ff.).

(81)   * Lee cut the knife dull.
       'Lee made the knife dull by cutting [something].'

Nothing names what is sung in (79a). But again this matches the distribution of the verb, here sing, when it exhausts the clausal predicate. In a simple clause like (77a), sing is fine without an O to name what is sung. It is not highly transitive. As a final example, consider freeze. On its own it can occur in an intransitive clause, as in (82), but only if S names what freezes. And again the same is true when it occupies M. Sentence (83) below entails that the lake froze and (84) is accordingly impossible.

(82)   The lake froze.

(83)   The lake froze solid.

(84)   * The pier froze apart last winter (despite never freezing).
       'The pier came apart from something [say, the surrounding water] freezing.'

Thus in English, MR inherits the behavior of M, in addition to properties associated with the resultative structure itself.

This pattern has a tidy explanation if arguments project from the verb. Suppose that cut in (76) has the cutter and cut as obligatory DP arguments, syntactically and semantically. Arguments must be satisfied wherever the verb occurs; and all else being equal, by phrases of a selected syntactic category, such as NP, and not by a passive or antipassive morpheme. So if this same cut occurs not only in (76a) but also the resultative (78a), both sentences will have S and O as content arguments of cut, and both will entail that Lee cut the bones. Correspondingly, both (80) and (81) are impossible for the same reason, namely that cut has an inappropriately unsatisfied internal argument. The same points go for sing and freeze, *mutatis mutandis*. English resultatives therefore provide a good case for a projectionist treatment of argument relations, a point made very influentially in Levin and Rappaport (1995).

What if thematic relations were instead separated from the verb? Concretely, what if (76a) had an underlying structure something like (85), with Agent and Patient relations introduced by silent morphemes AG and PT?

(85)   [Lee [AG [the bones [PT [cut]]]]]

The observed facts would then be expected only if, in a resultative, there were to be AG and PT morphemes *inside* of M, as in (86) for example. For only in this position would AG and PT introduce relations to the event of M, to be bound by S and O.

(86)   [Lee$_j$ [the bones$_k$ [^{MR} [^{M} ϵ_j AG [ϵ_k PT cut]] [^{R} open]]]]

Outside of M, as in (87), AG and PT would instead introduce relations to the event of MR, the process of cutting open. Since the cutting open is distinct from its constituent cutting (Section 13.4), (87) will not then entail that Lee cut the bones.

(87)   [Lee [AG [the bones [PT [^{MR} [^{M} cut] [^{R} open]]]]]]

So, if we want to capture this apparent entailment formally, as seems desirable, we will have to adopt (86), with AG and PT inside of M. But there are two problems with (86). First and most important, it contradicts the assumption, both standard and well justified, that M in English contains no more than the verb. Second, (86) leaves unclear why the agent-of-M role, here the role of cutter, should be bound by S rather than O (here, Lee rather than the bones) when O is structurally the nearest binder for this role. These two problems push against the separationist analysis for English.

The facts of Mandarin and Igbo, however, push in the opposite direction for exactly the same reasons (Williams 2005, 2008a). Here I will only discuss Igbo, as Mandarin is the same in the relevant regards (Williams 2014b; compare Li 1995, 1999, and Huang *et al.* 2009). And, for simplicity, I will just discuss the interpretation of O in resultatives; on the trickier case of S, see Williams (2014a).

Systematically, O in an Igbo resultative may be unselected, even when the verb in M is transitive. That is, even a verb that on its own must occur with an O naming its patient need not do so when in M. For example, in Igbo the verb bi 'cut' can occur only in transitive clauses where O names what got cut, as in (88a). O cannot be dropped, as in (88b), or bind some other relation to the cutting, as in (88c).

(88) a   Eze   bi   -ri   osisi.
          E.   cut -FACT   wood
          'Eze cut a stick.'
      b * Eze   bi   -ri   (ebi).
          E.   cut -FACT   (BVC)
          'Eze cut [stuff].'
      c * Eze   bi   -ri   mma   (n'   osisi).
          E.   cut -FACT   knife PREP   wood
          'Eze cut with a knife (at wood).'

Yet the same restrictions do not apply when bi 'cut' is in M. In (89) bi is part of bi kpụ 'cut dull.' The sentence entails that the knife is what became dull as a result of some cutting, but not that it got cut. Thus no overt dependent in (89) names the patient of cutting; nor does Igbo have pronouns that could do the job inaudibly.[12]

(89) Eze   bi   kpụ -rụ   mma.
      E.   cut dull -FACT   knife
      'Eze made the knife dull from cutting.'

This has a good explanation if bi 'cut' does not have what is cut as an argument. Semantically, it may be simply a predicate of cuttings, as in (90).

(90) $[\![$ bi 'cut' $]\!] = \lambda e[$ Cutting(e) $]$

The Patient relation is then introduced instead by some other part of the derivation, let us again say PT. When the predicate of the clause contains just the verb bi 'cut,' as in (91a), PT will introduce the patient of cutting. Derivation (91a) will have the meaning in (91b).

(91) a [Eze [AG [osisi 'stick' [PT [bi 'cut']]]]]
      b $\lambda e[$ Agent(e, Eze) & Cutting(e) & Patient(e, the stick)]

Now consider resultatives. For Igbo, as for Mandarin (Thompson 1973, Li 1990, Huang 1992), it is standard to assume that M contains just the verb, and no dependents (Lord 1975, Hale et al. 1995). For us this implies that M does not contain PT either; see Section 13.3. And, as a

[12] Most likely, the reason that the knife got dull from cutting is because it was the instrument of that cutting. But presumably this is just a plausible inference, and not an aspect of sentence meaning. The instrument relation does not project from the verb, given (88c). And it is implausible to say that the construction is ambiguous, with one of its meanings imposing an instrumental relation on the object.

consequence, MR will not state any patient relation to the event of M. Instead it will mean something like (92).

(92) $[\![$ bi kpụ 'cut dull' $]\!]$
$= \lambda e_1 \exists e_2 \exists e_3[\ K(e_1, e_2, e_3)\ \&\ \text{Cutting}(e_1)\ \&\ \text{Dullness}(e_3)\ ]$

This complex predicate may occupy a clause whose O is introduced by PT, as in (93). Then O will name the patient of the event of bi kpụ 'cut dull,' as in (94).

(93) [Eze [AG [mma 'knife' [PT [^{MR} bi kpụ 'cut dull']]]]]
(94) $\exists e[\ \text{Agent}(e, \text{Eze})\ \&\ [\![\text{bi kpụ}]\!](e)\ \&\ \text{Patient}(e, \text{the knife})\ ]$

This says only that the knife is the patient of a process that is brought about by cutting, and ends with dullness. This entails that the knife got dull, but not that it got cut. We are free to infer any relation between the knife and the cutting that is compatible with what (94) does say: Eze dulled the knife by means of a cutting. One plausible inference is that the cutting had the knife as its instrument.

So if verbs in Igbo characteristically have no arguments, we understand why O in this language may in general be unselected – even with verbs with meanings like 'cut,' 'poke,' 'carry,' 'tread on' or 'throw.' Attractively, the prediction depends only on the uncontroversial assumption that M contains only the verb. Were we to assume instead that verbs do have arguments in Igbo, we would have to stipulate they are eliminated exactly in the context of M, lest Igbo be just like English. But this stipulation has no clear basis. For further discussion see Williams (2008a, 2014a and 2014b).

DISCUSSION POINTS

1 Do you know a language with a resultative construction, other than English? What combinations of M and R are natural in that language? Does the language differ from English in which combinations are natural? Does it allow cut open, cook soft or fry crisp? How about cook white, punch unconscious or drag smooth? Can you see patterns in what works and what doesn't?

2 From examples like (89) in Section 13.7, we learned that Igbo is a language where, quite generally, O in a resultative need not be selected. Can this be reconciled to the hypothesis that children acquiring Igbo are guided by Participant-to-Argument Matching, discussed in Chapter 11? If not, why not? If so, how? In answering, think carefully about the difference between our rival semantic

analyses for resultatives, the causing event semantics and the process semantics.

3 What does (1) below show about the structure of resultatives? (See Beck and Snyder 2001, Beavers and Koontz-Garboden 2012.) Consider the question first from the perspective of a fully syntactic analysis of resultatives, and then from the perspective of the partly or fully lexical analysis.

(1) a   Today Al pounded the cutlet flat, after pounding it yesterday to no
          effect whatsoever.
     b ⊭ Today Al pounded the cutlet flat again.

Many speakers agree with (2). Reconsider your responses to (1) in light of this. Does the relevance of (2) differ between the syntactic and lexical views?

(2) a   The dough was flat. After it rose, Al pounded it flat.
     b ⊨ Al pounded it flat again.

4 Synder (2001) makes two remarkable generalizations. First, languages that productively allow resultatives also productively allow "endocentric root compounds," such as English frog man or glove box. Second, compounds and resultatives emerge together in child language acquisition. What does this suggest about the child's analysis of these constructions? Does it suggest anything about the derivation of resultative clauses in the adult language – and, if so, is there other evidence that pushes against these suggestions?

5 In Mandarin, as in English, the subject of a clause whose predicate means 'sing' must name the singer: (3) is impossible. Under a projectionist treatment, this implies that chang 'sing' has a singer argument that projects to the subject.

(3) * Nashou   gequ   chang -le   wo.
       that   song   sing -PFV   1s
       'I sang that song.'

In clauses with chang ya 'sing hoarse,' however, the referent of the subject can be either the singer, (4), or the song, (5). So if chang 'sing' does have a singer argument, it projects differently here (Li 1995). But why would that be? Can you think of another account of these data, on which arguments do not project differently in different contexts?

(4) Wo   chang   ya   -le   sangzi.
     1s   sing   hoarse -PFV   throat
     'I made my throat hoarse from singing.'

(5) Nashou gequ chang ya   -le   wo.
    that   song   sing   hoarse -PFV 1s
    'That song made me hoarse from singing.'

Now consider event structure. What analysis would a causing event semantics assign to (4), and to (5)? On that semantics, why might (6) be a problem? (See Williams 2009.)

(6) Bu shi ni chang -de   ge   chang ya   -le   nide
    NEG COP 2s sing -NMOD song sing hoarse -PFV your
    sangzi! Shi ni ziji!
    throat COP 2s SELF
    'It's not the song you sang that sang your throat hoarse! It's you yourself!'

6 Suppose that the subject of a clause whose event is an action always names the agent of that action. Under a causing event semantics for resultatives, the entailment in (7) then follows immediately. But this is not so under a process semantics. Say why.

(7) a Al cut the bone open.
     b ⊨ Al cut something.

What options are open to the proponent of the process semantics, for capturing (7)? How is the range of options affected by (8), or Mandarin (5)?

(8) The bone dulled Al's knife.

7 Wechsler (2005a) gives an account of contrasts like that in (9). He says that, when O is "a semantic argument" of M, as it is by assumption in (9), R must express a property with a maximal degree. Cleanness has a maximal degree, but things can always get dirtier.

(9) a He wiped the table clean.
     b * He wiped the table dirty.

To motivate this proposal, Wechsler makes two further claims. First, "telicity is a constructional feature of resultatives," so that a resultative must imply an intrinsic conclusion for its event. Second, the resultative predicate will be telic only if R expresses a property with a maximal degree. Wiping a table dirty could go on forever, since a table can always get dirtier.

Many other languages, including Mandarin and Igbo, are not like English. In constructions that appear to be resultatives, one finds predicates in R with meanings like 'dirty,' 'bad,' 'wet,'

'angry' or 'tired,' none of which have maximal degrees in principle. Mandarin allows the equivalent of (9b), for instance

Because his account of (9) has several parts, there are several
ways Wechsler might respond to such facts. Try to think of a few of
them. Are there some you find plausible? To assess the plausibility
of a certain response, what facts would you want to know about
the relevant language?

8 Sentence (10) is an example of the *way*-construction. Is this a kind
of resultative construction? What facts suggest a positive answer?
(See Marantz 1992.) Do (11) and (12) (Jackendoff 1990b:212) suggest
a negative answer?

(10)   Al slashed his way through the dense bush.

(11)   Al slashed his way slowly and angrily through the dense bush
        (#rapidly).
        'Al (#rapidly) got through the bush slowly and angrily by slashing.'

(12)   * Al pounded the cutlet slowly and angrily flat.
        'Al made the cutlet flat slowly and angrily by pounding it.'

SUGGESTIONS FOR FURTHER READING

Beavers 2012 is an excellent overview, touching on many topics I do
not address in this chapter. Levin and Rappaport Hovav 1995 and
Rappaport Hovav and Levin 2001 are central discussions. Rothstein
2004 illuminates resultatives in the light of a broader class of complex
predicates. Kratzer 2005 is very clear about both the theoretical and
empirical motives for a version of the Small Clause analysis. On the
acquisition of resultatives, read Snyder 2001. Larson 1991 discusses
resultatives in the context of verb serialization, cross-linguistically.
Washio 1997 makes important observations about variation in which
combinations of M and R are acceptable. On resultatives in Mandarin,
see Huang *et al.* 2009 and Williams 2014a, 2014b.

Glossary

Terms in SMALL CAPS have a glossary entry.

A-checking rule A rule of derivation that combines HEAD B and DEPENDENT A, eliminating a minor category feature of B when its value matches a category feature of A (see SYNTACTIC CATEGORY: MINOR).

A-feature A category feature that may be targeted (checked) by an a-checking rule.

A-list A list of a-features. "Subcategorization frames" are a kind of a-list.

Being a syntactic argument of A is a SYNTACTIC ARGUMENT *of* B just when B takes A as a syntactic argument.

Having a syntactic argument Expression B *has* a syntactic argument exactly when it has an a-feature.

Taking a syntactic argument Head B *takes* dependent A as a SYNTACTIC ARGUMENT just when they combine under an a-checking rule, eliminating an a-feature of B that matches a category feature of A. If B HEADS C, and C takes D as an argument, then B also takes D as an argument.

Actor An individual viewed as initiating an *act*, an event that issues from the will or is "intentional under some description" (Davidson 1971).

Agent An individual viewed as directly involved in bringing about an event, given what sort of event it is taken to be. Other names for a similar category are "Effector" and "Initiator."

Ambiguity See INDETERMINACY.

Analytic entailment X ENTAILS Y 'just because of what it means,' or since X has Y as 'part of its meaning.'

Strict Y can be proven from X, using rules of (some pertinent) logic, just with reference to form. This is the relation of SYNTACTIC CONSEQUENCE, which I write as X ⊢ Y. A strict analyticity is *overt* when the formal structure in X that licenses the proof of Y is obvious. Otherwise it is *covert*.

Application A semantic operation that, given function f and a member of its domain a, returns b whenever $\langle a, b \rangle \in f$.

Argument diagnostics Observable patterns that provide conditional evidence for whether or not a DEPENDENT is a SYNTACTIC ARGUMENT in its phrase.

Iterability If expression C has a part A in semantic role R, and [C D] (order irrelevant) is acceptable with dependent D in exactly the same role as R, this is evidence that D is a SYNTACTIC ADJUNCT.

Movement If extraction out of a non-subject dependent clause A is acceptable, this is initial evidence that A is a SYNTACTIC ARGUMENT.

Omissibility If removing a dependent A results in unacceptability, this is initial evidence that A is a SYNTACTIC ARGUMENT.

Strandability If a rule of derivation applies acceptably to [B A] (order irrelevant) but not to HEAD B alone, this is initial evidence that A is a SYNTACTIC ARGUMENT.

Substitution by pro-forms If a pro-form can substitute for [B A] (order irrelevant) but not for head B alone, this is initial evidence that A is a SYNTACTIC ARGUMENT.

Argument sharing A single overt dependent (seemingly) binds relations to the events of two distinct predicates.

In resultatives A single overt dependent, subject or object, (seemingly) binds relations to the events of at least two of the predicates M, R or MR.

A-theory (of reason clauses) The claim that CONTROL of REASON CLAUSES is mediated by a syntactic dependency to the TARGET CLAUSE, and determined with reference to a syntactic property of that clause, namely its list of syntactic arguments.

Base Argument Theory (BAT) of passives Some syntactic part of a SHORT PASSIVE, and some part of the host in a LONG PASSIVE, has a FUNCTIONAL SEMANTIC ARGUMENT in the DEEP-S ROLE. In general this corresponds to a SYNTACTIC ARGUMENT OF that part as well. An analysis that is not a BAT is a NoBAT.

Adjunct-by variety The syntactic derivation of a short passive eliminates the argument in the deep-S role.

Argument-by variety In a long passive the deep-S role is bound by the by-phrase.

Pronominal variety The deep-S role is instantiated by a silent pronoun.

Bound reading When an expression with an UNREALIZED ROLE is in the scope of a quantifier, the role has a bound reading just when its values are in the set denoted by its restriction. For example, *No contest was enjoyed by the guy who won* has a meaning which entails that the contests won, an unrealized role, are exactly the contests in the domain for *no*.

Canonical correspondence The assumption that every SYNTACTIC ARGUMENT of an expression is also a FUNCTIONAL SEMANTIC ARGUMENT, and vice versa.

Causing event semantics Describes a transitive clause as meaning that one event e_1 causes another e_2, where e_1 involves the subject-referent and e_2 involves the object-referent. E.g., Floyd hardened the glass might mean 'Floyd's actions (e_1) caused the glass's hardening (e_2).'

For resultatives A RESULTATIVE clause with predicate MR means: 'an M event caused (the coming about of) an R event.'

Complex event structure See EVENT STRUCTURE.

Composition A semantic operation that, given two functions f and g, yields a new function $\lambda x[f(gx)]$.

Compositional semantics The theory of DERIVED MEANINGS.

Conjunction A semantic operation that, given two functions f and g, yields a new function $\lambda x[fx \& gx]$.

Content (semantic) argument A is a content argument of B just when, in the derivation, A binds a relation that 'comes from' B. That is, B HAS a FUNCTIONAL ARGUMENT that it 'contributes' to a containing expression D, and D then *takes* A as a FUNCTIONAL ARGUMENT.

Contextual features See SYNTACTIC ARGUMENT.

Control of a reason clause Semantic role R controls a REASON CLAUSE expressing predicate P when we understand that the same individual x satisfies both R and P. With the ship was sunk to collect insurance, we understand that the same individual is both the ship-sinker (R) and the insurance-collector (P).

Control of a result predicate A RESULTATIVE with result predicate R entails that some individual x changes, ending up in a state defined by R. The overt dependent that names x controls R. E.g., in pound it flat, it controls flat.

Covarying reading When an expression with an UNREALIZED ROLE is in the scope of a quantifier, the role has a covarying reading when its understood values vary with the individuals in the set denoted by the quantifier's restriction. E.g., in Every guy who put chips on 17 won, the contests won vary as a function of the guys in the domain of every.

Covert analyticity See ANALYTICITY.

Deep-S(ubject) role The semantic role associated with the surface subject in an ordinary active clause.

Demotion Two clauses with the 'same' verb are related by demotion of the DEEP-S ROLE only if: that role is bound by the subject in one, but neither the subject nor the object in the other; the role is existential when unrealized (see UNREALIZED ROLE: EXISTENTIAL); and the two clauses are satisfied by the same sorts of events.

Dependent An immediate part of an expression that does not HEAD it. If A is a dependent in C, and C immediately heads D, then A is also a dependent in D.

Derivational part A token primitive, or a token application of a rule, in a derivation. Also referred to as a *part of a derivation*.

Derived meaning When an expression has meaningful parts in SYNTAX or in LEXICON, its meaning is derived.

Direct causation   A transitive clause describing a change is sometimes said to ENTAIL that events involving the subject referent cause a certain condition in the object referent, in a way that is somehow *direct*. E.g., Floyd hardened the glass is said to entail that events involving Floyd *directly caused* the glass's becoming hard.

Direct Object Restriction   R in a RESULTATIVE clause is CONTROLLED by the underlying direct object.

Displacement   Two expressions are displaced when they are syntactically and/or semantically related, but separated in the surface string by 'unrelated' material, as the chair and carry are in The chair tends to seem to be easy to carry.

Endocentricity   Every expression with syntactic parts has a head.

Entail   See ENTAILMENT.

Entailed role   Relative to predicate B, an entailed role is a relation that any B must bear to something. E.g., if it is necessary that every dog is *at* some place, then "At" is an entailed role for dog.

Entailed role argument   A is an entailed role argument of B just when, in the derivation, A binds a relation that is an entailed role for B.

Entailment   X entails Y when every circumstance where X is true is also one where Y is true. This is the relation of *semantic consequence*, which I write $X \models Y$.

Event semantics   The assumption that a clause is a predicate of an event ($\lambda e[\, P(e)\,]$), which comes to be existentially quantified ($\exists e[\, P(e)\,]$).

Event structure   An event structure is a description of the clause as an event predicate, one which may relate the main event to one or more other events.

> **Complex event structure**   An event structure with more than one event predicate.
>
> **Main event**   A clause is a predicate of events, $\lambda e[\, P(e)\,]$. That predicate, P, is a predicate of the clause's 'main event.'
>
> **Subevent**   An event to which the main event is related in the event structure.

Event structure, motives for

> **From adverbs**   Sometimes an adverb can describe either the main event or a subevent. If those events are described by separate parts of the clause, this can be described as an ambiguity in which part the adverb attaches to.
>
> **From form**   Structure in the event-structural SEMANTIC DECOMPOSITION corresponds to morphological structure, as in hard-en.
>
> **From inferences**   Complexity in the event structure allows us to generalize over patterns of inference, like from The glass hardened to The glass was hard, or from The glass melted to The glass was liquid.
>
> **From unattested meanings**   Sometimes event-structural SEMANTIC DECOMPOSITION is claimed to limit what content a word can have.

Event-structural thematic relations The semantic relation bound by a dependent A is the composition of two relations, Θ and R, where Θ relates A's referent x to an event e_1, while R relates e_1 and another event e_2.

Framing A predicate occupies a *frame* of semantically related satellite phrases, an argument structure. Framing generalizations describe patterns in which predicates occupy which frames.

Functional (semantic) argument A is a functional semantic argument of B in [B A], order irrelevant, just in case the value of the latter is derived as $[\![B]\!]([\![A]\!])$.

> **Having a functional argument** B has a functional argument just when there is a derivation of [B A] or [A B] where A is a functional argument of B.
>
> **Taking a functional argument** B *takes* A as a functional argument just when A is a functional semantic argument of B.

General rules Rules that do not refer to specific categories, such as *verb* or *noun*. Rules that are not general are specific.

Generality See INDETERMINACY.

Head An immediate part B of an expression C from which C INHERITS its category. If B heads C, and C immediately heads D, B also heads D. A LEXICAL ITEM that heads an expression is *the head* of that expression.

Implicit argument in the broad sense An UNREALIZED ROLE associated with some linguistic generalization, syntactic, semantic, pragmatic or psychological.

Implicit argument in the narrow sense An UNREALIZED ROLE that participates in some grammatical dependency, semantic or syntactic, that is otherwise available only to an overt dependent.

Indeterminacy The form of the expression does not on its own make clear what the speaker means to (literally or directly) say in using the expression.

> **Ambiguity** Two expressions with the same sound but different meanings, like franks with mustard and Franks with mustaches.
>
> **Generality** The meaning of a predicate subsumes that of some relevant others, as with meat relative to venison.
>
> **Polysemy** A single expression that is not indexical (me, here) or deictic (him, that), but still has various possible values on different uses, even relative to the same domain of discourse. Potential examples include France (nation or territory), book (content or object) and sad (person or music).
>
> **Vagueness** The boundary between satisfying and not satisfying the predicate is intrinsically uncertain, as with tall.

Inheritance Expression C with immediate part B inherits its category from B when it is derived by a rule that sets its major category to that of B. The inverse of inheritance is *transmission*. When B transmits its category to C, it HEADS C.

Instrumental subject   The subject of a clause made true by a situation in which the subject's referent was in fact wielded as an instrument.

Ambiguity theory   An instrumental subject binds a different relation than does a noninstrumental subject with the same verb. A nonambiguity theory denies this.

Lexical item   A primitive part of a derivation in SYNTAX.

Lexicalist encoding (of arguments)   Encodes argument relations by means of A-FEATURES and highly general A-CHECKING RULES.

Lexicalized primitives   Derivational primitives that have a phonetic interpretation, if only as the empty string. A syntax with only lexicalized primitives is itself *lexicalized*.

Lexicalized syntax   A syntax all of whose primitives are lexicalized.

Lexicon   A level of analysis whose domain is the set of primitives for SYNTAX, the LEXICAL ITEMS.

Linking   The grammatical association of a semantic with a syntactic relation. Linking generalizations describe patterns in linking.

Major category   See SYNTACTIC ARGUMENT.

Meaning   The invariant contribution an expression makes to restricting the SEMANTIC VALUES of its uses.

Mentalist semantics   SEMANTIC VALUES are inside the mind.

Minor category   See SYNTACTIC ARGUMENT.

Movement   A syntactic operation on an expression E that takes a part of E, and attaches it elsewhere, standardly to E itself (that is, at its root). Often movement is used to encode DISPLACEMENT relations.

Nonlexicalist encoding (of arguments)   Not a LEXICALIST ENCODING of argument relations.

   Rule-based   Encodes argument relations by means of category-specific rules of derivation.

   Constructional   Encodes argument relations by means of NONLEXICALIZED PRIMITIVES, which themselves have arguments that may be category-specific.

Nonlexicalized primitives   Derivational primitives that are not phonetically interpreted. A syntax with some nonlexicalized primitives is itself *nonlexicalized*.

Nontransformational semantics   A semantics whose rules of combination (derivation) do not refer to any structure in what they apply to, or to their derivational history. Every common linguistic theory presupposes a nontransformational semantics, which is often regarded as an aspect of *compositionality*.

Objectivist semantics   SEMANTIC VALUES are in general outside the mind.

Obliqueness Hierarchy   An ordering of syntactic relations used in grammatical generalizations, including LINKING rules. One common version is: Subject < Object < Obliques.

Outside Object syntax for resultatives   The direct object in a RESULTATIVE clause is outside of MR, c-commanding both M and R. For *pound it flat*, this would give: [it [pound. . . flat]].

Outside Relations semantics for resultatives   Subject and object in a RESUL-
TATIVE clause bind semantic relations to the event of MR, besides any
relations they might bind to the events of M or R.

Overt analyticity   See ANALYTICITY.

Participant   An individual viewed as related to event *e* by a PARTICIPANT ROLE
for predicate B.

Participant role   A participant role for B is one that is represented by an
explicit constituent of the SKETCH for B.

Participant argument   A is a participant argument of B just in case, in the
derivation, A instantiates a relation that is a PARTICIPANT ROLE for B.

Participant-to-Argument Matching (PAM)   The assumption that argument
NPs in a clause exactly match the PARTICIPANTS in its event, one-to-one.
This has been claimed to guide language acquisition in young children.

Passive   One kind of a construction where the DEEP-SUBJECT ROLE is demoted.
In general, the demoted role is claimed to be an IMPLICIT ARGUMENT,
when it is UNREALIZED (that is, in a short passive).

> **Long passive**   A passive with an overt dependent binding the DEEP-
> SUBJECT ROLE, like the English by-phrase.
>
> **Short passive**   A passive with no overt dependent binding the DEEP-
> SUBJECT ROLE.

Patient or Theme   Generally, a PARTICIPANT viewed as 'undergoing' the event
as it is described by the verb.

> **Changee**   In a change, the participant whose properties determine its
> end, like the glass in an event of its melting. Often called the
> patient or theme of the change.
>
> **Happenee**   The participant in a non-change that is viewed as "having
> something happen to it," like the glass in an event of Floyd touch-
> ing it. Often called the patient or theme of the event.
>
> **Holder**   The holder of a state is sometimes called its patient or theme,
> like the glass in an event of its being liquid.

Polysemy   See INDETERMINACY.

Prelexical item   A primitive part of an analysis (derivation) in LEXICON.

Prelexical syntax   Rules that relate LEXICAL ITEMS to PRELEXICAL ITEMS; speaking derivationally, rules that derive LEXICAL from PRELEXICAL ITEMS.

Principle of Interpretability   Each syntactic part of an expression must have
a meaning, and thus "be in the domain of the interpretation function"
(Heim and Kratzer 1998).

Process/Means distinctness   The event of MR in a RESULTATIVE need not satisfy M.

Process semantics   Describes a transitive clause as a predicate of a process
with the subject- and object-referents as its agent and patient.

> **For resultatives**   MR means: 'An event ending with an R event was
> achieved by means of an M event.'

Projectionist analysis   The semantic relation bound by a dependent A – due
to which A's referent has an ENTAILED relation to the event of a nearby

verb V – is introduced lexically by V itself, linked to a FUNCTIONAL SEMANTIC ARGUMENT of V. An analysis that is not projectionist is SEPARATIONIST.

Promotion   The surface subject binds a role, said to be promoted, other than the demoted DEEP-S role.

Rationale clause   See REASON CLAUSE.

Reason clause   Also called a *rationale clause*. This is a nonfinite clause construed as giving a teleological explanation for the fact expressed by its TARGET CLAUSE. In The ship was sunk to collect the insurance, the reason clause to collect the insurance is adjoined to its target clause, The ship was sunk.

Remote control   Cases where a REASON CLAUSE is CONTROLLED across sentences, thus neither by a role that is linked to an argument in its syntactic host, nor by the fact expressed by its host. E.g., the sinker of the ship may be the understood collector of insurance in: The ship was sunk. It was horrible. The only reason was to collect the insurance.

Responsibility theory (of reason clauses)   CONTROL of REASON CLAUSES is discourse anaphora, with the understood subject of the reason clause construed as ranging only over parties viewed as explanatorily responsible for the fact expressed by the TARGET CLAUSE.

Resultative   A resultative is a single clause, like Al pounded it flat, comprising two overt predicates, neither introduced by a conjunction or adposition, where one describes the end of a process (flat), and the other, the means by which it was achieved (pound).

> **M**   The part of a resultative that describes the means of achieving its event, like pound in pound flat.
>
> **R**   The part of a resultative that describes the end of its event, like flat in pound flat.
>
> **MR**   The smallest constituent containing both M and R.

Role Exhaustion   When a dependent is assigned a relation to some (group of) event(s), it identifies *all and only* the individuals in that relation to that (those) event(s). Something like this is also known as *Thematic Uniqueness*.

Role Iteration Generalization (RIG)   Generally or always, two distinct dependents do not bind the exact same type of semantic relation to the same event.

Semantic bootstrapping   Inferring something about the syntactic distribution of an expression based on its apparent meaning, in the process of language acquisition.

Semantic consequence   See ENTAILMENT.

Semantic decomposition   The SEMANTIC VALUE of an expression is described using a formula that has more parts than the expression itself seems to have.

> **Strict**   The complexity of the formula matches nonobvious structure in the MEANING or SEMANTIC VALUE itself.
>
> **Representational**   The complexity is only in a SEMANTIC REPRESENTATION.

Metasemantic The complexity corresponds to nothing in the language.

Semantic representation A formula representing the MEANING of an expression, used in some grammatical generalization or rule, but not the meaning itself.

Semantic value Something outside the language for which (the use of) an expression stands. Notationally, the semantic value of A is written ⟦A⟧.

Semantic wedge An expression which, placed between two others, A and B, shows on semantic grounds that A is not a FUNCTIONAL or even CONTENT SEMANTIC ARGUMENT of B.

Separation, syntactic Two (thematic) relations are introduced by two separate parts of the derivation.

Separationist analysis The relation bound by a dependent A – due to which A's referent has an ENTAILED relation to the event of a nearby verb V – is introduced by something other than the verb. More generally, separationism proposes STRICT SEMANTIC DECOMPOSITION, and treats the structure in the 'decomposed' meaning as syntactically DERIVED.

Separationist analyses, motives for

From adnominal modals When a modal word like possibly attaches to one conjunct within a dependent, the best paraphrase is arguably one where the modal scopes over just the thematic relation associated with that dependent. This requires syntactic separation of that relation.

From alternations Separation allows us to say that exactly the same lexical item occurs in two 'synonymous' alternates.

From complex predicates The distribution of a thematic relation is best stated with respect to not the verb itself, but the potentially complex clausal predicate that contains it. This suggests that the relation is introduced separately from the verb.

From idioms In general, special meanings for verbs are conditioned only by satellites in a certain syntactic domain. This might be explained by treating only these as FUNCTIONAL ARGUMENTS of the verb.

From linking There are linking generalizations that relate thematic to grammatical relations. This would follow, if the former were the meanings of (DERIVATIONAL PARTS underlying) the latter.

From plurals On cumulative readings of clauses with two plural dependents, neither has the other in its scope. This can be explained if they bind thematic relations introduced by separate parts of the derivation.

Single headedness An expression has no more than one HEAD.

Sketch A privileged psychological representation, associated with a predicate B, of things that satisfy that B. E.g., the sketch associated with carry might explicitly represent only the carrier and the carried.

Small Clause syntax (for resultatives) The direct object in a RESULTATIVE forms a constituent with R, to the exclusion of M. For pound it flat, this would give: [pound [it flat]].

Structured value A SEMANTIC VALUE with structure (that is psychologically or metaphysically relevant). When structure in a semantic value corresponds to syntactic or lexical structure in the expression, it is DERIVED. Otherwise it is *underived*.

Syntactic adjunct A dependent that is not a SYNTACTIC ARGUMENT.

Syntactic argument When C has HEAD B and DEPENDENT A as immediate parts, A is a syntactic argument in C just in case C differs in (minor) category from B.

Syntactic bootstrapping Inferring something about the meaning of an expression based on its apparent syntactic distribution, in the process of language acquisition.

Syntactic category The properties of an expression to which rules of SYNTAX may refer.

> **Contextual features** Minor category features of an expression that encode what arguments occur in relation to it. A-FEATURES are one kind of contextual feature, used in LEXICALIST ENCODINGS of argument relations.

> **Major category** A syntactic classification that encodes very general patterns, often in where the expression can occur as an argument, such as VERB or NOUN.

> **Minor category** A syntactic classification that encodes less general ˉpatterns, such as TRANSITIVE or PLURAL.

Syntactic consequence An ENTAILMENT from A to B that can be proven just with reference to form, written A ⊢ B. See ANALYTIC ENTAILMENT, STRICT.

Syntax A level of analysis that has at least the sentences in its domain; speaking derivationally, a level that builds at least the sentences.

Target clause The clause expressing the *target fact* which a REASON CLAUSE is meant to explain. In The ship was sunk to collect the insurance, the target clause is The ship was sunk.

Telic sentence A sentence that describes its event as having a natural conclusion, hence a nonarbitrary duration. With telic sentences, in X time modifiers measure the start-to-finish duration of the event.

Telicity, thematic analysis of The claim that, when the telicity of a sentence depends on the meaning of a dependent A, then A binds a "gradual" thematic relation (Krifka 1992), one that maps increments on some scalar measure of the participant to temporal progress in the event.

Thematic Hierarchy An ordering of semantic relations that must be preserved in an ordering of syntactic relations they link to. One common version is:

Agent < Patient/Theme < Goal < Instrument/Manner/Location/Time.

Thematic relation A semantic relation that is predicated of just one dependent and not more. Often expressed as a relation between an event and an individual.

> **General** A thematic relation, such as Agent, that has many different sorts of events in its domain.

Structured A thematic relation that is said to have semantic structure that is not DERIVED; advocated by Jackendoff.

Thematic relations, motives for

From cognition It plays a privileged role in nonlinguistic cognition.

From inferences It is useful in representing an inference as a SYNTACTIC CONSEQUENCE, a STRICT ANALYTIC ENTAILMENT.

From linking It is useful in stating a generalization about the LINKING of semantic to grammatical relations.

From separation It is introduced by a separate part of the derivation.

Thematic relations, objections to

From inferences It leads to invalid inferences, notably with symmetrical predicates (opposite to), or pairs of nearly inverse predicates (buy and sell).

From obscurity Its content cannot be satisfactorily explicated, or even distinguished from that of others.

Thematic relations, popular types

Agent Viewed as directly involved in bringing about an event.

Experiencer Viewed as the sentient locus of a mental event.

Goal Viewed as something towards which a certain participant moves.

Instrument Viewed as helping the agent bring the event about.

Location Viewed as the location of an event.

Patient Viewed as significantly affected by the event. The term is often used interchangeably with Theme.

Source Viewed as something from which a certain participant moves.

Theme Originally, a participant whose location, movement or change is described by the verb. More generally, a participant viewed as 'undergoing' the event.

Theta Criterion "Each [syntactic] argument bears one and only one Θ-role, and each Θ-role is assigned to one and only one [syntactic] argument" (Chomsky 1981).

Θ-role A syntactic feature of an expression B that marks a syntactic argument of B as being linked to a semantic argument of B. A list of Θ-roles is a Θ-grid.

Transformation A derivational operation that refers to a part of what it applies to, or to its prior derivation.

Transmission See INHERITANCE.

Unaccusativity, deep At a level of 'underlying syntax,' the surface subject of an intransitive clause has the same syntactic relation to the predicate as does the direct object of a transitive clause.

Unaccusativity, sign of The surface subject of an intransitive clause displays some property that, in transitive clauses, is shown by the direct object, and not the subject.

Unarticulated constituent   A part of the content of a direct speech act performed in using expression E, that is not the value (relative to the context of use) of any derivational part of E. That such content exists is controversial.

Uniformity of Theta Assignment Hypothesis (UTAH)   Universal Grammar provides a function from individual thematic relations to LINKINGS of those with syntactic relations.

Universal Alignment Hypothesis (UAH)   Universal Grammar provides a function from the meaning of the clause, or sets of semantic relations, to LINKINGS of those with syntactic relations.

Unrealized role   An entailed relation that is not separately expressed or instantiated by any obvious derivational part of the clause. Examples include the location, thief or victim of theft in The necklace was just stolen.

> **Existential**   Initially paraphrased with a narrow-scope indefinite like stuff or someone. But unlike an indefinite, existential unrealized roles cannot antecede subsequent pronouns, and do not permit BOUND or COVARYING readings in the scope of a quantifier.
>
> **Definite**   Initially paraphrased with a definite like the guy, the thing or that. Prone to BOUND or COVARYING readings in the scope of a quantifier.
>
> **Restricted**   An unrealized role is restricted when it has a narrower range of values than do overt dependents of the same predicate.

Vagueness   See INDETERMINACY.

References

Ackema, Peter, and Maaike Schoorlemmer. 2006. Middles. In *The Blackwell companion to syntax*, ed. M. Everaert, H. van Riemsdijk, R. Goedemans and B. Hollebrandse, volume III, 131–203. Malden, MA: Wiley-Blackwell.

Ajdukiewicz, Kazimierz. 1935. Die syntaktische Konnexität. *Studia Philosophica* 1:1–27. Reprinted in *Polish Logic*, ed., S. McCall, 207–231. Oxford University Press, 1967.

Alexiadou, Artemis, Elena Anagnostopoulou, and Martin Everaert. 2004. Introduction. In *The unaccusativity puzzle*, ed. A. Alexiadou, E. Anagnostopoulou and M. Everaert, 1–21. Oxford University Press.

Alexiadou, Artemis, and Florian Schäfer. 2013. Non-canonical passives. In *Non-canonical passives*, ed. A. Alexiadou and F. Schäfer, 1–20. Amsterdam: John Benjamins.

Allen, Cynthia. 1995. *Case marking and reanalysis*. New York: Oxford University Press.

Anagnostopoulou, Elena, and Anastasia Giannakidou. 1996. Clitics and prominence, or why specificity is not enough. In *Papers from the 31st Regional Meeting of the Chicago Linguistic Society*, ed. P. M. Peranteu, J. N. Levi, and G. C. Phares, 1–14. Chicago Linguistic Society.

Anderson, Steven R. 1971. On the role of deep structure in semantic interpretation. *Foundations of Language* 7:387–396.

Andrews, Avery. 1985. The major functions of the noun phrase. In *Language typology and syntactic description*, ed. T. Shopen, volume I: *Clause structure*, 62–154. Cambridge University Press.

Anscombe, G. E. M. 1957. *Intention*. Oxford: Blackwell.

Arad, Maya. 2006. The spray/load alternation. In *The Blackwell companion to syntax*, ed. M. Everaert, H. van Riemsdijk, R. Goedemans and B. Hollebrandse, volume IV, 466–478. Malden, MA: Wiley-Blackwell.

Arregi, Karlos. 2003. Clitic left dislocation is contrastive topicalization. In *Proceedings of the 26th Annual Penn Linguistics Colloquium*, ed. E. Kaiser and S. Arunachalam, 31–44. Philadelphia: Penn Linguistics Club.

Arunachalam, Sudha, and Sandra R. Waxman. 2010. Meaning from syntax: Evidence from 2-year-olds. *Cognition* 114:442–446.

2011. Grammatical form and semantic context in verb learning. *Language Learning and Development* 7:169–184.

Austin, John L. 1950. Truth. *Proceedings of the Aristotelian Society, Supplementary Volume* 24:111–128.

1961. Unfair to facts. In *Philosophical papers*, ed. J. O. Urmson and G. J. Warnock, 102–122. Oxford: Clarendon Press.

1962. *Sense and sensibilia.* Oxford University Press.

Aze, F. Richard. 1973. Clause patterns in Parengi-Gorum. In *Patterns in clause, sentence, and discourse in selected languages of India and Nepal*, ed. R. L. Trail, 235–312. Norman, OK: Summer Institute of Linguistics.

Bach, Emmon. 1980. In defense of passive. *Linguistics and Philosophy* 3: 297–341.

1982. Purpose clauses and control. In *The nature of syntactic representation*, ed. P. Jacobson and G. K. Pullum, 35–37. Dordrecht: D. Reidel.

Bach, Kent. 1994. Semantic slack: What is said and more. In *Foundations of Speech Act Theory*, ed. S. L. Tsohatzidis, 267–291. New York: Routledge.

2000. Quantification, qualification, and context: A reply to Stanley and Szabó. *Mind and Language* 15:262–283.

Baker, Mark C. 1988. *Incorporation: A theory of grammatical function changing.* University of Chicago Press.

1989. Object sharing and projection in serial verb constructions. *Linguistic Inquiry* 20:513–553.

1997. Thematic roles and syntactic structure. In *Elements of grammar: Handbook in generative syntax*, ed. L. Haegeman, 72–137. Dordrecht: Kluwer.

Baker, Mark C., Kyle Johnson and Ian Roberts. 1989. Passive arguments raised. *Linguistic Inquiry* 20:219–251.

Bar-Hillel, Yehoshua. 1953. A quasi-arithmetical notation for syntactic description. *Language* 29:47–58.

Barker, Chris, and David Dowty. 1993. Non-verbal thematic proto-roles. In *Proceedings of the North Eastern Linguistics Society 23*, ed. A. Schäfer, 49–62. Amherst: GLSA, University of Massachusetts.

Beavers, John. 2006a. Argument/oblique alternations and the structure of lexical meaning. Doctoral dissertation, Stanford University.

2006b. Semantic underspecificity in English argument/oblique alternations. In *Proceedings of the 33rd Western Conference on Linguistics: WECOL 2004*, ed. M. Temkin Martínes, A. Alcázar and R. Mayoral Hernández, 26–33. Fresno, CA: Department of Linguistics, California State University, Fresno.

2010. The structure of lexical meaning: Why semantics really matters. *Language* 86:821–864.

2012. Resultative constructions. In *The Oxford handbook of tense and aspect*, ed. R. I. Binnick, 908–933. Oxford University Press.

Beavers, John, and Andrew Koontz-Garboden. 2012. Manner and result in the roots of verbal meaning. *Linguistic Inquiry* 43:331–369.

Beck, Sigrid. 2005. There and back again: A semantic analysis. *Journal of Semantics* 22:3–51.

Beck, Sigrid, and Kyle Johnson. 2004. Double objects again. *Linguistic Inquiry* 35:97–123.

Beck, Sigrid, and William Snyder. 2001. The resultative parameter and restitutive *again*. In *Audiatur vox sapientiae: A festschrift for Arnim von Stechow*, ed. C. Fery and W. Sternefeld, 48–69. Berlin: Akademie Verlag.

Beier, Jonathan, and Elizabeth Spelke. 2012. Infants' developing understanding of social gaze. *Child Development* 83:486–496.

Belletti, Adriana, and Luigi Rizzi. 1988. Psych-verbs and Θ-theory. *Natural Language and Linguistic Theory* 6:291–352.

Bennett, Jonathan. 1988. *Events and their names*. Indianapolis: Hackett.

Bhatt, Rajesh, and Roumyana Izvorski. 1998. Genericity, implicit arguments and control. Paper presented at SCIL7, available at fttp://ling.upenn.edu/studenterpapers/bhatt/PROarb.ps

Bhatt, Rajesh, and Roumyana Pancheva. 2006. Implicit arguments. In *The Blackwell companion to syntax*, ed. M. Everaert, H. van Riemsdijk, R. Goedemans and B. Hollebrandse, volume II, 554–584. Malden, MA: Wiley-Blackwell.

Bierwisch, Manfred. 2003. Heads, complements, adjuncts: Projection and saturation. In *Modifying adjuncts*, ed. E. Lang, C. Maienborn and C. Fabricius-Hansen, 113–160. Berlin: Walter de Gruyter.

Bittner, Maria. 1999. Concealed causatives. *Natural Language Semantics* 7:1–78.

Blevins, James P. 2003. Passives and impersonals. *Journal of Linguistics* 39:473–520.

2006. Impersonals and passive. In *Elsevier encyclopedia of language and linguistics*, ed. K. Brown, volume IX, 236–239. Amsterdam: Elsevier.

Boas, Hans C. 2003. *A constructional approach to resultatives*. Stanford, CA: CSLI.

Boas, Hans C., and Ivan A. Sag. 2012. *Sign-based construction grammar*. Stanford, CA: CSLI.

Bolinger, Dwight L. 1961. Contrastive accent and contrastive stress. *Language* 37:83–96.

1968. Postposed main phrases: An English rule for the Romance subjunctive. *Canadian Journal of Linguistics* 14:3–30.

1972. Accent is predictable (if you're a mind-reader). *Language* 48:633–644.

1977. Another glance at main clause phenomena. *Language* 53:511–519.

Booth, Amy E., and Sandra R. Waxman. 2003. Mapping words to the world in infancy: Infants' expectations for count nouns and adjectives. *Journal of Cognition and Development* 4:357–381.

2009. A horse of a different color: Specifying with precision infants' mappings of novel nouns and adjectives. *Child Development* 80:15–22.

Borer, Hagit. 1994. The projection of arguments. *University of Massachusetts Occasional Papers in Linguistics* 17:19–47.

2003. Exo-skeletal and endo-skeletal explanation: Syntactic projections and the Lexicon. In *The nature of explanation in linguistic theory*, ed. J. Moore and M. Polinsky, 31–67. Stanford, CA: CSLI.

2005. *The normal course of events*, volume II. Oxford University Press.

2010. Root bound. Handout for a talk at the University of Maryland, April 16, 2010.

Borer, Hagit, and Yosef Grodzinsky. 1986. Syntactic cliticization and lexical cliticization: The case of Hebrew dative clitics. In *The syntax of pronominal clitics*, ed. H. Borer, Syntax and Semantics 19, 175–217. New York: Academic Press.

Borg, Emma. 2004. *Minimal semantics*. Oxford University Press.

Brandone, Amanda, Dede A. Addy, Rachel Pulverman, Roberta M. Golinkoff, and Kathy Hirsh-Pasek. 2006. One-for-One and Two-for-Two: Anticipating parallel structure between events and language. In *Proceedings of the 30th Annual Boston University Conference on Language Development*, 36–47. Somerville, MA: Cascadilla Press.

Bresnan, Joan. 1978. A realistic transformational grammar. In *Linguistic theory and psychological reality*, ed. M. Halle, J. Bresnan and G. A. Miller, 1–59. Cambridge, MA: The MIT Press.

Bresnan, Joan. 1980. Polyadicity. In *Lexical grammar*, ed. T. Hoekstra, H. van der Hulst and M. Moortgat, 97–121. Dordrecht: Foris Publications.

Bresnan, Joan. 1982. The passive in lexical theory. In *The mental representation of grammatical relations*, ed. J. Bresnan, 3–86. Cambridge, MA: The MIT Press.

Bruening, Benjamin. 2012. By-phrases in passives and nominals. *Syntax* 16:1–41.

Burgess, Alexis G., and John P. Burgess. 2011. *Truth*. Princeton University Press.

Büring, Daniel. 2004. *Binding theory*. Cambridge University Press.

Burzio, Luigi. 1981. Intransitive verbs and Italian auxiliaries. Doctoral dissertation. Massachusetts Institute of Technology.

Calabrese, Andrea, and Joan Maling. 2009. *Ne* cliticization and auxiliary selection: Agentivity effects in Italian. Unpublished manuscript University of Connecticut.

Camacho, José. 2000. Structural relations in comitative constructions. *Linguistic Inquiry* 31:366–375.

Cappelen, Herman, and Ernie Lepore. 2005a. *Insensitive semantics*. Malden, MA: Blackwell.

2005b. Radical and moderate pragmatics: Does meaning determine truth conditions? In *Semantics versus pragmatics*, ed. Z. G. Szabó, 45–71. Oxford University Press.

2007. The myth of unarticulated constituents. In *Situating semantics: Essays on the philosophy of John Perry*, ed. M. O'Rourke and C. Washington, 199–215. Cambridge, MA: The MIT Press.

Carlson, Greg. 1984. Thematic roles and their role in semantic interpretation. *Linguistics* 22:259–279.

1998. Thematic roles and the individuation of events. In *Events and grammar*, ed. S. Rothstein, 35–51. Dordrecht: Kluwer.

Carnap, Rudolf. 1928. *Der logische Aufbau der Welt.* Leipzig: Felix Meiner Verlag.

1956. *Meaning and necessity.* University of Chicago Press.

Carrier, Jill, and Janet H. Randall. 1992. The argument structure and syntactic structure of resultatives. *Linguistic Inquiry* 23:173–233.

Carston, Robyn. 1988. Implicature, explicature, and truth-theoretic semantics. In *Mental representations: The interface between language and reality,* ed. R. Kempson, 155–181. Cambridge University Press.

2002. *Thoughts and utterances.* Oxford: Blackwell.

2004. Explicature and semantics. In *Semantics: A reader,* ed. S. Davis and B. S. Gillon, 817–845. Oxford University Press.

Carter, Richard. 1976. Some linking regularities. In *On linking: Papers by Richard Carter,* ed. B. Levin and C. Tenny, 1–92. Cambridge, MA: Lexicon Project, MIT Center for Cognitive Science.

Castañeda, Hector-Neri. 1967. Comments on D. Davidson's "The logical form of action sentences." In *The logic of decision and action,* ed. N. Rescher, 104–112. University of Pittsburgh Press.

Cattell, Ray. 1976. Constraints on movement rules. *Language* 52:18–50.

Champollion, Lucas. 2010a. Cumulative readings of *every* do not provide evidence for events and thematic roles. In *Logic, language and meaning, lecture notes in computer science,* ed. M. Aloni, H. Bastiaanse, T. de Jager and K. Schulz, 213–222. Berlin: Springer.

2010b. Parts of a whole: Distributivity as a bridge between aspect and measurement. Doctoral dissertation. University of Pennsylvania.

Chierchia, Gennaro, and Sally McConnell-Ginet. 1990. *Meaning and grammar.* Cambridge, MA: The MIT Press.

Chomsky, Noam. 1957. *Syntactic structures.* The Hague: Mouton.

1965. *Aspects of the theory of syntax.* Cambridge, MA: The MIT Press.

1970. Remarks on nominalization. In *Readings in English transformational grammar,* ed. R. Jacobs and P. Rosenbaum, 184–221. Waltham, MA: Blaisdell.

1971. Some empirical issues in the theory of Transformational Grammar. In *Goals of linguistic theory,* ed. S. Peters, 63–130. Englewood Cliffs, NJ: Prentice Hall.

1975[1955]. *The logical structure of linguistic theory.* New York: Plenum Press.

1981. *Lectures on Government and Binding.* Dordrecht: Foris.

1982. *Some concepts and consequences of the theory of Government and Binding.* Cambridge, MA: The MIT Press.

1986. *Barriers.* Cambridge, MA: The MIT Press.

1995. Categories and transformations. In *The Minimalist Program,* Chapter 4. Cambridge, MA: The MIT Press.

2000a. Minimalist inquiries: The framework. In *Step by step: Essays on Minimalist syntax in honor of Howard Lasnik,* ed. D. Michaels, R. Martin and J. Uriagereka, 89–156. Cambridge, MA: The MIT Press.

2000b. *New horizons in the study of language and mind,* Chapter 6, Language from an internalist perspective, 134–163. Cambridge University Press.

Chomsky, Noam, and Howard Lasnik. 1993. The theory of principles and parameters. In *Syntax: An international handbook of contemporary research*, ed. J. Jakobs, A. von Stechow, W. Sternefeld and T. Vennemann, 506–569. Berlin: Walter de Gruyter.

Cinque, Guglielmo. 1990. Ergative adjectives and the lexicalist hypothesis. *Natural Language and Linguistic Theory* 8:1–39.

Clapp, Lenny. 2012. Indexical color predicates: Truth-conditional semantics vs. truth-conditional pragmatics. *Canadian Journal of Philosophy* 42:71–100.

Clark, Robin. 1990. *Thematic theory in syntax and interpretation*. New York: Routledge & Kegan-Paul.

Collins, Chris. 2005. A smuggling approach to the passive in English. *Syntax* 8:81–120.

Comrie, Bernard. 1976. *Aspect: An introduction to the study of verbal aspect and related problems*, volume II. Cambridge University Press.

Condoravdi, Cleo, and Jean-Mark Gawron. 1996. The context-dependency of implicit arguments. In *Quantifiers, Deduction, and Context*, ed. M. Kanazawa, C. Piñón and H. de Swart, 1–32. Stanford, CA: CSLI.

Conklin, Kathy, Jean-Pierre Koenig and Gail Mauner. 2004. The role of specificity in the lexical encoding of participants. *Brain and Language* 90:221–230.

Coppock, Elizabeth. 2009. The logical and empirical foundations of Baker's Paradox. Doctoral dissertation. Stanford University.

Creary, Lewis G., J. Mark Gawron and Jon Nerbonne. 1989. Reference to locations. In *Proceedings of the 27th Annual Meeting of the Association for Computational Linguistics*, 42–50. Association for Computational Linguistics.

Crimmins, Mark, and John Perry. 1989. The prince and the phone booth: Reporting puzzling beliefs. *The Journal of Philosophy* 86:685–711.

Croft, William A. 1998. Event structure in argument linking. In *The projection of arguments: Lexical and compositional factors*, ed. M. Butt and W. Geuder, 21–63. Stanford, CA: CSLI.

2012. *Verbs: Aspectual and causal structure*. Oxford University Press.

Cruse, D. A. 1973. Some thoughts on agentivity. *Journal of Linguistics* 9:11–23.

1995. Polysemy and related phenomena from a cognitive linguistic viewpoint. In *Computational lexical semantics*, ed. P. Saint-Dizier and E. Viegas, 33–49. Cambridge University Press.

Culicover, Peter. 2009. *Natural language syntax*. Oxford University Press.

Culicover, Peter W., and Ray Jackendoff. 2005. *Simpler syntax*. New York: Oxford University Press.

Dale, Robert, and Nicholas Haddock. 1991. Content determination in the generation of referring expressions. *Computational Intelligence* 7:252–265.

Dalrymple, Mary, Irene Hayrapetian and Tracy King Holloway. 1998. The semantics of the Russian comitative construction. *Natural Language and Linguistic Theory* 16:597–631.

Davidson, Donald. 1967a. Causal relations. *Journal of Philosophy* 64:691–703.

1967b. The logical form of action sentences. In *The logic of decision and action*, ed. N. Rescher, 216–234. University of Pittsburgh Press.

1967c. Truth and meaning. *Synthese* 17:304–323.

1969. The individuation of events. In *Essays in honor of Carl G. Hempel*, ed. N. Rescher. Dordrecht: D. Reidel.

1970. Events as particulars. *Noûs* 4:25–32.

1971. Agency. In *Agent, action, and reason*, ed. R. Binkley, R. Bronaugh and A. Marrias. Dordrecht: Kluwer.

Davies, Mark. 2008–. *The Corpus of Contemporary American English: 450 million words, 1990–present*. Available online at http://corpus.byu.edu/coca/.

Davis, Anthony R. 2011. Thematic roles. In *Semantics*, ed. C. Maienborn, K. von Heusinger and P. Portner, HSK Handbooks 33.1, 399–420. Berlin: Walter de Gruyter.

Davis, Henry. 2000. Salish evidence on the causative–inchoative alternation. In *Morphological analysis in comparison*, ed. W. U. Dressler, O. E. Pfeiffer, M. Pöchtrager and J. R. Rennison, 25–60. Amsterdam: John Benjamins.

2010. Teaching grammar of St'át'imcets. University of British Columbia book manuscript.

Davis, Henry, and Hamida Demirdache. 2000. On lexical meanings: Evidence from Salish. In *Events as grammatical objects*, ed. C. Tenny and J. Pustejovsky, 97–142. Stanford, CA: CSLI.

Davison, Alice. 1980. Peculiar passives. *Language* 56:42–66.

Déchaine, Rose-Marie. 1993. Predicates across categories. Doctoral dissertation. University of Massachusetts at Amherst.

Delancey, Scott. 1984. Notes on agentivity and causation. *Studies in Language* 8:181–213.

1991. Event construal and case role assignment. *Berkeley Linguistics Society (BLS)* 17:338–353.

Deo, Ashwini. 2012. Morphology. In *The Oxford handbook of tense and aspect*, ed. R. I. Binnick, 155–183. Oxford University Press.

Depiante, Marcela. 2000. The syntax of deep and surface anaphora. Doctoral dissertation. University of Connecticut at Storrs.

Dixon, R. M. W. 1988. *A grammar of Boumaa Fijian*. University of Chicago Press.

1994. *Ergativity*. Cambridge University Press.

Dölling, Johannes, Tatjana Heyde-Zybatow and Martin Schäfer. 2008. *Event structures in linguistic form and interpretation*. Berlin: Walter de Gruyter.

Dowty, David. 1972. On the syntax and semantics of the atomic predicate CAUSE. In *Papers from the Eighth Regional Meeting of the Chicago Linguistic Society*, ed. P. M. Peranteu, J. N. Levi, and G. C. Phares, 62–74. Chicago Linguistic Society.

1979. *Word meaning and Montague Grammar*. Dordrecht: Reidel.

1981. Quantification and the lexicon. In *The scope of lexical rules*, ed. M. Moortgat, H. van der Hulst and T. Hoekstra, 79–106. Dordrecht: Foris.

1988. Type raising, functional composition, and non-constituent coordination. In *Categorial Grammars and natural language structures*, ed. R. T. Oehrle, E. Bach and D. Wheeler, 153–197. Dordrecht: Reidel.

1989. On the semantic content of the notion of "thematic role." In *Properties, types and meanings*, ed. G. Chierchia, B. H. Partee and R. Turner, volume II: *Semantic issues*, 69–130. Dordrecht: Kluwer.

1991. Thematic proto-roles and argument selection. *Language* 67: 547–619.

2001. The semantic assymmetry of "argument alternations" (and why it matters). In *Making sense: From lexeme to discourse*, ed. G. van der Meer and A. G. B. ter Meulen, 171–186. Groningen: Center for Language and Cognition.

2003. The dual analysis of adjuncts and complements in Categorial Grammar. In *Modifying adjuncts*, ed. E. Lang, C. Maienborn and C. Fabricius-Hansen, 33–66. Berlin: Walter de Gruyter.

Dowty, David, Robert Wall and Stanley Peters. 1981. *Introduction to Montague Semantics*. Dordrecht: Reidel.

Dretske, Fred. 1967. Can events move? *Mind* 76:479–492.

Dryer, Matthew S. 1994. The discourse function of the Kutenai inverse. In *Voice and inversion*, ed. T. Givon, 65–99. Amsterdam: John Benjamins.

Égré, Paul. 2008. Question-embedding and factivity. *Grazer Philosophische Studien* 77:85–125.

Elbourne, Paul. 2005. *Situations and individuals*. Cambridge, MA: The MIT Press.

2008. The argument from binding. *Philosophical Perspectives* 22:89–110.

2011. *Meaning: A slim guide to semantics*. Oxford University Press.

Embick, David. 2004a. On the structure of resultative participles in English. *Linguistic Inquiry* 35:355–392.

2004b. Unaccusative syntax and verbal alternations. In *The unaccusativity puzzle*, 137–158. Oxford University Press.

Embick, David, and Rolf Noyer. 2007. Distributed morphology and the syntax/morphology interface. In *The Oxford handbook of linguistic interfaces*, 289–324. Oxford University Press.

Engelberg, Stefan. 2011. Frameworks of lexical decomposition of verbs. In *Semantics*, ed. C. Maienborn, K. von Heusinger and P. Portner, HSK Handbooks 33.1, 358–399. Berlin: Walter de Gruyter.

Evans, Gareth. 1982. *The varieties of reference*. New York: Oxford University Press.

Fagan, Sarah M. B. 1992. *The syntax and semantics of middle constructions: A study with special reference to German*. Cambridge University Press.

Faraci, Robert. 1974. Aspects of the grammar of infinitives and for-phrases. Doctoral dissertation. Massachusetts Institute of Technology.

Farkas, Donka F. 1988. On obligatory control. *Linguistics and Philosophy* 11: 27–58.

Fillmore, Charles J. 1968. The case for case. In *Universals in linguistic theory*, ed. E. Bach and R. T. Harms, 1–90. New York: Holt, Rinehart and Winston.

1970. The grammar of *hitting* and *breaking*. In *Readings in English transformational grammar*, ed. R. Jacobs and P. Rosenbaum, 120–133. Waltham, MA: Ginn.

1971a. Some problems for Case Grammar. In *Report on the 22nd Annual Round Table Meeting on Linguistics and Language Studies*, ed. R. J. O'Brien, 35–56. Georgetown University Press.

1971b. Types of lexical information. In *Semantics*, ed. D. D. Steinberg and L. A. Jakobovits, 370–392. Cambridge University Press.

1977. The case for case reopened. In *Grammatical relations*, ed. P. Cole and J. Sadock, Syntax and Semantics 8, 59–81. New York: Academic Press.

1978. The organization of semantic information in the lexicon. In *Proceedings of the 14th Regional Meeting of Chicago Linguistic Society*, ed. D. Farkas, W. M. Jacobsen and K. W. Todrys, 148–173. Chicago Linguistic Society.

1982. Frame semantics. In *Linguistics in the morning calm*, 111–137. Seoul: Linguistic Society of Korea.

1986. Pragmatically controlled zero anaphora. *Berkeley Linguistics Society (BLS)* 12:95–107.

Fisher, Cynthia. 1996. Structural limits on verb mapping: The role of analogy in children's interpretations of sentences. *Cognitive Psychology* 31:41–81.

2002. Structural limits on verb mapping: The role of abstract structure in 2.5-year-olds' interpretations of novel verbs. *Developmental Science* 5:55–64.

Fisher, Cynthia, Yael Gertner, Rose M. Scott and Sylvia Yuan. 2010. Syntactic bootstrapping. *Wiley Interdisciplinary Reviews: Cognitive Science* 1:143–149.

Fisher, Cynthia, Henry Gleitman and Lila R. Gleitman. 1991. On the semantic content of subcategorization frames. *Cognitive Psychology* 23:331–392.

Fodor, Janet Dean, Jerry Fodor and Merrill F. Garrett. 1975. The psychological unreality of semantic representations. *Linguistic Inquiry* 6:515–531.

Fodor, Jerry. 1970. Three reasons for not deriving "kill" from "cause to die." *Linguistic Inquiry* 1:429–448.

1975. *The language of thought*. Cambridge, MA: Harvard University Press.

Fodor, Jerry, and Janet Dean Fodor. 1980. Functional structure, quantifiers and meaning postulates. *Linguistic Inquiry* 11:759–769.

Fodor, Jerry, and Ernie Lepore. 1998. The emptiness of the lexicon: Reflections on James Pustejovsky's "the Generative Lexicon." *Linguistic Inquiry* 29:269–288.

1999. Impossible words? *Linguistic Inquiry* 30:445–453.

2006. Analyticity again. In *The Blackwell guide to the philosophy of language*, ed. M. Devitt and R. Hanley, 114–130. Malden, MA: Blackwell.

Foley, William A., and Robert D. Van Valin. 1984. *Functional syntax and universal grammar*. Cambridge University Press.

Foster, John A. 1976. Meaning and truth theory. In *Truth and Meaning: Essays in semantics*, ed. G. Evans and J. McDowell, 1–32. Oxford: Clarendon Press.

Fox, Danny, and Yosef Grodzinsky. 1998. Children's passive: A view from the by-phrase. *Linguistic Inquiry* 29:311–332.

Francez, Itamar. 2010. Context dependence and implicit arguments in existentials. *Linguistics and Philosophy* 33:11–30.

Francez, Nissim, and Mark Steedman. 2006. Categorial grammar and the semantics of contextual prepositional phrases. *Linguistics and Philosophy* 29:381–417.

Frank, Robert. 2002. *Phrase structure composition and syntactic dependencies.* Cambridge, MA: The MIT Press.

Frege, Gottlob. 1884. *Die Grundlagen der Arithmetik.* [The foundations of arithmetic.] Breslau: W. Koebner. Translated by J. L. Austin, 1974, Oxford: Blackwell.

1891. Funktion und Begriff. [Function and concept.] Translated by P. Geach in *Translations from the philosophical writings of Gottlob Frege*, ed. P. Geach and M. Black, 21–41. Oxford: Blackwell 3rd edition, 1980.

1892. Über Sinn und Bedeutung. [On sense and reference.] Translated by M. Black in *Translations from the philosophical writings of Gottlob Frege*, ed. P. Geach and M. Black, 56–78. Oxford: Blackwell, 3rd edition, 1980.

Fukui, Naoki, and Margaret Speas. 1996. Specifiers and projections. *MIT Working Papers in Linguistics* 8:128–172.

Gafter, Roey. 2014. The distribution of the Hebrew possessive dative construction: Guided by unaccusativity or prominence? *Linguistic Inquiry* 45:482–500.

Gagliardi, Annie. 2012. Input and intake in language acquisition. Doctoral dissertation. University of Maryland.

Gagliardi, Annie, Erin Bennett, Jeffrey Lidz and Naomi H. Feldman. 2012. Children's inferences in generalizing novel nouns and adjectives. *Proceedings of the 34th Annual Conference of the Cognitive Science Society*, ed. N. Miyake, D. Peebles and R. P. Cooper, 354–359. Austin, TX: Cognitive Science Society.

Gamut, L. T. F. 1991. *Logic, language, and meaning*, volume I. University of Chicago Press.

Gao, Tao, and Brian Scholl. 2011. Chasing vs. stalking: Interrupting the perception of animacy. *Journal of Experimental Psychology: Human Perception and Performance* 37:669–684.

Garey, Howard B. 1957. Verbal aspect in French. *Language* 33:91–110.

Gauker, Christopher. 2012. What is Tipper ready for? A semantics for incomplete predicates. *Noûs* 46:61–85.

Geach, P. T. 1969. *God and the Soul.* London: Routledge & Kegan Paul.

Gergely, György, Zoltán Nádasdy, Gergely Csibra and Szilvia Bíró. 1995. Taking the intentional stance at 12 months of age. *Cognition* 56:165–193.

Gillon, Brendan S. 2004. Ambiguity, indeterminacy, deixis and vagueness: Evidence and theory. In *Semantics: A reader*, ed. S. Davis and B. S. Gillon, 157–187. Oxford University Press.

2006. English relational words, context sensitivity and implicit arguments. Unpublished manuscript. McGill University.

2012. Implicit complements: A dilemma for model theoretic semantics. *Linguistics and Philosophy* 35:313–359.

Ginet, Carl. 1990. *On action*. Cambridge University Press.

Gleitman, Lila. 1990. The structural sources of verb meanings. *Language Acquisition* 1:3–55.

Goldberg, Adele. 1995. *Constructions*. University of Chicago Press.

2001. Patient arguments of causative verbs can be omitted: The role of information structure in argument distribution. *Language Sciences* 23:503–524.

2006. *Constructions at work*. Oxford University Press.

Goldberg, Adele, and Ray Jackendoff. 2004. The English resultative as a family of constructions. *Language* 80:532–568.

Goodall, Grant. 1997. θ-alignment and the by-phrase. In *Papers from the 33rd Regional Meeting of the Chicago Linguistic Society*, ed. K. Singer, R. Eggert and G. Anderson, 129–140. Chicago Linguistic Society.

Goodman, Nelson. 1955. *Fact, fiction, and forecast*. Cambridge, MA: Harvard University Press.

Gordon, Peter. 2003. The origin of argument structure in infant event representations. In *Proceedings of the 27th Annual Boston University Conference on Language Development*, ed. A. Brugos, L. Micciulla and C. E. Smith, 189–198. Somerville, MA: Cascadilla Press.

Green, Georgia. 1972. Some observations on the syntax and semantics of instrumental verbs. In *Papers from the Eighth Regional Meeting of the Chicago Linguistic Society*, ed. P. M. Peranteu, J. N. Levi, and G. C. Phares, 83–97. Chicago Linguistic Society.

Grice, H. Paul. 1969. Utterer's meaning and intentions. *The Philosophical Review* 68:147–177.

Grimshaw, Jane. 1979. Complement selection and the lexicon. *Linguistic Inquiry* 10:279–326.

1981. Form, function, and the language acquisition device. In *The logical problem of language acquisition*, ed. C. L. Baker and J. J. McCarthy, 183–210. Cambridge, MA: The MIT Press.

1990. *Argument structure*. Cambridge, MA: The MIT Press.

2005. *Words and structure*. Stanford, CA: CSLI.

Groenendijk, Jeroen, and Martin Stokhof. 1991. Dynamic predicate logic. *Linguistics and Philosophy* 14:39–100.

Gropen, Jess, Steven Pinker, Michelle Hollander, Richard Goldberg and Ronald Wilson. 1989. The learnability and acquisition of the dative alternation in English. *Language* 65:203–257.

Gruber, Jeffrey. 1965. Studies in lexical relations. Doctoral dissertation. Massachusetts Institute of Technology.

Guerssel, Mohamed, Ken Hale, Mary Laughren, Beth Levin and Josie White Eagle. 1985. A cross-linguistic study of transitivity alternations. *Papers from the Parasession an Causatives and Agentivity at the Twenty-First Regional Meeting of the Chicago Linguistic Society*, ed. W. H. Eilfort, P. D. Kroeber and K. L. Peterson, 48–63. Chicago Linguistic Society.

Gutiérrez-Rexach, Javier. 1999. The formal semantics of clitic doubling. *Journal of Semantics* 16:315–380.

Hacker, P. M. S. 1982. Events and objects in space and time. *Mind* 91: 1–19.

Hale, Ken, Uzodinma Peter Ihionu and Victor Manfredi. 1995. Igbo bipositional verbs in a syntactic theory of argument structure. In *Theoretical approaches to African linguistics*, ed. A. Akinlabi, 83–107. Trenton, NJ: Africa World Press.

Hale, Ken, and Samuel J. Keyser. 1993. On argument structure and the lexical expression of syntactic relations. In *The view from Building 20* ed. K. Hale and S. J. Keyser, 53–109. Cambridge, MA: The MIT Press.

1997. On the complex nature of simple predicators. In *Complex predicates*, ed. A. Alsina, J. Bresnan and P. Sells, 29–65. Stanford, CA: CSLI.

Hall, Barbara. 1965. Subject and object in modern English. Doctoral dissertation. Massachusetts Institute of Technology.

Halle, Morris, and Alec Marantz. 1993. Distributed morphology and the pieces of inflection. In *The view from Building 20*, ed. K. Hale and S. J. Keyser, 111–176. Cambridge, MA: The MIT Press.

Hankamer, Jorge, and Ivan Sag. 1976. Deep and surface anaphora. *Linguistic Inquiry* 7:391–428.

Harley, Heidi. 2002. Possession and the double object construction. *Linguistic Variation Yearbook* 2:29–68.

2011. An alternative to deficiency approaches to the manner alternation parameter. Handout from the Workshop on Verbal Elasticity, Universitat Autònoma de Barcelona.

Harman, Gilbert. 1996. Analyticity regained? *Noûs* 30:392–400.

Hart, H. L. A., and Tony Honoré. 1959. *Causation in the law*. Oxford: Clarendon Press.

Hay, Jennifer, Christopher Kennedy and Beth Levin. 1999. Scalar structure underlies degree achievements. In *Proceedings from Semantics and Linguistic Theory IX*, ed. T. Matthews and D. Strolovitch, 127–144. Ithaca, NY: Cornell Linguistics Club.

He, Angela Xiaoxue, Alexis Wellwood, Jeffrey Lidz and Alexander Williams. 2013. Assessing event perception in adults and prelinguistic children: A prelude to syntactic bootstrapping. Poster presented at the 38th Annual Boston University Conference on Language Development.

Heim, Irene. 1982. The semantics of definite and indefinite noun phrases. Doctoral dissertation. University of Massachusetts at Amherst.

Heim, Irene, and Angelika Kratzer. 1998. *Semantics in generative grammar*. Cambridge, MA: The MIT Press.

Heycock, Caroline, and Anthony S. Kroch. 1999. Pseudocleft connectivity: Implications for the LF interface. *Linguistic Inquiry* 30:365–397.

Hirsh-Pasek, Kathy, Roberta M. Golinkoff and Letitia Naiglas, 1996. Young children's use of syntactic frames to derive meaning. In *The origins of grammar: Evidence from early language comprehension*, ed. K. Hirsh-Pasek and R. M. Grinkoff, 123–158. Cambridge, MA: MIT Press.

Hoekstra, Teun. 1988. Small clause results. *Lingua* 74:101–39.

Hopper, Paul J., and Sandra A. Thompson. 1980. Transitivity in grammar and discourse. *Language* 56:251–295.

Hornstein, Norbert. 1999. Movement and Control. *Linguistic Inquiry* 30:69–96.

⎯⎯. 2002. A grammatical argument for a Neo-Davidsonian semantics. In *Logical form and language*, ed. G. Preyer and G. Peter, 345–364. Oxford: Clarendon Press.

Hornstein, Norbert, and Jairo Nunes. 2008. Adjunction, labeling, and Bare Phrase Structure. *Biolinguistics* 2:57–86.

Hornstein, Norbert, Jairo Nunes and Kleanthes K. Grohmann. 2005. *Understanding Minimalism*. Cambridge University Press.

van Hout, Angeliek. 1996. *Event semantics and verb frame alternations: A case study of Dutch and its acquisition*. Tilburg Dissertations in Linguistics.

Huang, C.-T. James. 1982. Logical relations in Chinese and the theory of grammar. Doctoral dissertation. Massachusetts Institute of Technology.

⎯⎯. 1988. *Wo pao de kuai* and Chinese phrase structure. *Language* 64: 274–311.

⎯⎯. 1992. Complex predicates in Control. In *Control and grammar*, ed. R. K. Larson, S. Iatridou, U. Lahiri, and J. Higginbotham, 109–147. Dordrecht: Kluwer.

⎯⎯. 1999. Chinese passives in comparative perspective. *Tsing Hua Journal of Chinese Studies* 29:423–509.

Huang, C.-T. James, Audrey Li and Yafei Li 2009. *The Syntax of Chinese*. Cambridge University Press.

Huddleston, Rodney. 1970. Some remarks of case-grammar. *Linguistic Inquiry* 1: 501–511.

Hunter, Tim. 2011. *Syntactic effects of conjunctivist semantics: Unifying movement and adjunction*. Amsterdam: John Benjamins.

Iwata, Seizi. 1999. On the status of an implicit argument in Middles. *Journal of Linguistics* 35:527–553.

Jackendoff, Ray. 1972. *Semantic interpretation in generative grammar*. Cambridge, MA: The MIT Press.

⎯⎯. 1976. Toward an explanatory semantic representation. *Linguistic Inquiry* 7:89–150.

⎯⎯. 1977. *X-bar theory: A study of phrase structure*. Cambridge, MA: MIT Press.

⎯⎯. 1983. *Semantics and cognition*. Cambridge, MA: The MIT Press.

⎯⎯. 1987. The status of thematic relations in linguistic theory. *Linguistic Inquiry* 18:369–411.

1990a. On Larson's treatment of the double object construction. *Linguistic Inquiry* 21:427–456.

1990b. *Semantic structures*. Cambridge, MA: The MIT Press.

1996. The proper treatment of measuring out, telicity, and perhaps even quantification in English. *Natural Language and Linguistic Theory* 14: 305–354.

Jacobson, Pauline. 1990. Raising as Function Composition. *Linguistics and Philosophy* 13:423–475.

Jones, Charles Foster. 1985. Syntax and thematics of infinitival adjuncts. Doctoral dissertation. University of Massachusetts at Amherst.

Joshi, Aravind K. 1987. An introduction to Tree Adjoining Grammars. In *The mathematics of language*, ed. A. Manaster-Ramer, 87–115. Amsterdam: John Benjamins.

2004. Starting with complex primitives pays off: Complicate locally, simplify globally. *Cognitive Science* 28:637–668.

Joshi, Aravind K., and Yves Schabes. 1997. Tree-adjoining grammars. In *Handbook of formal languages*, volume III: *Beyond words*, ed. G. Rozenberg and A. Salommaa, 59–123. Berlin: Springer.

Juhl, Cory, and Eric Loomis. 2010. *Analyticity*. New York: Routledge.

Kako, Ed, and Laura Wagner. 2001. The semantics of syntactic structures. *Trends in Cognitive Science* 5:102–108.

Kamp, Hans. 1981. A theory of truth and semantic representation. In *Formal methods in the study of language*, ed. J. Groenendijk, T. Janssen and M. Stokhof, 277–322. Amsterdam: Mathematical Centre.

Karttunen, Lauri. 1969. Pronouns and variables. In *Papers from the Fifth Regional Meeting of the Chicago Linguistic Society*, ed. R. Binnick, A. Davison, G. Green and J. L. Morgan, 108–116. Chicago Linguistic Society.

1976. Discourse referents. In *Notes from the linguistic underground*, ed. J. D. McCawley, Syntax and Semantics 7, 363–386. New York: Academic Press.

Kay, Paul. 2002. An informal sketch of a formal architecture for Construction Grammar. *Grammars* 5:1–19.

Kayne, Richard. 1985. Principles of particle constructions. In *Grammatical representation*, ed. J. Gueron, H. G. Obenauer, and J.-Y. Pollock, 101–140. Dordrecht: Foris.

Keenan, Edward L., and Matthew S. Dryer. 2007. Passive in the world's languages. In *Language typology and syntactic description*, ed. T. Shopen, volume I: *Clause structure*, 325–361. Cambridge University Press.

Keenan, Edward L., and Edward Stabler. 2003. *Bare grammar: Lectures on invariance*. Stanford, CA: CSLI.

Kemmer, Suzanne. 1993. *The middle voice*. Philadelphia: John Benjamins.

Kennedy, Christopher, and Louise McNally. 2010. Color, context, and compositionality. *Synthese* 174:79–98.

Keyser, Samuel Jay, and Thomas Roeper. 1984. On the middle and ergative construction in English. *Linguistic Inquiry* 15:381–416.

Kim, Jaegwon. 1976. Events as property exemplifications. In *Action theory*, ed. M. Brand and D. Walton, 310–326. Dordrecht: Reidel.

King, Jeffrey C. 1995. Structured propositions and complex predicates. *Noûs* 29:495–521.

1996. Structured propositions and sentence structure. *Journal of Philosophical Logic* 25:495–521.

Kiparsky, Paul. 2013. Towards a null theory of the passive. *Lingua* 125: 7–33.

Klein, Ewan, and Ivan A. Sag. 1985. Type-driven translation. *Linguistics and Philosophy* 8:163–201.

Klein, Wolfgang. 1994. *Time in language*. London: Routledge.

Koenig, Jean-Pierre, and Gail Mauner. 2000. A-definites and the discourse status of implicit arguments. *Journal of Semantics* 16:207–236.

Koenig, Jean-Pierre, Gail Mauner and Breton Bienvenue, 2002. Class Specificity and the lexical encoding of participant information. *Brain and Language* 81:224–235.

Koenig, Jean-Pierre, Gail Mauner, Breton Bienvenue and Kathy Conklin. 2008. What with? The anatomy of a (Proto)-Role. *Journal of Semantics* 25:175–220.

Koopman, Hilda, Dominique Sportiche and Edward Stabler. 2013. *An introduction to syntactic analysis and theory*. Malden, MA: Wiley-Blackwell.

Kracht, Marcus. 2002. On the semantics of locatives. *Linguistics and Philosophy* 25:157–232.

2011. *Interpreted languages and compositionality*. Dordrecht: Springer.

Kratzer, Angelika. 1996. Severing the external argument from its verb. In *Phrase structure and the lexicon*, ed. J. Rooryck and L. Zaring, 109–37. Dordrecht: Kluwer.

2000. The event argument, chapter 2: Schein's argument. Manuscript available from www.semanticsarchive.net.

2002. The event argument, chapter 1: Verb meanings and argument structure. Manuscript available from www.semanticsarchive.net.

2003. The event argument, chapter 3: Theme arguments. Manuscript available from www.semanticsarchive.net.

2005. Building resultatives. In *Event arguments: Foundations and applications*, ed. C. Maienborn and A. Wöllstein, 177–212. Tübingen: Max Niemeyer Verlag.

Krifka, Manfred. 1989. Nominal reference, temporal constitution and quantification in event semantics. In *Semantics and contextual expressions*, ed. R. Bartsch, J. van Bentham and P. van Emde Boas, 75–115. Dordrecht: Foris.

1992. Thematic relations as links between nominal reference and temporal constitution. In *Lexical matters*, ed. I. Sag and A. Szabolcsi, 29–53. Stanford University.

1998. The origins of telicity. In *Events and grammar*, ed. S. Rothstein, 197–235. Dordrecht: Kluwer.

Kripke, Saul. 1977. Speaker reference and semantic reference. *Midwest Studies in Philosophy* 2:255–276.

Kroch, Anthony S. 1987. Unbounded dependencies and Subjacency in Tree Adjoining Grammar. In *The mathematics of language*, ed. A. Manaster-Ramer, 143–172. Amsterdam: John Benjamins.

Lahiri, Utpal. 2002. *Questions and answers in embedded contexts*. Oxford University Press.

Lakoff, George. 1965. On the nature of syntactic irregularity. Doctoral dissertation. Indiana University.

———. 1970. Linguistics and natural logic. *Synthese* 22:151–271.

———. 1971. On Generative Semantics. In *Semantics: An interdisciplinary reader in philosophy, linguistics, and psychology*, ed. L. A. Jakobovitz and D. D. Steinberg, 232–296. Cambridge University Press.

Landau, Barbara, and Lila R. Gleitman. 1985. *Language and experience: Evidence from the blind child*. Cambridge, MA: Harvard University Press.

Landau, Idan. 1999. Possessor raising and the structure of VP. *Lingua* 107: 1–37.

———. 2000. *Elements of control: Structure and meaning in infinitival constructions*. Berlin: Springer.

———. 2010. The explicit syntax of implicit arguments. *Linguistic Inquiry* 41:357–388.

Landman, Fred. 2000. *Events and plurality*. Dordrecht: Kluwer.

Langacker, Ronald W. 1984. Active zones. In *Proceedings of the Tenth Annual Meeting of the Berkeley Linguistics Society*, 172–188. Berkeley Linguistics Society.

Larson, Richard. 1988. On the double object construction. *Linguistic Inquiry* 19:335–391.

———. 1991. Some issues in verb serialization. In *Serial verbs*, ed. C. Lefebvre, 185–210. Philadelphia: Benjamins.

Larson, Richard, and Gabriel Segal. 1995. *Knowledge of meaning*. Cambridge, MA: The MIT Press.

Lasersohn, Peter. 1995. *Plurality, conjunction, and events*. Dordrecht: Kluwer.

Lasnik, Howard. 1988. Subjects and the Theta Criterion. *Natural Language and Linguistic Theory* 6:1–18.

Lasnik, Howard, and Robert Fiengo. 1974. Complement object deletion. *Linguistic Inquiry* 5:535–571.

Laughren, Mary. 1988. Towards a lexical representation of Warlpiri verbs. In *Thematic relations*, ed. W. Wilkins, 215–242. San Diego: Academic Press.

Lavine, James. 2013. Passives and near-passives in Balto-Slavic: On the survival of the accusative. In *Non-canonical passives*, ed. A. Alexiadou and F. Schäfer, 185–211. Amsterdam: John Benjamins.

van der Leek, Frederike. 1996. The English conative constuction: A compositional account. *Papers from the 32nd Regional Meeging of the Chicago Linguistic Society*, ed. M. Aucoin and L. McNair, 363–378. Chicago Linguistic Society.

Lees, Robert, and Edward Klima. 1963. Rules for English pronominalization. *Language* 39:17–28.

Lee-Schoenfeld, Vera. 2007. *Beyond coherence: The syntax of opacity in German.* Philadelphia: John Benjamins.

Leslie, Alan M. 1994. ToMM, ToBy, and Agency: Core architecture and domain specificity. In *Mapping the mind: Domain specificity in cognition and culture*, ed. L. A. Hirschfeld and S. A. Gelman, 119–148. Cambridge University Press.

Levin, Beth. 1993. *English verb classes and alternations: A preliminary investigation.* University of Chicago Press.

2012. *Slap, give a slap, slap a slap*: Cross-linguistic diversity in hitting event descriptions. Tenth Biennial Conference of the High Desert Linguistics Society, University of New Mexico, Albuquerque.

Levin, Beth, and Malka Rappaport-Hovav. 1995. *Unaccusativity.* Cambridge, MA: The MIT Press.

2005. *Argument realization.* Cambridge University Press.

Lewis, David. 1970. General semantics. *Synthese* 22:18–67.

Li, Yafei. 1990. On V-V compounds in Chinese. *Natural Language and Linguistic Theory* 8: 177–207.

1995. The thematic hierarchy and causativity. *Natural Language and Linguistic Theory* 13: 255–282.

1999. Cross-componential causativity. *Natural Language and Linguistic Theory* 17: 445–497.

Lidz, Jeffrey. 2000. A three-legged chicken. *Snippets* 1:3–14.

2001. The argument structure of verbal reflexives. *Natural Language and Linguistic Theory* 19:311–353.

Lidz, Jeffrey, Henry Gleitman and Lila R. Gleitman. 2003. Understanding how input matters: The footprint of universal grammar on verb learning. *Cognition* 87:151–178.

Lidz, Jeffrey, and William Idsardi. 1998. Chains and phonological form. *Penn Working Papers in Linguistics* 5:109–25.

Lidz, Jeffrey, Paul Pietroski, Justin Halberda, and Tim Hunter. 2011. Interface transparency and the psychosemantics of *most*. *Natural Language Semantics* 19:227–256.

Link, Godehard. 1983. The logical analysis of plurals and mass terms: A lattice-theoretical approach. In *Meaning, use, and interpretation of language*, ed. R. Bäuerle, C. Schwarze and A. von Stechow, 302–323. Berlin: Walter de Gruyter.

1998. The ontology of individuals and events. *Algebraic semantics in language and philosophy*, Chapter 13. Stanford, CA: CSLI.

Lombard, Lawrence B. 1985. How not to flip the prowler: Transitive verbs of action and the identity of actions. In *Actions and events: Perspectives on the philosophy of Donald Davidson*, ed. E. LePore and B. P. McLaughlin, 268–281. New York: Basil Blackwell.

1986. *Events: A metaphysical study.* New York: Routledge.

Lonzi, Lidia. 1986. Pertinenza della struttura tema-rema per l'analisi sintattica. In *Tema-rema in Italiano*, ed. H. Stammerjohann, 99–120. Tübingen: Gunter Narr Verlag.

Lord, Carol. 1975. Igbo verb compounds and the Lexicon. *Studies in African Linguistics* 6:23–48.

Lyons, John. 1966. Towards a "notional" theory of the "parts of speech." *Journal of Linguistics* 2:209–236.

1977. *Semantics*. Cambridge University Press.

Mahajan, Anoop. 1995. ACTIVE passives. In *Proceedings of the Thirteenth West Coast Conference on Formal Linguistics*, ed. R. Aranovich, W. Byrne, S. Preuss and M. Senturia, 286–301. Stanford, CA: CSLI.

Maienborn, Claudia. 2011. Event semantics. In *Semantics*, ed. C. Maienborn, K. von Heusinger, and P. Portner, HSK Handbooks 33.1, 802–829. Berlin: Walter de Gruyter.

Maienborn, Claudia, and Angelika Wöllstein. 2005 *Event arguments: Foundations and applications*. Tübingen: Max Niemeyer Verlag.

Maling, Joan, and Sigríður Sigurjónsdóttir. 2002. The "new impersonal" construction in Icelandic. *Journal of Comparative Germanic Linguistics* 5:97–142.

Manning, Christopher D., and Ivan A. Sag. 1998. Dissociations between argument structure and grammatical relations. In *Lexical and constructional aspects of linguistic explanation*, ed. G. Webelhuth, J.-P. Koenig and A. Kathol. Stanford, CA: CSLI Publications.

Marantz, Alec. 1984. *On the nature of grammatical relations*. Cambridge, MA: The MIT Press.

1992. The *way* construction and the semantics of direct arguments in English. In *Syntax and the Lexicon*, ed. T. Stowell and E. Wehrli, Syntax and semantics 26, 179–188. New York: Academic Press.

1997. No escape from syntax: Don't try morphological analysis in the privacy of your own lexicon. *Penn Working Papers in Linguistics* 4(2): 201–226.

Martí, Luisa. 2006. Unarticulated constituents revisited. *Linguistics and Philosophy* 29:135–166.

Mauner, Gail, and Jean-Pierre Koenig. 2000. Linguistic vs. conceptual sources of implicit agents in sentence comprehension. *Journal of Memory and Language* 43:110–134.

May, Robert. 1977. The grammar of quantification. Doctoral dissertation. Massachusetts Institute of Technology.

McCawley, James D. 1971. Pre-lexical syntax. In *Report on the 22nd Annual Round Table Meeting on Linguistics and Language Studies*, ed. R. J. O'Brien, 19–33. Georgetown University Press.

1972. A program for logic. In *Semantics of natural language*, ed. D. Davidson and G. Harman, 498–544. Dordrecht: Reidel.

1978. Conversational implicature and the lexicon. In *Pragmatics*, ed. P. Cole, Syntax and Semantics 9, 245–259. Academic Press: New York.

1979. Presupposition and discourse structure. In Presupposition, ed. C.-K. Oh and D. Dinneen, Syntax and Semantics, 371–388. New York: Academic Press.

McCourt, Michael, Aleksandra Fazlipour, Ellen Lau and Alexander Williams. 2014. Implicit agents and remote control of reason clauses. Poster presented at the 27th Annual CUNY Conference on Human Sentence Processing, March 14.

McFadden, Thomas. 2002. The rise of the *to*-dative in middle English. In *Syntactic effects of morphological change*, ed. D. Lightfoot, 107–123. Oxford University Press.

McNally, Louise. 1993. Comitative coordination. *Natural Language and Linguistic Theory* 11:347–379.

Merchant, Jason. 2010. These kinds of ellipsis. In *Context-dependence perspective, and relativity*, ed. F. Recanati, I. Stojanavic and N. Villanueva, 141–192. Berlin: Mouton de Gruyter.

ter Meulen, Alice G. B. 2004. Dynamic definite descriptions, implicit arguments, and familiarity. In *Descriptions and Beyond*, ed. M. Reimer and A. Bezuidenhout, 544–557. Oxford University Press.

Michaelis, Laura. 2013. Sign-based Construction Grammar. In *Oxford handbook of Construction Grammar*, ed. T. Hoffmann and G. Trousdale, 133–152. Oxford University Press.

Mittwoch, Anita. 1982. On the difference between eating and eating something: Activities versus accomplishments. *Linguistic Inquiry* 13: 113–122.

Montague, Richard. 1973. The proper treatment of quantification in ordinary English. In *Approaches to natural language*, ed. J. Hintikka, J. Moravcsik and P. Suppes, 221–242. Dordrecht. Reidel.

1974. *Formal philosophy: Selected papers of Richard Montague*, ed. R. H. Thomason. New Haven, CT: Yale University Press.

Moortgat, Michael. 2012. Typelogical grammars. In *The Stanford encyclopedia of philosophy*, ed. E. N. Zalta. Winter 2012 edition, available at http://stanford.edu/archives/spr2014/entries/typelogical-grammar.

Morgan, Jerry L. 1969. On the treatment of presupposition in transformational grammar. In *Papers from the Fifth Regional Meeting of the Chicago Linguistic Society*, ed. R. Binnick, A. Davison, G. Green and J. L. Morgan, 167–177. Chicago Linguistic Society.

Morreall, J. 1976. The nonsynonymy of "kill" and "cause to die." *Linguistic Inquiry* 7:516–518.

Moulton, Keir. 2009. Natural selection and the syntax of clausal complementation. Doctoral dissertation. University of Massachusetts at Amherst.

Müller, Stefan. 2006. Phrasal or lexical constructions? *Language* 82:850–883.

Naigles, Letitia. 1990. Children use syntax to learn verb meanings. *Journal of Child Language* 17:357–374.

1996. The use of multiple frames in verb learning via syntactic bootstrapping. *Cognition* 58:221–251.

Neale, Stephen, 1990. *Descriptions.* Cambridge, MA: The MIT Press.

2004. This, that, and the other. In *Descriptions and Beyond*, ed. M. Reimer and A. Bezuidenhout, 68–188. Oxford University Press.

2007. On location. In *Situating semantics: Essays on the philosophy of John Perry*, ed. M. O'Rourke and C. Washington, 251–393. Cambridge, MA: The MIT Press.

Nilsen, Don L. F. 1973. *The instrumental case in English: Syntactic and semantic considerations.* The Hague: Mouton de Gruyter.

Nishiyama, Kunio. 1998. V-V compounds as serialization. *Journal of East Asian Linguistics* 7:175–217.

Noble, Claire H., Caroline F. Rowland and Julian M. Pine. 2011. Comprehension of argument structure and semantic roles: Evidence from English-learning children and the forced-choice pointing paradigm. *Cognitive Science* 35: 963–982.

Nunberg, Geoffrey, Ivan A. Sag and Thomas Wasow. 1994. Idioms. *Language* 70:491–538.

Nunes, Jairo. 2001. Sidewards movement. *Linguistic Inquiry* 32:303–344.

Nwachukwu, P. Akujuobi. 1987. The argument structure of Igbo verbs. Technical Report 18, MIT Lexicon Project Working Papers.

Odijk, Jan. 1997. C-Selection and S-Selection. *Linguistic Inquiry* 28: 365–371.

Oehrle, Richard. 1976. The grammatical status of the English dative alternation. Doctoral dissertation. Massachusetts Institute of Technology.

Oliver, Alex, and Timothy Smiley. 2001. Strategies for a logic of plurals. *The Philosophical Quarterly* 51:289–306.

Panagiotidis, Phoevos. 2003. One, empty nouns, and θ-assignment. *Linguistic Inquiry* 34:281–292.

Pandharipande, R. 1981. Syntax and semantics of the passive construction in selected South Asian languages. Doctoral dissertation. University of Illinois, Urbana-Champaign.

Parsons, Terence. 1990. *Events in the semantics of English.* Cambridge, MA: The MIT Press.

Partee, Barbara. 1989. Binding implicit variables in quantified contexts. In *Papers from the 25th Regional Meeting of the Chicago Linguistic Society*, ed. C. Wiltshire, R. Grazyte and B. Music, 342–356. Chicago Linguistic Society.

Partee, Barbara, Alice ter Meulen, and Robert Wall. 1990. *Mathematical methods in linguistics.* Berlin: Springer.

Perlmutter, David M. 1978. Impersonal passives and the unaccusative hypothesis. In *Proceedings of the 4th Annual Meeting of the Berkeley Linguistics Society*, 157–189.

Perlmutter, David M., and Paul M. Postal. 1983. Toward a universal characterization of passivization. In *Studies in Relational Grammar 1*, ed. D. M. Perlmutter, 3–29. University of Chicago Press.

1984. The 1-Advancement Exclusiveness Law. In *Studies in relational grammar 2*, ed. D. M. Perlmutter and C. Rosen, 81–125. University of Chicago Press.

Perry, John. 1986. Thought without representation Part 1. *Proceedings of the Aristotelian Society, Supplementary Volumes* 60:137–151.

Pesetsky, David. 1982. Paths and categories. Doctoral dissertation. Massachusetts Institute of Technology.

1995. *Zero syntax: Experiencers and cascades*. Cambridge, MA: The MIT Press.

Pietroski, Paul. 2000. *Causing actions*. Oxford University Press.

2003. Small verbs, complex events: Analyticity without synonymy. In *Chomsky and his critics*, ed. L. Antony and N. Hornstein, 179–214. Malden, MA: Blackwell.

2005a. *Events and semantic architecture*. Oxford University Press.

2005b. Meaning before truth. In *Contextualism in philosophy*, ed. G. Preyer and G. Peter, 253–300. Oxford University Press.

2010. Concepts, meanings, and truth: First nature, second nature and hard work. *Mind and Language* 25:247–278.

2011. Minimal semantic instructions. In *Oxford handbook of linguistic Minimalism*, ed. C. Boeckx, 472–498. Oxford University Press.

to appear a. *Conjoining meanings: Semantics without truth values*. Oxford University Press.

to appear b. Framing event variables. *Erkenntnis*.

Pietroski, Paul, Jeffrey Lidz, Tim Hunter, Darko Odic and Justin Halberda. 2011. Seeing what you mean, mostly. In *Experiments at the interfaces*, ed. J. Runner, Syntax and Semantics 37, 187–224. New York: Academic Press.

Pinker, Steven. 1979. Formal models of language learning. *Cognition* 7:217–283.

1984. *Language learnability and language development*. Cambridge, MA: Harvard University Press.

1987. The bootstrapping problem in language acquisition. In *Mechanisms of language acquisition*, ed. B. MacWhinney. Hillsdale, NJ: Erlbaum.

1989. *Learnability and cognition: The acquisition of argument structure*. Cambridge, MA: The MIT Press.

1994. *The language instinct*. New York: William Morrow and Company.

Pollard, Carl, and Ivan Sag. 1987. *Information-based syntax and semantics*. Stanford, CA: CSLI.

Postal, Paul. 1971. *Cross-over phenomena*. New York: Holt, Rinehart and Winston.

Primus, Beatrice. 2011. Animacy and telicity: Semantic constraints on impersonal passives. *Lingua* 121:80–99.

Prince, Ellen F. 1981. Towards a taxonomy of given–new information. In *Radical Pragmatics*, ed. P. Cole, 223–256. New York: Academic Press.

Pylkkänen, Liina. 2002. Introducing arguments. Doctoral dissertation. Massachusetts Institute of Technology.

Quine, Willard van Orman. 1953. *From a logical point of view*. Cambridge, MA: Harvard University Press.

Events and reification. 1985. In *Actions and events: Perspectives on the philosophy of Donald Davidson*, ed. E. Lepore and B. McLaughlin, 162–171. Oxford: Basil Blackwell.

Ramchand, Gillian. 2008. *Verb meaning and the Lexicon: A first phase syntax*. Cambridge University Press.

Ramsey, Frank. 1925. Universals. *Mind* 34:401–417.

Rapp, Irene. 1997. *Partizipien und semantische Struktur: Zur passivischen Konstruktion mit dem 3. Status*. Tübingen: Stauffenburg.

Rappaport Hovav, Malka, and Beth Levin. 1998. Building verb meanings. In *The projection of arguments: Lexical and compositional factors*, ed. M. Butt and W. Geuder, 97–134. Stanford, CA: CSLI.

2001. An event structure account of English resultatives. *Language* 77:766–796.

2010. Reflections on Manner/Result complementarity. In *Syntax, lexical semantics, and event structure*, ed E. Doron, M. Rappaport Hovav and I. Sichel, 21–38. Oxford University Press.

Rayo, Augustín. 2002. Word and objects. *Noûs* 36:436–464.

Recanati, François. 2002. Unarticulated constituents. *Linguistics and Philosophy* 25:299–345.

2004. *Literal meaning*. Cambridge University Press.

2010. *Truth-conditional pragmatics*. Oxford University Press.

2012. Pragmatic enrichment. In *The Routledge companion to the philosophy of language*, ed. D. Graff Fara and G. Russell, 67–78. New York: Routledge.

Reinecke, Brigitte, and Gudrun Miehe. 2007. Diathesis alternation in some Gur languages. In *Studies in African linguistic typology*, ed. F. K. Erhard Voeltz, 337–360. Amsterdam: John Benjamins.

Rey, Georges. 2013. The analytic/synthetic distinction. In *The Stanford encyclopedia of philosophy*, ed. E. N. Zalta. Winter 2012 edition, available at http://plats.standford.edu/archives/fall2013/entries/analytic-synthetic.

Ritter, Elizabeth, and Sara Thomas Rosen. 1998. Delimiting events in syntax. In *The projection of arguments: Lexical and compositional factors*, ed. M. Butt and W. Geuder, 135–164. Stanford, CA: CSLI.

Rizzi, Luigi. 1986a. Null objects in Italian and the theory of *pro*. *Linguistic Inquiry* 17:501–557.

1986b. On chain formation. In *The syntax of pronominal clitics*, ed. H. Borer, Syntax and Semantics 19, 65–95. Academic Press: New York.

Roeper, Thomas. 1987. Implicit arguments and the head–complement relation. *Linguistic Inquiry* 18:267–310.

Rosen, Carol. 1984. The interface between semantic roles and initial grammatical relations. In *Studies in relational grammar 2*, ed. D. Perlmutter and C. Rosen, 38–77. University of Chicago Press.

Rosen, Sara Thomas. 1996. Events and verb classification. *Linguistics* 34:191–223.

Ross, John R. 1972. Act. In *Semantics of natural language*, ed. D. Davidson and G. Harman, 71–126. Dordrecht: Reidel.

Rothstein, Susan. 1983. The syntactic form of predication. Doctoral dissertation. Massachusetts Institute of Technology.

— 2001. *Predicates and their subjects*. Dordrecht: Kluwer.

— 2004. *Structuring events*. Oxford: Blackwell Publishing.

Russell, Bertrand. 1903. *Principles of mathematics*. New York: Norton.

— 1905. On denoting. *Mind* 14:479–493.

— 1911. On the relations of Universals and Particulars. *Proceedings of the Aristotelian Society* 12:1–24.

— 1918. The philosophy of logical atomism. Reprinted 1956 in *Logic and knowledge*, ed. R. C. Marsh. London: Allen and Unwin.

Ryle, Gilbert. 1949. *The concept of mind*. London: Hutchinson.

Saccòn, Graziella. 1993. Post-verbal subjects: A study on Italian and its dialects. Doctoral dissertation. Harvard University.

Safir, Ken. 1985. Missing subjects in German. In *Studies in German grammar*, ed. J. Toman, 193–229. Berlin: Walter de Gruyter.

— 1987. The syntactic projection of lexical thematic structure. *Natural Language and Linguistic Theory* 5:561–601.

Sag, Ivan A. 1985. *Grammatical hierarchy and linear precedence*. Stanford, CA: CSLI.

— 2012. Sign-based construction grammar: An informal synopsis. In *Sign-based construction grammar*, ed. H. C. Boas and I. A. Sag, 69–202. Stanford, CA: CSLI.

Sag, Ivan A., Hans C. Boas and Paul Kay. 2012. Introducing sign-based construction grammar. In *Sign-based construction grammar*, ed. H. C. Boas and I. A. Sag, 1–30. Stanford, CA: CSLI.

Sag, Ivan A., and Thomas Wasow. 1999. *Syntactic theory: A formal introduction*. Stanford, CA: CSLI.

Salkoff, Morris. 1983. Bees are swarming in the garden: A systematic synchronic study of productivity. *Language* 59:288–346.

Scha, Remko. 2013. Collections and paradox. In *The dynamic, inquisitive, and visionary life of ϕ, $?\phi$, and $\Diamond\phi$: A festschrift for Jeroen Groenendijk, Martin Stokhof, and Frank Veltman*, ed. M. Aloni, M. Franke, and F. Roelofsen. Available at www.illc.uva.nl/Festschrift-JMF.

Schein, Barry. 1993. *Events and plurals*. Cambridge, MA: The MIT Press.

— 1997. Conjunction reduction redux. Unpublished manuscript. University of Southern California.

— 2002. Events and the semantic content of thematic relations. In *Logical form and language*, ed. G. Preyer and G. Peter, 263–344. Oxford University Press.

— 2006. Plurals. In *The Oxford handbook of philosophy of language*, ed. E. Lepore and B. Smith, 716–767. Oxford University Press.

— 2012. Event semantics. In *The Routledge companion to the philosophy of language*, ed. D. Graff Fara and G. Russell, 280–294. New York: Routledge.

Schlesinger, Izchak M. 1989. Instruments as agents: On the nature of semantic relations. *Journal of Linguistics* 25:189–210.

1995. *Cognitive space and linguistic case: Semantic and syntactic categories in English.* Cambridge University Press.

Searle, John R. 1978. Literal meaning. *Erkenntnis* 13:207–224.

1980. The background of meaning. In *Speech act theory and pragmatics*, ed. J. R. Searle, F. Kiefer and M. Bierwisch, 221–232. Dordrecht: Reidel.

Sgall, Petr, Eva Hajicová and Jarmila Panevová. 1986. *The meaning of the sentence in its semantic and pragmatic aspects.* Dordrecht: Reidel.

Sher, Gila, 1990. Ways of branching quantifiers. *Linguistics and Philosophy* 13:393–422.

Shibatani, Masayoshi. 1976. The grammar of causative constructions: A conspectus. In *The grammar of causative constructions*, ed. M. Shibatani, Syntax and Semantics, 6, 1–40. New York: Academic Press.

1998. Voice parameters. In *Typology of verbal categories: Papers presented to Vladimir Nedjalkov on the occasion of his 70th birthday*, ed. L. Kulikov and H. Vater, 117–138. Tübingen: Niemeyer.

2002. Introduction: Some basic issues on the grammar of causation. In *The grammar of causation and interpersonal manipulation*, ed. M. Shibatani, 1–22. Amsterdam: John Benjamins.

Shopen, Timothy. 1972. A generative theory of ellipsis. Doctoral dissertation. University of California Los Angeles.

1973. Ellipsis as grammatical indeterminacy. *Foundations of Language* 10:65–77.

Siewierska, Anna. 1984. *The passive: A comparative linguistic analysis.* London: Croon Helm.

Simpson, Jane. 1983. Resultatives. In *Papers in Lexical-Functional grammar*, ed. L. Levin, M. Rappaport and A. Zaenen, 143–157. Bloomington: Indiana University Linguistics Club.

Smith, Carlota S. 1972. On causative verbs and derived nominals in English. *Linguistic Inquiry* 3:136–138.

1997. *The parameter of aspect.* Berlin: Springer.

Snyder, William. 2001. On the nature of syntactic variation: Evidence from complex predicates and complex word formation. *Language* 77:324–342.

Soames, Scott. 1987. Direct reference, propositional attitudes and semantic content. *Philosophical Topics* 15:47–87.

Sorace, Antonella. 2000. Gradients in auxiliary selection with intransitive verbs. *Language* 76:859–890.

Sperber, Dan, and Deirdre Wilson. 1986. *Relevance: Communication and cognition.* Oxford: Blackwell.

Sproat, Richard. 1985. On deriving the lexicon. Doctoral dissertation. Massachusetts Institute of Technology.

Stabler, Ed. 1997. Derivational Minimalism. In *Logical aspects of computational linguistics*, ed. C. Retoré, 68–95. Berlin: Springer.

2010. Computational perpectives on Minimalism. In *Oxford handbook of linguistic Minimalism*, ed. C. Boeckx, 617–642. Oxford Unversity Press.

Stainton, Robert J. 2006. *Words and thoughts: Subsentential ellipsis and the philosophy of language*. Oxford University Press.

Stanley, Jason. 2000. Context and logical form. *Linguistics and Philosophy* 23:391–434.

von Stechow, Arnim. 1995. Lexical decomposition in syntax. In *Lexical knowledge in the organisation of language*, ed. U. Egli, P. E. Pause, C. Schwarze, A. von Stechow and G. Wienold, 81–177. Amsterdam: John Benjamins.

1996. The different readings of *wieder* "again." *Journal of Semantics* 13:87–138.

Steedman, Mark. 1996. *Surface structure and interpretation*. Cambridge, MA: The MIT Press.

2000. *The syntactic process*. Cambridge, MA: The MIT Press.

Steedman, Mark, and Jason Baldridge. 2011. Combinatory categorial grammar. In *Non-transformational syntax: Formal and explicit models of grammar*, ed. R. Borsley and K. Borjars, 181–224. Malden, MA: Wiley-Blackwell.

Stolz, Thomas, Cornelia Struh and Aina Urze. 2006. *On comitatives and related categories: A typological study with special focus on the languages of Europe*. Berlin: Mouton de Gruyter.

Stone, Matthew, and Bonnie Webber. 1998. Textual economy through close coupling of syntax and semantics. *International Conference on Natural Language Generation (INLG)* 98:178–187.

Stowell, Tim. 1981. Origins of phrase structure. Doctoral dissertation. Massachusetts Institute of Technology.

Strawson, Peter F. 1950. On referring. *Mind* 59:320–344.

1959. *Individuals*. New York: Routledge.

Sybesma, Rint. 1999. *The Mandarin VP*. Dordrecht: Kluwer.

Talmy, Leonard. 1976. Semantic causative types. In *The grammar of causative constructions*, ed. M. Shibatani, Syntax and Semantics 6. New York: Academic Press.

2004. *Toward a cognitive semantics*, volume I. Cambridge, MA: The MIT Press.

Tarski, Alfred. 1944. The semantic conception of truth. *Philosophy and Phenomenological Research* 4:341–375.

Taylor, Barry. 1985. *Modes of occurrence: Verbs, adverbs and events*. Oxford University Press.

Tenny, Carol. 1987. Grammaticalizing aspect and affectedness. Doctoral dissertation. Massachusetts Institute of Technology.

1994. *Aspectual roles and the syntax–semantics interface*. Dordrecht: Kluwer.

Tenny, Carol, and James Pustejovsky. 2000. *Events as grammatical objects*. Stanford, CA: CSLI.

Tesnière, Lucien. 1959. *Éléments de syntaxe structurale*. Paris: Klincksieck.

Thalberg, Irving. 1972. *Enigmas of agency: Studies in the philosophy of human action*. New York: Routledge.

Thomason, Richmond. 1976. Some extensions of Montague Grammar. In *Montague Grammar*, ed. B. Partea, 77–118. New York: Academic Press.

Thompson, Sandra. 1973. Resultative verb compounds in Mandarin Chinese: A case for lexical rules. *Language* 42:361–379.

Thomson, Judith Jarvis. 1971a. Individuating actions. *Journal of Philosophy* 68:774–781.

1971b. The time of a killing. *Journal of Philosophy* 68:115–132.

1977. *Acts and other events*. Ithaca, NY: Cornell University Press.

Travis, Charles. 1996. Meaning's role in truth. *Mind* 105:451–466.

Tuyn, Harry. 1970. Semantics and the notion of transitivity in passive conversion. *Studia Neophilologica* 42:60–71.

van Oosten, Jeanne 1977. Subjects and agenthood in English. In *Papers from the Thirteenth Regional Meeting of the Chicago Linguistic Society*, ed. W. Beach, S. Fox and S. Philosoph, 459–471. Chicago Linguistic Society.

1986. *The nature of subjects, topics and agents: A cognitive explanation*. Bloomington: Indiana University Linguistics Club.

Van Valin, Robert D. 1990. Semantic parameters of split intransitivity. *Language* 66:221–260.

2004. Semantic macroroles in Role and Reference Grammar. In *Semantische Rollen*, ed. R. Kailuweit and M. Hummel, 62–82. Tübingen: Gunter Narr Verlag.

2005. *Exploring the syntax–semantics interface*. Cambridge University Press.

Van Valin, Robert D., and Randy J. LaPolla. 1997. *Syntax: Structure, meaning and function*. Cambridge University Press.

Van Valin, Robert D., and David P. Wilkins. 1996. The case for "effector": Case roles, agents and agency revisited. In *Grammatical constructions: Their form and meaning*, ed. M. Shibatani and S. Thompson, 289–322. Oxford: Clarendon.

Vendler, Zeno. 1957. Verbs and times. *Philosophical Review* 66:143–160.

Verkuyl, Henk. 1993. *A theory of aspectuality*. Cambridge University Press.

Verspoor, Cornelia. 1997. Contextually-dependent lexical semantics. Doctoral dissertation. University of Edinburgh.

de Villiers, Jill, and Peter de Villiers. 2000. Linguistic determinism and the understanding of false beliefs. In *Children's reasoning and the mind*, ed. P. Mitchell and K. J. Riggs, 199–228. Hove, UK: Psychology Press.

Vincent, Nigel. 2013. Conative. *Linguistic Typology* 17:269–289.

Vinet, Maria-Teresa. 1987. Implicit arguments and control in middles and passives. In *Advances in Romance linguistics*, ed. D. Birdsong and J. P. Montreuil, 427–437. Dordrecht: Foris.

Waismann, Friedrich. 1945. Verifiability. *Proceedings of the Aristotelian Society, Supplementary Volumes* 19:119–150.

Washio, Ryuichi. 1997. Resultatives, compositionality and language variation. *Journal of East Asian Linguistics* 6:1–49.

Waxman, Sandra R. 1998. Linking object categorization and naming: Early expectations and the shaping role of language. In *The psychology of learning and motivation*, ed. D. L. Medin, 249–291. San Diego, CA: Academic Press.

Waxman, Sandra R., and Dana B. Markow. 1998. Object properties and object kind: 21-month-old infants' extension of novel adjectives. *Child Development* 69:1313–1329.

Wechsler, Stephen. 1995. *The semantic basis of argument structure*. Stanford, CA: CSLI.

——— 1997. Resultative predicates and control. In *Texas Linguistic Forum* 38, 307–321.

——— 2005a. Resultatives under the "event–argument homomorphism" model of telicity. In *The syntax of aspect*, ed. N. Erteschik-Shir and T. Rapoport, 255–273. Oxford University Press.

——— 2005b. What is right and wrong about little *v*. In *Grammar and beyond: Essays in honour of Lars Hellan*, ed. M. Vulchanova and T. A. Åfarli, 179–195. Oslo: Novus Press.

——— 2008. A diachronic account of English deverbal nominals. In *Proceedings of the 26th West Coast Conference on Formal Linguistics*, ed. C. B. Chang and H. J. Haynie, 498–506. Somerville, MA: Cascadilla Proceedings Project.

Wellwood, Alexis, Annie Gagliardi, and Jeffrey Lidz. 2014a. Syntactic and lexical inference in the acquisition of novel superlatives. University of Maryland manuscript, submitted to *Language Learning and Development*.

Wellwood, Alexis, Angela Xiaoxue He, Jeffrey Lidz, and Alexander Williams. 2014b. Participant structure in event perception: Towards the acquisition of implicitly 3-place predicates. Paper presented at the 38th Penn Linguistics Colloquium, March 2014.

Westerståhl, Dag. 1985. Determiners and context sets. In *Quantification in Natural Language*, ed. J. van Bentham and A. G. B. ter Meulen, 45–71. Dordrecht: Foris.

Wexler, Kenneth, and Peter W. Culicover. 1981. *Formal principles of language acquisition*. Cambridge, MA: The MIT Press.

White, Aaron Steven, Rachel Dudley, Valentine Hacquard and Jeffrey Lidz. 2014. Discovering classes of attitude verbs using subcategorization frame distributions. In *Proceedings of the 43rd Annual North Eastern Linguistics Society*, volume II, ed. H.-L. Huang, E. Poole and A. Rysling. Amherst, MA: Graduate Linguistics Student Association.

Williams, Alexander. 2005. Complex causatives and verbal valence. Doctoral dissertation. University of Pennsylvania.

——— 2008a. Patients in Igbo and Mandarin. In *Event structures in linguistic form and interpretation*, ed. J. Dölling, T. Heyde-Zybatow, and M. Schäfer, 3–30. Berlin: Mouton de Gruyter.

2008b. Word order in resultatives. In *Proceedings of the 26th West Coast Conference on Formal Linguistics*, ed. C. B. Chang and H. J. Haynie, 507–515. Somerville, MA: Cascadilla Press.

2009. Themes, cumulativity, and resultatives: Comments on Kratzer 2003. *Linguistic Inquiry* 40:686–700.

2011. On from. Unpublished manuscript. University of Maryland.

2012. Null complement anaphors as definite descriptions. *Proceedings of SALT 22*: 125–145.

2013. Remote control of reason clauses. University of Maryland manuscript.

2014a. Agents in Mandarin and Igbo resultatives. In *Chinese syntax in a cross-linguistic perspective*, ed. A. Li, A. Simpson and W.-T. D. Tsai, 270–289. Oxford University Press.

2014b. Causal VVs in Mandarin. In *The handbook of Chinese linguistics*, ed. C.-T. J. Huang, Y.-H. A. Li, and A. Simpson. Malden, MA: Wiley-Blackwell.

Accepted. Objects in resultatives. *Natural Language and Linguistic Theory*.

Williams, Edwin 1974. Rule ordering in syntax. Doctoral dissertation. Massachusetts Institute of Technology.

1980. Predication. *Linguistic Inquiry* 11:203–238.

1985. PRO and subject of NP. *Natural Language and Linguistic Theory* 3:297–315.

1987. Implicit arguments, the binding theory, and control. *Natural Language and Linguistic Theory* 5:151–180.

Wilson, Deirdre, and Robyn Carston. 2007. A unitary approach to lexical pragmatics: Relevance, inference and *ad hoc* concepts. In *Pragmatics*, ed. N. Burton-Roberts, 230–259. London: Palgrave.

Wolff, Phillip. 2003. Direct causation in the linguistic coding and individuation of causal events. *Cognition* 88:1–48.

von Wright, Georg H. 1968. *An essay in deontic logic and the general theory of action*. Amsterdam: North Holland.

Wunderlich, Dieter. 1997. Argument extension by lexical adjunction. *Journal of Semantics* 14:95–142.

Yi, Byeong-uk. 1999. Is two a property? *Journal of Philosophy* 96:163–190.

Yuan, Sylvia, and Cynthia Fisher. 2009. "Really? She blicked the baby": two-year-olds learn combinatorial facts about verbs by listening. *Psychological Science* 20:619–626.

Yuan, Sylvia, Cynthia Fisher, and Jesse Snedeker. 2012. Counting the nouns: simple structural cues to verb meaning. *Child Development* 83:1382–1399.

Zaenen, Annie. 1988. Unaccusative verbs in Dutch and the syntax-semantics interface. *Report No. CSLI-88-123*. Stanford, CA: CSLI.

1993. Unaccusativity in Dutch: Integrating syntax and lexical semantics. In *Semantics and the Lexicon*, ed. J. Pustejovsky, 129–152. Dordrecht: Kluwer.

Zhang, Niina. 2007. The syntax of English comitative constructions. *Folia Linguistica* 41:135–169.

Zubizaretta, Maria Luisa. 1982. On the relationship of the lexicon to syntax. Doctoral dissertation. Massachusetts Institute of Technology.

Zweig, Eytan. 2008. Dependent plurals and plural meaning. Doctoral dissertation. New York University.

Zwicky, Arnold. 1971. In a manner of speaking. *Linguistic Inquiry* 2:223–233.

Zwicky, Arnold M., and Jerrold M. Sadock. 1975. Ambiguity tests and how to fail them. In *Syntax and semantics 4*, ed. J. P. Kimball, 1–36. New York: Academic Press.

Index